VICEREINE

The Indian Journal of Mary Minto

Edited by
Anabel Loyd

Anabel Loyd has lived and worked in India and is a constant visitor to the sub-continent from the UK. She is fascinated by Indian history and culture with a particular interest in the first half of the 20th century leading at last to Independence. She writes a regular column for the *Indian Telegraph* on British current events with occasional excursions in other directions. When she read Mary Minto's journal over a wet weekend in the Scottish Borders, it was at first with fellow feeling for another Mother of five who further suffered corsets and complicated Edwardian clothes whatever the Calcutta heat. There proved to be far more to Mary than minor domestic irritations and Anabel has greatly enjoyed her company, however gaspingly reactionary some of her opinions appear today.

VICEREINE

The Indian Journal of Mary Minto

Edited by

Anabel Loyd

ACADEMIC FOUNDATION

LIMITED EDITIONS

First published in 2016
by
LIMITED EDITIONS
an imprint of

ACADEMIC FOUNDATION

Delhi Sales Office:
4772-73 / 23 Bharat Ram Road,
(23 Ansari Road), Darya Ganj,
New Delhi - 110 002 (India).
Phones : 23245001 / 02 / 03 / 04.
Fax : +91-11-23245005.

Corporate Office:
No. 35, Sector 7,
IMT Manesar,
Gurgaon - 122050.
Haryana (India).
Tel: +91-124-4215070 / 71.

E-mail : books@academicfoundation.com
www.academicfoundation.org

Cataloging in Publication Data--DK
Courtesy: D.K. Agencies (P) Ltd. <docinfo@dkagencies.com>

Vicereine : the Indian journal of Mary Minto / edited by Anabel Loyd.
pages cm
Includes bibliographical references.
ISBN 9789332703278

1. Minto, Mary Caroline, Countess of, 1858-1940--Diaries. 2. Minto, Gilbert John Murray Kynynmond Elliot, Earl of, 1845-1914. 3. Viceroys' spouses--India--Diaries. 4. Viceroys--India--Biography. 5. Great Britain--Colonies--India. 6. Great Britain--Colonies--Administration. 7. India--History--20th century. I. Loyd, Anabel, editor.

DS480.2.V53 2015 DDC 954.0356 23

Printed and bound by The Book Mint, New Delhi.
www.thebookmint.in

For Mary's descendants,
especially Frankie, Michael and Clare

CONTENTS

ACKNOWLEDGEMENTS

This book would not have got beyond an overweight ring bound print out for friends and family without the help and enthusiasm of Philip Ziegler who used his spectacularly quick cutting eye to shorten and improve the final edit; David Knox of UK Archiving in Edinburgh who digitised both the text of the journals and all Mary's photographs and made my life a great deal easier as a result and Barnaby Rogerson who took a liking to Mary and encouraged a very uphill process to publication of her Indian story. So many thanks to them and to Mala Singh who thought of another possible publisher every week, showed unfailing interest and introduced me to Sanu and Rituraj Kapila who agreed to take the journals and then did a fantastic job on the design of the book. The whole idea of publishing Mary's Indian Journal started with a weekend at Minto in the Scottish Borders with Timothy and Diana Minto. I am enormously grateful to them for introducing me to Timothy's great grandmother, showing me her glorious Indian photographs and endlessly supporting the whole journal project with a lot of meetings in our local Wiltshire pubs.

— A.L.

INTRODUCTION

Mary Minto was born in 1858, the youngest of the five children of General, the Honourable Charles Grey, Private Secretary to Prince Albert. She married Gilbert John Elliot-Murray-Kynynmound, Viscount Melgund in 1883. Known to his friends as Rolly,[1] Lord Melgund was 14 years older than Mary and was heir to the 3rd Earl of Minto. In 1905, Rolly, by then the 4th Earl, succeeded Lord Curzon of Kedleston as Viceroy and Governor General of India. *The Indian Journals* are Mary Minto's record of her five years as Vicereine from 1905-1910.

When the Minto's left for India, the best known images of life at the summit of British India had come from the journals written by Emily Eden, sister and companion of the Earl of Auckland and Governor General of India from 1835-1842. They had been published as *Up the Country* in 1867 and one may guess that the book was prescribed reading for later empire wives.[2] Mary Minto, unlike Miss Eden, was neither a poet nor an artist and the pace of Viceregal life had changed in the 70 years that separate their Indian journeys, but Mary's journals resonate with a similar desire to communicate her experiences and keen interest in everything she saw to her family at home.

Whereas in the 21st century the British Raj is distanced to a chapter in a history book; a fascinating image of power, heat and painted elephants; a confusion of uniforms, clerks, Kipling, treasure, tigers and princes; and, ultimately, Partition and bloodshed; at the beginning of the 20th century, it was the jewelled finial on the vast edifice of an Empire whose dismemberment remained unthinkable to its rulers and to many of its ruled.

Mary was an articulate witness to the glitter of high Imperial service and to the darning needed to repair the fraying fabric of Empire as the glow of the British sun dimmed in a time of change. In the twilight of the golden Edwardian age passengers and mail still took over three weeks to travel between Britain and Calcutta but the telegraph had long since carried more immediate notice of triumphs and disasters, births and deaths, between continents. Communications were speeding forward into a world recognisable to us today; Viceregal tours and visits were made by train and cars were becoming a more common part of life for the privileged. We are struck therefore by less familiar elements of life a century ago.

---

1. A school nickname, apparently from his rolling gait; he rode as an amateur jockey under the name 'Mr Rolly' and was called Berty by his Mother and brothers.
2. Ruby was reading *Up the Country* when she arrived in India after her husband, Rowland Baring, joined Lord Hardinge's staff in 1915.

MM on Waitress.

It is difficult to imagine the fear of any illness in those pre-penicillin days when an attack of 'enteric' could so quickly be fatal. Death still hovered over childbirth and childhood, and children died of diphtheria, whooping cough and other contagious diseases whether in the streets of Calcutta or the dormitories of the great British boarding schools. In India, where the heat and dust exacerbated every fever, good health was never taken for granted.

Mary's journals were first a regular newsletter of Viceregal events, sent in the mail to her sisters for dissemination among relatives and close friends. Secondly, with the assistance of the Viceroy's Private Secretary, Sir James Dunlop Smith, they were written as a record of the Minto viceroyalty, compiled with a clear eye to posterity and Minto's place in British and Imperial history after Lord Curzon's complicated Indian reign. The originals include photographs; copies of personal and official letters; speeches; newspaper cuttings; bills, programmes and plans for dinners, camps, concerts and plays; shooting diaries and game lists; records of gymkhanas, polo and racing; even the rainfall statistics for Simla. The journals were printed in 1910 as the Mintos were leaving India, Mary's sharp eye for economy may have spotted the relative savings in leather bound volumes in Calcutta over London.

In the preface to his 1924 memoir of her husband, John Buchan, wrote of Lady Minto's "delightful Indian diary" and wished it could be "given intact to the world". As keeper of the flame after Minto's death, Mary used the journals as the basis for her 1934 book, *India, Morley and Minto*. John Morley, later 1st Viscount Morley of Blackburn was Secretary of State for India during Minto's Viceroyalty and joint author of the 1909 legislation that increased the participation of Indians in their country's government and became known as the Morley/Minto Reforms. Mary and Rolly shared an almost obsessive concern that the greatest credit for the reforms had been appropriated by Morley and Mary never missed a chance to puff Rolly's reputation, sometimes to an irritating degree. Her book was intended to redress the balance in Rolly's favour after Lord Morley published his one-sided Recollections.

As it happened the majority of the vernacular press at the time of the Reforms did believe Morley solely responsible. They saw little in the Viceroy beyond the public ceremonial image, the big game hunting that he loved and the grand tours and camps that were so great a part of the Viceregal role. Rolly was a modest man. He might have expected to receive his fair dues but he was no great orator demanding public acclaim for his achievements and considered his private intercourse with the home government including Morley, just that. Rose tinting aside, the journals give an occasionally quite despairing picture of the Viceroy wearing himself out in hard pursuit of his duty as he suffered from the growing demands and interference in his administration by the micro-managing intellect of the Secretary of State.

Occasionally used as source material by historians, Mary's Journals have largely been forgotten. They are not among the papers of the large Minto archive held in the National Library for Scotland but, separately, among a smaller collection in the Bodleian Library. The somewhat random Bodleian archive includes a visitors' book that travelled with the Mintos on tour and a diary with a record of distances covered from their departure from Britain to their return. Other copies of the journals were rediscovered recently at Minto with a remarkable collection of photograph albums going back to the 1870s. Those volumes, annotated in pencil in Mary's hand are, with her 'kodaks' of life behind the official scenes in India, the starting point for this edition of her journals.

On India's long timeline, the British Raj was a mere moment, each Viceroy's term no more than an eye blink. 65 years after Independence, we remember few of the great imperial administrators by name other than, perhaps, the last Viceroy, Lord Mountbatten, and the remarkable Curzon. The Morley/Minto reforms have been both criticised for their meagre concessions to Indian governance by Indians and praised as an important step forward on the long path of constitutional progress. For students of the Raj, they may have memorialised the Minto name more successfully than endless dusty plaques on the clock towers, parks and hospitals that were mostly officially renamed after Independence. Mary's Journals, not quite as intact, for the impatient modern reader, as John Buchan might have liked, give an animated picture of five years at the pinnacle of imperial service and a personal view of the individuals behind long defunct legislation and crumbling imperial architecture.

Mary and her older sisters, Sybil St Albans, who died in 1871, Victoria Dawnay, and Louisa Antrim, were inveterate journal keepers and letter writers, communicating regularly with each other and a wide circle of friends throughout their lives. In similar large handwriting they shared news, good, bad and sometimes mildly scurrilous, of friends and relations; concerns about children, illness, education and entertainment; going ups and coming outs, passings out and passings on, pleasures and pains. Mary and Louisa in particular exchanged political news and gossip gleaned from a wide acquaintance in the corridors of power. Louisa, who died in 1949 aged 94, outliving all her siblings, was a Lady-in-Waiting to two Queens, Victoria and Alexandra, and wife of the decidedly eccentric 'Buzzard', Earl of Antrim.

When Mary died in 1940, Margot Asquith, Lady Oxford and Asquith, widow of the Liberal Prime Minister, H.H. Asquith, described her as "one of the few survivors of a group of my friends called the 'Souls'."[3] In her memoir *Such Were the Years*, Mary's daughter, Ruby, remembered peeping down from the archways of the nursery floor at Minto, with her sister Eileen to watch guests from that group such as Lady Desborough, like a 'pink carnation', and the beautiful Lady Helen Vincent sweeping down the stairs in their swishing gowns and being 'rather mystified' by the 'Burne-Jones' type of beauty of the talented artist, Violet Granby, later Duchess of Rutland. Ruby remembered too the 'vast trunks' of these 'fleeting guests' in which presents for the children were usually found. These included, "little Tyrolean hats from Austria, of which we were immensely proud", from Lady Randolph

3. The 'Souls' were a group of friends described by Consuelo, Duchess of Marlborough as "A brilliant company, a select group in which a high degree of intelligence was to be found happily allied to aristocratic birth." See, *The Souls* by Jane Abdy and Charlotte Gere, Sidgwick and Jackson Ltd., London, 1984.

Churchill, whom Ruby recalled receiving letters from her son Winston, then in captivity in a Boer prisoner of war camp.

In this bright and beautiful circle, Lord Curzon and Arthur Balfour, the future Prime Minister, were the two greatest stars. That Mary and Rolly suffered from Curzon's inability to let go entirely of India is certain: perceived slights on their arrival at Bombay and irritations with the ongoing Indian schemes of their predecessor were fanned by partisan press, family and society gossip. Worst of all, Curzon's blustering enemy, the Commander-in-Chief, Lord Kitchener remained in India to play a bizarre Iago, twisting the wires and fuelling the fire of ill-feeling between his fellow soldier, the new Viceroy, and the statesman nursing injured pride in England. The fact that Mary was accused by Curzon and his supporters of purposely commandeering recognition for Curzon's dead wife's planned nursing improvement scheme when she established the Lady Minto Indian Nursing Association suggests a remarkable level of petty rivalry. In Mary's introduction to *India, Minto and Morley*, she wrote:

> *"In the following account of our five years in India, some reference to the attitude adopted by our predecessor is necessary. All that I have quoted in these chapters is merely history and in no way a personal criticism of one whose brilliant talents are universally recognised. Throughout his public life he experienced much ill-health and suffering and in the last year of his administration in India he had to face great personal anxiety which ended in the death of his wife. In spite of the views he publicly expressed on Indian affairs during Minto's Viceroyalty, I can never forget that he was one of our oldest friends."*

Mary was brought up entirely in Royal circles among Queen Victoria's extended brood; home was the Norman Tower at Windsor with holiday trips to Osborne on the Isle of Wight for skating in the winter and swimming in the summer. After Prince Albert's death in 1860, her Father continued in royal service as Private Secretary to Queen Victoria. He was the second son of the 2nd Earl Grey, of Great Reform Bill and scented tea fame and one of a Northumberland family whose members littered the lists of army, foreign service, political and court appointments. Childless for the first 12 years of her marriage, Mary's Mother, Caroline Farquhar, was supposed to have had her constitution changed by catching smallpox on a journey to Gibraltar, whereupon she managed to produce 6 children, all born at St James's Palace, between 1848 and Mary's birth in 1858.

The Grey children may have been bred as courtiers but Louisa Antrim's Recollections suggest theirs was far from the rigid and proscribed Victorian upbringing but, on the contrary, one where the children in her family achieved far more freedom than most. The word 'don't' was seldom heard. Governesses came and went with greater or lesser success; a vicious Hanoverian woman had to be suffered until her distressing methods were discovered. She was rumoured to have gone insane after her departure, from fury at the annexation of Hanover by Prussia. In spite of such educationally unpromising events, Mary learnt to speak German and French to add to accomplishments as an excellent skater and dancer. By the time she married, she was known for her charm and grace and was described by Vanity Fair magazine as both the best waltzer and the best-dressed of her contemporaries.

The Greys had very little money after the General died in 1870 aged only 66. His widow was given life occupancy of a grace and favour house at St James's Palace, a home where his three younger unmarried daughters learnt habits of economy. These would stand Mary in good stead when married to a relatively impoverished husband and trying to uphold Viceregal splendour without exceeding the expense account. It was assumed that the social standing of those aristocratic gentlemen chosen to be Viceroy would be buttressed by a degree of financial plenitude. Minto's great-grandfather's service as Governor General of India 100 years earlier and resulting earldom; 16,000 acres of Scottish borderland and a career mainly as a soldier and sportsman had granted him no such cushion.

When Rolly married Mary, he was 39 to her 25, with a hard-riding reputation as the gentleman jockey, 'Mr Rolly'; a wide collection of friends and a busy social life. His on and off army career included a stint in the Scots Fusilier Guards, the raising of a volunteer corps of mounted infantry and a mixed bag of foreign adventures as a war correspondent or soldier in the available wars of the later 19th century. His first experience of India was as A.D.C. to Major-General Frederick Roberts[4] during the Second Afghan War. He conceived a huge respect for his Anglo-Indian military colleagues and considerable contempt for the politicians and do-gooders at home who did not understand the reality of ruling India or the problems of the frontier and its lawless tribes. Rolly himself had seen and heard enough of them to avoid the chance of adding his name, gilded by "dauntless bravery,"[5] to the honours roll of dead Victorian heroes. Declining to join Sir Louis Cavagnari on the Great Game mission to Kabul that ended with a massacre when he and his men "fell victims to the treachery of a fanatical nation, destitute of all sense of truth and honour,"[6] he saved his skin to fight his own more diplomatic frontier battles at a later date.

Born in 1845 and brought up at Minto, near Hawick in the Scottish borders, Rolly was considered by his mother the least bright of her four sons, whose early education she undertook. He was tough, sporting, competitive and popular; running and rowing his way through Eton and, via tutors and crammers, into Cambridge. Here racing, hunting, fishing, shooting and mountaineering in Switzerland, took precedence over less physical and more intellectual pursuits. In his unsurprisingly partial memoir of a great friend, John Buchan pointed out[7] that "Melgund never failed to pass the requisite exams" and he duly received his degree in December 1866 in spite of some discouraging entries in his journals:

> *"Had a trigonometry paper this morning, which of course, I did not attempt to do a word of. In the afternoon we had a Livy translation paper. I think I could have managed most of it with the help of the man next to me, but unluckily I got throwing pens about, one of which cut over one of the examiners. Hudson, the other examiner got in a great rage."*

---

4. Later 1st Earl Roberts of Kandahar.
5. From the description of a statue of 23 year old Lt. W.R. Pollock in the Dublin Museum in Pictures of Ireland.
6. From *The Story of the Guides*, by Colonel G.J. Younghusband, C.B.
7. *Lord Minto, A Memoir*, John Buchan.

It is hard to spot the pen thrower behind the walrus moustache and uniform in the official photographs Rolly and Mary both disliked. Rolly was a Conservative and an imperialist to his bootstraps but, by the time he arrived in India, the stiff, wooden image presented to the world was something of an official carapace on the man who inspired the love and loyalty of his staff and of friends of all nationalities. He possessed a sometimes schoolboyish sense of fun and had a remarkably close and warm relationship with his children. Mary described him as the "Gentleman Rider, the keen follower to hounds, the soldier who had served in many parts of the World, rather than the politician." While his critics in India were unimpressed by the arrival of a Viceroy who was "a pleasant spoken gentleman who jumps hedges," Sirdar Ayub Khan, victor of the Battle of Maiwand against the British in the 2nd Afghan War said "His Excellency rained gentlemanliness upon me." The Viceroy always appreciated a fellow soldier.

Untroubled by Curzon's torturing intellect or tortured body,[8] by the time he arrived in India Rolly's own autocratic convictions had been smoothed by experience to make him less a tyrannical enforcer of colonialism and more a pragmatic administrator and reformer. It was the fit and pleasant gentleman, determined to do his straightforward and honest duty, who ultimately deserved the laudatory farewells on his departure. An article in *The Spectator*, written in 1932 with the wisdom of hindsight, noted:

> *"One who has ridden in the Grand National is rarely a fount of political apothegms but Lord Minto was responsible for two which deserve to be remembered. One was that to govern with the consent of the governed is not so much a moral as a physical necessity—the opposite is simply not possible. The other was that the strongest man is he who is not afraid to be called weak."*

Mary and Rolly spent the first two years of their married life in Canada when Rolly took his first step on the ladder of Empire administration as Military Secretary to the Governor General, Lord Lansdowne, in whose footsteps he would later follow in Ottawa and as Viceroy of India. Their eldest daughter, Eileen, was born in Canada in 1884, the Melgunds returning to Britain in 1885. Ruby was born in 1886 followed by Violet, Larry, and finally Esmond in 1895. Rolly hoped for further public office but his mild ambition for that career to be in the House of Commons was dashed by his defeat in the Hexham constituency of Northumberland in the 1886 General Election. His stand as a Liberal Unionist candidate on an anti-Home Rule ticket began with a personal detestation of Gladstone and was fought with rhetoric that played on fear of Irish immigration and loss of local jobs and on national security implications if so near a neighbour as Ireland became independent. The voters were unpersuaded by their candidate's single plank platform and he lost by 967 votes to his orthodox Liberal opponent. Anti-disestablishment and the abolition of the House of Lords, he had no opinion on matters of greater local importance such as perpetual pensions or Sunday closing, pleading lack of knowledge due to his time abroad.

8. Curzon suffered ill health, often due to overwork; in particular a chronically bad back.

The next 12 years were a mixed bag of peripheral political excursions, journalism and continued military involvement with the War Office through the command of the Scottish Lowland Brigade of volunteers. Rolly's Father's death and his resulting succession to local, parochial and estate duties also brought financial concerns over the Minto estate that were exacerbated by death duties and the need to renovate the house. An outbreak of typhoid had drawn attention to the unfortunate state of the drains and required the family to move out for two years while the house was remodelled and redecorated.

The social and sporting round whirled on; the London season and weekends staying with friends interspersed with fishing, shooting and hunting, supported by some judicious horse-coping on Rolly's part. The children all rode from an early age and the family took to energetic bicycling when it became a fashionable pursuit. Mary's skating style on the artificial rink, Niagara, in Westminster was described as 'abandoned' by a spectator. Once back in Minto, there was open house for friends en route to or from the Highlands. Rolly's views on this sound very similar to those later expressed by Mary about guests in India who expected to shoot tigers almost from their bedroom windows.

> *"We are now alone: a relief after the constant coming and going of visitors. They are by way of shooting deer and catching salmon but shooting has become so much more luxurious nowadays: they want all the game to play round them and my own idea is that few of them would do a good day's walking and certainly would not remain in the river all day without waders, as I used to do."*

Middle age and domesticity had not blinded Rolly to opportunities for preferment. He was well thought of by the War Office and the return of a Conservative-Unionist government in 1895 led him to seek the post of Under-Secretary of War. When the post went to a sitting MP, St John Brodrick,[9] Brodrick promised to support Rolly's ambition to become Governor General of Canada, a role of which both his and Mary's supporters believed them suited. They succeeded the Marquess and Marchioness of Aberdeen whose democratic reformist views of society were not approved of by the old Queen. Mary, steeped in court etiquette, was considered by the Royal Family to be the ideal person to restore the dignity of the crown to Rideau Hall, Government House in Ottawa, while Rolly's candidacy was bolstered by an influential coterie led by Lord Curzon.

The Mintos went to Ottawa in 1898. Rolly's initially stiff official image and lack of experience of high office combined with Mary's enforcement of court precedent and official propriety at Rideau Hall did not give them universal popularity. Canada was changing and its people were none too sure they wished to be under the hand of a British pro-consular puppet of far away Downing Street. While "in the presence of pompous politicians and bureaucrats, Minto seemed often to stand on his fragile sense of viceregal dignity."[10] This dignity lapsed

9. Later Secretary of State for War, 1900-1903: Secretary of State for India, 1903-1905. 1st Earl of Midleton.
10. *The Canadian Career of the Fourth Earl of Minto, The Education of a Viceroy*, Carman Miller, 1940, Wilfrid Laurier University Press, Ontario.

in private and in the relationships with ordinary individuals where both Mintos excelled. The outdoors, healthy, hearty life suited a sporting family and they remembered their six years in the country with nostalgia. Rolly successfully took up the cudgels on behalf of minorities such as Native Canadians and the Yukon goldminers and Rideau Hall held "a very jolly household.....a stark contrast to the pious band of concerned people which had haunted the Aberdeen establishment."[11] The A.D.C.s sound a wild bunch: "jovial, frolicking schoolboys, bent on a lark who were brought out for their decorative and entertainment value rather than any practical talent."[12] The Mintos, viceregal dignity notwithstanding, were unmoved by shocked reports from the caretaker of the Banff Hot Springs Hotel's swimming tank of the staff's early morning nude bathing.

The New York Times of 1903 gives a rather mawkish picture of the Elliot children and their parents at home in Canada although comments on Mary's careful housekeeping ring true. It congratulates Lady Minto on bringing up her children so successfully in the criticised "American method." These children are both seen and heard at all events barring functions of state, their parents appear more like an elder brother and sister. Mary, "tall and slight", always dressed "artistically" and with "flowers about her", is often confused with Eileen, aged 18, and is 'the most sympathetic of confidantes' for childish troubles. The Governor General "can romp like a schoolboy in the privacy of his home" and his heir, young Lord Melgund, had achieved fame by giving his boots away after the great Ottawa fire to a boy who had lost everything. Mary's economical bent is noted in complaints from Ottawa tradesman that the Governor General's wife "knows the price of everything" and does not, as she properly should, leave the housekeeping to the steward and the comptroller who "being men, would be more agreeable to deal with."

Ruby's letters to her father when she left India to be married, repeatedly thank her parents for a "radiantly happy childhood", for being 'so wonderful to us' and giving their children such "marvellously happy lives". Mary and Rolly's relationships with their children were certainly unusually close at a time when parents of their class were often more distant figures than nannies and governesses. Their letters to friends and relations proudly report the children's triumphs, trials and idiosyncrasies. Violet, her father's favourite, a dashing rider, who professed a dislike of parties and wanted to be a boy, was a down to earth child. Visiting the Yukon with her Father:

> *"a poor man was brought in horribly mutilated by a blast on the new railway near here. He was quite insensible and practically dead and they put him in the booking office. I hoped Vi had not seen him, but she had and assumed he was in frightful agony and asked me angrily why they did not kill him now, at once: 'Do have him*

---

11. *The Canadian Career of the Fourth Earl of Minto, The Education of a Viceroy*, Carman Miller, 1940, Wilfrid Laurier University Press, Ontario.

12. Carman Miller.

killed Father.' So thoroughly practical and so like old Vi—it would so often be the best plan."[13]

That Rolly's career in Canada got off to a rocky start was partly due to Larry becoming dangerously ill on board ship from Britain. On his entry to the country at Quebec City, Rolly cut the official reception to the briefest formalities and prevented any reception at all in Montreal or, finally, in Ottawa. Larry survived, although health problems throughout a long life were believed to date to his childhood in Canada and were of particular concern to his parents while they were in India. At the time it took longer to heal the perceived slight to Canadian dignity in a country already apprehensive of his father's untried ability, lack of experience and royalist sentiments.

The diamond maple leaf presented to Mary from the grateful people of Ottawa and the plaudits of endless farewell addresses on the Mintos' final departure from the city, signified a tenure of mixed successes interspersed with failures and petty disputes over issues such as the official memorial service for Queen Victoria in Ottawa. The family were criticised, as they were in India, for their addiction to 'aristocratic' sports such as shooting and racing although presumably energetic canoeing, lacrosse and the skating for which Mary was so famed were considered more democratic pursuits. Rolly was no public relations man and a famous photograph of the whole family dressed from head to foot in huge furs was taken as a slight to Canadian weather and modern Canadian civilisation. Mary was praised for her work in support of the Victorian Order of Nurses and for establishing cottage hospitals in outlying districts of the country. Aged 59 in 1903, with parlous finances and no promise of further employment, Rolly thought of settling in Canada permanently. It is probable, however, that the Mintos loved Canada more than Canada loved them or what they stood for.

Unexpectedly, Ottawa proved, instead of the end of a career, to be the Mintos' apprenticeship for the highest office of empire. By the time Rolly was appointed Viceroy to India he had experienced the Scylla and Charybdis of British colonial politics, the touchy sensibilities of a young energetic country and continual interference from distant Westminster. John Buchan wrote from personal experience when he said, "A Governor General in an autonomous Dominion walks inevitably on a razor edge."[14] If Rolly ever believed that the seat of Empire and its distant offshoots worked naturally in harmony or that soldierly virtues of duty and diligence were the only essential qualities for high Imperial office, he was disabused. Canada seasoned the wooden soldier and made a better diplomat of the "strong, impartial, imperial arbiter"[15] who reserved the right to "put my foot down if I

13. *Lord Minto, A Memoir*, John Buchan
14. *Lord Minto, A Memoir,* John Buchan.
15. Carman Miller.

suspected anything detrimental to Imperial interests."[16] John Buchan suggests that his imperialist dream "became a reasoned faith" and he "acquired perspective" that he would certainly need in India.

Mary, the courtier, was far from ripping off her stays in favour of the 'artistic' dress of the New York Times report. She continued in India to expect outward forms of respect for the crown in court trains and curtseys and her journals and letters are redolent with the beliefs and voice of her time and her class. She was by nature, nurturer and loyalty, a 'reasoned' imperialist who played her allotted part to perfection but the proper public trappings of viceregal grandeur do not disguise her private delight in people and places or the sense of humour she shared with those close to her. Mary was the perfect hostess and organiser and the indomitable Edwardian grande dame who was nonetheless, as a middle-aged vicereine and grandmother, unable to resist riding in a paperchase where she broke her arm in a "fearful smash"; and who was "little the worse except for a bruised hip and a good deal of skin off my elbow" after being "hurled to the ground with great violence" while dancing.

Her Journals suggest a level of energy few could manage. The Grey sisters had a considerable expectation and opinion of each other's stamina but after reading the first few instalments, Victoria wrote in 1906: "I never can understand how you do it all for even my days are so full that I write to you now at 1A.M." Mary played tennis and golf in India, was a good shot and an indefatigable walker; she was also as cool in the face of a bomb attack in Ahmedabad as she had been in Canada when part of Government House burnt down and she was helpless in bed with a broken leg. She may have expected others to live up to her standards but amusement seems generally to have triumphed over irritation when they did not.

As they relinquished office to the Hardinges, the Mintos' Viceroyalty was deemed as successful as the printed farewell speeches and John Buchan's memoir suggest. They had arrived when unrest was in the air; when they left, a Hyderabadi tradesman said the "Viceroy has sprinkled water on the people after the fire which he found." Mary's charity and social welfare work was honoured; Cornelia Sorabji, the great Indian lawyer[17] and Mary's friend, wrote of her successes with Indian women who had not previously been invited to Government House. Miss Sorabji was not an impartial observer but Mary's famous purdah parties were attended by more secluded women than "ever ventured forth in later years. They love her." Sorabji quoted a Hindu friend saying "God must have loved India very much to send us this Burra Lat and Lady Sahib."

On his return from India in 1813, Rolly's Great Grandfather had died at Stevenage in Hertfordshire. Rolly himself survived to see his Scottish hills and the border lands he and Mary both loved but their enthusiastic reception on arrival at Victoria station was the

16. Carman Miller, Minto Papers, Minto to Parkin, 26 September 1904.

17. Cornelia Sorabji was a Parsi Christian, the first woman to take the Bachelor of Civil Laws exam at Oxford and eventually the first woman barrister in India. She worked throughout her life on behalf of women, in particular those in purdah.

beginning of the end. A returning Viceroy was expected to continue to fulfil the obligations of great servants of state. There was little peace from the panoply of ceremonies, speeches and dinners attendant upon the great and good and Rolly never recovered his strength. He became seriously ill in 1913 and died on 1 March 1914, before the Great War changed the World he knew. Mary lived until 1940 but her reign as Vicereine was, as she had anticipated, the end of the dancing years and of the close family life she and Rolly had cherished.

After an unfortunate love affair in India with a temporary A.D.C., Eileen, who was an excellent amateur actress, married Francis Scott in 1915. A faithful A.D.C. throughout Rolly's Viceroyalty, Francis had earlier been hopelessly in love with Ruby. He was badly wounded in the Battle of Mons in 1914 and invalided out of the army. After the war Eileen and Francis moved as settlers to Kenya, a difficult life far away from friends and family that did not suit her well. She suffered from depression and died of cancer in London in 1938. Ruby returned to India, to the new capital, Delhi, in 1915 when her husband, Rowland Baring, was appointed to Lord Hardinge's staff. As the 2nd Earl Cromer, Rowland was later Lord Chamberlain and the keeper of British theatrical morals for 16 years. Violet's first husband, Charles Petty-Fitzmaurice, was killed in action in 1914 leaving her a widow at 25 with two small children. She married John Jacob Astor, 1st Lord Astor of Hever in 1916. Larry married a Canadian, Marion Cook in 1921; they had four children and he died in 1975. Esmond, Mary's beloved youngest son, was killed in action aged 22 in August 1917.

For Mary, the wheel had turned full circle in 1910 when Queen Mary invited her to become a Lady-in-Waiting. After Rolly died she left Minto to live at Hydon End, near Hambledon in Sussex. She went home at last to lie in the quiet graveyard at Minto with Rolly, Eileen and Francis. Nearby, the war memorial, a bronze statue of a private soldier with a face modelled on Edmund's, gazes out across older and newer Elliot graves towards Hawick and the border hills.[18]

18. The statue is by Thomas J. Clapperton also responsible for the Mungo Park memorial in Selkirk.

MY INDIAN JOURNAL

1905-06

Friday, November 17th, 1905, S.S. "Peninsular"

We are at last nearing our journey's end, although adverse currents have delayed us many hours and instead of reaching Bombay at 8 A.M. and landing at once for our public reception, we cannot get in before 4.30 in spite of throbbing engines doing their utmost to increase the speed; the ship feels like a furnace with its heated boilers. The last 3 days have been terribly hot, and S.S. Peninsular is not a well-planned boat. Wherever you sit the vibration almost jumps you out of your chair, and everything seems planned in opposition to all common sense. We have read a good deal, played bridge, and slept as much as the heat would allow. Every one has been most attentive, and the food on both ships has been quite excellent.

At 3 o'clock Bombay appeared like a white streak in the distance. At 4 o'clock we arrayed ourselves in our smartest clothes, and came on deck just as we were passing the Renown[19] and the Terrible. They looked beautiful so white and clean and smart with all their flags flying and the yards manned; innumerable little fishing smacks with one sail like the wing of a bird surrounding them. They boomed out their salute of welcome just as at the same hour on this day last year the guns on the terrace of the Parliament Buildings at Ottawa fired our farewell salute.

Shortly after we anchored, the Admiral and officers came on board, amongst them Captain Campbell whom we knew at Quebec on the Crescent. We then had a long wait, every one became impatient, the staff indignant at what appeared an unnecessary delay. At last Military Secretaries and Government officials put in an appearance, and we went off in a launch with all our Staff in white uniform, Rolly in a frock coat and tall hat. Shades of night were already beginning to fall, so it was impossible for us to have the public reception that had been planned. We therefore drove straight from the wharf to Malabar Point, about four miles. The streets looking intensely picturesque with the lamps and flags and weirdly attired natives. We found every one waiting on the steps of Government House, except Lord

Mary Minto, 1905. (Image © Victoria and Albert Museum, London)

19. Battleship refitted as Royal Yacht for Prince and Princess of Wales tour of India. The Renown was escorted by the cruiser HMS Terrible.

Curzon.[20] Lord Lamington,[21] Lord and Lady Ampthill,[22] Lady Curzon,[23] and all the various staffs to welcome us. Every one felt shy and awkward, and the diversion of tea was a relief. Lady Ampthill is doing the honours for Lord Lamington, and is a most excellent hostess.

We are all in different bungalows in the grounds to which we walked by a covered way shaded by bougainvillea-pointsettia and many other tropical creepers. Our luggage did not arrive till past 8, and I had to dress with windows thrown open to the verandah on which red coated men were stationed—some pulling punkahs, some standing ready to fly with a message, and none of them apparently interested in my toilette, so I tried to ignore them.

Rolly and Lord Curzon dined alone together in order to have as much time as possible to discuss things. On reaching the drawing-room I found that I had been keeping Lady Curzon waiting, a thing she does so often herself that no one regretted it. I sat between Lord Ampthill and Lord Lamington, a dinner of about thirty, consisting of the various staffs, and two or three of the Viceroy's council. Poor Lord Lamington is dreadfully anxious about his wife; he has had a bad account of her by this mail, so it is hard on him having this gigantic party. Everything exceedingly well done, dozens of servants and a huge punkah the whole length of the room kept it perfectly cool. Mary Curzon was very gorgeous in an embroidered gold gown with ropes of gigantic pearls. We talked for some time after dinner; she told me about the various charities she wants me to interest myself in, and rather resented Lady Ampthill bringing up Members of the Council for me to talk to. I see there is slight friction at Lady Ampthill doing hostess.

The girls went to bed at once, but I went with Mary to her rooms, where we had a long talk, and eventually Rolly and Lord Curzon joined us. From all she said to me of her enormous charities and ceaseless work, and the tone of things during this one evening I can fully understand the difficulties the staff have had to contend with. Lord Curzon has been most helpful in giving Rolly every sort of information; he seems rather knocked up and tired; he made a farewell speech at the Byculla Club dinner two nights ago of an hour and a half reviewing the whole of his seven years' regime; he had a great reception and his speech was most eloquent, but very egotistical.

The night was fearfully hot; beautiful red coated men regardless of my only being arrayed in my night gown brought me cooling drinks. I don't at all like this publicity. All the windows open to the ground, each room has about four doors, none of them seem to shut, and I feel black eyes are peering at me through the darkness from every aperture; one's bath-room hardly seems sacred.

---

20. George Curzon, 1st Marquess Curzon of Kedleston, Viceroy of India, 1899-1905.
21. Charles Cochrane-Baillie, 2nd Baron Lamington, Governor of Bombay, 1903-1907.
22. Oliver Russell, 2nd Baron Ampthill, Governor of Madras, 1900-1906, Acting Viceroy of India April-December 1904.
23. Mary Curzon, Baroness Curzon of Kedleston, Vicereine of India, 1899-1905. Died 1906.

1905 Arrival Group Bombay.

Saturday, 19th. Government House, Malabar Point, Bombay.

I was roused at 6 A.M. by an ayah bringing chota hazri,[24] and I felt terribly reluctant to rise from my bed from where I could watch the sun rise over the sea which was lovely with little sailing boats floating about framed by tall palms and luxuriant creepers hanging from the verandah. At 7.15 Rolly started with the Viceroy in a carriage-and-four with escort of the 10th Hussars. I followed with Mary Curzon, Major Adam[25] and Captain Lambert, our new extra A.D.C., in another carriage-and-four.

A glorious morning, but I was amazed at the streets being so empty, and they must have felt sad at not getting a cheer the whole way. We got out at the Apollo Bunder,[26] where several officials and many spectators were drawn up in line. Several rajas were there. They came forward and hung chains of flowers round Curzon's neck. The farewells were quickly said, and the Curzons bade good-bye to India, the launch giving a final shriek which covered the nearest spectators with black steam to the ruination of their white clothes. The girls had arrived and stood waiting for us with Mrs Crooke-Lawless.[27]

We then became the centre of attraction, and the President of the Corporation, Sir Pherozeshah Mehta, read the address of welcome, which was enclosed in a beautiful silver casket. Rolly made a very nice speech in reply, and we drove off to the Council Hall, where he was sworn in—it was not an impressive ceremony and not well managed. I fancy Colonel Dunlop Smith[28] has pointed out to several officials that they have not distinguished themselves. It seems our ship being late altered the arrangements, but they have not shown any organising powers, and Lord Lamington hardly seems to know who is responsible. Every Viceroy hitherto has been sworn in Calcutta, but for many reasons it was not advisable that Lord Curzon should go there, and the swearing in was arranged to take place here, but it has not been up to the mark, or in accordance with the prestige of the Viceroy.

Rolly and I, followed by the other carriages, then drove round the native town which was the most brilliant scene. Masses of gaily dressed people, some with little more than their rich brown skins, some with rings in the noses, painted foreheads and gleaming white teeth, Parsees with their curious shiny black hats, Arabs dressed entirely in white and many with huge gold and brilliant turbans. The melée of colour in the brilliant sunshine with the background of gaily painted houses with balconies packed with picturesque figures was a scene impossible to describe. I longed to drive through it all again, as I could not take in everything, and wanted to be able to see both sides of the streets at once. The whole way the crowd cheered and clapped their hands; my head was quite tired with the continual bows, and I felt my mouth assume a set smile of surprised delight. We returned very

The New Mahvat.

Mr Hindi Punch—Guide him gently, Mian Minto, and you will always find him obedient and docile, [Lord Minto, the new Viceroy of India, took the oath of office at the Bombay Secretariat on Saturday, 18th November 1905].

---

24. Bed tea.
25. Major Frederick Loch Adam, Military Secretary.
26. The wharf or seafront in Bombay.
27. Wife of Colonel Warren Crooke-Lawless, Surgeon to the Viceroy.
28. Lt-Colonel James Robert Dunlop-Smith, Private Secretary to the Viceroy.

hungry to breakfast at 10.15, which Rolly and I had alone, a gorgeous man in red and gold standing behind each of us with a huge fan, while six or seven others noiselessly handed us innumerable dishes.

I feel rather overwhelmed at this moment at my own importance—how am I to cope with all this formality? Letters are brought in from A.D.C.'s saying that they await my commands. At present, I have none to give them; apparently in future I shall have to send for anyone I may wish to see, as no one intrudes upon the sacred presence uninvited. I am bound to say a deep depression has taken possession of my soul. Reuter's telegrams are brought to me each hour, telling me the King has fallen into a rabbit hole and Prince Charles is King of Norway, if I raise my voice and say Qui hie, a red man appears to fulfil my commands.

A huge dinner of 110, mostly men. I put on my smartest clothes and new tiara, and began the familiar old game of making a complete tour of the room and shaking hands with everyone.

Certainly Canada has been a good training for all this. After dinner we had a few peaceful moments in the garden among the palms with the Japanese lanterns and small lights, and then the reception—an enormous assemblage passed before us—Europeans, Eurasians, Parsees,

Hindus of all sorts and descriptions, some with the most magnificent jewels, crowds of soldiers, and naval men. Two men with fans standing behind us made it just possible to endure the heat. We made a tour of the room having a word here and there with the most important people, and then retired thoroughly exhausted having begun our day at 6 A.M., and the heat makes one feel intensely limp.

Monday, 20th.

The luggage had to leave at 8 o'clock, so we were up betimes. I sent for the old housekeeper, who has been here 10 years, to thank her for making us so comfortable. She has been here with the Harrises, Sandhursts and Northcotes. I told her that Va now has a fringe and Parisian clothes but the news had already reached her. She said "Lady Sandhurst was a plain dresser while she was here." I wonder all the more having experienced the heat how Va can have endured a double starched collar. At 9.30 we started in three 4-horsed carriages with postillions, and an escort of the 10th Hussars, the streets very full, and a most cordial crowd. All the officials in full uniform drawn up in rows at the stations, the Maharajas in their gorgeous clothes and an enormous guard of honour.

The Viceroy's train is being used at present by the Prince and Princess of Wales, so we have got rather an antediluvian one, it is not a corridor train. Rolly and I have each our separate cars with bed-room, sitting-room, bath-room and servants' room. We can walk from one to the other, but are cut off from the rest of the world, so we feel rather lonely. The train shakes fearfully and the dust is appalling; the country is flat and uninteresting with curiously shaped mountains in the distance. We wait at the stations while we have our meals; two high officials of the railway and the chief of the police make us a party of 18. We can just sit down comfortably at the narrow long table in the dining car. I am told we have nearly a hundred servants with us, and certainly the train is a most amazing length. It looks so picturesque as at the station an army of red men appear, and the natives group themselves in most picturesque attitudes. The whole scene is so absolutely unlike anything one has seen before. I feel I belong to an army as we all emerge from the train arrayed in helmets, it is almost impossible to realise the power of the sun; when one drives one of the servants stands up holding a huge white umbrella over one, and if it goes for a second to the right or left the sun sends a burning ray which strikes one like a fire.

Wednesday, 22nd.

Arrived at Calcutta at 8.30 A.M., found the station beautifully decorated, and an enormous Guard-of-Honour composed of the volunteers from the railway employees. Rolly and I went in a great red and gold state carriage with Captain Bulkeley, the horses and outriders and escort looked magnificent. A very pretty sight crossing the Bridge over the Hooghly river, all the streets from the station to Government House lined with troops and packed with, people, but the crowds were very undemonstrative, I believe the Calcutta population is never enthusiastic. Government House is a very imposing building. The long flight of wide steps leading up to the massive columns that support the entrance, look most majestic. The great house so spotlessly white, the red carpet, the crowd of officials lining the steps from the top to the bottom made the scene immensely impressive. Sir Andrew Fraser, the Lieutenant-Governor, advanced to receive us, Lord Kitchener[29] standing by his side. The whole facade in front of the house was lined with soldiers in brilliant uniforms, the sunshine intensifying the lights and shades and illuminating the picture with the gorgeous colouring of the east. We wended our way up the long stair case, being introduced to various people as we went till we found ourselves in a magnificent marble hall. A long double line of pillars lead up to the throne-room which has just been done up beautifully by Turner Lord[30] with crimson silk, a heavy embroidered velvet canopy surmounts the throne; this has been copied from the palace at Munich, and is very fine indeed.

A perfect army of red-coated men were standing on each side of the entrance, all with deepest respect bowed to the ground; it seemed very like a fairy tale, and so impossible to realise that Rolly has such supreme authority, that this population of 300,000,000 people hang upon his slightest word. I feel terribly out of place and inadequate, it is impossible to realise in England the state that this position entails. We have actually 700 native servants counting the whole establishment; each has his appointed task and never trespasses on his neighbours' duties.

---

29. H.E. Lieutenant-General, the Right Hon. Viscount Kitchener GCB, OM, GCMG, Commander-in-Chief, India.

30. London decorators and purveyors of reproduction furniture.

INDIA'S NEW VICEROY: ARRIVAL OF HIS EXCELLENCY THE EARL OF MINTO AT GOVERNMENT HOUSE, CALCUT

His Excellency inspecting the Guard of Honour

The scene at Government House was very imposing as the carriage containing Lord and Lady Minto swung round the corner and entered the big gateway, for the stately Calcutta home of the Viceroy of India affords a fine spectacular effect on ceremonial occasions. At the foot of the great flight of broad steps which lead from the trim expanse of green lawns to the Throne Room were the Commander-in-Chief and Sir Andrew Fraser, waiting to receive the newcomers; and at the top of the staircase were grouped all the leaders of light and fashion in Bengal, a glittering array composed of Sir Francis Maclean and other legal luminaries (who did not follow the new fashion set by the Bombay Judges of appearing in wigs and gowns), Members of Council, foreign Consuls in gold, Maharajahs in diamonds, and Bishops and Archbishops, &c.

As soon as we had finished shaking hands with the people assembled to meet us, round tables appeared as if by magic in the marble hall with our breakfast. We have only 6 European servants, the headman Furness, Rolly's Valet, Fryer, the three maids, and the French chef. Immediately after breakfast Major Adam and Captain Bulkeley[31] conducted us round the house. At present we are in the opposite wing to the rooms we shall eventually occupy—these are being arranged for the Prince and Princess. All the rooms are immensely high, about 30 feet. They have enormous brown and gold doors and electric light has been put in quite recently, but my critical eye is terribly distressed by the unsightly white china switches which have been carefully placed in the most conspicuous part of the silk wall quite spoiling the effect of the panel. It took us an hour and a half to go through three sides of the house; it is depressingly large, and I tremble at the thought of unpacking and arranging.

Sir Louis Dane, Foreign Minister, came to luncheon. Cedard, the Prince of Wales' Chef—whom we have engaged till March—gives us the most supreme food—the temptation to eat too much will be very great. After luncheon we walked to the stables to inspect the horses—40 in all—a fine array, each horse's head is held by his own syce, so the number of grooms help to swell the army. We had tea in the garden, the girls and some of the staff played tennis, one stolid man stood as umpire shouting the score, while two indefatigable boys in white with red sashes flew about picking up the balls. Our next excitement was the Viceroy's band which played during dinner, and does so every night; the bandmaster comes from Munich, and has taught the men quite wonderfully.

Friday, 24th.

The staff seem to have an unlimited number of ponies which they kindly placed at our disposal, so Rolly, Ruby,[32] and Violet[33] rode with them at 7 A.M. I had been roused from my slumbers by the crows who seem to hold a durbar at dawn on my shutters, so regretted that I was not riding too. Another day devoted to unpacking, but it is terribly unsatisfactory as half the boxes have not come and King & Co, who packed for us seem to have taken delight in dividing volumes as nothing is complete and my rooms remain in dire confusion. At 4 when the heat of the sun is over we played tennis, the lawn is very good, I fancy an army water and fondle the grass all day long to keep it in good condition.

Saturday, 25th.

Eileen,[34] Violet and I rode with the staff at 7 A.M., the rank and fashion all assemble at that hour and gallop round the race course. H.E. the Commander-in-Chief cut me dead, and then

31. Captain T.H. Rivers-Bulkeley, Comptroller, Killed in Action, 1914.
32. Lady Ruby Elliot-Murray-Kynymound, youngest of Lord and Lady Minto's daughters.
33. Lady Violet Elliot-Murray-Kynymound, 2nd of Lord and Lady Minto's daughters.
34. Lady Eileen Elliot-Murray-Kynymound, eldest of Lord and Lady Minto's daughters.

in these circum-
ook referred to is

baric circus that the barbaric East has ever beheld in all its barbaric history.

THE NEW VICEROY OF INDIA AND HIS STAFF

The names, reading from left to right, are: Captain the Earl of Rocksavage, Captain Lambert, Major Fielding, Colonel Dunlop Smith, Captain R Minto (seated), Captain Bulkeley, Major Adam, Captain Lord Francis Scott, Colonel Crooke Lawless, Captain the Hon. A. F

came up to apologise. So we rode for the rest of the time together. I find him very pleasant to talk to and we discussed the impasse at home now that Campbell-Bannerman[35] has brought in the Home Rule[36] question. Everyone, however, tells me to beware of K______ as he is unscrupulous in the means he uses to obtain his ends. The temperature was perfect, but we wore our sun helmets.

At 1 o'clock the whole party drove off in four landaus to embark on the little steam launch Maud, which was to take us 16 miles up the Ganges to Barrackpore. The boats full of vegetables and grain look lovely, rowed by natives standing and swinging the oar as far as they can reach over their heads. Another man stands in the bow steering with a most unwieldy looking rudder. The landing stage leads straight up to the house through a bamboo avenue planted by Lady Ripon; on emerging from this I felt I must be in fairyland. One's dream of bliss would be to wander in this glorious garden, with all its tropical vegetable and grass parks stretching for miles along the banks of the river. We found our luncheon spread beside the historical banian tree, which each year increases its circumference by throwing down fresh roots from its branches into the ground; it is now quite a walk to go round it. About 20 red and gold men stood ready to serve Cedard's seductive dishes which appeared as if by magic. Two men stood waving long sticks to keep off the kites; it seems these great birds with the greatest effrontery swoop down and seize any meat they can get hold of. Then we sauntered through the house and grounds; saw the temple erected by Lord Minto in 1810,[37] in memory of the men who fell at the storming of Java.

At present it is winter here, which means the most perfect summer weather—and with no flies. This place will be an enchanting haven of rest—one feels one has for the moment escaped the watchful gaze of the public, and can be oneself. I have already got used to the body-guard, whom we never move without. We had to return before sundown, in five minutes the blackest darkness falls like a pall—there is no twilight at all—with this heavenly summer weather it seems strange to be in one's room with all the lights turned on before 6 o'clock.

Sunday, 26th. Calcutta

We discovered that going to church is quite a ceremony— escort, four horses outriders, and an A.D.C. in uniform who hands one the plate. The church was very empty, the season in Calcutta does not begin till December; it was rather an ordeal in spite of this as Rolly and I sit on a high dais facing the congregation above the rest of the world, and one felt every eye was turned critically in our direction. A Court mourning has put me out considerably, and I am afraid I am not sufficiently prepared to mourn the distant relatives of the whole Royal

The New Viceroy of India and his Staff. The names, reading from left to right, are: Captain the Earl of Rocksavage, Captain Lambert, Major Fielding, Colonel Dunlop Smith, Captain Ross, H.E. the Viceroy Lord Minto (seated), Captain Bulkeley, Major Adam, Captain Lord Francis Scott, Colonel Crooke Lawless, Captain the Hon. A.H. Strutt.

35. Sir Henry Campbell-Bannerman, Leader of the Liberal Party, Prime Minister, 5th December 1905-1908.
36. Campbell-Bannerman supported Irish Home Rule.
37. 1st Earl of Minto, Governor General India, 1807-1813.

family. So excited by the arrival of the mail—enchanted to receive letters from home at last. I had a delightful budget, but they made me feel terribly home-sick, and long intensely to see so many loved ones who are now so far away.

Monday, 27th

Ruby and I grappled with the drawing-room furniture, the Clerk of the works, a huge black man who rejoices in the name of Ram Das, stood in the centre of the room and directed a large army who eagerly pressed forward to move the chairs and tables. I had to exercise a great deal of self-control to content myself by giving Ram Das directions; it would have saved so much time to assist the angles of the chairs myself, but that would be unheard of. Ram Das talks beautiful English, and encouraged me by telling me he felt sure, as I took so much interest, we should make this house a paradise. Eileen and I and Lord Francis[38] partook of tea with the C-in-C; he has made his house charming and has got a cult for china. He has collected some beautiful old pieces, which his A.D.C.s have to dust! He doesn't allow the natives to touch them. He is also making a charming garden—nothing can be more friendly than he is, but Rolly fears there may be trouble in the future. The Viceroy's authority must be maintained and it depends how far K______ sees this.

Sunday, 3rd. Barrackpore.

Visited Lady Canning's tomb.[39] She is buried in a lovely spot overlooking the river. I believe it was a very favourite haunt of hers where she used to sit and sketch. She died in 1861 having gone through all the horrors of the Mutiny. Barrackpore was the first place to shew disaffection. After luncheon watched the kites flying around and swooping on bits of meat which they caught in the air as it was being thrown to them. They seemed extraordinarily tame but refused to be tricked into taking the meat which was tied to a string by an ingenious A.D.C..

Monday, 4th.

Rolly returned to Calcutta immediately after breakfast. Violet and I drove about the place in the little pony carriage with two fat ponies, Creepy and Crawly. The public road outside the park is extremely pretty, shaded by overhanging trees and palms. Weird little habitations are scattered here and there—Hindus in every variety of dress were squatting on the ground, some smoking unwieldy-looking pipes, others just basking in the sun enjoying life in idleness, children arrayed in every shade of coloured drapery, others with nothing

38. Lord Francis Montagu-Douglas-Scott, A.D.C., Married Eileen, 1915.

39. Charlotte Stuart, Countess Canning, artist, died of malaria 1861. Wife of 1st Earl Canning, Governor General, India, 1856-61, Viceroy, India, 1858-1861.

Village scenes near Barrackpore.

on but their rich brown skins harmonising with the bright foliage of the leaves. I am still astonished at the country being so green and fresh, it never rains, and yet the grass and the trees look brilliant.

There is a very heavy dew every morning which keeps the turf green and it is impossible to believe this is mid-winter. We returned to Calcutta in the afternoon very sorry to have left the peace and quiet. The noise of this town is bewildering; electric trams, shrill whistles from steamers, sirens, natives screaming to each other, dogs barking, crows cawing; there is no cessation day or night and it is very tiring.

Tuesday, 12th

Rode with Captain Bulkely to the Zoo. The brilliant masses of pointsettia looking gorgeous in the sunshine attracted me much more than the animals. Our ponies were much alarmed at the proximity of the lions and tigers and snorted with fear. One animal, called a Mandrill is too extraordinary—he looks as if his face had been painted like a clown—I could hardly believe nature was responsible for such a freak. He was furious at our looking at him and shook the bars of his cage with rage. Another amusing animal, whose name I forget, looked at us with a supercilious expression and then spat in our faces.

As several of the staff are dining out tomorrow, the auspicious day on which Eileen comes of age, we decided to have a little dance tonight to celebrate the occasion and also as a sort of rehearsal for the State Ball. For the last fortnight, 18 coolies in scant attire have been sitting in a line on the floor of the ball-room polishing the boards with bottles. It is a most comic sight; the final shine is obtained by several coolies running up and down the room with a mattress on which two semi-naked figures sit, apparently much enjoying their ride; the result is most successful as the floor shines brilliantly and is perfect for dancing. I was quite dazzled with the gorgeous effect of the room all lighted up. The crystal chandeliers are historical and were looted from a French ship about 100 years ago. Napoleon intended having a residence in India and sent chandeliers to decorate his house—the design was copied for the rest of the reception rooms, so they are the same throughout the house.

Tuesday, 19th.

The house was transformed into labyrinths of greenery, forming pens into which the ladies attending the drawing-room are to be herded; elaborate arrangements have to be made to avoid people crowding in together. The beautiful body-guard is relegated to the grounds, as the sight of so much beauty and splendour is supposed to have an injurious effect on the character of these puritanical Sikhs. As they mount guard every day in the passages and watch the ladies of the house party in the décolleté dresses which are supposed to offend their scruples, His Excellency most aptly remarked—"I suppose it is quantity, not quality, which they can't stand." The drawing-room commenced at 9.30. I wore a gold gown

embroidered with silver, with a lovely bouquet of dark red roses and orchids. Rolly looked very magnificent in his gold coat with his three stars, all his medals and light blue ribbon of the Star of India. I was not impressed by the beauty of Calcutta or the dresses; the age of the ladies who were presented struck me most and I wondered why they had delayed so long. About 700 attended, the husbands accompany them, but do not pass and wait in the ball-room and yellow drawing-room.

Sunday, 24th. Barrackpore

Received a very nice mail but hardly anyone has alluded to Christmas. Eileen, Violet, Major Feilding, Captain Lambert,[40] and I went for a ride in the afternoon; it was most interesting passing through the Indian settlements outside the park. When one sees this mass of

40. Major G. Feilding, Captain H. Lambert, A.D.C.s

Barrackpore.

humanity herded together like aimals one wonders why they are ever free from plague and disease, and how it will be possible to teach them the elementary rules of hygiene and sanitation.

Monday, 25th—Christmas Day.

We breakfasted, as usual, under the banyan tree, and the whole party went to church; it seemed so strange seeing the Christmas decorations composed of palms, poinsettias, bougainvilleas, marigolds, and nasturtiums. The Christmas hymns, however, were the same, and a lady sitting in the choir kept on a mink boa throughout the service, I imagine from sentiment as it must have made her uncomfortably hot. We had a large luncheon party from Calcutta, the launch bringing Lord Kitchener, Major Marker,[41] Captain Victor Brooke,[42] Sir H. and Lady Rawlinson,[43] Mr and Lady Noreen Bass,[44] and Lord Brooke.[45] Our table was decorated with mistletoe, and we ate turkey, mince pies, and plum pudding. Otherwise sitting under the shamiana with our tropical surroundings, we could hardly believe that it was Christmas Day and we thought of absent friends shivering in England in the cold, raw damp, and of others in Canada with their white world sparkling in the dazzling radiance of a typical winter's day with the thermometer at zero. After luncheon four conjurors spread a covering on the lawn and with a wonderful flow of unintelligible language made marked rupees come out of oranges and threaded rings on a stick which had never left the Viceroy's hands. Sundry other wonders were performed such as cutting off each other's tongues. The mango tree which I had always heard of as springing in five minutes from a seed to the size of Jack's bean stalk, I thought a dreadful fraud, as the seed was hidden underneath a wigwam and never grew more than three feet.

Wednesday, 27th. Calcutta.

At 8 A.M. the Tashi Lama[46] arrived with his retinue to pay his respects to the Viceroy. It was a very weird sight; the escort arrived on funny little shaggy ponies beating tom-toms, and making discordant noises. The Lama himself arrived in our carriage-and-four horses with a sergeant and six of the body-guard which had been sent to convey him here as a mark of respect for his high position; he seems a very ordinary young man with nothing remarkable in his appearance. On alighting from, the carriage he had to take off his round broad brimmed hat made of gold, and replace it by a yellow bishop's metre. Surrounded by his followers and all our staff in full uniform and hand in hand with Sir Louis Dane he mounted

41. Major Marker, C-in-C Staff.
42. Lt.Col.Victor Brooke. Killed 1915. Brother of Lord Alanbrooke.
43. Sir Henry Rawlinson, 1st Baron Rawlinson.
44. Sir William Bass, Racehorse owner.
45. Lord Brooke, Reuters correspondent Russo-Japanese War, 1904-05, Earl of Warwick, 1924-1928.
46. The 9th Panchen Lama, Thubten Choekyi Nyima.

the steps and was ushered into the throne-room where the Viceroy sat awaiting him. Not being a reigning prince protected by the Government of India, only a spiritual potentate, the etiquette is for the Viceroy to sit next to the Lama on an ordinary chair, not on the Throne. We flew from our point of vantage overlooking the entrance to the throne-room and watched the Durbar from behind screens—everyone sat in a great ring, the Lama's followers on one side, our staff on the other, and Sir Louis Dane as Foreign Secretary on the other side of the Viceroy. Then a conversation was carried on through an interpreter, a terribly difficult proceeding accompanied by many bows and interchanges of courtesies.

Tea was then brought in on trays and handed to the Tashi Lama and his suite. After this, the Tibetans came in laden with presents and laid them at the Viceroy's feet. These comprised bales of silk scarves, beautifully embossed silver and copper tea pots, silk embroideries, and lastly enormous bundles made of some animal's hide containing tea. It seems so ludicrous all these presents being brought, and it is such a farce as everything is paid for in full. The Viceroy has first choice, can select what he wants to buy; the other things go to a place called the Toshakhana, where they are kept and distributed when the occasion arises to give presents, or else sold and the money put into the treasury. Rolly told me afterwards the smell of these people was quite appalling, and nearly made him sick. The girls and I rushed upstairs to see the departure from the windows. The Tashi Lama climbed into a yellow palanquin carried by twelve and drawn with ropes by about twenty men. This palanquin was a present from the Emperor of China, only three of the imperial family have similar yellow ones, which is a royal privilege.

The Lama's procession was barely out of sight before more escorts appeared, and another of our carriages containing the Maharaja of Sikkim.[47] His followers were dressed in red and brown with hats looking like inverted flower pots, with a peacock's feather. The Maharaja was conducted to the throne-room; being a reigning protected prince this time the Viceroy sat on the throne. The Maharaja departed in his own carriage, his followers packing themselves like sardines into little native carriages, five or six people squeezing inside, while two or three more sat on the roof.

Snake Charmers, Barrackpore, Christmas Day, 1905.

47. Thutob Namygal, Maharaja Chogyal of Sikkim.

The comic element came in, when the final carriage remained stationary, owing to the horses refusing to move, this became serious as the third procession with the Tongsa Penlop of Bhutan[48] was waiting to draw up at the steps. Excited natives hurried forward, the horses were seized and almost carried out of the way in order to allow the Tongsa to alight. The

48. Sir Ugyen Wangchuck, became 1st Hereditary King of Bhutan, 1907.

same ceremony took place tea, dallies (sweets and fruits) and presents, and the durbars came to an end. I hope my kodaks may prove successful; but without the colour half the charm is gone.

Rolly and I went to the Horse Show after luncheon. On arrival we found that Violet had got first prize for the cobs and third for Rolly's mare Waitress. We watched the jumping for some time sitting under a cool and lofty shamiana. I then distributed the prizes, and a very long list made it nearly dark before we started to go home. Hearing that the Prince prefers a Quadrille to a Lancers at the State Ball, we felt it was needful to practise it. On my arrival in the drawing room I already found the people who take part in the State Quadrille drawn up ready to begin. A humble little teacher came to instruct us who knew less about it than I did, and I longed for D'Egville.[49] Found Colonel Crooke-Lawless awaiting me. Apparently Violet had felt the sun at the races yesterday having lent her thick sunshade to a lady who complained of the heat; this produced a bad headache and restless night, but being so anxious to drive and ride at the show today she said nothing about it. The result was her temperature went up to 104, and the pain in her head was very severe. I feel so unhappy that this should have occurred, but I am very thankful it is sun fever, and not a sunstroke.

The Tongsa Penlap and his ministers. (L to R) Punakha Jongpen, Thimbu Jongpen, Tongsa Penlop, Jung Dongu, and Debi Zimpen. The Tongsa Penlop, who is seated in the centre, is seen wearing the star and badge of the Order of the Indian Empire, of which he had just been made a Knight Commander (K.C.I.E.) when this portrait was taken. The badge of the Tudor rose and crown is hanging from a riband round his neck. Behind the other officials, who are standing, are some curious mural decorations representing elephants and winged symbolical figures.

Maharani of Sikkim.

Thursday, 28th.

Rolly had to start at 7.30 to return the Tashi Lama's visit and the other princes. The Tashi Lama lives in a huge tent—all hung round with snow leopard skins. The tea they gave Rolly was mixed with ghee—a sort of mutton fat—and nearly made him ill; the taste was so appalling.

During our absence at Barrackpore 700 men have been employed in painting, cleaning, and preparing the house for the Royal visit. I went round all the rooms, putting the finishing touches, and it looks very spick and span. The furniture has been polished, and my Chippendale pieces from Barrackpore are a great success. The grounds in front of the

49. Probably Louis Hervey D'Egville, dance teacher and choreographer, died 1892, or his son.

house have 50 large tents to accommodate the staff and servants—not our English idea of tents which one sees at Aldershot, but great rooms with a brick floor covered with mats and carpets; each person has a bed-room, sitting room, and bath-room, and even the valets have two arm chairs apiece; it is all beautifully thought out, and Captain Bulkeley deserves all praise; he has thought of everything down to the electric irons in each lady's maids rooms; the staff are all connected by telephone to their valet's tents. Sixteen guests to luncheon.

Friday, 29th.

Ruby and I, Lord Francis and Captain Strutt[50] drove to see the first match of the polo tournament, our staff against Calcutta. It was gratifying to find our staff were much the strongest team, they won by six goals to four. It is extraordinary how rash every one seems to be about the sun; ladies never wear sun-hats and sit with the burning rays playing on their backs with no protection but a linen shirt; I cannot imagine how they avoid sunstroke. Violet, I am thankful to say, is almost normal, and perhaps this warning will have the effect of making us all more careful.

The bustle of arrival seemed to permeate through the house. By luncheon time bullock wagons by the score, piled with Royal luggage, were to be seen at the back premises stretching as far as the eye could reach. Five hundred coolies have been engaged to handle the luggage, plans of the camp have been printed, large tickets with the owner's name adorn the tents, so no one has any excuse for making mistakes. At last the 15th Lancers turned into the gates at a trot with a battery of artillery, then a squadron in khaki—the Calcutta Light House. Next, the Cadet Corps composed of ruling Princes and cadets of princely houses who are being trained for the Army. They wear the most beautiful uniform I have ever seen; white coats with blue sashes, blue turbans with silver feathers and black chargers with white leopard skin saddle cloths. The bands all burst out in God Save the King as the carriage drove up with the Prince and Princess. There then seemed an endless amount of handshaking and introduction, but everyone seemed pleased and happy, and it all went with enthusiasm. The Prince and Princess were extremely cordial to everyone.

The girls with Bridget[51] and Molly[52] were waiting in the throne-room, which we passed through en route to the Prince's room where tea was waiting and which we partook of with them. They seem delighted at the success of the tour. We sat talking for over an hour. It seems almost incredible that difficulties should have been thrown in the way of the Prince and Princess' arrival, but from all they tell us this appears to have been the case. The train was not properly cleaned and over hauled because the Viceroy was on tour till four days before it was wanted. Their rooms were occupied at Bombay till the very last moment, and they almost found the servants putting clean sheets on the beds.

---

50. Hon. A. Strutt, A.D.C.
51. Hon. Mrs D. Keppel, wife of Hon.Derek Keppel, Equerry to the Prince of Wales.
52. Viscountess Crichton, wife of Captain Viscount Crichton, Equerry to the Prince of Wales, died 1914.

Violet on Lord Harry

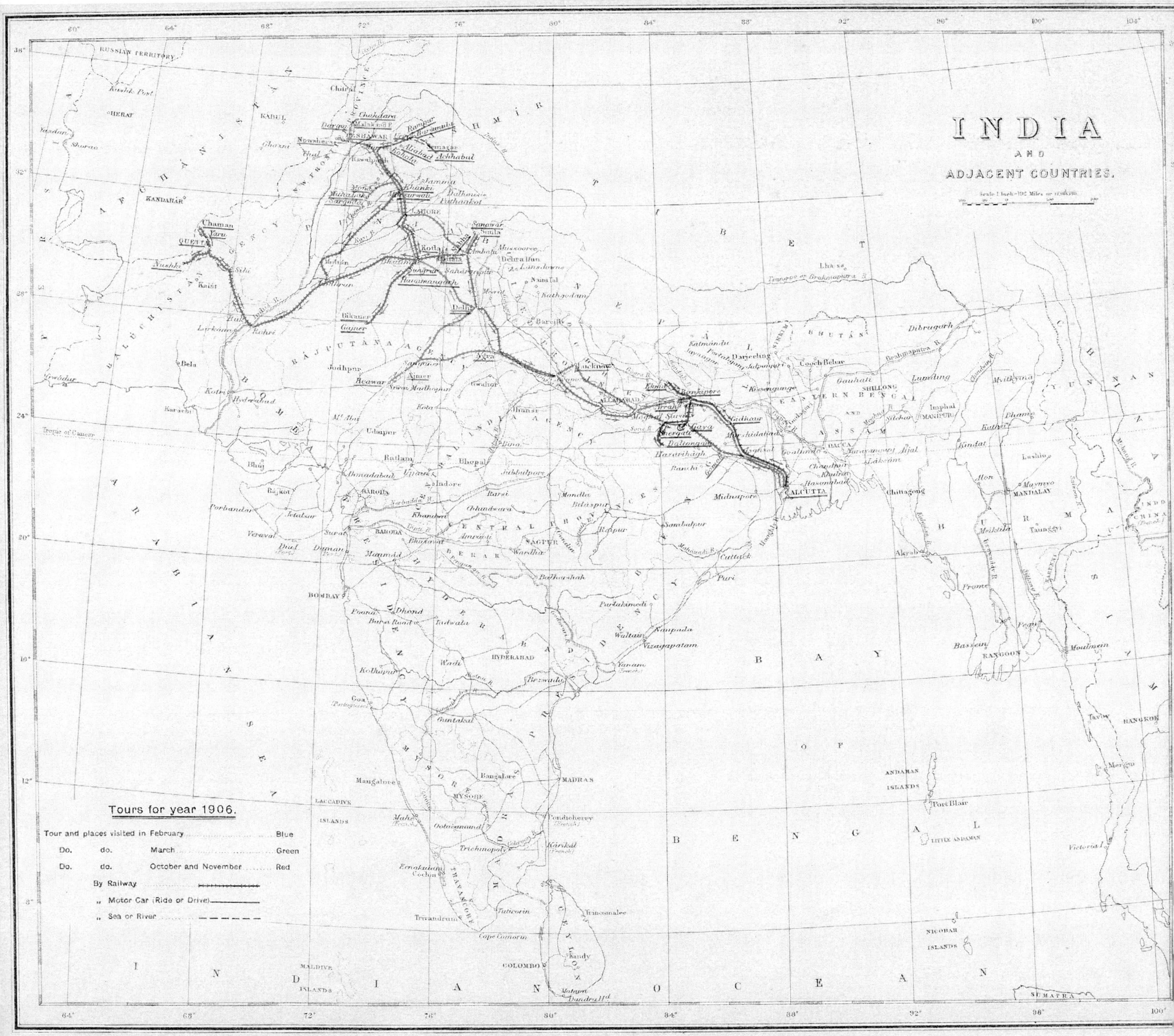

Viceregal Tours 1906.

1906

January 1st.

At 8.05 A.M. I fetched the Princess, and, with Lord Rocksavage[53] in attendance very beautiful in his uniform, we started for the Maidan in a carriage-and-four, and a large escort to witness the Proclamation Parade. We took up our position at the saluting point. Soon we heard the sounds of distant cheering and saw the dust of the escort as the cortege swung on to the ground. It was a proud moment when Rolly in his general's uniform with his waving plumes galloped on a showy little white Arab about 10 paces ahead of the Prince of Wales, Lord Kitchener and a host of other Generals. The two last Viceroys have hated riding and Lord Elgin[54] used to drive to the saluting point get on a horse which was held by about four grooms receive the salute and get off again.

Lord Curzon used to ride from Government House, but the pace was never accelerated, and when Minto first suggested cantering he was told it had never been done. Finding the Prince of Wales quite ready to fall in with his views the order was given and the appearance of the whole cortege cantering up was most effective. Nothing the natives adore so much as horsemanship, and I think they were pleased with the show this morning. On our return about five photographers appeared to photograph us in a group, and a formidable one it was.

Breakfast was very welcome at about a quarter to 11. We had barely time to swallow it before we were again under way this time to see a polo match between the 9th Lancers and the Golconda team. A tournament is going on all this week. I suppose this is about the finest

The Cadet Corps. His Highness General Sir Partab Singh of Idar.

53. George Horatio Charles Cholmondeley, Earl of Rocksavage, 5th Marquess of Cholmondeley, 1923-1968.
54. 8th Earl of Elgin, Viceroy 1861-1863, died in office.

polo you can see in the world; it was certainly wonderfully exciting. The best player was a Native officer called Shah Mirza Beg,[55] I felt rather sorry our English officers should be beaten by natives; they were all mounted on splendid ponies and rarely made a mistake, specially Shah Mirza, who was beautiful to watch.

Lunched alone with Their Royal Highnesses, and after started with the Princess, Lord Rocksavage, and the Dugdales[56] for a purdah party at Belvedere, the Lieutenant-Governor's; the two men remained outside. We three ladies went into the long drawing-room which was lighted with electric light, all the blinds being drawn down and several screens erected in the passage to prevent any possibility of a man seeing the *purdali* ladies even in the distance. Some of them had never seen a European lady or been out before. It is quite an operation for these ladies to get into their carriages in order to avoid the eye of the public. A folding screen is placed round them as unlike the Turkish women it is not considered sufficient for them only to hide their faces. About 60 ladies were assembled; the Princess went round first and was introduced, and I followed while she had the chief ladies brought up to her. Some had the most gorgeous jewels; large rings covered with precious stones through their noses and about six huge rings through their ears, others had large diamond solitaires stuck on their noses. One small child had a large pear-shaped diamond fastened in her nose which fell down right over her mouth. A group of three girls were standing together—their ages fourteen, fifteen, and nineteen; they were all married, the sign of marriage is a narrow red line down the parting of their hair; the fifteen-year old had one child, the one of nineteen three; one child of eleven was dressed in yellow satin covered with precious stones, ropes of pearls with large tassels hung from her head, and her arms were a mass of bangles and huge uncut emeralds and pearls which completely covered her. Jewels are not worn till after marriage; hers had taken place a year ago, but she was still living with her parents. A good many of them could speak English; some had been educated in schools and were not *purdali*. A native lady, a Mrs Gupta, went round with me and interpreted.

They were all immensely excited at seeing the Princess of Wales and also grateful for the great honour of being presented to me; it was explained to them that I was the Burra Lady Sahib. The Maharani of Cooch Behar told me many of them did not understand what life was outside the purdah, but once they got some knowledge of it they became rather dissatisfied. Some are so strict that even if they visit the Maharani they will not drink a drop of water in her house. I told many of them I hoped some day they would visit me in Government House; they looked rather alarmed, but said they would speak to their husbands about it.

Tuesday, 2nd.

Their Royal Highnesses lunched with the Maharaja of Cooch Behar, so for the first time Rolly and I had an opportunity of meeting the whole house party. All the Prince of 'Wales'

55. Major Shah Mirza Beg, Hyderabad Lancers, died on the polo ground, 1912.

56. Mr and Mrs F. Dugdale; he was Equerry to the Prince of Wales.

Staff are delighted with the success of his visit so far. At 4 o'clock the girls and I and Captain Strutt drove to the Maidan, where the native dances were to take place, a stage was erected in the centre, and the audience sat in the circular amphitheatre which is an exact copy in miniature of the Delhi Durbar. All the Native Princes were drawn up in line on each side of the steps of the Royal box in their most gorgeous clothes and jewels. The President of the entertainment, the Maharaja of Darbhanga, had the most magnificent crown on; it was originally bought in Paris for £80,000; it is now worth about £130,000. The Maharaja knelt down before me so that I might have the opportunity of examining his jewels more closely, and complained bitterly of the weight of his headdress.

The sports themselves were not very wonderful, nothing to approach a good show at Earl's Court. There were about four different dances—Sikkim, Bhutanese, Nagar Sankirtan, and the Tibetan ghost. An appalling discordant noise they made with their weird misshapen instruments. As evening closed in, the effect was very picturesque: the building with its towers and minarets stood out against the clear evening sky, and as darkness fell thousands of tiny lights outlined the whole structure, while in this mysterious light about 50 half-clothed savages performed extraordinary antics and belaboured each other with sticks. Attar and pan was then brought in jewelled vessels, and Imamzamin[57] was placed on His Royal Highness's arm according to the ancient custom of Muhammadans. The Maharajas then brought three wonderful golden chains made of threads and embroidered with seed pearls and placed them round our necks. I believe they are quite valuable. Their Royal Highnesses were cheered to the echo as they drove away. The whole of the Maidan was lighted up with myriads of little lamps hanging from the trees. The ponds looked like liquid fire, and on one of them a native boat entirely composed of silver lights floated on the golden waters. It was the most wonderful sight, and one which requires Eastern surroundings. A breath of wind would have played havoc, but in this marvellous climate nature does not play the vagaries we are accustomed to at home.

Thursday, 4th. Calcutta

Went with the Princess to see the Museum, which has a wonderful collection of Indian products and works of art. Lord Curzon has done a splendid job in collecting samples of handicrafts from all parts of India. We went on to St. John's Church which has several interesting monuments; there is a pedestal on which Lord Minto's name is inscribed—1810. Unfortunately his bust was thrown down in the great earthquake in the seventies and was smashed to atoms. We shall have to try and get a bust of the great grand-father to replace it. Doctor Ross[58] then drove with us round the sight of the old Port and showed us exactly where the Black Hole was; the new buildings almost entirely cover the ground, but it was interesting to see where the poor 243 victims were led through the fort expecting to find an

57. Decorated ceremonial armband—originally a gold coin tied in silk.

58. Sir Edward Denison Ross, Orientalist and Linguist.

exit on the other side. At 4 o'clock the laying of the Victoria Memorial Hall stone took place. This is to be a magnificent white marble building containing works of art. The ceremony commenced by Sir Andrew Fraser giving a history of the origin of the Memorial Building and Lord Curzon's desire to leave a monument to contain art treasures which would be worthy of our great Queen.

Friday, 5th.

We all lunched together—a party of about 60 had been summoned to say good-bye. Everybody received a present or photographs; our staff have been given lovely things; it is wonderful how everybody has been thought of. I believe about 40 servants have been given a souvenir—the Bandmaster, Büchner, a baton made specially. Rolly and I went with the Prince and Princess to his room; there we found the most gigantic silver bowl which he presented to Rolly; it is hammered out of one piece of silver and the inscription is beaten out instead of being engraved; it is a splendid piece of plate almost the size of a bath. I was given a diamond brooch with the Prince of Wales' feathers which makes a lovely badge.

We left at 4.30 for the Station and found their enormous train awaiting us; it is really the Viceroy's, so we were very glad to have an opportunity of seeing it. The Prince and Princess have each their separate carriage containing sitting-room, bed-room, bath-room, and servants' rooms, most luxurious and fitted up with green silk, but unfortunately the bed-rooms are not divided off and have to be used as passage-rooms which practically means the Staff can never pass through to the dining car, and the train has always to stop at stations, if people want to circulate. The journey to Barrackpore only took half an hour. Captain Bulkeley had slaved all day getting things straight. The European servants have been so difficult to accommodate.

Monday, 8th. Barrackpore

The Princess and I had our usual drive—Bridge in the evening. I think they are all sorry their visit to us is over and they have genuinely enjoyed themselves. The Prince on every occasion has insisted on the Viceroy taking precedence; it was really rather amusing to see them bowing to each other in the door-ways, each trying to make the other walk first. It is a great relief to know they have found everything to their satisfaction; we felt terribly handicapped having only been here five weeks, but I think everything has pass off without a hitch.

Tuesday, 9th. Calcutta

Their Royal Highnesses, myself, and the remainder of the Staff left by launch at 8.30; they are marvellously punctual people, and the Prince invariably appears a few minutes before the time, and attendants with anxious faces arrive on the scene at a run. I am thankful we have not kept them waiting once during their visit. Rolly was on board the Guide at Calcutta which takes them down the river to join the Renown. We all felt quite sad when the final partings came; everyone has been so particularly nice and grateful for all we have done, and both the Prince and Princess thanked us repeatedly for making things so easy. One feels very thankful all has passed off so well, as it has been a grave responsibility, and such a strain playing up for 10 whole days, as I have been with them continuously from morning to night. The house feels quite strange and empty, and well it may after the exodus that has taken place.

Friday, 12th

The Rani Sahibah of Wadhwan came to pay me a visit; she is a purdah lady, and I watched her arrival at the private entry door with great interest. She drove up in a hermetically sealed carriage—one man on the box and two men behind and two outriders. Once at the door the coachman threw down his reins, and the horses fortunately stood still. The outriders and two servants then ran out of sight, and the coachman stood with his back to the door covering his eyes with his hands. An ayah and an English nurse helped the little lady to alight, throwing a black shawl over her head; she was accompanied by two tiny children. Eileen and Ruby met her at the door, every sentry, policeman and *chaprassie*[59] having been ordered to absent themselves. Dwyer[60] was allowed to assist in throwing back the door of the lift, and the procession at length arrived in my sitting-room. I rose to receive her and shook hands, after which she went down on both knees and three times hit the floor with her hands and forehead. I was so embarrassed, I was not expecting this, and did not know how to receive such a salutation. I was greatly relieved to get her safely on the sofa beside me. She is a widow, and consequently was dressed in black embroidered with gold, and wore a mass of pearls and diamonds.

The two children were gorgeously attired in cloth of gold and wonderful embroideries and covered with ropes of pearls and emeralds; she told me when the silk of the embroidery wears out, the ragged material is burnt, and the gold and silver that remains is used again. This lady was not purdah before she married and does not approve of the custom which is not Hindu, but taken from the Muhammadans; but as her husband was very strict she doesn't like now to revert to her freedom. She tells me it is a great trial; she talks beautiful English and is interested in many philanthropic schemes. The children sang us songs in English and in two different Hindu dialects. The girls accompanied her to the door when she left, and to show them how purdah ladies manage at railway stations, &c.; a silk screen on four poles was produced which had been brought on the top of the carriage. This was placed all round her and was moved along with her by the ayah and nurse till the carriage

59. Orderly.

60. MM's Lady's maid.

was reached, the coachman again turning his back; he then whistled and the servants and outriders made their appearance. It seems incredible in these days that anyone can believe such an absurd performance is necessary.

Rolly had an address from the Indian Association, which means the agitators in connection with Lord Curzon's recent partition of Bengal; they came with a long petition which Rolly answered most carefully, saying it was impossible once the sanction of the Secretary of State had been obtained to reverse the policy. I believe they were considerably saddened, but pleased on the whole that he should have spoken out and not misled them; all the newspapers have supported the line he has taken.

Saturday, 20th.

Have nothing to record this week; have spent an absolutely quiet time at Barrackpore. I personally have been in bed most of the time with an awful cold. It is the greatest mistake to imagine it is always hot in India; the evenings and nights are very chilly, and I dislike these perpetual draughts, as in this country it never seems to occur to any one to shut a door. I have always forgotten to allude to the jackals; they abound here, and at night occasionally make the most hideous noise. If one begins, at least 10 join in the chorus, and give vent to the most unearthly sounds; it is my idea of the agonising moans and cries of spirits in torment. These jackals are frequently seen trotting about the grounds, Rolly once came on four or five together; they are a constant excitement to Dandy[61] and add greatly to his enjoyment of life.

Since I have been here I have had time to glance at my journal, and I must confess it makes me hot to read it consecutively. I hope my family will remember that I write it at any odd moment, and will make every allowance for the repetitions and mistakes, and the atrocious grammar wandering as I do from one tense to the other; it is only a hurried account of our every-day life, and seeing it in print gives it an undue importance and suggests a carefully written essay, which certainly does not describe my fragmentary phrases.

Tuesday, 23rd.

Small-pox is very prevalent in Calcutta, so Colonel Crooke-Lawless has vaccinated all the family and the whole establishment; it is now impossible to get *durzies*[62] to work for us, as no one is allowed into the compound unless they are vaccinated and they naturally refused to submit to this regulation. Rolly and I and the two girls dined with Cooch Behar. Mr Risley sat on my other side, it amused me to see how he has turned round to support the powers

61. Lord Minto's Dandie Dinmont terrier.

62. Tailors.

that be. He started by trying to make me run a proposed nursing scheme of Lady Curzon's which, in my opinion, does not meet the requirements of the country. I told him a month ago I thought a new scheme must be devised; he now tells me that his views absolutely coincide with mine, and that he admires the wise decision I have come to; I could hardly help laughing. Cooch Behar was very interesting about the feeling of the natives in connection with education and caste: they are a strange people and there is so much to learn about them. He mentioned the gratitude of the native if he is kindly treated; he said they would literally lay down their lives for you, which is more than you expect from a European. It seems to me so monstrous that young soldiers treat their bearers like dogs just because they happen to be black, and the idea that the native must he roughly handled to keep him sufficiently in subjection is, I am sure, mistaken.

Friday, 26th

A terrible morning of photography; the family and staff arranged in various attitudes by two different photographers. No one would remain quiet, at the same time the men all showing great anxiety as to the curl of their moustaches, and the correct sit of their tunics.

Sunday 28th.Barrackpore

The girls, Bridget, and Molly arrived in the morning having had a native banquet at Cooch Behar's on the previous evening. They were all dressed up in saris; sat on the floor and ate very disgusting dishes with their fingers, which they don't seem greatly to have appreciated! Ruby, Lord Francis and I had a lovely ride about four miles from home. We came on some temples and a gigantic pink god with a monkey face sitting on a platform over a pond; he is a most amazing apparition. We were quickly surrounded by a crowd of natives; two men could talk excellent English and proceeded to tell us their religious legends. I could only gather that the good god Rama had overcome a bad god Ravana, and encircling his neck with his tail hurled him into the sea. They were greatly excited on hearing who we were, and anxious to show us all their temples and gods, but the shades of night were falling and we had to gallop home.

Monday, 29th.

Drove Bridget round by some of the picturesque villages before breakfast, taking kodaks, it always amuses the natives, and they are usually delighted to pose, but they are a very sad race and it strikes me how seldom one sees them laughing; they are certainly devoid of *joie de vivre*. I think people out here catch the depression; it is so different to the colonies where people have their permanent homes. Here they are only birds of passage. Everyone's idea is to make enough money to enable them to get home. Most people have some sadness to contend with in the separation of wife or children; a united family in India seems hardly possible. Everywhere one sees monuments put up to great men who have lost their lives in building up this wonderful empire. There seems to be very little recreation for the community.

As for Rolly, his work is really beyond one man's strength. There is no small detail that is not brought before him; every day endless files come in, and have to be looked through. It seems ridiculous that he should be asked whether a thousand rupees should be spent on building an official his bath-room in a remote station in Madras, or whether a man at Nagpur may have leave to go to Bombay to visit his dentist. Mr Hewett, one of the Members of Council, told him the other day that he had no hesitation in saying the work was absolutely twice as much as in Lord Lansdowne's or Lord Elgin's time. Not a single Member was allowed to take any authority upon himself whatsoever by Lord Curzon, who insisted on knowing the minutest detail; the number of seats provided for the public in the various parks would be ordered by him, and endless equally absurd trivialities. I hope this will be changed ere long, and, by giving the Viceroy only things worthy of his notice, he will have time to give them fuller consideration. In reading over his despatches and private letters to Mr John Morley,[63] the knowledge that he is obliged to have of the country makes my brain reel.

The Military Administration, which must be most delicately handled—so as to satisfy those in authority here, and also be acceptable to the new orders of things at home is a fearful problem. So many difficult questions arise whether rebellious tribes should be treated with leniency, hoping to civilise them, which Rolly strongly advocates, or whether punitive expeditions should be sent which means decimating whole districts, destroying beautiful trees and orchards and crops, and driving women and children from their homes. Then there are all the questions of finance, the suggested Persian Loan, the Frontier Railway schemes, what route is to be selected. Everything means most careful study. Endless dissatisfaction has been caused by the partition of Bengal;[64] trouble crops up every day in connection with it. Besides the time engaged in discussions with Council come the perpetual interviews; everybody wishes to see the Viceroy and put his special grievance before him. Addresses have to be answered, and a thorough knowledge of the government of this gigantic empire must be displayed in every branch. Certainly the Viceroy with all his autocratic power has not a bed of roses; it is a most strenuous life which seems all work and no play.

Friday, February 2nd. Calcutta

Spent most of the morning looking into accounts. They seem to me appalling. I suppose the Prince's visit is answerable for a good deal, but at this rate most of our pay will be spent principally on food. The waste in the house is cruel; it seems any one belonging to

63. John Morley, 1st Viscount Morley of Blackburn, 1908, Secretary of State for India 1905-1910.

64. October 1905, Division of Bengal into 2 parts, East Bengal and Assam and West Bengal, highly unpopular among Hindu population in particular.

the establishment can have their food from our kitchen, so it is very difficult to keep a real check on the consumption and I know that twice the amount needed is cooked.

Went with Captain Strutt miles through the native town to a place where 800 Hindu school children were assembled sitting in rows on the grass. I had time while monotonous recitations, droning native songs, and flower dances were taking place to examine them minutely. Some children had beautiful faces—enormous eyes and feathery eye-lashes almost uncomfortably long—every child's hair was plastered with oil. Some had wonderful head dresses; golden nets with pearls placed coquettishly on one side of their heads; others with strands of hair taken in festoons from the brow giving the effect of the most parisian ondulations. Many of them had painted faces, carmine lips, rosy cheeks, and very black lines beneath their eyes. They came up in sections to receive their prizes—tiny tots staggered off with enormous bibles, although they appeared too young to be able to read. A great many of them had the line of red paint on their partings to show they were married. As you look at them collectively they have strangely impassive faces, and appear to take little interest in their surroundings. The teacher tells me they have marvellous memories and learn much quicker than English children.

I feel dreadfully aggrieved at my vaccination having taken. I have no recollection of this disagreeable experience before, but I suppose this proves it was necessary.

Monday, 5th. Calcutta

Worked all day to get through letters and business so as to be ready for our departure tonight. We left after dinner, by special train at 10 o'clock, a party of 12—Rolly, self, the 3 girls, Molly and Bridget and 5 of the Staff. Dwyer and I occupy one carriage, which consists of drawing-room, bed-room, bath-room, and Dwyer's room. I was fast asleep at 2 A.M., under my mosquito netting when in rushed Dwyer looking white and pinched, with her hair in curlers, with the disagreeable news that my carriage was on fire, and they could not keep the flames under control when the train was in motion. I had therefore to get out and leave the carriage behind—as they had already had four outbreaks. It was most provoking as Dwyer always unpacks my things on the train, and pretends I am in my own room at home. Everything had to be hurled back into the box in frantic haste. Major Feilding and Fryer fetched my bedding and made a bed for me in Rolly's sitting-room where I spent the rest of the night. Either the line or the carriage were at fault for seldom have I felt so churned up and I expected to fly off the rails at any moment; the fire having delayed them about two hours they went at a tremendous pace to make up time.

Wednesday 7th. Bankipore

Started in two motors at 7.30 A.M. to go and see the opium factory at Patna; it was very interesting; there is only this factory and one other in India. These two factories supply the whole demand in China and bring the country in a colossal revenue over three million pounds clear profit. All the labour is done by hand; there is no machinery at all, at the time of the harvest 3,000 hands are employed. We saw the whole process. The poppy, the liquid oozing from the pod, then the pure opium drying in the sun, and finally we watched them rolling huge round balls with their hands; after they are well dried these are packed and sent to China. Each case contains 40 cakes, the cost of each being Rs. 470, total 1,370 or 91 pounds. During the Japanese war these cases sold at Rs. 1,600 and Rs. 1,700.

Looked into the hospital and then to see a wonderful old library, the finest collection of Oriental works in India. There was a rolled copy of the Koran written by hand with the most minute letters on the thinnest parchment which measures 35 feet long; some of these illustrated books were beautiful, one copy had cost Rs. 75,000; this collection has been donated by a native, Khuda Baksh, Khan Bahadur, about a hundred years ago; the son continued collecting; he is now a very old man and immensely proud of these treasures.

Had to hurry back to array ourselves in our smartest clothes to attend the Durbar; everyone in uniform except the Viceroy. We ladies sat on the dais to the right of the throne—ladies are not considered worthy to take part in these proceedings, but are graciously allowed to be passive spectators. The tent was lovely; hung with transparent draperies of every hue, a scheme of colour blending all shades from light to dark which was most effective. Rolly, preceded by his staff, was ushered to the throne over which a golden canopy was spread, and a carpet of cloth of gold covered the steps. The Maharajas in their beautiful native dresses presented an address, to which he replied in cordial terms, and the ceremony terminated by pan and attar being carried round by the officials. This is the first Durbar we have attended, a function which the natives hold in the deepest reverence. The gathering was a very large one, and people had come from all parts of the country to attend.

Thursday, 8th.

Went out before breakfast with Lady Fraser to try a rifle Major Adam has lent me, a 270 Mannlicher, in case any wild animal comes my way when we are in camp. I was terrified of letting it off, but very relieved to find it didn't kick at all. Cleared off a lot of correspondence and started with Colonel Dunlop and Major Feilding at 6.45 for the station. We were only about a quarter of an hour in the train, then got on board a steamer to cross the Ganges from Digha Ghat to Paleza Ghat; we dined on the deck, several boat and railway officials joining our party. Our silver candlesticks were on the table, and we were waited on by our own *khidmatgars*;[65] the food was cooked by our own Chef. All these things seem to appear as if by magic, and I make no enquiries.

---

65. Servant or butler.

We then got into a special train—very comfortable carriages on a narrow-gauge line. We reached Ekma at 10:30. I understood we were going into an ordinary camp for two nights. I had taken my roughest clothes and was delighted at the prospect of airing my short flannel skirts and Strathcona boots which I had last worn camping at Qu'Appelle[66] a year and a half ago. Nothing since I have been in India has impressed me as much as this camp. The Viceroy signified his pleasure that he would go to Ekma for one day's duck-shooting; the Lieutenant-Governor undertook all the arrangements, and we have not had to trouble ourselves about any preparations.

On alighting at the station we found strings of imposing carriages awaiting us. Rolly and I and an A.D.C. got into the most gorgeous of these equipages, and drove off preceded by mounted troops. The whole road was lined with masses of silent figures huddled together looking ghostly in the moonlight muffled up as they were to protect them from the fresh night air. After a short drive in the open, we turned into a wood where everything assumed a more mysterious aspect. The great trees threw huge black shadows across our path and the groups of natives could only be dimly seen here and there, some half hidden, others standing out clearly in the silver light.

We could see in the distance rows of lamps outlining the avenue making a serpentine line of fire as they turned in and out among the trees. Picturesque as this had been, we were hardly prepared for the sight that met our gaze as an abrupt turn disclosed the camp. We seemed to be in a double avenue of mango-trees, on each side of which huge tents were pitched as far as the eye could reach. From every tree hung Chinese lanterns and rows of lights outlined the drive. Festoons of flags crossed and recrossed the road. We drove up to the door of a palatial tent banked on each side with palms, ferns, and eucharis lilies; the wide opening revealed a spacious drawing-room with sofas and chairs all covered in silk. Delicious bowls of roses stood on every table, while beyond this room was a passage which terminated in a huge dining-room, where a long table was glittering with silver and laden with food and flowers. Two rows of crimson and gold servants stood awaiting us. It took us some time to recover from the surprise occasioned by all this magnificence, but we contrived to eat a little supper before inspecting our sleeping apartments which were arranged on the same scale—bed-room, dressing-room, sitting-room, bath-room—a Turkish carpet, a brocaded sofa and chairs—adorned my room, while the dressing table was covered with masses of white anemones. My ayah had preceded us with the luggage; so all my things were unpacked and I had nothing to do but to get into bed. Dwyer was so astounded at the glories of her surroundings; we could hardly help discussing our previous experiences of camp life. The silver candlestick having now replaced the radnor water bottle which frequently made my candlestick at Qu'Appelle, while in my experiences on the St. John River and Yoho Valley I don't think we ran to such luxuries as candles.

66. Saskatchewan, Canada.

Friday, 9th.

The shooting was organised by a Mr Knyvett, and we all started off to drive to the lake; butts were arranged all along the shore, in which we took up our position. I established myself comfortably in No. 3 butt with a 28 and a 20 bore gun. I was most thankful that the day was still cloudy, as the temperature was perfect. The ducks were beaten up and soon began to fly in huge flights over our heads, but unluckily so high up that, although I blazed away, I only had a very moderate number of corpses lying round me, but I enjoyed it all thoroughly. I was so amused to see Rolly's *Khidmatgar* who always follows him endeavour to hide himself by climbing into a tree and curl himself round the branches in order to mislead the duck. After luncheon we went out in boats. I missed Leader and his canoe sadly; he was so wonderful in his knowledge of the best methods of approaching the duck. My native boatman insisted on poling me to such conspicuous places that I had no chance of getting near the birds and they invariably flew off in the most tantalising way. The result of the day's shoot was 300, of which I shot about 14 and some coot. We all sat round the camp fire after dinner; although I felt the additional heat unnecessary it added to the beauty of our surroundings.

Ekma duck shoot.

Monday, 12th

A three hours' run in the train brought us to Gaya where five motors awaited us, and where we were joined by Sir Andrew and Lady Fraser. We motored out about five miles, and arrived at old Gaya—here we alighted and were introduced to a row of priests, very smartly attired and covered with jewels, who were awaiting us. We walked through numberless streets, so tortuous that only two people could walk abreast. As we approached the temples we passed endless shrines with hideous images of distorted gods covered with offerings of flowers and garlands. As we entered the temple of Vishnu Pad, several priests came forward and hung garlands round our necks; they are made chiefly of jasmine and the sacred yellow flower like a marigold, which has an unpleasantly pungent smell. It looked too ludicrous seeing Rolly with at least four garlands hanging all over him, and Colonel Strutt in full uniform covered with flowers was a glorious sight.

In the centre of this building is a silver fountain where the footstep of Vishnu is imprinted. A priest poured some liquid into the water whereupon the footprint was clearly seen marked out in white, on the dark water. We then retraced our steps, pausing on our way to make sundry purchases of gods and idols which were displayed on a platform for our inspection. A terrible photograph of the Elgins was hung in the place of honour on the wall of this house; he with his sun helmet quite awry; his face and grisly

beard partly visible, the rest of his body completly hidden beneath innumerable garlands. We motored on through avenues of mango, neem and tamarind trees for about five miles till we reached the famous temple of Bodh Gaya. One motor passed through a swarm of bees, and the unfortunate victims had to alight and have them picked out of them; this most disagreeable experience was the only contretemps of the day. A whole army of priests received us dressed in deep orange draperies, the colour all devotees wear; it was a lovely sight, especially as this old temple which is supposed to date back to 513 B.C. is built on a succession of terraces. A very steep flight of steps leads down to where the image of Buddha is seated on a golden shrine inside a golden temple. The figure is beautifully preserved, but I couldn't remain for more than one second in the building as the smell of the burning ghee which they offer up to Buddha was so appalling, I felt it must make me ill. The Tashi Lama spent hours worshipping before Buddha's shrine and had four hundred pounds worth of oil burnt as an offering, perhaps it was still some of this extra supply that made the smell so terrible.

We reached our camp at Barachati, in time for tea. After dinner the excitement was to climb to the top of the dining tent, and slide down. Ruby and Violet managed to do this most successfully if not gracefully. Lord Rocksavage having got himself up for the evening was

The Tashi Lama and his staff.

considered too smart for a camp in the jungle, so during dinner in order to pay him out, one of the staff told his bearer to move his things to another empty tent. Three ayahs who had not yet been assigned sleeping accommodation were put into Lord Rock's vacated tent. He was quite unaware of what had been done, and we watched him from a neighbouring tent going off to bed without a light, and had the satisfaction of hearing wrathful exclamations as he fell over the first, second, and third prostrate form before he discovered his tent was occupied.

Tuesday, 13th.

The whole party started in motors at 8.30 and drove through lovely country with great wooded hills in the distance for about eight miles. The Raja of Takari owns this country, and he and his Manager, Mr Keith, have arranged this shoot for us; he is not a prepossessing youth—coal black with large lips and prominent eyes; he has lately returned from Paris, having bought three of the most up-to-date motors which we are now making use of. We drew up in front of five huge elephants, all beautifully painted and decorated; standing in line facing us with their mahouts in their brilliant turbans, and the elephant pads of green and crimson making still more brilliant patches of colour. The laughter, noise, and confusion can easily be imagined as our party of 15 disposed of themselves either on horse, or elephant back, to ride four miles into the jungle. Everyone talked at the top of their voices, and I, perched with three others on the tallest elephant, was terrified lest the seat called a "*charjarna*" on which we sat like an Irish jaunting car should slip round and hurl us to the ground. The motion of the elephant is abominable and shakes one to pieces. We were to shoot from "machans", platforms erected on trees and covered with leaves.

Everyone except Lady Fraser and myself had drawn lots for their places. We were followed by an army of coolies carrying rifles and ammunition, and it was no easy matter to put everyone into his allotted place, and find all his necessary belongings. A report had got about that a tiger was in the district. I was given a machan close to a gully they thought he might possibly come along, so with breathless excitement rifle in hand I waited and watched for three mortal hours. It is thrilling to feel one is really in the jungle with wild animals around, and though one is supposed to be safe in one's machan, there are always possibilities. The day was perfect; our huge helmets protected us from the sun ; we also wore pads on our backs, and had some shelter from the trees. The beaters came along beating tom-toms and drums, and shouting; we could hear them miles away; and I felt my heart thrill with excitement as I scanned every shrub, picturing a huge yellow tiger within a stone's throw of me. I however was doomed to disappointment, as not a living thing came my way and I experienced nothing more exciting than hearing the shots of others, but even that gave one quite a thrill.

We arrived terribly hungry in spite of some biscuits which Lady Fraser's forethought provided, for us to find, alas, that no luncheon had arrived; the coolies must have missed their way, so we could only say that the last thing we wanted was food, and that it was much nicer to rest without eating. Mr Keith somehow managed to produce luncheon from the Raja's camp which was about two miles away in a wonderfully short space of time and our spirits rose considerably after eating some cold meat, pate de foie gras, peaches, shortbread and drinking champagne. We had just disposed of this excellent food when our own luncheon made its appearance but by that time we had to return to our machans for the afternoon beat. This time Lady Fraser insisted on my occupying her place, and moved elsewhere herself, but again I watched in vain, and Lady Fraser was the only successful person. A great black bear walked deliberately towards her machan; she shot him through the heart and he rolled over stone dead. No one else got a shot.

Wednesday, 14th.

Awoke in the night to hear the rain on the tents but by breakfast time it seemed to have cleared so we all started full of hope for our shoot which was supposed to be over better ground than yesterday. After a couple of miles in the motors we found the elephants awaiting us, unfortunately the ladders had been forgotten, so there was nothing for it but to get on the elephant as best we could. A man made a loop of the elephant's tail in which we placed one foot, while another step on his back brought us with a terrific scramble up to the *charjarna*. It was a very funny sight to watch. Lady Fraser is not slight, and thinking the situation was one not to be missed with a kodak I begged her to wait with one foot in the loop of the elephant's tail as she was getting up, quite forgetting that the unfortunate man was supporting at least 13 stone, and was straining every nerve to prove equal to the task.

Again the guns were disposed of in the machans; these were not very substantial and swayed about with every movement. We had a good deal of laughter at the nervous expressions of the two people left like birds in a nest, prisoners till the elephants returned to relieve them. No sooner had we got settled than the rain began to come down in sheets; this interfered with the beating. The natives hate the rain and herded under trees in groups. We had mackintoshes, but it was very difficult to keep dry. We knew the beat was drawing to a close and again I had seen nothing and was beginning to relax the tension with which I had been watching when I saw something brown moving in the distance. Then three small deer bounded across an opening; thinking they were turning away from me I fired two hurried shots as they were moving. I knew at that distance, and being on the move, I couldn't expect to hit them. Suddenly I saw the third animal stand still and turn round for a second. I fired my third shot; he bounded away and I supposed I had missed him as the distance was quite 150 yards, and these deer, which they call chinkara, are very small, but I was horribly disappointed. The beat came to an end. Mr Woodman got down, found the tracts of the chinkara and came upon him not 20 yards from where I had fired shot through the heart. I was naturally delighted, as this is my first trophy.

Friday, 16th. Gidhaur.

Still raining. At 8.30 we alighted at Gidhaur station. The Maharaja had come to meet us; all his flags and decorations looked very sad and sodden, soaked through and through. We were driven to his house in a smart carriage-and-four; he himself is a very good-looking man, beautifully dressed, and with several ribbons and Orders. It was a very pretty sight being marshalled through the courtyard; in spite of the rain all the balconies round were crowded with natives; a band struck up ' God save the King,' and at the entrance we were greeted by rows of Rajas and an impressive retinue. We were led up through the hall to a dais on which two magnificent gold and silver chairs were placed. We were en route for the jungle so it really looked too absurd: Rolly in knickerbockers, with thick shooting boots reposing on a blue plush and silver stool, an enormous golden garland hanging round his neck over his rough tweed coat. The Maharaja made a charming little speech in excellent English, saying how proud he was to welcome the King's Representative and that he begged leave to erect a clock-tower to be called the Minto Tower to commemorate our visit, and which was the greatest event of his life, &c., &c. We were all photographed before leaving, and presented with lovely bouquets, and presents of native manufacture.

Friday, 2nd March. Calcutta

Began the scrap books. I miss MrSladen's[67] methodically dated envelopes sadly, with all the cuttings arranged in rotation. Lately Lord Francis has undertaken the job, but all the early extract of arrival in Bombay and Calcutta are in sad confusion and the chaos is deeply depressing. Rolly's book has also been neglected, which is really serious as he so often wants it for reference, but Colonel Crooke-Lawless has valiantly undertaken it. We shall not have amusing American newspaper heading here; the papers are most indifferent and very dull. An American paper has found its way here; the heading is "Lady Minto pitted against Lord Kitchener, the woman-hater." Rolly, Eileen and I went to have tea with him. I told him of this cutting which amused him very much.

We had Mary Hamilton, Mrs Cheney, Mr Landon[68] and Baron de Neuville to dinner. Mr Landon is a great supporter of Lord Curzon and he told me he was simply bewildered. He had seen Lord Curzon's papers in connection with the Army Scheme but Lord K and his staff maintained they were absolutely inaccurate as regards the line Lord Kitchener had taken. I didn't wish to discuss the question; the whole story of course is public property but hearing it, as I have done, from Lord Kitchener, makes it immensely interesting. The absurd thing is that all this terrible fuss need never have arisen. Lord Kitchener told me that at one time Lord Curzon himself had wished to make a reform in the Army Department. Later, when Lord Kitchener brought his scheme forward, he suggested that it should be called Lord

67. S.F. Sladen, Lord Minto's Private Secretary in Canada.

68. Perceval Landon, Special Correspondent of the Times for the Prince of Wales' visit to India.

Curzon's and not his own in order to satisfy public opinion and maintain the prestige of the Viceroy, but Lord Curzon would not agree to this once the suggestion came from Lord K-.

With regard to the unfortunate publication of this row, the Home Government telegraphed to Lord Curzon words to the effect that they would greatly deprecate Lord Kitchener's decision if he insisted on the publication of the whole controversy. Lord Kitchener told me he read this telegram for the first time in the newspapers and was never consulted about it before it appeared in print. In one of the despatches which Lord K- was by way of having seen and which he denied any knowledge of, it was discovered that the particular paragraph which caused the friction had been inserted at a later date and had never been before Lord K-. This Lord Curzon would not admit, which practically implied that Lord K- was not speaking the truth, hence the irreparable breach. They have never spoken to each other since, and I suppose never will.

Had a long talk to Mary Hamilton after dinner about her life in New York when she was training for the stage. When I think of her old Puritanical father, the Bishop of Ottawa, it amazes me that she should have been allowed to study for two years with actors and actresses who were not even gentlemen and ladies.

Sunday, 4th. Barrackpore.

This is the final day of the Mohammedan festival called Moharrum. We can hear drums and tom-toms across the river day and night. The feast lasts about 30 days; while it continues no Mohammedan may eat between sunrise and sunset and if they are specially devout, they will not even swallow. All our *khidmatgars* are Muhammedans so they must be terribly exhausted after this prolonged fast. The fanatics often end up with horrible orgies; they drink a peculiar liquor called bhang, which is immensely strong, and in their frenzy beat their breasts for hours and cut themselves with knives. The noise they make is appalling; the roads today have been thronged with men, women and children—all walking towards their place of rendezvous. The whole population of the countryside evidently take part in the final ceremony.

Saturday, 10th March. Calcutta

Spent the whole day sorting and packing. Every single thing has to be sent up to Simla:[69] not a book remains, not a picture is left on the walls; everything in the rains becomes mildewed. I am expected to leave my room intact with all my household goods about. A *baboo* then proceeds to make a drawing of the room and a list of every article that is on each table, &c., &c.; everything then is packed and sent to Simla, and next year everything will find its way

69. The annual move of the British administration from Calcutta to Simla during the hot summer months and the winter return had been part of the rhythm of life for the upper echelons of the British Raj since 1864.

back again to Calcutta, as if it had never been away. The Viceroy makes a spring and autumn tour during this time of packing, and returns to find everything as it was, thus avoiding the inconvenience and annoyance of even seeing packing cases. The three girls, Miss Salberg, and Colonel Strutt started at 7.30 for Dehra Dun—a journey of 60 hours.

Sunday, 11th March. Barrackpore

The house felt strangely empty and quiet without the girls and missed not having them to share my home news. The arrival of the mail is by far the most exciting moment of the week, and I breathe a sigh of gratitude if the letters contain good news. A message came after luncheon that a snake had been seen; so Major Feilding dashed off to fetch a rifle, and returned shortly with a pale grey snake nearly 6 feet long, a horrid-looking reptile. It is quite harmless, and called the cow-milker as it has a habit of coiling itself round the hind legs of a cow which prevents it moving, and then sucking its milk. This is the first snake I have seen in India. Rolly and I had a long spell of landscape gardening after tea. We have left directions for great improvements, as this is my last visit to Barrackpore till next December.

Monday, 12th.

Returned to Calcutta by launch. About half-way saw a 'bore', a meeting of the tides which extended about half across the river, and lashed the waters into turbulent waves; a small boat would not have a chance of living in the seething foam. I believe notices are sent when these bores are likely to occur. Some of the boats had their sails dyed a brilliant red, others yellow, to celebrate one of the many festivals which are always taking place. The people here are just like children in their superstitions— the simplest things give them pleasure; one frequently sees a great man running with a kite which they seem to fly very well.

Rolly receives endless petitions, odes, and verses couched in the queerest language. I must give a few specimens as some are quite amusing.

To

HIS EXCELLENCY THE VICEROY,

Calcutta.

MAY IT PLEASE YOUR EXCELLENCY,

I beg most respectfully to inform Your Excellency that I am a poor native of Boulai, District Mymensingh, and possess nothing to personally present at such a golden opportunity of our Royal visit. So I shall most esteem it most glorious act of my life if Your Excellency should kindly allow me to sprinkle some blood of my own breast as a token of loyalty at the feet of our Prince of Wales when His Majesty reach Calcutta.

Your Excellency's most obedient servant,

(Sd.) SYED ZAHURUL HAQUE,

Boulai P. O., Mymensingh District,

Eastern Bengal and Assam.

An oath be to Your Highness to read it and act accordingly!

God bless my godfather and my godmother for their everlasting happiness.

MY AFFECTIONATE GODFATHER,

Your kind letter, dated the 23rd instant, is reached to hand; this is a keepsake to me for ever, and I have gladly gone through it, but I see that I am fully disappointed and there is no any service for my poor luck under you. Then I do not want any service. This is my only begging from your kind door that please call me to you to kiss the dust under your lily feet and of my mother, and let me plainly express my kill-joy of distressed life. If I be able to go before you, then I shall test that what is in my lack; if I am not fortunated, then I am ready to suicide myself before you, and how can a father and a mother are able to look their son's suiciding, because this present life is no other than a toy and a plaything and better to die than a cat and dog life, and in the day of resurrection, when everybody should be present before God for trial, I shall be asked for my suiciding great sin, and openly reply before Him that my unbearable condition committed so, only your kindness one me. So many applications I did for my chance, but not yet. Please think not me a mad one. My poverty made me so. I cannot bear it any more.

Your son,

(Sd.) HASTINGS.

Rolly has also received a large consignment of Manna which is made in Persia from the identical kind of Manna on which the children of Israel subsisted during their wanderings. It is found in Arabia, Syria, and North-West Persia. It is either the product of a worm or is produced from the young branches of a plant (*tamarit manninora*) caused by the action of the worm (*coccus nianniparus*).

Thursday, 15th

We had intended leaving the train at Daltonganj at 8 o'clock, but Rolly came to my room at 6.30, telling me there had been a kill about five miles away from Mohammedganj, where our special had been stopped, and that I must get up at once. Mr Lyall, the Commissioner, who is arranging the shoot, had arrived, and we all started full of hope directly after breakfast. All the men riding, Geoffrey[70] careering about on a huge white horse which he said had such perfect paces that he thought of buying it. As the horse refused to have a saddle on his back, and Geoffrey was sitting on a magenta and golden saddle-cloth with his legs wound round the animal, I didn't think the horse was suitable for riding on the Maidan in Calcutta. Colonel Crooke-Lawless and I mounted an elephant who ambled along at a terrific pace. When we reached the jungle the going became impossible for the elephant. We found ourselves always in danger of colliding with thorny branches of trees, so we alighted and began to ascend the side of the hill on foot. The heat was very great, so throwing *les convenances* to the wind I mounted Captain Ross's pony, leaving the reins absolutely loose, I allowed the pony to select his own way, while I clung on to the mane to prevent me slipping off over his back Arrived at the machan, Rolly and I and Mr Lyall climbed up the rickety ladder finding a purple velvet mattress for us to sit on. Alas the beat was a blank, although the tiger had killed that night and we saw swarms of vultures flying over the remains of the buffalo.

We found on our return to the train that Dwyer and Fryer had had an adventure. They started for an elephant-ride, taking a conductor of the train with them as interpreter for the mahout. Something evidently upset the elephant as he started to run away, and careered roaring and trumpeting down to the river filling his trunk with water which he flung back over his riders. Dwyer showed great courage, held on to the rope of the pad, and remarked to me afterwards that she could only die once and felt such an experience was worth the risk. Fryer, on the contrary, realised how important his life was not only to himself but to

70. Major Feilding, A.D.C.

the Viceroy and told Colonel Dunlop it was all very well when the elephant was galloping, but when it took to steeple-chasing, he gave up hope.

Forty minutes in the train brought us to Daltonganj during which time we lunched. Rolly and I started for the beat, driving till we came to the river which we crossed on an elephant, the empty carriage being assisted through the water by about a hundred coolies. We drove for some way; then the men got on ponies, and I was taken in a sedan chair, carried by four men, two in front and two behind. They rest the long pole that supports the chair on their shoulders and hurry along at an ambling sort of pace which is quite a smooth and pleasant motion, singing a weird kind of dirge, to the rhythm of which they swing along. Every five minutes four fresh coolies relieve the others; consequently a brisk pace is kept up, over the rough ground. This country belongs to the Raja of Chainpur; he has a son of 14, who accompanied us mounted on a tiny piebald pony. The boy is the most revolting object I have ever seen. His body had the circumference of a huge beer barrel, weighing at least 14 stone. I tried hard to get a snapshot of him, but he was evidently sensitive about his appearance and eluded me. As we approached the jungle silence was enforced; coolies encircled my sedan chair breaking off a branch or leaf for fear I should be annoyed by a single twig—sometimes in riding one is caught by cruel thorns—the branches are most deceptive as they look harmless till one discovers one is imprisoned by merciless fangs that rend one's flesh and clothes. We silently wended our way up the hill, and stole like criminals into the machan; this time there was no purple mattress, but we had serviceable little stools to sit on.

Tiger shoot at Kolibari.

Once the beat begins and one hears the distant sounds of tom-toms, drums, and cries gradually approaching, absolute silence is necessary, a falling leaf, the flight of a bird quickens ones pulses and one gazes with painful intensity into the depths of the jungle, so that nothing should escape one. Suddenly I heard a rustling in the leaves, a sharp crackling of twigs and through the trees I thought I caught sight of the stripes of a tiger's back. I gripped my rifle and felt my heart beat quicker; it is a curious feeling to know a tiger is roaming at large, never having seen one except through the bars of a cage in the zoo, it alters the case when one knows he can make mince meat of an unsuspecting coolie in about a second. The excitement was short-lived as Mr Lyall whispered to me it was only a hyena. Again we waited, another hyena passed us and the beaters were getting alarmingly near. I hardly dared breathe. Suddenly through a clump of bamboo on my right I saw a huge yellow head with great green eyes looking between the leaves. I nudged Rolly and Mr Lyall; they had not seen it, but my excited face expressed "tiger". I couldn't shoot then, as it was impossible to get my rifle round enough without interfering with Rolly. In a second we all saw the tiger through the bushes turning away and moving quickly. Rolly and I fired almost simultaneously. The tiger fell over, but with a mighty roar was up in a moment and over the brow of the hill before we could fire again.

Then Mr Lyall shouted in Hindustani "wounded tiger back", and in the twinkling of an eye every beater was up a tree. After about 10 minutes we heard another shot from a distant machan; this was Captain Ross, who caught sight of the tiger moving away, but thought he hit him in the hind quarters. The tiger must have been lying down till disturbed again by the beaters and his tracks were marked with blood. On seeing a coolie he made a wild spring at him, but luckily only got hold of his *pugree* which enabled the man to escape, none the worse except for a severe fright. Meanwhile, very sad and disappointed we retraced our steps; it is dreadfully unsatisfactory from every point of view. The wretched animal is left to suffer and it is not safe for people to enter the jungle, for a wounded tiger is terribly dangerous; the only way of securing him is by turning herds of buffalo into the jungle, they gradually surround a wounded tiger, and when he is once located some one manages to shoot him from an elephant or from a tree.

Friday, March 16th. Betla Camp.

Started riding at 8.30 for a near beat only about a mile and a half away. Again I went into a machan with Rolly. This time they felt certain of a tiger, there was his kill of the night before close by, and although the jungle seemed alive with game, we allowed everything to pass—a herd of samber, a hyena, endless peacocks and jungle fowl, and countless monkeys. The beat got nearer and nearer, till at last we saw the black bodies of the coolies approaching within a few yards of us. Alas, the tiger had escaped! While the ponies were being fetched we sat in a circle on our machan stools silent with disappointment. I looked up at the multitude of beaters, about a thousand in all—and was conscious that every pair of eyes were fixed with absorbed interest on the Viceroy. They had never seen the Burra Sahib so close before, and they wished to take every advantage of it.

Tiger cartoon by member of household Lalapura camp.

We had a splendid bonfire after dinner; a sort of ebony wood which they burn made the most attractive, long fiery serpents swirling into the inky sky like pyramids of liquid fire. Colonel Dunlop has written the following account, which is quite true, although to us it seems unbelievable:

> "The bonfire in the camp after dinner on the 16th was a little difficult to start, and Mr Lyall ordered a number of coolies to bring up quantities of straw and dry sticks to encourage the blaze. It was pitchy dark, and the effect of these dark men flitting about in the glare of the fire was very striking. They looked like a lot of gnomes, so Her Excellency called for her camera in the hopes of getting a good picture. It required rather a long exposure, so Lyall was told to arrange the men about the fire and tell them to keep still. The three who were nearest the fire at once took for granted they were going to be cast on the flames as a sacrifice to propitiate whatever particular deity in the Hindu Pantheon is concerned with the arrangements for bringing a Bengal tiger within shooting distance of a Viceregal machan. However, neither they nor their companions seemed to dispute the appropriateness of the idea, and when they were let go probably thought their release a distinct sign of weakness."

Saturday, 17th. Betla Camp.

As far as sport went our trip was disappointing, but I enjoyed every minute of it, and love the free life in the wilds, it has done Rolly a world of good. Colonel Dunlop has given me the following account of a conversation he had with a native:

The Private Secretary to Viceroy had to ride straight out to our camp at Betla as soon as we arrived at Daltonganj. On the way he overtook a sowar (trooper) in the service of one of the big landlords who had helped in making arrangements for our camp. The two got into conversation, and when the sowar found out that Dunlop Smith was in the service of the Viceroy he became most interested, and the following scrap of their conversation shows how they look on the Viceroy :

Sowar—"The Viceroy of India is a very great being."
Dunlop Smith— "Without doubt."
Sowar—"Will the Presence (i.e., Dunlop Smith) tell the humblest of his slaves if the Viceroy ever talks to other men. I was talking about this with my friends, and we all think that the Viceroy is so great a Badshah[71] he

71. Great King.

cannot talk with other men, but issues all his orders on the tar barki" (lit. "lightening-wire" the Telegraph).
Dunlop Smith—"This is not altogether the case, for sometimes the Viceroy does talk with other men, but you and your friends are right in thinking that he does issue a great many of his orders on the tar barki."

Sunday, 18th. Calcutta.

We have just been telegraphing our farewells to the Royal Party. I can't imagine who can have been wicked enough to start the report that the Prince drinks. There is not the dimmest foundation for such a scandalous canard. I heard from England the other day that the night of the Calcutta illuminations the Prince dined with Lord Kitchener; this is quite true as I sat next to him. The story went on that both the Prince and Lord Kitchener were so drunk they couldn't appear after dinner. I drove with the Prince for an hour that evening myself, and Lord Kitchener was in the next carriage. The Prince knows about these reports; he said I suppose they think the same thing in India because over one of the triumphal arches was written "God help the Prince." I don't think he really minds what people say, but one wonders who can originate such a story. I think it is cruel, especially as he touches any wine, no Champagne or liqueur, only a light Moselle.

Friday 30th

Thought of dear Aunt Clive[72] on her 91st birthday, and sent her a cable. Arrived at Lucknow at 8.30 and found the Lieutenant-Governor, Sir James LaTouche, waiting to receive me. Drove to Government House, which stands in a very pretty garden; found Lady LaTouche, two girls, a Canadian Miss Onslow, and an American Miss Caswell, whose accent you could cut with a knife. Had a quiet day till we went to the station at 5 o'clock to meet Rolly, who had a public reception with salutes and escorts, all the officials in uniform to meet him. The heat in Calcutta has been appalling; but Rolly's budget speech went off extremely well, and Colonel Dunlop tells me it made a very good impression.

Saturday, 31st.

Rolly and I and most of the staff started at 7.15 to see the Residency. It is such a lovely ruin, with masses of flowering shrubs growing in profusion. The bullet marks riddle the remaining walls, and how 1,600 men can have withstood 60,000 seems incredible. An old man called Hylton showed us round; he was in the Residency during the siege, and became so excited telling us all his experiences: he said the rebels could have rushed the defences

72. Ann Sibella Martha Farquhar, wife of George Clive M.P., Mary Minto's great-aunt.

at any moment, but they were such cowards. The besieged always tried to pick off the rebel leader, and the rest invariably ran away.

Sunday, April 1st. Lucknow.

Rolly began the day by telling me Lord Kitchener was engaged to be married, but I was not made an April Fool of. We started in a motor with General Sir E. Elliot to drive round the sights of Lucknow; the gardens here far surpass anything I have seen in India. I believe there is a gardener from Kew, and he has shown the greatest taste in laying out the grounds round these Palaces. We first visited the Dilkusha, a villa now in ruins, which stands in a lovely garden in the midst of a deer park. The surviving women and children were brought here during the Mutiny from the Residency after the relief. We then drove on to La Martiniere, an Italian structure, built about 1783 by a Frenchman who originally served as a private in the regiment of Lorraine; later he formed a company of chasseurs and garrisoned Chandernagore till taken by Clive. Then he entered the English Army and died a General, having amassed a huge fortune, so he had rather a curious career. Martiniere left funds to endow a school, and about 180 boys can get a most excellent education in this colossal Italian palace free of charge.

Lucknow residency spring tour 1906.

The next sight was the great Imambarah built by one of the Kings of Oudh in 1785; the whole structure is enormous with domes, minarets, and courtyards, and the silver tomb rests in a gigantic room placed obliquely in order to face Mecca. The grass that surrounds this building and the Jumma Musjid, the principal mosque, is very well kept and the vivid green enhances the beauty of the building. I am told that it is only of recent years they have discovered the secret of making lawns. This peculiar grass has roots 18 inches in the ground and sucks up nourishment a long way below the surface; so by digging trenches and by filling them with loam and rich soil the most beautiful results have been obtained.

We left Lucknow after dinner. We are now in the Royal train. It is most comfortable; my bath-room is enormous; the sofas and chairs in the drawing-room are covered with green silk; it is a joy to have got rid of my horrid old carriage which shook me to pieces, it has now become the perquisite of the Commander-in-Chief.

Monday, April 2nd. Agra.

Arrived punctually at 7 o'clock. I have not yet got used to the custom of this country, and much resent being called every morning at 6 A.M. The station was lined with officials. Sir James LaTouche having seen us off at Lucknow appeared on the platform to receive us at Agra owing to an acrobatic feat on the part of the Railway Company. The drive up to the Circuit House through a park which has been laid out within the last few years was beautiful; the Taj in the distance shone out with dazzling whiteness against the blue sky. After breakfast we went to a large shamiana where Rolly received the Municipal Address enclosed in a marble casket with his arms inlaid in the various stones with which so many of these palaces are decorated. The Maharaja of Orchha was invested with the K.C.S.I.[73] Rolly had to struggle to get the ribbon over his head the right way; he was a fine-looking old brigand and was already plastered with orders.

The heat was too great for us to leave the house before 4.30; we then drove off across the river to see the tomb of Itamad-ud-daulah. There are some exquisite marble carvings in the window recesses, and a lovely balustrade. The dust at Agra is appalling, and the penalty of driving about with an escort is very great; they water the roads, but the sun dries them up in a second; one becomes coated in a thick covering of dust, and one seems to breathe nothing else. The rest of the afternoon we devoted to the Taj; it is so perfect that it is quite useless my trying to describe it; but as one passes through the great gateway of the outer mosque, and stands facing this glorious marble palace, the beauty of this unrivalled monument quite overawes one. I hated seeing it with a herd of officials who dog our footsteps and quite prevent one enjoying such a sight as one would otherwise do.

73. Knight Commander of the Order of the Star of India.

Tuesday, 3rd.

Visited the Fort at 7.30—a strong contingent of officials again accompanied us. During the last four years, Lord Curzon has worked wonders in restoring ruins and broken balustrades. We have been so interested in hearing that Lord Minto was the first Viceroy who commenced restoring the Taj. Lord William Bentinck, his predecessor, had put it up to auction but fortunately the money offered was not considered sufficient; so it did not pass into the hands of a private individual. Tourists in the old days used to chip off pieces of the marble panels and carry them away as souvenirs, and no one attempted to stop such vandalism till Lord Minto's time.

Wednesday, 4th. Delhi.

Delhi is far more oriental than any city I have seen so far; the people all much more primitive, and it looks to me as if I was seeing continual scenes from the Bible. The bazaars are so narrow one can only just drive through, packed with people busily selling their merchandise, while the overhanging balconies of the second stories almost make a complete arch overhead. We drove to the Fort, which is built on the same scale as the one at Agra; but is wrecked inside by horrid modern barracks. I was much interested in seeing exactly where the great Durbar ball took place. An Italian was busily working at the recess which used to contain the Peacock Throne repairing the pietra dura work. It will take him three years to complete it.

Major Douglas, who showed us round gave me an account of the riot that nearly took place at the time of the Durbar. The Jumma Masjid, had been requisitioned for visitors to view the grand Durbar Procession and the fire-works in the evening. Tourists from all parts arrived having paid immense sums for their places; it was discovered that they had brought provisions often consisting of ham sandwiches which in the Mohammedans' eyes desecrated their temple, and a riot was averted with the greatest difficulty.

Another story which amused me was about Lord and Lady Dufferin, who went to pay an official visit to the Begum of Bhopal. The Begum being strictly purdah had thrown herself on the ground with a shawl over her head before Lord Dufferin entered—he being rather shortsighted advanced hat in hand, and bowing low was just about to sit down on what he thought was an ottoman. Lady Dufferin fortunately grasped the situation, and intervened just in time to avert catastrophe.

Friday, 6th April.

At 5 o'clock I started with Colonel Crooke-Lawless and a large escort Ceremony of Bengal Native Cavalry followed by Colonel Dunlop and Sir Louis Dane to drive to the Nicholson Gardens, where Rolly was to unveil his statue. The grounds were packed with spectators and troops, all the regiments who had served with Nicholson in the storming of Delhi were represented, and 15 veterans who had been through the siege of Delhi were present. General

Duff read a short address which Rolly answered, alluding to Nicholson's wonderful career and death in the hour of victory, and laying great stress on the Native and British soldiers, standing as they were shoulder to shoulder to do honour to the man they both venerated.

He was very careful to say nothing that could possibly arouse bad feeling. As he pulled the string which drew aside the Union Jack covering the statue, the guns boomed out a General's salute, the massed bands played "Auld Lang Syne" and the audience felt a thrill of emotion as they gazed at the magnificent monument. There was Nicholson sword in hand, his head turned with a keen look of intense eagerness towards the Kashmir Gate, and with such movement and decision that one felt how ready the soldiers must have been to follow him to the death. Rolly spoke to each of the veterans, and I think everyone felt the solemnity of the scene standing on the plot of ground where Nicholson had been 49 years ago just before he led the assault. We left Delhi on the train at 8 o'clock; it was stifling till we moved out of the station in spite of all the electric fans. I often think how poor old Lord Minto must have suffered without any of these modern inventions, there was no ice in those days and no *punkhas*; it must have been unendurable.

Sunday 8th April. Sargodha[74]

This place is absolutely flat; in fact, it was a great sandy desert before the irrigation works made the trees grow; dust-storms are very frequent—there was one in the night, the whole of my room had a thick coating of dust which was horrible. Had a quiet day till we all started off to see a tournament, the best managed sports I have ever seen. The ground was lined with thousands of natives; where they come from is a mystery, as there are no visible habitations.

The tent-pegging was splendid—about 6 competing teams in parties of four. They came along at a hand gallop, shouting weird cries, and generally 3 out of the 4 carried away the peg. Then we had a camel-race, which was too comic; these huge animals galumfing along, their riders sitting them with the greatest ease. There were two exciting tugs of war between Sikhs and almost naked Punjabis with long hair, looking as wild as hawks. These men are really professional cattle-stealers, and now the land is under cultivation they can no longer come with their camels and camp where they like; so they strongly disapprove of this process of civilisation. The sports terminated by a wonderful performance by a sort of Sadhu; he started by brandishing swords and blowing out his cheeks, and making appalling grimaces with flashing eyes; his hair and moustache were painted vermillion. Then he bent down, seized a ring in his teeth which hung in the middle of a huge railway sleeper and tossed it with ease over his head.

I presented the prizes to the winners; it was so strange to see a naked savage advancing with his matted raven locks hanging over his face to receive a small velvet bag full of money

Opening of Delhi Memorial.

74. Punjab, now in Pakistan.

DELHI.

DELHI, 3RD DECEMBER.

The Victoria Zenana Purdah Nashin Memorial Hospital, of which the foundation-stone was laid in February, 1904, was to-day formally opened by Her Excellency Lady Minto. The Viceregal party arrived at 3-30 p. m. accompanied by the Lieutenant-Governor and Lady Rivaz and the Commissioner, and were conducted to the Royal dais through a dazzling assemblage of Hindu and Mahomedan nobles and notabilities of all ranks of Indian society. The leading civil and military officers and residents of the district and many English visitors were present. Noticable in this brilliant and fashionable assembly were the modern Kings of Delhi, Rai Bahadur Lala Sheo Parshads, Rai Bahadur Shri Krishen Das, Rai Bahadur Lala Ishri Pershad, Mr. Radha Mohan, the Nawabs of Doorgana and Loharu, the Maharaj of Kulsia State, Khan Bahadur Mahomed Hossain Khan, Sultan Singh and others.

The Honorary Secretary, the Rev. S. S. Thomas, to whose labours so much is due, then read the address which notices the Memorial as a striking and happy instance of the cordial co-operation of all classes of the community, European and Indian, and testifies to the warm support received from the Government of India. The subscriptions total considerably over one lakh and a half. Careful financing adds some Rs. 21,000 as interest. The fund was helped largely by the sympathy of the late Commissioner, Mr. Fanshawe, and the untiring energy and enthusiasm of Major and Mrs. Douglas. The hospital's unique site to the left front of the Jama Musjid was granted on the strong recommendation of Lord Curzon. The design of the building was made by the Consulting Government Architect Mr. J. Ransome. Lala Babu Mal acted as honorary Engineer. The total cost of the land, buildings and equipment has been Rs. 96,000. Rs. 80,000 have been invested in Government paper and Calcutta Port Trust debentures as funded capital. Various Governmental annual contributions, etc., permit of an income of Rs. 17,000. It is hoped that the institution will meet the purdah needs of both Delhi city and District. Training classes will be established, fittingly connecting the hospital with the Victoria Memorial Scholarship Fund.

LADY MINTO'S REPLY.

Her Excellency replied :—"It has afforded me much pleasure to be present here to-day to open the Victoria Zenana Hospital. It is indeed a splendid tribute from the people of Delhi to the memory of our late beloved Queen whose keen interest and sympathy with every movement to help the women of India were so well known. The co-operation of all classes, European and Indian, in supporting such a memorial is assuredly a happy augury of its future success. The collection of funds and the general arrangements connected with the erection of such a building must have given considerable anxiety to the Committee and in this connection the admirable and self-sacrificing work of Mr. S. S. Thomas, its Honorary Secretary, must be mentioned, whilst the honorary Engineer Lala Babu Mal deserves hearty congratulations on the result of his labours. I can only echo the words just spoken in hoping that this hospital may prove a boon and blessing to the *purdah* women of Delhi and its sourroundings. I heartily wish it every success, and shall follow its work with much interest."

TWO POEMS.

A Sanskirit poem of eight verses was then chanted to Her Excellency by Pandit Biuke Rai Naval Goswan on behalf of the Hindu community, who preponderate at Delhi, followed by a poem of Hakim Ajmal Khan, recited by Ghulam Mahomed Hassan Khan on behalf of the Mahomedan Society. The former, an excellent poem, noticeable for its platonic reference to Hindu ladies as "better halves," refers to Her late Majesty as "ever-victorious Victoria, fountain of mercy and benevolence, impartially just to all and seeking the good of all her subjects alike and the goddess of love." The latter poem, equally good in its own appropriateness and poetry, contains many kind personal references and some philosophy. In this world womenkind are "nosegays of love and faith." When a man falls ill woman has to attend on him. Woman, however, when she falls ill, has to look to heaven for help, etc. "We pray that Lady Rivaz may never meet with any mishap for eternity and may ever remain engaged in picking thorns from the robe of humanity."

Various presentations were then made to Her Excellency of nobles, the Managing Committee and others including Miss Sorabji and the Nursing Superintendent Sister Winifred Thorpe. Her Excellency was then presented with a key as a souvenir of the occasion, and proceeded to inspect the hospital.

Her Excellency then drove to the new site of the Cambridge Mission Zenana Hospital to lay the foundation-stone.

THE OPENING OF THE

PROGRAMME OF HIS EXCELLENCY VICEROY'S VISIT TO DELHI, 1906.

December	
3rd, 8-0 A.M.	Private arrival.
12 to 1-30	His Excellency receives private of Ruling Chiefs and N Gentlemen.
	The Ladies and visitors see the and Jumma Musjid.
3-30 P.M.	Her Excellency will start to ope Victoria Zenana Hospital ar Cambridge Mission Hospita turning to the Circuit Hou 6 P. M.
4th, Morning.	Quiet.
	The Ladies to see sites of Mu seige batteries, &c., and sho the city.
Afternoon.	Ride and drive to Humayun's and the Kutb, have tea, then and drive back.
8-0 P.M.	Dine with the Commissioner. I at the Club.
5th, Morning.	Quiet.
Afternoon.	18th Tiwana Lancers "At Hom
Evening.	Leave for Calcutta about 6-30 Private departure.

F. L. ADAM, *Lieut.-Col*
Military Secy. to the Vice

from my white-gloved hand. The elite of Sargodha were present, about eight unfortunate women; it is a God-forsaken place to have to live in—-the heat next month is unbearable, and they have dust-storms every day till the rains come in June. They had a dreadful bout of plague four years ago. Mr Hailey looked after all the people and then caught it himself; his unfortunate wife, who is an Italian in some way connected with Napoleon's family, nursed him without a doctor or any European to help her, and pulled him through; but she told me it shattered her nerves and she was ill for a year afterwards.

Tuesday, 10th. Malakand.

We are no longer in British India; the tribesmen have been allowed to retain possession of the very fertile Swat Valley without taxation and administer their own laws. The real frontier of India extends considerably further through which we make our roads and build our forts, but the country is not under British administration. It is difficult to realise that these are the men that have so continually been fighting against us, and it is really comic that they should now be asking for a broad-gauge railway. Four years ago they had never seen a train and people thought building this railroad was throwing away money. Now there is so much traffic everyone experiences the greatest inconvenience at goods having to be detrained owning to the toy line which joins the Nowshera Railway.

Malakand Fortress occupies a splendid position on a succession of hills. Arrived at the foot of the fort—a strong guard of honour was waiting, and a dandy, to convey me up the narrow winding paths to the summit, which is about 800 feet. Meanwhile, the guns of the fort were booming out their salute. After the intense heat, the fresh crisp air as we ascended the mountain was most reviving. From the top of the fort we overlooked the Upper Swat Valley. This is a year of plenty—after five or six years of famine—the whole country looks most prosperous. A brilliant green plateau stretches up to the range of hills in the distance full of promising crops. Major Godfrey is going to house Rolly and me; his bungalow is perched on nearly the topmost pinnacle of the mountain. Mrs Godfrey received us. They seem very nice people and have made their house charming. It is quite tiny, but so soigné, pretty chintzes, very good china, masses of sweet peas and roses, and the verandah full of arums, sweet-smelling geraniums and other flowers in boxes.

It is so interesting to look round the range of hills where so much fighting has taken place. This is the road to Chitral, which is 140 miles further north. Another lot of tribesmen were assembled at the foot of the hill with offerings of sheep and flowers. I learnt two words of Pushtu: *Jorye*, "I hope you are well," and *Sture Musha*, "may you always be strong," which pleased them immensely. The rebel leader, a man with one eye, was among them. Rolly told him he was glad to hear he was such a good soldier, and he was wreathed in smiles when this was translated to him. We just managed to squeeze eight people into the little octagon dining-room; most of the staff dined at the officers' mess. I inspected their quarters, and found the dinner table groaning with silver and the room full of trophies.

Wednesday, 11th.

The natives had all received the intimation that the Viceroy was going to ride to Chakdara, 11 miles beyond Malakand, our last frontier post, and were asked to show their respect by turning out. Consequently we passed four relays of tribesmen; all gathered together on the heights of their mountain passes; they stood in groups holding out their standards which we could see were riddled with bullet holes made by our rifles. They are mostly Pathans and talk Pushtu. They claim to be descendents of the children of Israel, and they certainly look very Jewish. They are supposed to have invaded the country with Alexander the Great in 350 B.C., the original inhabitants being Buddhists.

The old Buddhist road from Dargai over the mountains to the frontier still exists; they cannot trace its date; but as Buddha was 600 B.C., it must be over 2,000 years old. All these tribes have been forced by the Amir of Afghanistan to turn Mohammedan. On arrival at the bridge which crosses the Swat River at the foot of the Chakdara Fort, a Hindu tribe, the Baiezai Khan Khels of Thana, was awaiting us formed up in line. Two old warriors came forward and said they wished to present two of their standards for the acceptance of the Viceroy. They had never before been carried except in warfare, and this gift was to mark their appreciation that the Viceroy had condescended to come among them.

I am told they were delighted at our trusting them and going down their lines without a guard. As a matter of fact, I believe they are not very trustworthy, and will be quite friendly one day and stick a knife into you the next. They simply fight for the love of fighting, and they say themselves that, though they are quite contented now, they must relieve the monotony sooner or later by having a rising. They don't mind rifles, but look upon our guns as taking an unfair advantage of them. They have 40,000 armed men they can put into the field any day.

Afghan prisoners.

Their mode of government is very interesting; it is not unlike ours. They have a sort of parliamentary assembly, and an upper house of elders. We could see the village, where their meetings take place, about three miles away in the hills. There is no road up to it, so we could not inspect their Houses of Parliament.

At the fort we were introduced to Colonel Vaughan, Captain Hume, and the six officers who garrison it. Beyond the walls on the other side we found the foster-brother of the Mehtar of Chitral dressed in velvet and embroidery. He had brought amongst his followers three men with hawks, one with a hood made of Chitral gold. As we stood on the top of the fortress, they let a macaw fly from the heights, the hawk was despatched and pinned it in a second. The most weird-looking people of all were a party of Kaffirs who had tramped six days over the mountain passes covered with snow from beyond Chitral, and now appeared in all the glory of their gala apparel—goat's hair fringed their boots, their hats were decorated with plumes and peacocks' feathers, and their raiment was of many colours. They suggested dancing in our honour, and then drums and squeaking pipes began, and the whole company jumped about to a long swinging step, clapping their hands and shouting. I felt I was once more watching my friends, the Blackfeet, on the prairie near Calgary.[75]

We lunched in the mess-room. The whole table was decorated with masses of Fortune Yellow roses. They have several trees, they told me, in this garden at the foot of the fort. I have never seen this particular rose except at Howick; so it is curious to meet it here on the frontiers of Afghanistan. No one knew its name and called it William Alan Richardson, so I undeceived them. After luncheon we saw some gun practice; it is curious what confidence the Natives have in our shooting. Several horsemen were watching in the fields close to where the shells were exploding, so that they might be near at hand to pick up the lead. The Swat Valley is quite lovely, and the river that runs through it makes everything so green and prosperous, it looks a land of plenty, bordered on each side by ridge after ridge of stony mountains with grand outlines.

Thursday, 12th.

Returned by the little toy train, and found it very hot and dusty in the plains, after the mountain air. Arrived at Mardan at 12 o'clock. Colonel Younghusband of the Guides received us. We drove from the station through country lanes which might have been in England—shaded with trees—and the hedges a mass of flowering roses. We stopped to see the memorial which has been raised to Cavagnari and the men who fell at Kabul. It gave me *chaire de poule*[76] to think how narrowly Rolly escaped their fate. He only gave up going at

75. Minto was a great supporter of the Native American tribes during his time in Canada, objecting to the 'narrow-minded' attempts of others to 'civilise' them and stop their traditional dances. As for attempts to make them wear European clothes, he told the Canadian Prime Minister he considered traditional dress far less barbaric than the highlander's kilt.

76. Goose bumps.

the last moment on Cavagnari begging him to do so. We drove on and inspected the little church which belongs to the Guides, and the beautifully kept churchyard.

There are two churchyards here with many interesting tombs—the two Battyes[77] who fell during the Afghan and Tirah Wars. There were a large number of graves belonging to my father's old regiment, the 71st, who were killed in the Ambela Campaign of 1863. Found a large number of ladies and crowds of officers in the Guides' quarters—such charming rooms, and so many interesting trophies. I believe the Guides have seen more service than any other Indian regiment, and have been quartered at Mardan since the Mutiny; so there is a home-like look about their surroundings. We knew the Younghusbands before as they came to Ottawa about five years ago; he is brother of Sir Francis of Tibet fame.

Friday, 13th.

One of the tribes raided a native village last night six miles from Peshawar. These people are under British protection. Four men were killed, and about 50 wounded. This sort of thing is continually happening, so we are living in the thick of these light-hearted gentlemen to whom life is of no account.

Monday, 16th, Peshawar.

Started by train at 8 o'clock and reached Jamrud about 9 o'clock, and started to drive up the Khyber Pass. The drive is 22 miles past Ali Musjid to Lundi Kotal. Immense precautions had been taken to ensure our safety—1,700 Khyber Guards on the Rifles were stationed along the road, and on the heights; the mountains are so difficult to scale, most of the men went up over night. We could see them on the sky-line standing to attention and presenting arms. We passed several villages, all made of mud; each little settlement has its loop-holed watch-tower from which to shoot the enemy. These villages appeared to be absolutely deserted, and we were told the inhabitants were forbidden to come out on pain of being shot, for fear of any doubtful characters roaming at large.

At Ali Musjid all the Chiefs of the tribes had assembled with some of their followers. Each Chief was made responsible for our safety. They are called Maliks of the Afridi tribes, and came up one by one, shook hands with Rolly, and delivered a speech of welcome in Pushtu. Some expressed themselves in the most courteous terms: "I am the Lord's servant—my head is his to do what he will with it. I place myself beneath the feet of the Lord," &c., &c. They brought offerings of sheep and goat-skins and honey. They all looked most

77. The 10 Battye brothers were legendary figures of Victorian heroism, 4 died fighting in various colonial wars including Quentin, second in command of the Guides, who was killed on the Ridge at Delhi during the Mutiny. His last words were said to have been *'dulce et decorum est pro patria mori'*, guaranteeing his place among the dauntless brave of Victorian legend.

amiable, kind creatures; one young boy looked rather scared, and no wonder; his father was murdered two months ago, and he is bound by law to avenge his death—a blood-feud goes on from generation to generation—each man has to look after himself; if he doesn't kill his opponent, he will be killed himself. All blood-feuds have been suspended for a fortnight to insure peace during our visit. The tribesmen all held Rolly's hand with both their own, and spoke in low hurried tones; they seemed very pleased that the Viceroy should have visited them so soon after his arrival in India. The British road for two days in the week is made neutral ground to allow the caravans of camels to pass to and from Kabul, laden with sugar and merchandise without being molested.

H.E. in pinstripes at Khyber Pass.

Tuesday, 17th.

Rolly and I in a landau and four horses, followed by Sir Harold and Lady Deane; the girls and staff drove with a huge escort right through the Native Bazaars to a building on a hill from the top of which one sees the most glorious panorama. All the houses are built of mud on account of the frequent earthquakes, the women in their gay-coloured garments were sitting on the flat roofs. We gazed at the snow mountains in the far distance, the nearer mountain range forms a complete horse-shoe encircling the plain; a beautiful sight. The streets were decorated and lined with troops, and the natives gave us a very friendly reception, but I think everyone was thankful when we got safe home again. As Sir Louis

Dane says, with these people one never knows when a "regrettable incident" may occur. Colonel Younghusband told Rolly he was playing polo one day near Chakdara, when he heard a lot of firing, and saw his syces running away with his polo ponies. There quite close was a band of Afridis popping away across the polo-ground at another tribe whom they had elected to quarrel with. The polo players had to gallop off as fast as they could to avoid being shot, but no attempt was made to stop them; they were busy with their own fight, which went on merrily. Colonel Younghusband spoke to the Chief before riding off, and asked him particulars about the fight. His answer was: "Oh! Sahib, we are only fighting about a piece of land, there are only eight corpses at present, but by the grace of God there will soon be more".

Since leaving Peshawar I have heard more details as regards the precautions taken for Rolly's safety. The whole compound, besides the usual guard, was surrounded by police in disguise—I cannot say in plain clothes—as probably they had very few on, but in spite of this two men with petitions got inside the grounds, and nearly reached the house before they were detected. The Prince and Princess went through the same programme as ourselves. I fancy most of the officials nearly had nervous prostration from the anxiety they endured during their visit. They all said it was the greatest relief to get rid of us, safe and sound; but of course every Viceroy has had to take the same risk.

Thursday, 19th.

Arrived at Kalka during the night. Most of the staff started by train for Simla at 6 A.M. but we had decided to drive the 60 miles, and started at 9 A.M. Rolly and I went first in a most comfortable landau with India-rubber tyres; the horses were decorated with paper-flowers of gold and silver, and all colours of the rainbow. The three girls were in another landau; two more carriage-loads and a tonga with the ayahs made up the procession. It was a splendid drive. We mounted altogether 7,000 feet, but the road is a great deal down-hill as well. I have never been so fast in my life; these little horses go at a hand gallop the whole time. We occasionally stood up to see how the coachman was holding his reins to make sure that the pace was intentional and that we were not being run away with. We changed horses every five miles, and the average pace was well under 5 minutes a mile; so we went at the rate of about 15 miles an hour. Changing horses occupied 1 minute and 20 seconds.

About two miles from Simla some tents had been pitched where we put on smart hats and had the dust brushed off to present a tidy appearance on arrival. Here our little victoria with postillions and a body-guard escort met us, and we drove up the narrow, winding roads to the summit of the hill on which Viceregal House stands. On the lawn in front of the house we found a huge concourse of people—all the Council and their wives and families, and crowds of Simla people we have never seen before. We shook hands with everyone we knew. The whole place was bristling with Generals; amongst others Sir F. Younghusband,[78] General Beatson,[79] General Duff,[80] General Bayly,[81] General Martin, &c., &c.

We then made a tour of inspection round the house. My sitting-room is quite charming with the most divine view, and a little turret-room beyond with six windows facing every way. Lovely cream-watered silk walls and a plain green carpet—really pretty, but the furniture is very bad, and the electric light fittings criminal. The Finance Minister had a fit of economy when this house was being built, and reduced the hall by half, which quite spoils the proportions of the house. The outside is hideous—I believe the Dufferins[82] are answerable for it. It is quite bare without one creeper, and reminds me of a nouveau riche house on the 1000 Islands.[83] The distant views of the snow mountains are beyond words beautiful. The garden is disappointing; there is a new man who has only been out since July, but he has planted daffodils and iris in single plants, and has not made the most of the wonderful surroundings. I am planning to ask for huge sums, and shall endeavour to make these grounds a sight of beauty. I am sure till a Viceroy asserts his authority the officials have no respect for him. I imagine they cannot understand any one having the power to spend money without exercising it, I hope to put this right very soon. The drawing-room has pale blue silk walls and might be lovely but the carpet is cruel, vermilion with the most aggressive pattern that hits one in the face and spoils any attempt to make the room look comfortable.

Sunday, 22nd. Simla.

Only three people are allowed carriages in Simla: the Viceroy, Lieutenant-Governor, and the Commander-in-Chief; the rest of the world have either to ride or go in rickshaws. Our carriages only hold two people. We have two Victorias, a landaulette and a pony carriage, and they were all out to convey the party to church, which is situated on the other side of Simla—not an impressive service and a very young Curate irritated me by saying we should confess our sins to God in the presence of a clergyman. Hard at work arranging the house; it is rather strange to find the hall hung with the same red and white curtains as we had in the dining-room at Ottawa. The baths in the house are constructed on the most peculiar

---

78. Lieutenant–Colonel Sir Francis Younghusband of Tibet fame.
79. Brigadier-General S.B. Beatson whose disciplinarian instincts created problems during the Boer War when he accused the Australian troops under his command of cowardice, expressing the unfair view that they were "a damned fat, round shouldered, useless crowd of wasters" and "white-livered curs".
80. General Sir Beauchamp Duff, Kitchener's Chief of Staff, later Commander-in-Chief, India, 1914-1916.
81. Brigadier-General A.W.L. Bayly, First Commandant of the Command & Staff College established at Deolali in 1905, before its permanent move to Quetta.
82. First Marquess and Marchioness Dufferin, he was Viceroy 1884-1888, Viceregal Lodge was finished in 1888.
83. In the 19th century, the 1,864 islands in the St Lawrence River on the US/Canadian border became a popular summer destination for the wealthy, New Yorkers in particular, resulting in a rash of summer homes or occasionally 'castles'.

principle. They stand about four feet above the floor, which necessitates two ladders to climb in and out. My ladder is covered in ordinary felt, but the Viceroy's presents a very royal appearance covered with red velvet—singularly inappropriate, I should imagine, on emerging dripping from a bath.

Monday, 23rd.

The San Francisco disaster is perfectly appalling. These earthquakes make one rather nervous. The world seems in a very unsettled condition. Formosa practically destroyed, and this ghastly eruption of Vesuvius. His Royal Highness the Grand Duke of Saxe-Weimar arrived with a large retinue of Germans to luncheon—found him a most disagreeable pompous little man. His chief topic of conversation was his annoyance that the Viceroy had not arranged a tiger shoot for him. As it happens, all the Native Princes refused to entertain him; they have done quite enough for one year having had the Prince of Wales and we only got notice of this man's arrival when he landed at Ceylon. However, he found fault with anything, the mode of travelling in India, &c.&c., but he always reverted to his great grievance that he was returning to Germany minus a tiger. I am glad to say this cross little Princelet leaves Simla tomorrow; his staff were most civil and told us we all spoke German *aber ganz vortreflich*.[84]

Played tennis with Rolly in the covered court; it is much smaller than the Government House court at Ottawa and meant only for a single set. It has a splendid arrangement for the balls; they fall into a trough at the net, and run down into a basket. Two little boys are constantly emptying the basket into the recess near the server. I don't know how I shall ever do anything for myself again. If we play lawn tennis, we have at least four men and two boys picking up the balls—no one ever dreams of exerting themselves in India. I am sure it is very bad for one.

Saturday, 5th May.

We had another Gymkhana; Viceregal Lodge was not so successful as last week. I am afraid my journal will become intensely monotonous, now that we are stationary at Simla, there is nothing to record. Rolly has just received the following account from our Kabul Agent, who met us at Lundi Kotal. The story he relates he witnessed two days after leaving us; it makes it difficult to realise such things can occur in the 20th century.

> "At Kala-i-Yakub Khan, on the 11th April 1906, a girl of thirteen or fourteen years of age slaughtered, like a goat, the murderer of her father, under the orders of His Highness the Amir, I myself was present on this occasion, and the place was surrounded by a (military) guard. After slaughtering the man, the girl licked the

---

84. But admirably.

blood-stained knife with which she had committed the deed. The girl then invoked the blessings of God on His Highness, saying that she had revenged her father's murderer with her own hands. It is stated that the man who has thus been butchered had committed theft in the house of the girl's father, had put the latter to death, and had carried away all the property in the house. The girl complained of this atrocious deed of the deceased to Sahib Gul, the Kazi, and Abdul Aziz, the Mufti of Tirgarhi, but the deceased got the case decided in his favour by bribing the Kazi and the Mufti. On the Amir's arrival at Kala-i-Yakub Khan, the girl complained to His Highness. The latter has placed the Kazi and the Mufti under arrest, and has ordered all the property of the Kazi to be made over to the girl."

Monday, 21st May. Simla.

Colonel Crooke-Lawless and I are very busy planning our new Nursing Scheme. It requires a tremendous amount of thought. I believe that people never attempt to get nurses until they are at death's door, owing to the difficulty in obtaining them; consequently, when the nurse arrives, it is usually too late. We shall need a Government grant for at least five years and then, I hope, the nurses will earn sufficient to run the Association without assistance. We have a great scheme *en l'air*—a week's fête at Calcutta during the winter—a kind of Earl's Court with a water shoot and a switch-back railway, which, we hope, will bring in some funds towards endowing the "Indian Nursing Association".

Friday, 25th May

Spent a tiring morning at the photographers while Rolly was photographed. I am furious at seeing horrible caricatures produced in the English papers which were taken in Calcutta, but which I forbade them to publish. They so arranged the light as to make his head look like a billiard ball. If all I hear of the effect of the Simla climate is true, I suppose this will soon came to pass, but at this moment it is a libel. The "on dit" is the first year you lose your hair, the second year your teeth, and the third your reputation. I am sorry to say I am experiencing the first item, and find most of my hair remains in my hand when I brush it. I suppose the intense dryness of the mountain air produces this disastrous effect; if you are not bald, you become snow white in a few weeks, so Simla is not an encouraging place as far as appearance goes.

H.E. with Sir Pertab Singh.

Friday, 28th May.

The Swedish explorer, Doctor Sven Hedin, has come to stay with us. He has made five most interesting journeys through Central Asia. His experiences are blood-curdling; it is hard to believe he can really have been 7 days without water and food when he was travelling in 1895 through the Takla-Makan Desert in Eastern Turkestan but he appears most accurate in relating his adventures. He now wishes to explore the unknown parts of Tibet, but the Home Government will not give him permission to cross our frontier. It seems very short-sighted as of course he can go round and enter through China; it will only delay him six weeks. Sir F. Younghusband is longing for him to get the desired permission and see Tibet opened up. It is so interesting meeting a man who has endured such terrible hardships. He hopes to be in Calcutta in 18 months time after exploring the northern part of Tibet.

Saturday, 9th June

Mrs Annie Besant came to luncheon. She is an extraordinary woman. She started life by marrying a clergyman of the Church of England, but shortly afterwards obtained a separation from him, then she went about with Bradlaugh,[85] preaching free thought. Later she embraced the Roman Catholic faith, then became a Theosophist. Now she professes the Hindu religion, and is at the head of a large Hindu school for boys at Benares, which is a most remarkable position for a woman. She has been giving lectures here, and all the rank and fashion have attended them. The Bishop told me her eloquence was amazing, although he didn't think there was much matter in what she said.

Wednesday, 13th. Mashobra

Have spent a very quiet time at Mashobra. Rode after tea to the top of a mountain on which a small bungalow is built; it is called the Patiala Observatory House. The view from the top is quite magnificent. It is almost frightening to gaze on such a grand vista and wonder what appalling volcanic upheaval produced these limitless ranges of mountains. One feels such a poor atom surrounded by such natural magnificence. At 11.15 P.M. I was lying in bed, and Rolly had that moment come upstairs and had walked into my room, when I suddenly felt as if an unseen presence was lifting my bed into the air. It was a horrible sensation; the earth seemed to give vent to a groan of agony, the curtains blew into the room, I felt a violent swaying, and we realised we had experienced a very violent earthquake. We rushed to Eileen's room where the family assembled in nightgowns. All the rooms had cracks in their walls, and the water in the fire-buckets hanging in the passage was all splashed over. The shock lasted seven seconds, and is the worst they have had since April last year, when the very bad earthquake took place, and the tower of Viceregal Lodge fell down. It is the

85. Charles Bradlaugh, M.P., atheist, political activist and founder of the National Secular Society.

most alarming sensation and I felt my heart thumping long after it was over. This is not an experience I want repeated often.

Thursday, 14th

I attended Mrs Annie Besant's last lecture. It was called "The Science of the Emotions". She spoke for an hour with brilliant fluency, but what she said was not original. She enlarged on the importance of influencing the world by the love we should show to mankind. It was only the old story, a soft word turning away wrath, but it was certainly very well put. Many people have told me that she learns her lectures by heart, but I think this is impossible, although she was never at a loss for a word.

Monday, 25th.

We attended a ball given by a Club called "The Black Hearts". These gentlemen were dressed in ordinary evening clothes with breeches and a red garter round their black silk stockings. A little black heart was suspended from a red ribbon round their necks, and the entire room was decorated with red garlands. Red roses were arranged in the most effective manner, and black hearts played a prominent part in the supper-room on the red walls, on the candle shades, and programmes. The Grand Master who looked after me was promoted to a golden heart—such a nice man called Gamble, whom I had not met before. A few years ago, when he was quite young, he was called "The Greek god," and he still answers to the description.

The monsoon has broken with alarming violence. In five days 13 inches of rain have fallen; a thick blanket of mist pours in through any open door or window, and the whole house smells musty. My time has been wholly employed in writing letters in connection with my Nursing Scheme. I am asking the Queen and most of the Royal Family to patronise it. I have

The Retreat Mashobra. Breakfasting under the Shamiana.

appealed to the public in England, but I don't suppose I shall get much of a response, and in India people feel that they are migratory, and grudge any money invested in the country; so I see I shall have great difficulty in raising the necessary endowment fund, but I mean to persevere and put the nurses on a permanent basis, if possible.

Tuesday, July 3rd.

Gave a small dinner for Lord Kitchener and a few chosen friends, followed by a musical evening. A Mrs Ross played divinely with the whole orchestra; she was a professional before she married. A Mrs Yates Hunter also sang to the orchestra; she has performed in the Gilbert and Sullivan operas, and has quite a good voice. Herr Buchner, the Band Master, plays the violin himself beautifully. When one thinks one is living on the top of the Himalyas, it seems rather wonderful that we should be able to collect so much talent; it would have been an excellent concert even in London.

Friday, 6th.

The tremendous rainfall has played havoc with the roads—many embankments have been washed away, the railway service has been suspended, and the mails got through with the greatest difficulty, coolies carried the bags across the chasms where the roads had been demolished, and a succession of tongas just managed to cover the 60 miles in time to catch the train at Kalka on the main line. Some unfortunate people going to England on leave were stranded, and of course missed their boat at Bombay.

Monday, 9th. July.

Rolly's birthday; but alas he was quite unable to indulge in the holiday which was the privilege of our childhood; the files arrived thick and fast and had to be attended to, but I insisted on a ride after tea. Our two selves, the three girls, and three staff clattered through Simla, looking more like a riding school than a party of pleasure. We made the ascent of Jacko, and very steep we found it. An old Fakir lives on the summit of the mountain in charge of the sacred monkeys whom he feeds. Captain Ross, who talks Hindustani like a native, asked the Fakir the history of these monkeys. It seems that the chief monkey, or "Raja" as the Fakir called him, arrives with about 30 queens and countless numbers of children, and takes up his abode for a week or so on the top of Jacko. They never remain long, and one tribe is succeeded by another. We asked how the monkeys selected their "Raja." The Fakir's answer was—"He is appointed by God," and certain it is that the monkeys all obey him. The monkey children were killing, tiny babies with harassed wrinkled faces, and yellow fluffy hair parted in the middle clung on to their mothers as they swung from branch to branch. No attention was paid to the child who seemed in peril of its life as its tiny arms clutched either the neck or arm or tail of the mother, who appeared totally indifferent with regard to its safety, unless an enterprising infant advanced within reach of our horses hoofs, when a skinny arm was outstretched, the unfortunate little victim seized, and a severe reprimand administered.

Friday, 13th.

Mr Chang, a Chinese Emissary, lunched with us. He is going on a trading mission to Thibet. I found conversation through an interpreter for the whole of luncheon, an exhausting operation. In the afternoon, I called on several ladies whose husbands are connected with our huge establishment. They all have such comfortable little houses. We had tea at the Tennis Court, and watched a match between Major Shepherd, champion racquet player of the world, and our marker. The match was to be the best of five sets. It was a beautiful sight to watch the amazing rallies, but Major Shepherd entirely defeated the marker, who has never been beaten before. The staff offered the latter sums of money to encourage him to play his level best, but five games was the utmost he could get, and he retired after three sets completely exhausted.

We dined with the Lieutenant-Governor; the evening terminated in quite a pleasant little dance. I had a long discussion with Count Quadt[86] as to the propriety of curtseying to the Viceroy as the ladies leave the dining-room. Curiously enough this was not done in Lord Curzon's time, and the first dinner party we gave the ladies were all agog at seeing me go through this performance. Articles were written in the papers, and the question was raised why Lord Curzon, who was so anxious to assert his position, had never thought of having this mark of respect paid him. I answered Quadt by telling him I was treating the Viceroy as I should the King, that I should curtsey to any Royalty on rising from the table, and the proof that it was the correct thing to do was that the Princess of Wales herself was most punctilious in always curtseying to the Viceroy. Quadt's contention was that they observed stricter etiquette on the continent, and, of course, on meeting Royalty ladies would curtsey, but not on leaving the dinner table. I replied that I had not been much on the continent, but was under the impression that the foreign custom was for the gentleman to escort the lady from the room and that, therefore, they had no occasion to curtsey. Poor Quadt after this retired discomforted. These Foreign Consuls are too absurd about their own precedence, and last year, because Lord Curzon didn't put Countess Quadt in the State Quadrille at a ball at Viceregal Lodge, they left the house in a huff. Countess Quadt being a very charming and

86. Count Albert von Quadt, German diplomat

H.E. and Eileen at Narkanda

pretty lady, His Excellency had her admitted this year into the magic circle. The smallness of these official quarrels is past belief, and reduces society to the level of the house-keeper's room.

Thursday, 19th.

Horrified at hearing that poor Mary Curzon is dead; it came as the most dreadful shock, and I cannot say how deeply I feel for him. I fear that the last few months of her life were not very happy; it was naturally a terrible disappointment to her everything going wrong in the end; but she was wonderfully brave and supported every word and action of George Curzon's with loyal devotion. I am told by the staff who were with her that she never had a very happy disposition, that something always seemed to occur to mar her thorough enjoyment of the moment. All the native servants have shown a great deal of feeling, and it has cast a gloom over the whole of Simla. She was so beautiful and seems so young to die. We have cancelled all our engagements till after the funeral.

Friday, 20th.

Rode down to Annandale for tea. We had a rifle practice. The Maharajas of Scindia and Bikaner are staying in Simla and came and joined us. They are both admirable shots but I felt very proud of Rolly as he got the highest score. I think they were impressed. Lord Kitchener was made to compete much against his will; he is not brilliant, but I don't think his sight is very good. Scindia came and dined alone with us; he is very clever, most pleasant to talk to, and wonderfully go ahead; he has put electric light throughout Gwalior; he is building tram-cars and making every modern improvement throughout his province; he is one of the richest Princes in India. His appearance is peculiar; he was dressed in a mauve embroidered silk coat with green trimmings; it was beautiful, but was far too tight for his very fat body. A curiously-shaped cap, covered with red Turkey twill and a bit of gold braid, was placed obliquely on his head, and he evidently suffered a great deal from heat, which, owing to his size, was not surprising.

Saturday, 21st.

These are anxious times in India. The effect of the sudden and radical changes that were made during the last regime are bearing fruit. As old Pertab Singh[87] said: "Lord Curzon has strewn Lord Minto's bed with thorns, and he must lie on them." Sir Denzil Ibbetson,[88] a Member of Council and a great admirer of Lord Curzon's, said "Never has a Viceroy

Rickshaws waiting outside Christ Church, Simla.

87. Lieutenant-General Maharaja Sir Pratap [Pertab] Singh of Idar, British Indian Army officer and twice Regent of Jodhpur.

88. Indian Administrator, anthropologist and author.

found such a tangled web or such a heritage of difficulties as Lord Minto." He was alluding, amongst other things, to the alarming and ever-increasing agitation owing to the partition of Bengal. Radical changes have taken place which are a direct menace to our supremacy in India. Reforms must come, but it needs expert steering, rocks abound, and a breath may cause us to come in contact with them. The Military organisation is working without a hitch, but there are many anxious questions connected with our frontier in which Thibet, Afghanistan, Persia, and Aden are involved. The Home Government have very decided views which do not coincide with Rolly's. He has written urgent letters to Morley, who always answers him with the greatest courtesy. This paragraph in one of his letters pleased me: "It is with the liveliest satisfaction that I perceive how much cool, equitable, and penetrating reflection you are giving to all our puzzles." (You won't suspect me of vulgar flattery.)

The last letter of July 6th contained this paragraph: "Your letter of last mail was of the very first order in its interest and importance. It does not carry me with you, but this makes no difference whatever in my appreciation of its great clearness, ability, and force as a statement of a case. I will let Grey and the Prime Minister see your two letters." That any Government should contemplate a rapprochement with Russia in its present state of seething unrest is incomprehensible, and to my mind Rolly's views are so obviously the sound ones that I cannot fancy any Government taking the responsibility of adopting other measures, which would appear to my poor comprehension as a danger to the Empire.

Monday 23rd. Mashobra.

We all drove in for the Memorial Service for poor Mary Curzon at Christ Church at 6 o'clock. The church was very full. I was disappointed in the service, which was rather ordinary, and did not impress one as a special service connected to her at all. It left one quite cold and unmoved.

Tuesday 24th.

The Maharaja of Bikaner dined—such a charming man! He speaks English absolutely as well as I do; and has only once been to England at the time of the Coronation. I remember hearing that his head was in danger of being turned as all the ladies made such a fuss about him. He looked very splendid in his gorgeously embroidered clothes and *pugree*, and one couldn't wish for a pleasanter companion. He has two wives in purdah. He told me his mother was very old-fashioned, and any idea of a woman emancipating herself was abhorrent to her—in fact, even the young women really prefer remaining in their seclusion, and, if they have no desire to alter their mode of living, changes are not likely to occur very rapidly.

Friday, 27th, Simla.

A luncheon party, including Lady Grizel Hamilton. Lady Dundonald wrote to me saying she hoped we should be kind to her daughter, but that I must understand that this request did not include her son-in-law, whom she wished to have nothing to do with. The said son-in-law is luckily not here. There are all sorts of rumours going about; one being that the unfortunate youth has incurred Lord Kitchener's displeasure, who has refused him any leave. He is the Hamilton who was forced to leave the Guards by his brother officers, and I fancy he is hated in his present regiment. We were all very agreeably surprised by Lady Grizel: she was very pleasant and didn't insist on walking out of the dining-room before me. We heard that she never forgets for a moment that she is the daughter of the 12th Earl of Dundonald, and that, when she invites guests to dinner, they assemble first and she then makes an entrance and a royal progress round the room. She is supposed to put Indian society on a plain miles below her, and alludes to anyone connected with the peerage as "one of us." These traits were not apparent during my short conversation with her after luncheon.

Monday, 30th

There have been a great many bothers in connection with the government of the new Province of Eastern Bengal. The Lieutenant-Governor, Sir Bampfylde Fuller, has several times been tactless, thereby increasing the agitation and he has had to be reproved. A blunder was made recently when a murderer, who was justly sentenced to death, but who had appealed to the Viceroy, was hung before the appeal had been received. The agitators made a great to do—questions were asked in the House of Commons, and Mr Morley said that "the case had not been conducted according to the traditions of the distinguished Indian Civil Service." This snub was not at all liked by the official community in India. At this moment Sir Bampfylde resigned over a question of school policy.

The Members of Council, whom Rolly consulted, feared that, if his resignation was accepted, the impression throughout India would be that the agitation had brought about the desired result and that they would howl all the louder in order to obtain further concessions. Rolly decided that this danger was preferable to the risk of keeping on Sir Bampfylde with the probability of having to recall him at some future date, so accepted the resignation. The difficulty was to find the right man to succeed Fuller. A Mr Hare,[89] who is at present officiating at Calcutta in Sir Andrew Fraser's absence, was ordered to come at once to Simla to be inspected. Mr Hare arrived with a Private Secretary, Financial Secretary, and an A.D.C., not having the dimmest idea why he had been sent for. The party remained two days and Rolly decided to appoint Mr Hare to this very difficult post. Having to deal with a disaffected province is not an enviable position. It is to be hoped he will act with more discretion and tact than his predecessor. I don't think he will allow his tongue to run away with him. I found him one of the most silent individuals I have ever sat next to at dinner.

Friday 3rd August. Simla

A few days ago I happened to be on the balcony outside my sitting-room, giving directions to the gardener about our new terraces. I suddenly saw the air thick with what looked like dead leaves; there was no wind, and I expressed great astonishment at this queer phenomenon. The gardener enlightened me—it was a swarm of locusts! He told me if they alighted they did a great deal of damage. Fortunately, they continued their flight. Had I been John the Baptist, I should have contented myself with the wild honey. The locust does not look as if he would be an appetising morsel.

Saturday, 18th.

A year today since Rolly was appointed Viceroy of India. It seems much longer since we were living in the factor's little house at Cleughhead[90]—going down each day to try to hurry on the installation, of electric light and the building of the new wing. How well I recollect the mixed feelings with which I received the news when Rolly told me that a messenger from St. John Brodrick[91] had arrived, bringing the letter offering him the great post of Viceroy of

---

89. Sir Lancelot Hare, Lieutenant Governor East Bengal and Assam, 1906-1911.

90. At Minto, Roxburghshire.

91. Secretary of State for India, 1903-December 1905.

India. We had strolled into the garden after breakfast on one of those divine fresh August days when the sunlight sparkles through the trees, and the shimmering haze dances over the grass, and makes one realise that no country is so lovely as the British Isles on a really glorious summer morning. So much has happened since then, that it seems to me much more than a year ago.

For the first time for about six weeks the sun has pierced through the veil of mist, and the flood-gates of heaven have at length given us a few hours' respite. Since the end of June, 70 inches of rain have fallen. Every one has been affected by the weather. I took advantage of a bad cold and remained in my room for three days, feeling very unsociable, and rejoicing at not having to meet any inmates of the house except my family.

Saturday, 25th.

Our first real performance of "Cynthia" took place. The audience was quite excellent and the applause very encouraging. Eileen was overwhelmed with compliments. "Isn't she a real princess?" someone exclaimed just behind me when she made her entrance in a lovely gown which does great credit to the Simla dressmakers, adorned by my tiara and most of my jewels. The whole burden of the play falls upon her and I hear the impression in Simla was that she had been given the leading part because she was the Viceroy's daughter but they went away saying she was the best lady amateur that had ever acted in Simla. I don't know where she gets this talent from but her voice, expression, movements are really quite professional. The whole cast is excellent. Captain Young, Cynthia's husband, has inherited his acting powers from the Youngs of histrionic fame. I think everyone left at the close of the entertainment thoroughly delighted, especially as we had been careful to administer to the needs of the inner man.

Sunday, 2nd September.

On the 15th we are going to Narkanda, about 50 miles from here, for a week's camping in the pine woods, we shall make expeditions and explore the country. On the 6th October we start for Quetta and Kashmir. The Amir[92] is by way of coming to Agra on the 8th December, where we shall have a really big show for him. His visit is a great coup politically, and entails an enormous amount of arrangement. A colossal camp will have to be planned at Agra, as every high official throughout India has to be invited to meet him. The staff are already beginning to look agitated and harassed, as there are so many details to be considered.

Friday, 7th.

Visited the Auckland school. The head mistress, Miss Strong, is a most charming lady; she came from the Baker Street School in London where she left a great reputation. On arrival here, she was naturally rather dismayed to find that half the pupils were Eurasians and that the Government provides this education for Rs.3 a head per week; for this absurd sum they get practically the same tuition that would cost £200 in England. It seems these Indian Provincial Governments are more inclined to spend money on Native than on European education and Miss Strong is much too good for the place. The building was the Government house in Lord Auckland's time and, judging from its appearance, I don't think it can ever have been repaired since. I never saw such a disgraceful condition as it is in.

Friday, 14th.

Went to the Chelsea Convent, which is the same sisterhood as the Convent at Scillery, Quebec. They received me with the same kind of address, recitations, music, and bouquets, and I was able to imagine myself back again in Canada, as I watched the little bowing forms with their hands on their hearts each time my name was mentioned. It is so extraordinary how the Catholics always contrive to collect sufficient funds for educational purposes and for buildings, while the Protestants spend their lives in fighting poverty. I quite enjoyed my inspection of the spick and span establishment, and there was heartiness in the reception which, as a rule, seems lacking in India.

We all attended the great Masonic Ball in the Town Hall, a most imposing affair. We were received by gorgeously apparelled individuals belonging to their various lodges, and processed up the room under a steel arch of drawn swords held by the Knights Templar who looked as if they were ready to start for the crusades. I was presented with a wonderful enamel medal which they suggested I should wear when attending philanthropic functions; also a cushion and a pair of gloves, the latter gift being a relic of an old-time custom. It was naturally a very mixed assemblage, and I enjoyed seeing Dwyer in a décolleté cream silk "confection" floating round in the giddy waltz in the embrace of a military gentleman. Judging from the number of her partners, she seemed in great request.

---

92. Habibu'llah Khan, Emir of Afghanistan, 1901-1919.

Costume list for Cynthia.

Monday, 10th.

Mr Francis Grenfell,[93] 9th Lancers, arrived from Rawal Pindi to stay a week with us. I have never seen such a strong family likeness as all the Grenfells have. Francis got into a row lately. A native insulted him and he knocked him down. Luckily the matter has been arranged and the native has withdrawn his case. Lord Curzon usually sided with the native against the British soldier and feeling consequently runs very high owing to Tommy Atkins resenting the partiality with which the natives are treated. It is a common trick now for natives to come and insult a soldier who can no longer defend himself. Mr Grenfell said to me "If Lord Curzon had been Viceroy, I should now be out of the Army." All these young soldiers talk with the greatest bitterness of the difficulties that have been created for soldiers in India and, once a feeling has been aroused, it takes years to eradicate: they are so slow to detect a change of policy.

Saturday, 15th.

The day appointed for our departure for the mountains. A few rays of fitful sunshine raised our hopes that the break in the weather was about to take place, although a mass of black clouds looked ominous on the horizon, and the most sanguine hesitated before embarking on our first march of 33 miles. We made an imposing procession winding up the Mashobra Hill on our ponies. Rolly, self, the three girls, Freddy Adam,[94] Colonel Dunlop, and Tommy Bulkeley. Francis Scott and Francis Grenfell were to ride with us as far as the luncheon bungalow at Fagu. We hadn't been riding half an hour before down came the rain in pitiless sheets, but on we plodded curling round and round the mountain side, no view visible, nothing except a thick cloud of white vapour.

A sorry spectacle we presented on arrival at Fagu at 2 o'clock. An army of sodden-looking syces relieved us of our ponies. The rain seemed to have penetrated everything—collars, cuffs, boots, &c.; but at any rate we found blazing fires in the tiny rooms of the bungalow, and we were able to dry some of our soaked garments. The luncheon revived our spirits. The scarlet servants with immovable faces stood round the table as usual, looking as if they had never left Government House—Francis Grenfell told me he expected a picnic luncheon, but I informed him that the Viceroy must have his silver plate, his Star of India China, and every variety of wine, even if he happens to be on the highest pinnacle of the Himalaya Mountains, and somehow they always appear as if by magic.

Sunday, 16th. Matiana.

The oldest inhabitant never recollects the rains at Simla lasting beyond September 12th. In three months 101 inches have fallen, and we had begun to despair of its ever being fine

93. Francis Octavius Grenfell, VC 1914, polo player, killed in action May 1915.

94. Lt.Col. F.L. Adam, Military Secretary to the Viceroy, Died of fever 1907.

again, so our joy was great on Sunday morning to awake to find the sun pouring in through the tiny windows of our bungalow. News of a bear in the neighbourhood had been brought us, and the Raja Sahib with his retainers arrived to conduct us to the place. I never saw anything more comic than the appearance we presented. The Viceroy headed the procession, mounted on a tiny but wicked-looking pony, about 12 hands high, which would have been a valuable asset to any circus, as it was white marked with strange black spots, and its evil eyes being encircled with large pink rims gave it an unnatural expression of countenance. It was caparisoned with a large blue velvet saddle-cloth, trimmed with gold braid, on which was placed a small white saddle. The bridle and reins were also white, and looked as if they might have been used by the pampered progeny of a millionaire in Rotten Row.

The Viceroy in a very workman-like shooting suit perched on this prancing steed was a spectacle we all enjoyed. I followed on a diminutive white rat. The girls and staff, all mounted on mules and ponies, accompanied by the Raja, marched in solemn procession down the road. Barnum would have paid a good deal to exhibit us. I stuck to my pony until we began climbing down a perpendicular mountain torrent, and then I felt I should be safer on my own feet. The excitement was intense; the bear had been located and we all took our different stands looking into a ravine. In the previous experience we have had of shooting we have waited during a beat for hours, and usually seen nothing at the end of it. We had barely seated ourselves, before an army of men rushed down the glen and commenced throwing stones into a thicket not 10 yards from the path which we had crossed a quarter of an hour before. To my amazement a huge black bear jumped out of the bushes and was lost to sight in the jungle under the hill. In a second more he re-appeared and was bowled over instantly by Rolly, who caught him behind the shoulder—a very fine shot. The babel that then arose was deafening. Every one shouted and screamed: "The Lord Sahib with a magnificent shot had killed the bear!" All was joy and excitement, the Raja was a proud man. We all mustered on a small plateau to rest after our exertions; drinks and fruit were offered us; the Raja, with fat fingers that had lately been engaged in searching for the bullet-mark on the bear's corpse, pulled the most tempting-looking grapes from the bunch, and presented them to me in the palm of his extremely dirty hot hand!

Monday, 8th October. Quetta.

During the whole of Sunday the train was running through Bahawalpur. This is the second most important Mohammedan State in India. The Nawab is a young man of 24, and so far is very promising. At the first long halt the Chief Minister of the State and three other high officials were on the platform to welcome the Viceroy to the State. They had brought *dalis* of flowers and fruit for everyone from the Viceroy down to the junior A.D.C. There were 31 baskets for His Excellency corresponding to the number of guns in his salute. Each A.D.C. got four!

We arrived at Quetta at 1:30. The General Officer Commanding was not present as he is out on the Yaru manoeuvres. Mr Tucker, Agent to the Governor General, and all his staff

were there The two great Baluchi Chiefs were also present: His Highness Sir Mahmud Khan, G.C.I.E., the Khan of Kelat, we took over the Bolan and Quetta from him or rather from his father. He stands high among the Feudatory Chiefs of India and receives a salute of 15 guns. The other Chief was Mir Kamal Khan, known as the Jam of Las Bela. He is a much smaller person with a salute of only 9 guns. We were introduced to sundry people, and then drove off with Mr Tucker to the Residency. It has been done up from top to bottom for the Royalties, the Government paying £15,000 for the furniture. Mr Tucker is evidently rather an old maid over his household arrangements, and looks after things very well.

Tuesday, 9th.

Rolly was out with the troops at 5 A.M. Drove at 5 o'clock to the Sandeman Hall, where a big Durbar was to take place. These Baluchis are very weird looking, with long black

On the train at Quetta.

tresses, wild and unkempt, falling down each side of their faces. This gives them rather a cut-throat appearance, but the better classes oil and crimp their long raven locks and they are magnificent men, very tall and powerful. We had a horrid little gallery from which to view the proceedings. All the Sirdars sit on the floor, except the two Chiefs who have been nicknamed Ham and Jam, which abbreviations I find easier to recollect than their unpronounceable titles. I was much impressed by each Commissioner who introduced all the men belonging to his district without a note reeling out such names as:

Sirdar Pasand Khan, Zarakzai,
Sirdar Sir Nauroz Khan, Naushirwani,
Malik Baz Khan, Haikalzai Tarin,
Seth Muhammad Ali Alibhoy Hony, &c., &c., &c.,

with great fluency. There were altogether 118 presentations. They all came up and bowed to the Viceroy, who sat on a great silver throne; after which he read them a speech and presented some with medals, others with wonderful golden embroideries, as marks of appreciation for their good services. We hurried home as soon as we could, and went out riding with Mrs Smith-Dorrien; the opening meet takes place tomorrow, and we thought it wiser to try our mounts.

Wednesday 10th.

The meet was barely a mile away. There were a large number of riders, and we soon trotted off to Woodcock Spinny. The hounds at once gave cry and the scent seemed quite good, as they streamed away. How can I possibly describe the country which I found myself galloping over? In England we should certainly get off and lead our horses over such rough ground. It consists of a net-work of ridges and blind ditches interspersed with deep drains—small streams with high rotten banks, but above all "*karezes*"; these are the old irrigation works of the natives who brought water from the hills through these under-ground tunnels, some 40 feet deep. One must be continually on the watch to avoid falling into a sudden opening in one of these chasms. I soon found my black horse was an old hand at the game, flew like a bird over quite a wide and very deep ditch with a rotten mound of mud on each side, and manipulated his feet with the greatest dexterity.

I soon missed Violet, and was much concerned to hear she had fallen to the bottom of the above-mentioned ditch. The pony fell backwards into the water, with poor Violet underneath. I was re-assured as to her not being hurt, and told she had gone home. Three others fell at the same place. On we galloped sometimes climbing down into a gorge and scrambling up perpendicular mud-walls, for 30 minutes we went a good rattling pace over innumerable ditches. During a check, what was my surprise to see Violet and Geoffrey join the chase, having galloped wildly in pursuit and managed cleverly to cut us off. Violet was a mass of mud from head to foot, but was quite pleased with her experience. She really had a merciful escape, as in rolling free from the horse he put his hoof on her back demolished all

the steel and whale-bone of her under-garments, and left a bruise in the shape of a horse-shoe. The Master, Major Sarel, gave me the brush. They were all so delighted at our coming out.

Saturday, 13th.

We drove for about an hour along an exceedingly dusty road, to witness the final attack of the troops. As we neared the position, the incessant roll of musketry was tremendously impressive. I must get some one with military knowledge to write the account for me, I can only give my own impressions in a most amateur way, though General Smith-Dorrien[95] was most kind in explaining the position to me. After a murderous fire had been kept up for about half an hour, the whole line fixed bayonets, the bugle sounded the charge, and the troops advanced with drums beating, all shouting as they went, right on up the rocky slopes to assault the heights. Men fell on all sides, it was tremendously realistic, they lay in motionless heaps just as they fell, in impossible positions. The Medical Corps were hard at work removing the wounded, if they could do so under cover. Special trenches had been dug for them, and the surgeons were busy extracting imaginary bullets and dressing wounds. The attack was made entirely on the lines of the experience gained from the Russo-Japanese War, and all the officers declared that they had never seen a more realistic fight. It was interesting to see a party detailed to throw hand grenades, a practice which most people supposed to be obsolete until its recent revival by the Japanese.

A peaceful afternoon till 5 o'clock, when we went to the Horse Show, and Rolly gave the prizes to the winners. They looked so picturesque advancing to receive their gifts. Fierce-looking Baluchis with their tangled hair and dust-coloured rags draped round them, a brilliant scarf round their waist, or *pughree*, invariably redeemed their otherwise insipid colouring. The Khan of Kelat looking murderous, accompanied by his brother, sat facing us a little to one side. He had on a splendidly embroidered coat and head dress, and over all a dirty old white Kashmir shawl which he hugged around him, burying his face almost to his eyes; he is certainly a villainous-looking object. We all dined with the Smith-Dorriens—such a pretty house, a wonderfully decorated dinner table and excellent food. All the soldiers are highly delighted at the success of the manoeuvres. General Smith-Dorrien tells me he hasn't had four hours' sleep for the last 10 nights. After dinner we had quite a pretty little military tattoo in the garden.

95. General Sir Horace Lockwood Smith-Dorrien, one of the few survivors of the Battle of Isandlwana during the Zulu Wars, Commander of the BEF 11 Corps and Second Army WWI.

Khan of Kelat.

Sunday, 14th.

Baluchistan is full of old legends, and a little story told me by Sir Archibald Hunter[96] of how these wild tribes account for the existence of the horse and the camel is worth recording. God, they say, first made man, next woman, then the horse, the king of all animals. But the horse far from being satisfied with his creation complained of it to God: "You", he said, "have given me small feet which sink into the sand, a short neck so that I can barely reach my food, and a back so round that nothing will stick on it, but immediately rolls to the ground." So God scratched his head and thought with, the result that he made an. animal with great large feet that wouldn't sink into the sand, with a long, long neck so that it could eat its food with ease, and with great big hump on its back so that things wouldn't roll off; then God brought his new creation to be inspected by the horse, to show him what he might have been, at which the horse was so horrified that he shied, and shied; and has shied at the camel ever since. Another rather strange custom of the Baluchis is to bury their dead along the roadsides with the idea that on the day of Resurrection when God walks along all the highways collecting the dead spirits He cannot fail to see their graves and take them with Him.

Monday, October 15th. Quetta

Rolly had the gratification of walking on Afghan soil at Chaman and went part of the journey on a trolley. After dinner he held a Levée; meanwhile the ladies came into the drawing-rooms, and I endeavoured to go the rounds and talk to them, but they were packed like sardines and the room was terribly hot. As soon as the men joined us, we repaired to the refreshment-tent, which was icily cold. Our poor host is not very successful with his entertainments; in fact I have seldom seen such a hopeless person. He never seems to do the right thing, although, I am sure, his intentions are excellent. The Quetta climate is very trying; the air is so transparent that the sun seems more powerful than in other parts of India. In the day-time the thermometer is about 80°, and in the evening it falls to 40°. It has not agreed with the girls. They have all taken it in turns to faint, which is not uncommon here.

Wednesday, 17th

Our journey through the Scinde desert seemed like a voyage in the infernal regions. In spite of electric fans, the thermometer was 90° in our carriages, and the whole of the dust of desert seemed to penetrate through every aperture, eyes, nose, and mouth seemed full of it, and thick layers of dust covered us from head to foot. At meals the drinks were thoroughly iced, but the glasses felt so hot to one's lips that it was quite disagreeable touching them.

96. General Sir Archibald Hunter, GOC Southern Army in India.

The train stopped for dinner, and the windows being open, all the insects of the desert were attracted by the light. Locusts innumerable alighted on our faces and hands, springing with marvellous agility from person to person, and caused a most disagreeable diversion during our evening meal. The Staff made a large collection which would no doubt be of great value to an etymological museum. The dinner was a noisy one, many and varied screams frequently rent the air, as none of the family can be calm under the determined attack of an army of insects. The climax was reached when an enormous sort of flying frog suddenly alighted on Colonel Dunlop's shirt front. With great valour he caught the animal, in spite of a severe sting. It was hastily drowned in whiskey, and the scientists of Quetta are endeavouring to discover to what species it belongs. It was the most revolting object I have ever seen—a large scaly back, gigantic antiller, very long legs and feet composed of spreading brown coral, rather like cauliflower leaves. Had such a creature alighted on me, I doubt my still being in possession of my senses.

Thursday, 18th.

The country we have been passing through is cultivated and looks quite green owing to the irrigation works. Sir Louis Dane was telling me he knew the country well before it was irrigated; he travelled through it with his wife in tongas soon after they married before the days of railways. They drove entirely at night owing to the heat, which even then was 106°. Lady Dane was so overcome that she fainted from exhaustion and he had to lay her down on the boiling sand and pour water over her till she recovered. He also told me that a fortnight after his first child was born he was obliged to start for a station in the wilds, 13 marches from Simla. His wife accompanied him. The road was so rough, over-hanging such alarming precipices, that they didn't dare risk carrying the baby, so it was slung native fashion on a cooly's back. His wife is alive, and hale and hearty, which shows what people can live through.

Saturday, 20th. Kohala

We have become the guests of the Maharaja of Kashmir. After luncheon we drove 35 miles to Uri, pausing at Chakoti for tea. An amazing spectacle greeted us on arrival at Uri. A great round enclosure had been made, entirely surrounded by the most magnificent tents. These were connected by wide passages all hung with brocades and Eastern draperies. The drawing-room was beautifully furnished with every modern luxury, and the dining-room was a sort of banqueting hall, the table groaning with plate and artistically arranged flowers. Besides this, the Viceroy's private dining-room was prepared for the special use of himself and his family. In the centre of the enclosure a large shamiana was erected, and in front of every tent a square garden was laid out with shrubs and evergreens, with the name of the owner of the tent marked in countless white pebbles, while broad grass-paths led from the centre of the ground to the door of each tent.

When one realises that there are at least 20 suites of apartments, everyone has a bed-room and dressing-room, our maids have tents quite near ours, and the ayahs and native servants all have suitable accommodation, one can realise what an enormous amount of planning this camp has entailed. We sleep here again on our return journey, which is some consolation, as it would be cruel to have given so much trouble for a single night. Sundry officials received us all sent by the Maharaja, and the gentleman who laid out the camp beamed with joy when we praised his arrangements. Each tent had a great stone fireplace which was certainly needed, as the night was bitterly cold. A magnificent snow-capped mountain, the Haji Fir, towered above us at the head of the valley, and one could hardly believe we had been melting with the thermometer at a 100° only two days ago.

Sunday, 21st.

Spent a most comfortable night, but the cold was so great I had to get up and find a Shetland shawl in which to envelope my head. The drive into Baramulla leads through an avenue of poplar trees; for the last couple of miles we galloped at racing pace, swinging from side to side; the throngs of natives that stood salaaming on each side of the road looked a blurred mass, so great was our speed. I imagine the pace was in accordance with the prestige of the Viceroy. The Jhelum at Baramulla becomes quite a wide, imposing river, and here a huge flotilla awaited us, as we proceed to Srinagar by boats. The Maharaja's brother, Sir Amar Singh, and staff stood on the steps awaiting us in full uniform; large medals of various members of our Royal Family adorned his breast. We talked to him while the string of landaus, victorias, tongas, and ekkas gradually arrived, each one making a desperate effort to produce a final furious dart in order to arrive with sufficient éclat.

The maids' appearance was splendid, Dwyer with a huge sun-hat, floating grass-green veil, a short tweed coat and skirt, which makes her look broader than she is long, always heads the procession. She is followed by Eileen's very tall and lean-looking attendant Cook, while Beams, whose proportions are of a medium kind, brings up the rear with a colossal amount of white chiffon floating down her back—and sundry bags and packages hung on to various positions of her person. Fryer with ruffled 'hair, a plaid round his shoulders, always in frantic haste to reach the Viceroy's side, arrives at a trot, hanging on to Dandy's chain, who prefers moving leisurely, and therefore considerably retards his progress.

The Viceroy has a boat to himself, with drawing-room, dining-room, and bed-room; on the flat roof a shamiana with luxurious chairs is placed. Tied to the side of the boat is a smaller vessel with a throne of green velvet and gold, over which is placed a crimson and gold dome-like canopy. An officer in blue and gold embroidery stands beside the throne, and 12 men dressed in white with red sashes and lunghis rest on their oars, ready at any minute to convey the Burra Lord Sahib to any other boat he may wish to visit.

View from the Dal Lake.

Monday, 22nd.

It is not altogether unmixed happiness to live in a houseboat on the Jhelum River. The 1,500 coolies have been drilled for weeks past to keep silence while at work, but they had evidently profited but little by their tuition, and the bustle and noise that arose at 5 A.M., in connection with our departure, was enough to wake the dead. Another drawback is the uncertainty of meals—if the kitchen boat lags behind, the whole organisation crumbles. We hadn't much to complain of in the way of food, but members of the staff were perpetually being searched for, as they were either too far in front, or too far behind. It was rather amusing to see the Viceroy trying to take a little exercise by walking along the bank. He was surrounded by a concourse of people. A huge escort in front, soldiers bringing up the rear, policemen to the right and left of him, scouts on ahead, and skirmishers surveying the country on either side. Had we been marching through an enemy's country, it would have been impossible to take more drastic precautions.

Tuesday, 23rd.

The morning was cold and rainy which created general consternation, on account of our public arrival in Srinagar. Sat in our houseboats cowering over the fire, writing for the mail which leaves today in order to reach Bombay by the 27th. Luckily the weather cleared after luncheon, and our entry into Srinagar was the most picturesque scene I have ever beheld. The Maharaja awaited us with a huge retinue of officials at the entrance of the city. He is an insignificant little man dressed in pink and gold embroideries with a huge lunghi bigger than himself. The Viceroy and staff received him on the roof of the State barge painted in papier-mâché work, very pretty in the sunshine.

The etiquette is for the Viceroy and Maharaja to occupy two thrones at the end of the boat, while their respective staffs sat in two rows on either side facing each other. About 50 men paddled the boat along. They have a great variety of strokes, and at the word of command

Srinagar.

they vary their style, which is exceedingly graceful. Their paddles are different to anything I have seen before and are made like spades. We advanced up the river through the town of Srinagar, lovely old houses with carved balconies of all sizes and shapes rising from the water's edge. Temples with silver domes and spires shone out here and there, but what made the scene so surpassingly beautiful, were the vast crowds of people that lined the banks. One gazed and gazed trying to imprint the scene on one's memory. We passed a variety of bridges and chinar trees, some of which were turning a brilliant crimson, and reminded me of the Canadian maples. The roofs of the houses were covered with tall grasses, and gave the appearance of gardens; I am told in the spring that they are a mass of iris.

There were long graceful gondolas with crews of 20 men in gay uniforms—boats with matting roofs, common boats called shikars; big boats and little boats, smart boats and shabby boats, some with crews of schoolboys wearing mauve lunghis, all holding their oars upright at the salute, others with boys with yellow lunghis. Crowds of school children were waving banners on the banks, while strange mottoes hung from gaily decorated houses and one felt one was receiving a really warm welcome. On a wide expanse of red bunting were the words: "God save the King mildly and firmly." The uninitiated would hardly understand where the loyal prayer ended and our motto began.[97]

After paddling up the river for five miles, we alighted at some wide steps profusely decorated. A large escort of Native Chiefs formed the escort, and Rolly drove off in a crimson silk-lined carriage-and-four with the Maharaja, while I went in another equally beautiful with Sir Amar Singh. Eileen followed with the little heir, Mian Sahib, son of Sir Amar. There are terrible complications going on as to the succession. The story is thrilling, and would serve for the plot of a melodrama. I cannot go into details, but nothing seems wanting to assist the imagination. The reality is quite sufficient; jealous brothers, fictitious babies, sudden deaths, hints of poison, intriguing officials. The Viceroy is expected to act as a sort of Solomon and arrive at some conclusion to please all parties. I shall use my influence in favour of the fascinating youth of 10 who escorted Eileen; he talks beautiful English, and seems able to converse on any subject.

Wednesday, 24th.

The girls and I went to the Museum, where all the merchants have collected their best goods for our inspection. The carving is excellent, and the papier-mâché things are fascinating. After luncheon Rolly inspected the Imperial Service Troops, and we went to watch a game of native polo, which was the most dangerous entertainment I have ever assisted at, played by Gilgit Frontier Chiefs. The enclosed ground is long and narrow with a mud wall about 2 feet high on either side off which the ball ricochets. The teams belong to wild tribes who are accustomed to play up and down their bazaars; barbaric music was played by the

Dachigam camp, the camp comprised 200 horses, 6,000 coolies and an electric light installation.

97. The Elliot Clan motto is "*Fortiter et Recte*" meaning Boldly and Rightly.

different tribesmen to encourage their clansmen and cheer them to victory. The teams had no distinguishing mark, their clothes were grotesque, some wore embroidered breeches, others flowing white trousers, some had long hair floating down their backs, many had ornamented their bridles with coloured beads.

The audience were enthusiastic, the excitement was intense. I soon realised this polo was fraught with the greatest danger: the players hit very straight; but the ground was so narrow, and they played in such deadly earnest, hitting with all their might, that to prevent the ball going occasionally over the barrier amongst the crowd was unavoidable. At one moment I realised that 14 ponies and men, with uplifted sticks were whirling perilously near my head, a second later a poor little boy was removed from the audience with a broken nose and his lip split right in two.

After the game was over, the losing teams assembled in front of our stand. The band made a ring round them, and the populace surged round and watched them dance to the banging of tom-toms, and the squeaking of pipes. The spectators became intoxicated with excitement, they shouted, waved, and screamed, while the performers revolved at first solemnly and then with desperate frenzy round and round. It was scene savouring of the middle ages. Near at hand a tall bronzed man was pointed out to me by Sir F. Younghusband as being the most successful raider of the district. He had taken part in about 150 escapades.

Major de Lotbiniére[98] came to dinner and told me many interesting facts. The Maharaja had wanted to stop certain lime works that employ several thousand coolies 10 days before we drove past them on the way to Baramulla, in case the Viceroy galloping past in his carriage should be inconvenienced by the smell!! Major de Lotbiniere ventured to suggest that the smell was very slight, and would at any rate not inconvenience the Viceroy for more than two or three minutes. The works therefore were only shut for two days. He also told me that literally thousands of coolies had been employed in putting the 100 miles of road that we travelled over on Kashmir territory in good repair. They did so with excellent success, the road was like a billiard table. For 10 days before our arrival at Uri, all provisions for miles around had been commandeered—all milk, eggs, poultry, walnuts, apples, &c., &c., grown in the district, were carted to the camp at Uri. This is an old custom. The people cheerfully give everything they have, and the Government officials take them as a perquisite, eat some and sell the remainder. The people never question the justice of this; and although the State is supposed to pay, it is doubtful whether the money ever finds its way into the proper channels.

Wednesday, 31st

Left Dachigam Camp, which has now been christened Minto Park, at 9.30 and rode to Harwan, where we went to see a trout hatchery. They netted up trout of l0 lb for us to see. Drove on to Nishat Bagh Gardens, which are still more lovely than the Shalimar, planned in the same style. Seven long terraces through which a stream of water runs with numerous fountains. At the top of the garden is a grove of magnificent chenar trees, and from this terrace one sees the most divine view of the Dal Lake, the old fort and the snow mountains—a truly romantic spot laid out by Nur Mahal.[99] We drove on to Pampar for luncheon; here we found an elaborate camp with gardens, wonderfully designed flower-beds and fruit trees stuck into the ground, all arranged for one luncheon, which was laid out in a spacious shamiana. The Maharaja always goes on ahead to see that everything is satisfactory. He is a great autocrat. You hear people say on all sides: "This is the order of the Maharaja," and somehow it has got to be accomplished. Roily opened a new experimental

98. Brigadier-General Henry Gustave Joly de Lotbinière.

99. Wife of Emperor Jehangir, also known as Nur Jahan.

farm at the Maharaja's request, and made a little speech about stock and farming generally. A bull was produced which Rolly admired. The Maharaja turned round to the Manager of the farm and said: "The Viceroy admires this bull, see that all bulls in future are exactly like this one." The Manager bowed acquiescence. I don't know what further measures he will take to carry out the Maharaja's orders.

Sangam Camp is on the banks of the river, and we sleep in our house-boats. Tea was spread for us under a splendid chinar tree. Rolly casually asked the Maharaja the circumference of the tree. "The Viceroy desires to know the size of this tree," and at once 10 people rushed forward to measure it. A bowing official advanced and humbly begged to say "the tree is 25 feet round." The Maharaja adds "this is nothing; the Viceroy must see a tree 50 feet in circumference." Since we started on our tour a private dining-room has always been provided for us, where the family eat alone. It is a great relief, and makes it much more of a holiday. As we sat down to dinner, the Maharaja's band struck up. The entire band consisting of 80 men has been sent out to play to us for the three evenings we are here! One really is quite taken aback by all the attentions one receives.

Friday, November 2nd, Sangam Camp.

The anniversary of our departure from London. I shall never forget the strain of the last few days. The house was a pandemonium, ceaseless streams of boxes containing our various trousseaux made every nook and corner of the house appear like a lumber-room. Friends occupied each room and tradesmen lined the stairs. I remember having to sit up till 4 A.M., finishing off all sorts of letters and necessary orders, and finally all the misery of the farewells shattered one's constitution, and makes the recollection, especially of the last day, a nightmare. It is satisfactory to feel that a year has passed, and that several of the vexed questions which we found on arrival in India have been smoothed over.

Saturday, 3rd.

Had another charming ride; everything is beautiful in this country. The Kashmiris have a strange custom and always carry a small basket lined with tin, full of burning charcoal called kangri, which they place inside their garments on their chests, and I am told there is hardly a man without severe scars from burns; they go to sleep with this stove on their bodies with the most disastrous results. It very frequently produces cancer. It does not add to the beauty of their figures. I could not understand at first why they all had such strange contours. Another custom is to dye the beard a bright vermilion, as soon as it begins to turn grey; this is done all over India, but the colour is more subdued in other parts; here it is alarmingly brilliant.

Sunday, 4th. Achabal Camp.

A huge crowd was congregated at Islamabad. We visited a very interesting temple with arcades and carving, and a beautifully-shaped spire; also great tanks of water containing sacred fish. We then rode on about 6 miles to Achhabal Camp. The country must be densely populated, as masses of people were congregated along the road. All the patriarchs seemed to be assembled with long flowing beards, and staves in their hands, while their flocks and herds grazed on the hill-side. It is a pity that in this part of India the men all wear dust-coloured garments; they say that the clothes they are wrapped in as babies are added and added to as they grow, and makes the foundation for their apparel through life. It must be depressing never to make a fresh clean start; but if asked how old they are, they just count their bits of blanket which mark the years.

This is the last of our camps in Kashmir, and it is certainly the loveliest. A stream of clear water gushes out of a solid rock, and this with one or two similar streams forms the source of the Jhelum River. Temples have been built with bridges to span the water, and in the centre of the largest tank an oriental pavilion stands hung with Eastern draperies, sumptuous carpets, and luxurious arm-chairs—an ideal spot to sit and read with the sound of the falling water making pleasant music in one's ears. There is only one disagreeable moment in camp, and that is facing the moment when the time comes to leave one's warm bed, but even then consolation is at hand, as one finds an enormous bath full of the hottest water awaiting one—not the apology for a bath which was produced for me while camping in Canada, which consisted of a flat saucer made of India-rubber which collapsed if one leant against the side and upset its thimble full of lukewarm water in which there was a large percentage of grass and mud. By the time one is ready for breakfast the sun has melted the hoar frost, and the temperature is perfect.

His Highness arrives every morning in his enormous white lunghi, white puttees, gold embroidered shoes turned up at the toes, and over all an old check frock-coat, one button of which is fastened with evident labour across his chest. Each morning he comes to Sir F. Younghusband and says, "Is the Viceroy satisfied? Does he express any wish? You are responsible for His Excellency's comfort. I am responsible for yours." I am getting quite fond of the old man, but his one idea is the Viceroy; he is quite bored at having even to say "How d'ye do ?" to me. His love of state is a great nuisance; it would be so much pleasanter not to have quite so many triumphal arches and flags wherever we go; it quite spoils the natural beauty of the various places, and the huge lamp-posts with incandescent light, most suitable for the refuge at the bottom of St. James' Street, is quite out of place near Jehangir's sacred pavilion. Colonel Ward, who manages the shooting, told me when he was out with the Duke of Connaught some years ago they had just located three fine bears, when a regiment of sowars galloped up through the middle of the beat with an offering of fruit and vegetables from His Highness for the Duke. The latter's feelings can easily be imagined.

Monday, 5th.

Rolly went to a meeting of the village authorities and heard exactly how the land revenue is collected. It seems that all trades descend from father to son, priests, cobblers, blacksmiths, carpenter, potters, &c., to whom each land-owner pays a small fixed percentage of his income for the support of each trade upon which he depends for his own requirements. Rolly inspected a piece of land which was the property of five men; with great magnanimity he remitted their rent for ever which consisted of Rs.8 a year paid to the State amongst the five of them which constitutes the land revenue. They were quite beside themselves with joy, and behaved as if he had presented them with a fortune.

Wednesday, 7th.

We had a great rush to get ready in time for the banquet at the Palace. I sat next to Sir Francis and a Mr Field, rather a nice man; he told me in one small district 1,500 chickens had been slaughtered for our consumption. I feel our visit must produce a famine in the land, as all the animals must have been exterminated. At dessert, the Maharaja, Sir Amar Singh, and all the Native officials filed into the room and took up their position behind Rolly. The Maharaja read a very nice speech and proposed our health; it was rather a fine performance on the part of the old man reading it himself, as he doesn't speak English over well. They all seemed very pleased with Rolly's reply. He did his best to tell them how deeply we appreciate the magnificent hospitality they have shown us which has certainly been beyond anything I could have imagined. He also congratulated them on their various progressive enterprises and the general prosperity of the State. We then proceeded to a balcony overlooking the river, and looked at a line of boats which were illuminated and a great display of fireworks which were very pretty with the reflections in the water.

Sunday, 11th. Aliabad Camp

Left after breakfast and rode up over a pass called the Haji Pir, which is 8,900 feet high. The most amusing incident was witnessing Dandy's departure from camp. He had a specially made wooden bedstead with a mattress which was being carried by four coolies, with four relief men, and one man in a red uniform to see that he didn't fall out of his carriage. I hear that the Viceroy's dog is called Dandy Sahib by the household, and he seems quite to realise his own importance and gives himself absurd airs. We lunched at a Dak Bungalow half-way up the mountain, and were met at the top of the pass by the Raja of Poonch. There was a glorious view of the distant valley from the top. Descended a most precipitous road in a rickshaw, and reached Aliabad Camp at dusk which is in a most picturesque situation in the pine woods. There is a Eurasian overseer called Bredon, who has an appalling wife and niece; they received us in white cloth coats trimmed with lace and bedraggled ostrich feathers in their hats, most out of place in the jungle. The boss of the place is a Captain

Hamilton, a charming man with a very nice wife and sister, and they have made everything most comfortable for us.

Thursday, 15th.

Left camp at 11 o'clock. The road to the top of the pass is nearly perpendicular. I rode on a man's saddle; we have all worn divided skirts since we have been in Kashmir. They look very neat walking, or riding, and are so convenient as one feels prepared for every emergency. I see that people in England are riding astride in long coats and top boots without any skirts at all. There is a huge photograph of Lady Castlereagh in one of the picture papers in this attire. I remember feeling rather shocked about 12 or 14 years ago at seeing the Duchess of Manchester practising riding a bicycle in front of the pantry windows at Taplow; so when it comes to ladies wearing no skirts at all it shows how times are changing.

The Viceroy has acted the part of a Solomon during his stay in Kashmir; his decree has gone forth. The Maharaja is to recognise his brother, Sir Amar Singh, and his son as the heirs to the throne, but if for religious purposes he wishes to adopt a son he may do so. The Raja of Poonch's second son has been selected, and should the Maharaja die tomorrow he will have a son to close his eyes. The fact that this gentleman is only 18 months old does not signify. Everyone is pleased all round. The Maharaja is glad to have matters settled for him, the ladies of the harem have given him a bad time lately on account of this question of succession, but the adopted son gives the wife a status in the country even after the death

The Viceroy's Tour. Bikaner shooting trip, Hanumangarh, 1906.

of the Maharaja. The ladies are never mentioned, they are alluded to as the "inner palace," and everything connected with them is veiled in mystery.

Saturday, 17th.

I have been reading extracts from Lord Lytton's letters while he was in India which have just been published; his criticisms on the Indian Civil Service are expressed with great freedom. A great deal of the feeling connected with the resignation of Sir B. Fuller is caused by resentment that the administration of this sacred brotherhood should have been adversely criticised. The official world holds up its hands in horror saying that the prestige of all Lieutenant-Governors has been destroyed owing to the acceptance by the Viceroy of the resignation of a member of their service in the face of agitation. The real reason of Rolly accepting Sir B.'s resignation is very simple but cannot be told to the public. Although an extremely able man, he is utterly lacking in tact; he is a hot-head and impetuous Irishman totally unfitted to rule over a disaffected

province. He has been described by a colleague as an "hysterical windbag." While he was in power, Rolly was kept on thorns lest some hasty word or action might land them into a really serious difficulty. What wonder then that when Sir B. resigned of his own accord, that his retirement was viewed with satisfaction.

The predictions of the pessimists have not been verified; on the contrary, Bengal is calming down under the same policy but administered by Mr Hare with a calm and fair determination which always tells with the natives.

Sunday, 18th. Camp Hanumangarh, Rajputana

Arrived at Bhatinda at 2 o'clock; it is in the Patiala State, and is simply a railway junction. It is here that we meet Esmond and Victoria and Lewis on Monday, 26th. Moved into the narrow-gauge train which is exactly like our own train, only everything is in miniature, gorgeous silk coverings for the sofas and chairs, and rich velvet pile rugs and all details most carefully thought out. Arrived at Hanumangarh at 5.50, found the Maharaja of Bikaner awaiting us at the station. Here we are in the midst of an endless desert, the only landmark for miles around being a huge red brick fort which has many historical traditions. A ten minutes' drive brought us to a perfect town of tents. We occupy a very comfortable bungalow, with every conceivable luxury. Had a most pleasant dinner, just ourselves and the Maharaja; he is such a perfect host and absolutely European in all his ideas. His wife died of consumption a short time ago; his little girl of 7 received us beautifully dressed and covered with jewels; the boy of 4 was in hunting kit, and looked delicious in the tiniest Jodhpur breeches I have ever seen.

Monday, 19th.

Rolly had the most wonderful day's sport; he shot 149 ducks to his own gun, 72 in the first half hour. He could have got more in the evening, but his cheek had got so tender from constant firing that he had to give it up. The Maharaja got 199, by far the biggest bag ever obtained. The total bag for 5 guns was 666. After dinner there was a war dance and wrestlers performed by torch light. Their sinewy black bodies were most interesting to watch as they got hopelessly entangled in their endeavours to land their opponent on the broad of his back in the dust. Mrs Herbert, wife of the Agent, was sitting beside me, and I think from her face I detected that she rather resented the almost entire absence of garments worn by the wrestlers. It recalled a story of an enthusiastic admirer of India trying to extort some appreciation of the beauties of the gorgeous East from the demure wife of a Scotch minister; the temples, colouring, traditions, were appealed to in vain and the only retort she made in response to the glowing picture of Eastern magnificence was "Aye, but Mistress—the heathen are bare."

Wednesday, 21st

We arrived at Bikaner punctually at 8.30. The platform was a blaze of colour; Native Chiefs galore sparkling with jewels and embroideries. Bikaner[100] himself, resplendent in brocaded silk, looked magnificent in his rainbow lunghi decorated with a beautiful jewelled aigrette. The drive through the town was a thrilling experience—quite the most Eastern pageant I have yet seen. The Palace must be about a mile and a half out of the town, and the road the whole way was lined with troops, mounted mostly on camels; some were encased in chain armour from head to foot, with visors over their faces. There were silver bullock carts drawn up in line, the bullocks harnessed with silver trappings, and their horns covered with embossed silver casings. A line of horses came next with golden saddles and massive bridles, and velvet saddle-cloths emblazoned with elaborate designs. As we passed the crowds shouted: "Koumay" the translation of which is "Pardon, Mighty Lord." Bikaner is one of the few places in India where they cheer, and their greeting to the Maharaja is "Hail King of the Desert"—he is so European in ordinary life that it seems strange that this should be his title. The town is a mass of white buildings with the huge fort built of dull red sandstone. The Palace itself was only finished a few years ago; it is a huge building of which every atom is covered with elaborate carving and very fine designs. As we drove up under the arch of the main entrance, Bikaner's little boy stood on the top of the steps dressed in an officer's uniform—he looked like General Tom Thumb. He remained at the salute while we alighted, and behaved with the greatest dignity. This baby has his own carriages, escorts, and officials to look after him; they are always ready to obey his orders, so it is not to be wondered at if these Native Princes acquire domineering manners.

The rooms in the Palace are beautiful, and full of every conceivable luxury. The writing table might almost vie with the provision of pens, pencils, knives, scissors, strings, pins, and elastic bands, &c., &c., for which Newton Don[101] is so famed. My dressing table besides being covered with silver bottles, trays, and pin-cushions has a most attractive selection of Floris's[102] best perfumes, while my bath-room has a ledge with a profusion of Eau de Toilettes, powders, and salts for softening the water. As no women come about the house, I must find out from the Maharaja what fairy looks after our comfort with such luxurious forethought.

At 11 o'clock the three girls and I repaired to the Durbar Hall—a beautiful room—full of gorgeous beings seated in rows in order of precedence awaiting the arrival of the Viceroy. I passed through an avenue of soldiers presenting arms to the strains of "God save the King ", which is an honour to which I am not entitled, but having no red-tape official with me the band was not interfered with. The Viceroy sat on a throne with the Maharaja on his left, and prince after prince advanced bowing, and presented the Viceroy either with

100. HH General Sir Ganga Singh, 1880-1943, reformer and soldier, member of the Imperial War Cabinet WWI, represented India at the Paris Peace Conference and the League of Nations.

101. Newton Don, Kelso, Roxburghshire, house belonging to the Balfour family.

102. Famous perfumier, first shop founded in 1730 and remaining at 89 Jermyn Street, London SW1.

money in a napkin or his sword-hilt which he just touches. No native ever turns his back on his superior, so each one retired backwards, and I felt so nervous as they approached the steps, lest some catastrophe should occur. However, fortunately everything went off excellently. The Maharaja then placed a golden garland round the neck of the Viceroy, and anointed him with attar of roses, while lesser officials decorated the staff. We watched with some amusement their evident anxiety as to the condition of the handkerchiefs which had to be produced to be anointed. I was so impressed by the splendid carriage and courteous dignity with which these Rajputs came to make their obeisance. They one and all advanced in an easy graceful way with the deepest respect and without a vestige of false pride or self-consciousness. After luncheon a review took place, 1,200 troops in all, of which 400 were the Camel Corps.[103] The silence with which these huge animals move over the sand, is very impressive; they glided by absolutely noiselessly except for the words of command.

Our next function was to open the new power-house of electric installation. The Maharaja made a speech, I pressed a button on the howdah of a little silver elephant and the power-house was suddenly illuminated in a blaze of light. Rolly then made them a little speech congratulating them on the scientific advances they were making and we examined huge boilers and indicators which conveyed nothing to me. When we returned to our carriages all the principal buildings of the city were outlined with thousands and thousands of tiny lights, the fort with its arches and battlements was a beautiful sight; its perfect architectural lines delineated in liquid fire. As we drove towards the city, a succession of fountains and wheels of fire formed an avenue which we passed through, the horses were severely tried and the escort became sadly scattered. From the fort a water-fall of liquid fire was pouring, and from either end bouquets of rockets whirled glittering serpents into the sky. Pictures of Rolly and me in flames were not exactly flattering likenesses, but the tout ensemble was one of the prettiest displays I have ever seen.

I am quite losing my heart to Bikaner. I have never seen such a thoughtful, attentive host. He told me at dinner last night how he disliked the purdah system; he said: "You can imagine what one's feelings are when one sees one's wife for the first time after the marriage ceremony; she may be charming, but her looks may not appeal to one, but we have to make the best of it." I said that I thought it equally trying for the wife, and he agreed, but said the lady probably looks from behind the purdah and gets to know her future husband, at any rate, by sight. Bikaner was engaged to marry a daughter of the Maharaja of Udaipur, the greatest of all the Rajput Princes. It is supposed to be the highest honour to marry into his family. Bikaner discovered the lady was only 10 years old, and had a harelip into the bargain, so he promptly broke off the engagement, and fell into terrible disgrace in consequence. He was devoted to the wife who died three months ago; he told me all about her illness; she was in bed seven months, gradually dying of consumption. His other wife now becomes the chief wife with an allowance from the State. She unfortunately is also an invalid, and I suppose ere long he will marry again, as he has only the one rather delicate little boy.

---

103. The Bikaner Camel Corps, founded by Maharaja Ganga Singh, fought in the Middle East in WWI and WWII.

Sunday, 25th, Bikaner

After luncheon motored with the Maharaja to Devi Kund, where we saw all the cenotaphs of the Maharajas and their wives for the last few hundred years. They are mostly made of beautifully carved marble. All the Maharajas whose wives committed sutti burning themselves on the funeral pile of their husbands have a peculiar tablet representing a man on a horse holding a drawn sword and the ladies who perished with him are represented standing beside the horse raised on a little step. There was not much beauty in the modelling; they looked like a family of Mrs Noahs. At the entrance of the fort, there are rows and rows of hands carved on the walls which represent each woman as she passed into the fort in order to commit sutti. The custom is very seldom observed now, but women occasionally insist on doing it when their husbands die. Went with the Maharaja to visit his wife and his mother. Violet was able to carry on a little conversation in Hindustani, which delighted them. I don't think he pretends to care much about his wife, he said: "She is quite a good sort, but my mother misses my late wife dreadfully." We left Bikaner after dinner, having had a most successful time and thoroughly enjoyed the Maharaja's princely hospitality.

Monday, November 26th.

Reached Bhatinda at 8 o'clock and had the happiness of seeing a small white figure awaiting us on the platform, and soon Esmond,[104] Victona, and Lewis[105] were all bundled into our carriage, and we found ourselves all talking at once, while nobody listened in the confusion and excitement of our first greeting. Esmond looks gloriously well, and we all thought him decidedly grown. I only wish Larry was here to complete the party. Arrived at Maler Kotla at 12 o'clock; was received by the Nawab; he is acting Regent for his father, who is mad. Rolly drove off in a magnificent carriages and I followed with the brother, a poor little *chétif*[106] creature to look at, but quite intelligent. We only lunched here and spent two hours, yet every member of the party had a tent prepared with sofas, chairs, and writing tables. We then drove round the city and left Maler Kotla at 5. It is a tiny State which no Viceroy has ever visited before. Curiously enough it is a Mohammedan settlement in the middle of this Sikh country. The Nawab had on ropes and ropes of splendid pearls, I am afraid their beauty caused me to break the 10th Commandment.

H.E. the Maharaja of Bikaner.

104. Hon.Esmond Elliot-Murray-Kynynmound, Lord and Lady Minto's youngest son, died of wounds 1917.
105. Lady Victoria and Lt. Col. Hon. Lewis Dawnay, Mary's eldest sister and brother-in-law.
106. Sickly.

Wednesday, 28th. Nabha

Arrived at Nabha about 12 and found the old Raja[107] waiting for us on the platform; he belongs to the old school and dresses in the same style as his ancestors have done for hundreds of years past. He is a splendid old warrior to look at, and is intensely proud of his Sikh soldiers. We drove up to the guest-house which is quite an impressive building outside with a very broad staircase covered with crimson cloth. On entering the hall I literally gasped with dismay; I was confronted with such an appalling chamber of horrors. It seemed as if some demon had for a joke collected the most terrible assortment of rubbishy monstrosities. The hall was painted an impossible yellow, bad buttered eggs describes it best, with lines of vivid blue and red painted here and there, which finished off with arabesques of arsenic green. The pattern of the carpet was so violent with its orange ground, crimson roses, green, and blue ribbons that one felt giddy in looking at it. The chandeliers were red, brown, yellow, blue, and green. On a ledge making the complete circle of the hall were thousands and thousands of coloured glass jars with terrible paintings of lilies and jasmine, which one sometimes sees reposing on a woollen mat in a very second-rate boarding house. The walls were plastered with cromos and distorted lithographs of celebrities evidently painted in Native Bazaars, as all had crooked eyes, snub noses, and impossible mouths.

Colonel Dunlop has given me the following memorandum which he wrote out for Rolly:

> "On the night of the 28th the Raja of Nabha said he wanted to have a talk with me the next morning. I went over to the outer palace at 7.30, and our interview lasted till 9 A.M. The old Chief was most interesting. He had already had a Punjabi translation made of Your Excellency's speech at the State Dinner, and was full of the historic significance of the visit. He is much aged and kept on repeating himself, but he had all the facts of the relations of the first Lord Minto with the Phulkian States clearly in his head. He described the famous interview of Metcalfe—then a lad of 23—with Ranjit Singh when he delivered the Governor General's ultimatum to the Ruler of the Punjab, and it was most interesting to see how his national pride in Ranjit Singh as a Sikh King wrestled with his thankfulness to Lord Minto for delivering his State with Patiala and Jind from the hated Lord of the Manja. He then appealed to me whether the Viceroy, who had seen both the Manja and the Malwa Sikhs, didn't as a soldier think the latter were by far the best material for the army. This was rather a poser, and I had to avoid the issue and remind him that now there was no talk of the Sutlej, and that under the British Raj the dream of Teg Bahadur and Govind Singh[108] was realised and all the Khalsa[109] were one. This set him off on to the deterioration in the physique of men and cattle. Horses, he said, were as good as ever they were, but men were deteriorating because of early marriages."

---

107. Sir Hira Singh of Nabha, moderniser of his state, 1843-1911, ruled for 40 years.

108. Father and son, the 9th and 10th (last) of the Sikh Gurus.

109. Founded by Guru Gobind Singh, the last Guru of the Sikhs, in 1699, the Khalsa is the Community of Singhs and Kaurs, the baptised Sikhs.

Next morning, just before we left for Patiala, the old Raja went up to Esmond, who could hardly be seen under his enormous sun-hat. He bent low down so that he could see the boy's face, and said in Punjabi: "Your father is kind to the 'Phulkian misl' (confederation) because God, the Immortal, has caused the noble spirit of his ancestor, who saved their forefathers, to pass, into him. You must never forget this and must be kind to my grandchildren as your father is to me. My sword is yours." He then put out his sword for Esmond to touch. He meant it all.

Thursday, 29th. Patiala.

Reached Patiala at 12. The Maharaja is a boy of 15, nearly 6 feet high and very fat, but with a very pleasing expression, he weighs 14 stone.[110] In Rolly's tent is a picture of Lord Minto; under it is printed in gold letters: "Saviour of the Patiala State." In the centre of our garden

His Excellency with H.H. the Maharaja of Patiala.

110. Maharaja Bhupinder Singh, 1891-1938.

is a silver house, built originally for the King in 1876, to sleep in, but I believe he very wisely preferred a tent to the somewhat limited proportions of the silver cage. The Durbar in the afternoon was a splendid sight. The magnificent hall was crowded with nobles and soldiers. A very good full-length picture of the King and Queen hung on the walls. Young Patiala walked up with Rolly through lines of soldiers; his clothes were superb, a velvet coat worked all over with real pearls. A parure of huge pear-shaped diamonds hung over his brow, and from his neck to his waist he wore ropes of gigantic pearls; also a diamond necklace, originally the property of the Empress Eugénie with a single diamond which is the fourth biggest in the world. Numberless trays with offerings were brought in and laid at the Viceroy's feet; five elephants and two horses were also presented; but everything has to be given back—a practice I greatly deplore.

Sunday, 2nd.

Left Patiala after dinner, the Maharaja and suite all coming to see us off. We have had a most successful time in every way, and they have spared no pains to show that they genuinely feel that they owe the existence of the State to the support given them by Lord Minto when threatened by Ranjit Singh.

Saturday, 8th. Calcutta.

A busy day, arranging the house; the chaos is depressing and old horrors in the shape of furniture, table-cloths, cushions, &c., &c., &c., that I threw away last year have re-appeared. My strength and temper have been severely tried. Our wardrobes have also suffered greatly owing to the incessant travelling, and the whole family seems to require a new trousseau, which is very difficult to procure out here. The *durzies* work beautifully, but they require an exact copy, and are terribly slow, and the dresses from Paris I was counting on are a distinct disappointment.

Sunday, 9th.

The new 40-horse 6-cylinder Napier Motor made her maiden trip with us to Barrackpore. The chauffeur has not yet arrived, but a Mr Ross Craik drove her beautifully. The car is perfection, every detail most carefully thought out, and she runs quite silently. This is the first car I find I can carry on a conversation in with comfort. All the improvements have been carried out excellently in the house, I am delighted with the electric light and the panelling on the walls, and the white paint instead of the drab and mustard colour with stencilling which previously was the decoration of the house is a vast improvement. The rose garden also will be charming, and I felt all my labour has been thoroughly repaid.

Tuesday, 25th. Christmas Day.

Receiving and distributing presents nearly made us late for half past 10 church. Esmond hung up rows of stockings in which Father Christmas fortunately placed sundry objects, but what gave him the greatest joy was a mongoose, a small snapping creature which terrified me. I received some lovely presents, and found Santa Claus had also not overlooked my stockings. Larry sent me a charming album of his Kodaks with a cover beautifully painted by Gertrude—such a delightful souvenir to possess. Our additional party for luncheon included Sir Francis Maclean,[111] Captain Holden,[112] Captain and Mrs Keighley,[113] Judge Robertson, Lily Seymour's boy, who is Lieutenant on the Hermes, Lady Chetwode,[114] Miss Bruce, Sir E. and Lady Locke Elliot, and Mr Hewett, making us a party of 45. We had three round tables for dinner—the contents of the crackers caused a great diversion, a huge spider was arranged as a centre stud for Lord Kitchener, and innumerable little pieces of china produced from the crackers were sent him with suitable messages from his staff to add to his collection. He thoroughly entered into the spirit of the Christmas festivities, but I thought it was rather an achievement to find him sitting on the floor beside me holding up a sheet and blowing at a feather. We had quite a rowdy evening with games and dancing.

Friday, 28th.

The house has become a perfect maze barricaded with screens, pens, and palms for the drawing-room. All our guests passed, Lilian Adam was presented and then 800 extremely plain women filed by, which was most wearying. It was encouraging having Laurence and one or two friends standing opposite me with whom I could exchange an occasional eye-meet. Kitty[115] looked splendid, the girl's toilettes of silver tissue was most successful, and I induced Rolly to wear his gold coat with white legs, which he detests, but which pleases the Civil Service who always feel jealous of any military preference.

Monday, 31st

This closes a very eventful year for us. I hope it may prove to have been the most difficult and arduous of our regime in India. Rolly, I am thankful to say, has borne the strain of the incessant work better than I could have expected. He has now got a grasp of the country, and therefore can get through the business much more rapidly. I think he may well feel

---

111. Chief Justice.
112. Captain H.N. Holden, Governor General's Bodyguard.
113. Captain V.A.S. Keighley, Governor General's Bodyguard.
114. Wife of Sir Philip Chetwode, Field Marshall and 1st Baron Chetwode, Commander-in-Chief India, 1930.
115. Mrs Laurence Drummond, of whom Lord Minto wrote in 1880: "met my cousin, Kitty Antrobus, the most beautiful girl I ever saw but over six feet high".

relieved that the conditions throughout India are more satisfactory than they were a year ago. The army system is working excellently. The 66 million Mohammedans look to him as a champion of their rights. The Native Princes have been treated with courtesy and consideration, and for the first time several Maharajas have been asked to take part in the State Banquet: this is a new departure and has given immense satisfaction amongst the Natives. The agitation in Bengal still continues, but with less violence.

The following is an extract from Sir Arthur Godley's letter. He has been Permanent Secretary at the India Office for many years.

> "When you receive this, you will be at a season which is, I suppose, to all of us a time of retrospection and prospection. As for the first, I think you have every cause for satisfaction. You came into an office at a time of unusual difficultly, and at the end of 12 months you can not only say like Sièyes,[116] 'J'ai vécu',[117] but you can look round upon a greatly improved state of things, and look back upon some thoroughly good pieces of work. And the prospect before you is, I hope and believe, a satisfactory one."

116. French priest and revolutionary.

117. "I survived".

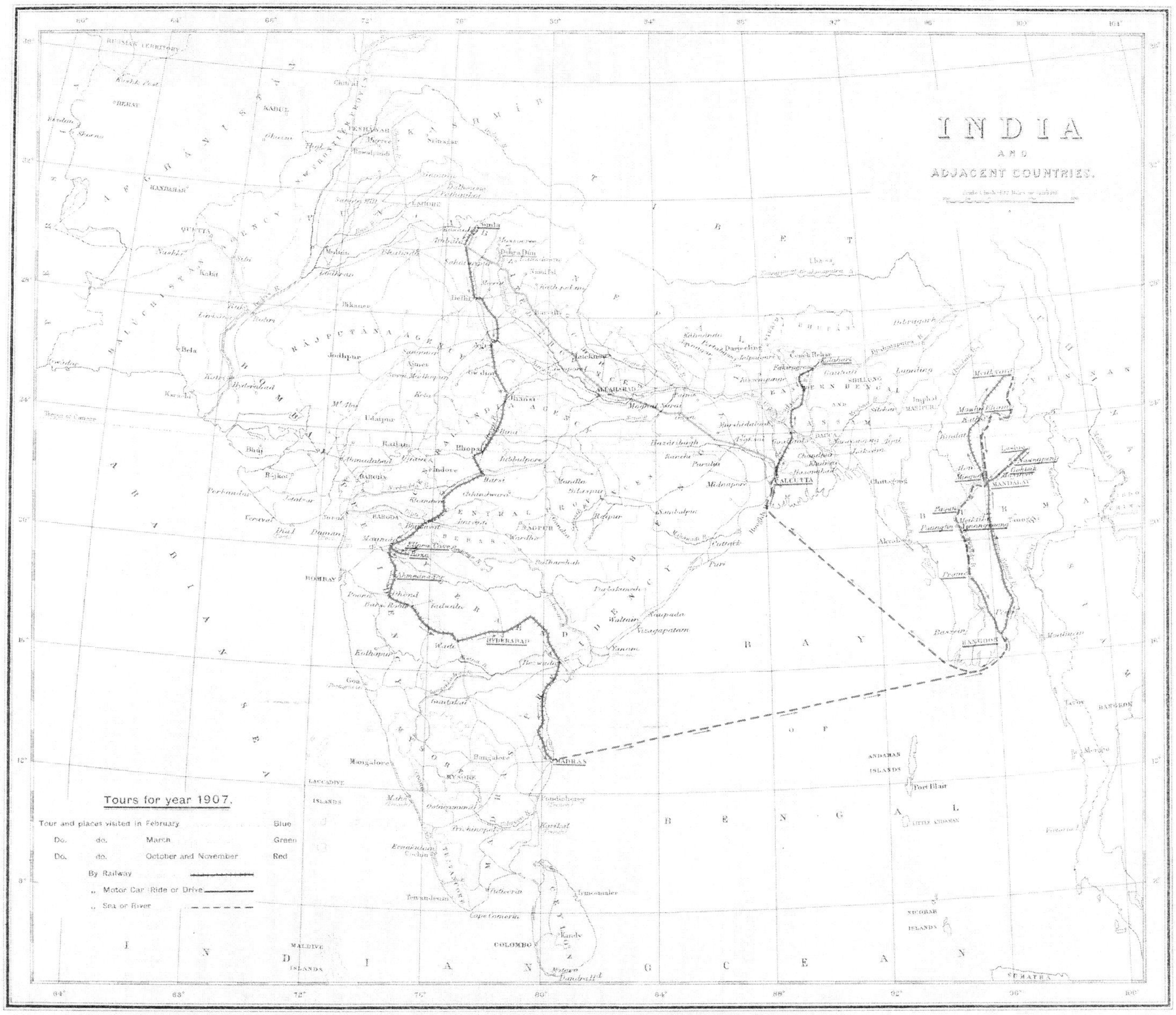

Map of tours, 1907.

1907

Tuesday, 8th January.

Reached Agra at 10:30. The Lieutenant-Governor Sir John Hewett and Staff, the Commander-in-Chief and Staff, and all the Native Princes were there; also the Begum of Bhopal,[118] completely hidden by a blue satin mask and looking exactly like a chess castle. The streets were a seething mass of humanity; there were crowds of Europeans, and I occasionally recognised a familiar face. Three regiments were on escort duty—first came the landaus, then 2 barouches and teams, and lastly our State carriage, with old Sir Pertab, in his beautiful Cadet Corps dress, riding on one side, and Captain Holden of the Body-Guard on the other. It was a magnificent sight—troops lining the entire route to the Circuit House. The view from the house is splendid, the Taj shining out in one direction, and the great Red Fort in the other.

In the afternoon, Victoria, Kitty, Sybil, Count Sala[119] and I went to look on at the Polo. I was so glad to see Bikaner again. I am sorry to say his polo team has been beaten. We drove on to see Lord K-'s camp. We had tea with him, and had great fun chaffing him; he has been quite overcome by Kitty, and so regrets that she can't become Lady Kitchener; he thinks they match so well in size and would make an imposing entry into a room. I heard a certain Lady Stewart, who was sitting next to me at the polo, ask him who was the very tall lady. He replied: "Oh that's Lady Kitchener," and hastily marched off to speak to Kitty. The poor lady was quite bewildered and turned to me with a puzzled look, and said: "What does Lord Kitchener mean?" I had to explain his joke, which naturally a stranger would not grasp at once. I saw Lady Stewart was wondering how he had contrived hitherto to conceal such a conspicuous wife.

The Amir's Camp is colossal; huge silver poles support the great Durbar shamiana where about a dozen gorgeous silver chairs are arranged in a circle. There is a large empty room with prayer carpets, where his devotions will be said; his bed is a silver four-poster with gold and silver embroideries instead of sheets; and his bath is a large inlaid marble tombstone with an iron pedestal beside it, on which a man stands and pours water over him. His other toilet requisites are all encased in plush and embroideries. On his dressing table is a golden case full of scents—one bottle containing the pure extract of attar of roses. This small amount cost £10.00. A great many of the tents, carpets, &c., &c., have been borrowed from Native States, otherwise, Sir Louis Dane told me, the camp would have cost about £80,000.

Wednesday, 9th.

A most depressing day, pouring with rain. The camp at once becomes a quagmire. The Amir arrived at 10:30. Many of the party went to see him drive past in an open carriage; he

118. HH Sikander Saulat, Iftikhar ul-Mulk, Nawab Dame Sultan Kaikusrau Jahan Begum Sahiba, Nawab Begum of Dar-ul-Iqbal-i-Bhopal, G.C.I.E., K.I.H., ruler of Bhopal, 1901-1926.

119. Count Maurice Sala, French Diplomat.

appeared quite smiling in spite of the weather, and he fortunately looks on rain as a good omen. I met our guests for the first time at luncheon; we had our large table in the centre of the tent and four or five smaller round tables, so that we can by degrees sit next to the principal people. The huge entrance shamiana was a sorry sight, rain pouring through in rivers, and baths and basins formed the chief decoration of the room. After luncheon Kitty, who has the most infectiously high spirits, insisted on playing games and running obstacle races. We sent for the band and made them play all our favourite tunes and by tea time the rain cleared off. Rolly meanwhile spent the entire day returning the calls of the Native Princes; his poor escort was literally soaked to the skin, and all their uniforms were ruined.

A few extra guests to dinner, amongst others Sir John Hewett; he had received the Amir at the station, and drove to the camp with him. He told me he had asked him to put on his great-coat in the pouring rain; he was wearing a General's uniform with Admiral's epaulettes. The Amir replied: "The Emperor's soldiers have no over-coats in spite of the rain. I am also a soldier, and will do the same as they do." Princess Lucien Murat[120] sat next to Rolly. She was a daughter of the Duc de Rohan; she has the strangest manners, lies with both arms on the table, and stuffs things into her mouth with both hands. Her hair was coiffed mountains high and the huge pink bird of paradise in it hit Rolly in the eye each time she moved her head. I sat between Sir John Hewett and Scindia. Sir James Willcocks[121] came afterwards and told me the wild Afridi men all know I have shot some bears. It has

120. Writer, traveller and art patron.

121. Major-General, later commanded the Indian Corps in France in 1914 and became Governor of Bermuda, 1917-1922.

H.E. with Amir of Afghanistan.

produced a great effect; they call me "Lady Sahib the Lion-hearted one." I feel my reputation has been easily gained.

Thursday, 10th.

The Amir arrived to pay his visit of ceremony; he came with a large retinue in our carriages and with the Viceroy's body-guard. Rolly, when he pays his return visit, is escorted by the Amir's personal body-guard; the Amir distinctly scores by the transaction. Rolly met him at the entrance of the shamiana and in a very loud voice the Amir said, in rather halting English, that it gave him the greatest pleasure to visit a friendly country and receive such a friendly reception. The Amir himself introduced the whole of his suite, then they sat on two silver thrones exchanging formalities and sipping coffee. The room was full of officials, and we ladies looked on from a distance.

The afternoon was very threatening, but luckily held up for the garden party. Masses of people came to it. We received the Amir and his retinue at the entrance of the garden. The girls and I were introduced to him, and then we walked round the grounds. He stammers before he begins to speak and bellows out his remarks in an autocratic manner, as if there could be no question about their being obeyed. If he doesn't understand an English word, he waves his hand for his interpreter. He is a thick set cheery-looking man with a very intelligent face. I expected to see a tribe of barbarians, but the Afghans he has brought with him are dressed in very smart uniforms; they have quite fair complexions and might easily pass for Spaniards. They have mostly a very Jewish type and look far less Oriental than the Indians.

I introduced as many people as I could, and finally we sat down and drank tea. After about half an hour I alluded to the twilight, to the damp; in short, I gave him every possible hint I could to make him go, but he was apparently enjoying himself and seemed in no hurry to move. He looked at his watch, and said: "It is not time to go," and rather commanded me to walk again. Kitty produced the most tremendous effect upon him. I introduced her as my cousin who was only paying us a short visit. The Amir said: "You must order her to remain for a month and a half. When I go, then she go too." It was very difficult to remain grave under the circumstances. I foresee complications with the Amir, who at once made these declarations, and the Commander-in-Chief, who clearly has designs on Lawrence's life; we shall soon be in the midst of a jealous intrigue. A lady came up to me at the garden party and said: "Lady Minto, happy to meet you again; my name is Miss Stevens. I was introduced to you, some years ago, at Washington." I am afraid my memory failed me, but her next remark amused me. She pointed to the Maharaja of Bharatpur, a sinister-looking man with a head dress entirely composed of pearls with a fringe of pear-shaped emeralds, and said: "Do you think I could suggest to that gentleman that he should exchange hats with me? He might not think it civil to refuse a lady." I replied if that had been possible I should have effected the exchange already.

Saturday, January 12th, Agra. The Grand Review

The most divine morning. Motored out to the review ground with Sir John Hewett and Victoria; passed thousands and thousands of people en route. On arrival we took up our position in a carriage just behind the saluting point, and the sight was a most magnificent one. I felt very proud of Rolly as he rode on to the ground escorted by the dazzling array of Generals glittering with decorations. The Amir's seat on a horse is not pretty, he rides with a perfectly straight leg, and his feet sticking out beyond his horse's shoulders; he was evidently immensely impressed. It seems he had been told the Indian Army was not of much account, and that his own army was fully equal to it. The Amir was very excited on seeing a balloon, and declared he must go up in one: "not higher than I can reach," said Lord K-. A wag has further added that the Amir remarked: "It will take me quite a year to get my army to this state of perfections." I believe it is true that the Commander-in-Chief, a man of gigantic proportions, with a waist like a barrel, will have to fly the country before the Amir returns to Afghanistan to avoid being beheaded for having misled his royal master. I am told the two Commanders-in-Chief made a killing picture standing talking together at the State Dinner—one tall and broad-shouldered, but with a minute waist, which looks a little suspicious, and as if corsets were in some measure answerable for such a wonderful result, and the other very short and with the contour of a tub. Unfortunately the light prohibited the possibility of a Kodak. At the review I took several snap shots of the Amir; he would lean up in close proximity against the Viceroy, who was always being jostled out of his position. The whole display was a wonderful sight, the like of which I am not likely to see again.

The great function of the week took place this evening in the Fort. There are only two entrance gates, so it was decided that all our guests should dine there to avoid difficulties in conveying them to the Durbar Hall in time for the investiture. How it was managed I cannot imagine. A minute kitchen was arranged to heat the food, and dinner was produced for a party of a 100. Everything was transported in mule wagons, and the guests tell me that the dinner was not only hot, but excellent. Rolly walked up the centre aisle in his massive blue velvet robe covered with the Star of India with great dignity, and Esmond in a page's dress, made the same as the Queen's pages, but of blue silk and silver, held one side of the robe, the 13-year old brother of the Maharaja of Dholpur the other.

Rolly spoke in a clear, audible voice which must have been heard throughout the hall. It was a moving spectacle, and one wished the walls could speak and tell us of the glories of the old Mogul dynasty in the past. There were the white race occupying all the seats of the hall with the exception of the few Native Princes, such as Sir Pertab Singh, Scindia and Nabha, the old Sikh Chief, the Begum of Bhopal, and Bikaner, the head of the Rajputs. They sat in the front row wearing the robes of their Orders. It was a sight which made one's pulse beat, and it seemed so strange that I should have any connection with these grand proceedings, and that my husband should be occupying this great historical throne. I have heard since that the Sardars[122] disliked seeing the Amir making an obeisance; he had never done so before except to God, but he understood the situation, and told them that it was right to bow to the King-Emperor in the person of his representative who was doing him honour.

After the ceremony was over we repaired to the Jasmine Hall. The Water Tank and fountains were illuminated underneath; giving the water a transparent effect and making the spray sparkle like a shower of diamonds. The whole building was lighted in the most admirable manner; no lights showed any where—mouldings had been fixed along the cornices to conceal the globes, and every hall was brilliant with a flood of mellow light most becoming to the guests and illuminating without a single jarring note every detail of the marble carvings and arches of this unrivalled structure. The guests filed through the hall called the Dewan-i-Am[123] and passed us as we stood surrounded by the native princes and Sardars in one of the fine raised courtyards, the whole of which had been roofed over. After talking for some time we formed a procession and went up a wide staircase, made for the occasion, to the banqueting hall. It all seemed like fairy-land.

Rolly sat between the Amir and Sir John Hewett; I opposite them. The Amir suddenly enquired across the table what my Orders were, and I hoped he was going to take off a magnificent diamond sun that shone upon his breast and present it to me, but alas I was doomed to disappointment. The fountain in the court-yard was composed of rose-water, and a sparkling cascade trickled over the marble carvings in the grooved wall. One could not feast one's eyes sufficiently on such a scene.

Monday, 14th.

In the afternoon the final of the polo tournament took place, won by the XVth Hussars who were presented by me with the Viceroy's magnificent cup. We sat in a raised stand, and seeing a young officer in the crowd, who shall be nameless, I sent an A.D.C. to ask him to come and speak to me. He came, and hardly touched his cap as he sat down beside me, puffing a newly-lighted cigarette in my face. A few minutes afterwards the Amir arrived and occupied the same seat. When cigarettes were handed to him; he took one, but did not light it. "Won't Your Majesty smoke?" I asked. "No," was the answer, "I smoke when I leave you." I couldn't help comparing the manners of the 20th century young English officer, with those of an Afghan barbarian who has never before mixed in civilised society, and I felt ashamed for my country, as our manners undoubtedly compare unfavourably with those of other nations.

Lord K- entertained the Amir at dinner last night and it seems to have been a great success. The Amir became most hilarious, drank three bottles of soda-water and a tub of plain water,

122. Noblemen or high-ranking officers.

123. Hall of public audience.

and the effect could not have been more invigorating, had the liquid been wine. He led Lord K- to a sofa and said: "You my friend, I your friend; now we joke." Lord K- had the greatest difficulty in getting rid of him towards midnight. Every night besides our own guests in camp we have had from 20 to 40 guests, and dinner has varied from 100 to 150. Everyone seems delighted and cannot say enough about the comfort of our camp and the attention they have received from, the A.D.C.'s. We have had six extra ones: Captain Hill, Captain King, Captain Cheyne, Captain Caryl Baring, Captain Fisher and Charlie Fitzmaurice.[124]

Tuesday, 15th.

The Amir came to see us at 10 o'clock. He brought with him a stereoscopic machine and a lot of photographs of Kabul taken by himself. They are really very good, and his garden seems quite artistically laid out. He is a great photographer and a keen gardener. He is much enjoying the food he is getting. He says in Afghanistan he eats no sweets on account of gout, but he has told his doctor that for two months he will eat everything. It is strange to think of the chaos the Amir's brain must be in when one takes into consideration that he is seeing everything for the first time. Trains, motor cars, polo, social gatherings, the balloon that was sent up during the review, and all the modern inventions which we take as a matter of course, but which to him are unknown quantities.

He is evidently delighted at the respect which has been paid him, and the title of Your Majesty used by the King in his telegram of welcome. The Amir is undoubtedly a very shrewd man with a good deal of ability. I hear he wouldn't allow his principal Sardars to come to the review, as he did not wish them to make comparisons, which would be unfavourable to the Afghan army.

Left Agra in our special at 11 P.M. absolutely tired out, General Gaselee[125] and sundry officials at the station to see us off.

Sunday, 20th. Calcutta.

My cough very bad and finding I had a temperature of over 100 remained in bed, though I had to ask Mrs Crooke-Lawless and Lilian to come and see me to settle endless question in connection with the Fête. Colonel Crooke-Lawless[126] is also ill; Sybil Lascelles is in bed with influenza, Gilbert Elliot is supposed to have pleurisy, Captain Mackenzie, fever; so we are a sorry household.

---

124. Married Violet 1909. Killed 1914.

125. Commander Bengal forces.

126. Surgeon to the Viceroy.

Fête programme.

Monday, 28th.

A day of anxiety for me and Colonel Crooke-Lawless; we had made a bold venture and the question as to the success of the undertaking meant everything to us. A lakh of rupees had been expended and to make the Fête a great financial success, the public would have to come in their thousands and the Calcutta crowd are queer customers. Spent the whole morning in the grounds making final arrangements. Mrs Crooke-Lawless and Lilian have slaved during the last two days. Captain Bulkeley and Captain Mackenzie have got the decoration of the stall completed, which to my mind looks most attractive, draped with the Star of India blue. The goods appear to be a mixture of Hatchard, Goodes, Walter Jones, Les Trois Quartier and the Bon Marché.[127] The sellers were dressed in white with broad sashes of pale blue fastened across like an Order. The day was unfortunately hot but I think that everything was a gigantic success.

We walked round most of the shows in order to throw the light of our countenance upon them; patronised the Café Chantant where they have an excellent troupe of amateur singers got up as Viennese minstrels. It is difficult to believe everything has been carried out by amateurs; the place has the business-like appearance of Earls Court about it. I only got home at 7 and we dined at 7.45 at Prince's Restaurant in the grounds; we entertained a party of 30, mostly connected with the Fête. After dinner we watched the military display, concluding with a sanguinary attack on the fort which is demolished and burnt to the ground where the bodies of the dead and dying are strewn—a great performance.

127. London and Paris stores.

Thursday, 31st.

So far the gate-money and returns have been greatly in excess of our expectations. The wild rush for tickets for the lucky bag has caused endless disappointments and the crush in drawing the 50,000 tickets has been terribly difficult to cope with. Many people with 20 tickets have drawn blanks. A private in a Highland Regiment with two tickets drew first Rs.10 and then the diamond ornaments worth a hundred pounds. Another soldier has won the buggy and Lord Kitchener the baby elephant! If only Punch could get hold of this, what a cartoon they could draw!

Friday, February 1st.

I had to receive the Amir at the Fête at 4 o'clock. He had warned me that he did not care about small, inexpensive things, so a huge glass-case was filled with jewellery from a native shop. The first thing he did was to pick out a necklace worth Rs. 2,000 and various brooches and earrings, spending, I suppose, about Rs. 4,000 at the stall. I offered to have the purchases sent to Hastings House, where he is staying. "What!" he said, "pack up these cases—too heavy, I cannot have all this luggage. No, I give away now," upon which he proceeded to present Kitty with the necklace, Ruby and Violet with the earrings, and the Duchess of Manchester, who happened to be in the stall, with the brooch. Eileen was very sad at not having been present. He then went to the Medical Stall making several purchases; then the Military one; there he saw a certain lady, called Mrs Villiers, who attracted him, upon which he said: "Kindly let me buy everything from your hand." The lady was so flurried that she didn't make the most of her time. She certainly might have sold him a great deal more. The last stall was Lady Fraser's, where he purchased lavishly and presented Lady Fraser with an enamel brooch in the shape of a serpent. Suddenly he said: "I have forgotten something at the other stall," and off he went by himself, and we all waited patiently for him. On emerging he came up to me and presented me with a really beautiful ring, a huge ruby surrounded by brilliants. "I give you this as a little souvenir of your Fete," he said. He did it so nicely, he evidently didn't wish to buy a present for me while I was with him, so eluded us and hurried to the other stall without any of his attendants. We had tea in the Café Chantant, and he poured about 20 sovereigns into the Manager's hands. In the middle of his tea he realised it was time to pray; so he asked if he could be shown to some secluded spot, and added "As everything here is done for charity, my room must cost me at least Rs. 100." He is enjoying himself so much that he insists on remaining at Calcutta and giving up his tiger-shoot much to our depression, as he comes down to Barrackpore on Sunday, and is to dine with us another night, and the strain of playing up to him is very great.

Lord K- has sold his elephant for Rs. 500, and has placed all his money in a motor raffle, the fact of his having won it is so unutterably funny. Several allusions were made to him during the evening in the topical songs:

"So the baby elephant's been won by Lord------! Hush
His staff have to nurse it by night and by day! Hush,"
&c., &c., &c. This quite brought down the house.

Sunday, 3rd February. Barrackpore.

The Amir arrived at 1 o'clock and remained till 6 o'clock; he enjoyed himself so enormously. I was so exhausted after looking after him for all those hours that I went straight to bed, having had a terrible week of fatigue with the Fête. The Adams, Clem, Violet Crawley, and Lena Ashburton all came to help us to entertain the Amir, but what he really enjoyed was playing croquet with Eileen; he had never seen the game before, and enjoyed it so much that to my horror he suggested returning the next day to have another lesson. Sir Henry McMahon came to our assistance and put difficulties in the way.

After luncheon he said he had a few presents he wished to give us; he took the greatest delight in giving us each individual thing. The girls waited while he made me my presentations: first

M.M. with Amir at Viecregal Stall.

a lovely diamond and ruby bird of paradise, then some Astrakhan skins and other furs, and innumerable stuffs all made in Afghanistan, a shawl he insisted on pinning round me, and lastly two beautiful Persian rugs. Each girl had exactly the same in smaller numbers: Eileen a lovely ruby and diamond riband ornament, Ruby five small diamond stars, and Violet one larger one, unfortunately all set in gold. Rolly was given the presents on a previous occasion. Gigantic carpets, furs, stuffs—and some Indian silver; also a silver cigarette-case with Venus in coloured enamel, a most startling apparition, but these will have to go to the Toshakhana.

Tuesday, February 5th, Calcutta.

Tonight the Amir has continued the flirtation with Eileen which he commenced during his game of croquet at Barrackpore. The oriental comes out in the way he devotes himself first entirely to one person, then to another, quite ignoring his previous attraction. We walked him through the house, showed him the ball-room, &c., &c., and he threw out such terribly broad hints to be asked to the State Ball that is to take place on Friday that at last we were obliged to invite him. This means he is postponing his visit again and causing untold inconvenience, but he doesn't consider any one but himself. He sat down to the piano and sang us Persian love songs. It was fortunate we could not understand the language, as I believe the poetry was of a most peculiar description. We couldn't get rid of him till 12 o'clock.

Friday, 8th.

Our State Ball took place in the evening. We marched in procession up the room, danced the State Lancers, then the Amir arrived; he has never seen dancing in his life, and I was terrified he was going to ask me to teach him. He has a way when sitting with one of gradually encroaching on one's side of the sofa, and I found it very difficult to sit with dignity at an oblique angle trying to avoid being scratched by the huge epaulettes on his uniform. I told him at supper it was our custom to put our knife and fork together if we had finished and wanted our plate removed. He said: "You teach, I learn." Then he showed me their custom of crossing their knives and forks, but afterwards he never forgot to do as I had told him. He said: "Please you tell me, I been heavy guest or light guest?" Of course I said: "You've been a light guest," whereupon he added: "Then I come and stay with you next year, not official. I come as your friend for long time." With a sickly smile I told him that we should look forward to that pleasure, privately praying that the Government will never allow this experiment to be repeated oftener than once in five years.

He told me it took him 12 days' riding and driving from Kabul to Landi Kotal. Then added: "Now I make good motor-road. I come in two!" Before we knew he was coming to the State Ball we had invited him to luncheon on Saturday at 2 o'clock to say good-bye to us. Sir Henry

MacMahon came up to me and said: "His Majesty suggests arriving at 11 o'clock tomorrow." I recovered from my shock as quickly as I could and hastily said that a previous engagement would occupy me till 12 o'clock; and I hoped His Majesty would not arrive before that hour.

Saturday, 9th.

Sir Henry managed well, and it must have been 12.20 before the Amir turned up. Rolly very meanly never appeared till luncheon was ready. The Amir is becoming so affectionate to the whole family that I am thankful to think they have at last persuaded him to leave Calcutta. I bade him farewell with many expressions of mutual friendship and left the room. On reaching the passage I found he was running after me. "I come to ask," he said, "can I write you private letters?" "Not in Persian," I said, "as I fear I should not understand them." "No, no," he answered "with translation, but private, not official; and you answer me. Then I write to you and to Lady Eileen." I suppose my whole time in future will be taken up corresponding with the Amir. Sir Henry told me he really felt very much upset at saying good-bye. He thought we had been so kind to him, and the whole mode of living was so different to what he had anticipated.

Sunday, 10th.

There are many stories current about the Amir: one is that if his interpreter makes any mistake he at once cuts off one of his toes. Another that he refused to allow a certain marriage to take place, the couple consequently eloped, but were soon caught and brought into the Amir's presence, who said: "If you are so fond of this lady, you shall have her all to yourself," and there and then he had her boiled, and a cup of the liquid was offered to the unfortunate husband, who was made to take a draft before being put to death. Of course these tales have really been invented. I should dislike to think I had been sitting next to such a monster; he has quite a kind face, though a very determined one. It is rather curious that he has never been attended by his own Sirdars; he evidently does not want them to glean as much information as himself. From things he said to me he evidently sees the English newspapers. He knew all about the agitation in Bengal. One day at the Cafe Chantant at the Fête the crows were making a tremendous babel in the trees, and he said, "that is just like the Bengalee Baboos always shrieking for no reason." He promised before leaving Afghanistan that he would not discuss politics, and he has kept his word, and never showed any desire to introduce business into this pleasure trip.

Wednesday, 13th.

Received the following telegram, a duplicate was also addressed to both Eileen and Ruby. It really is a priceless thing to possess:

“I have arrived at Bombay today, Tuesday, 12th February 1907. Thank God, I am quite well. I hope you will give me the pleasure of knowing about your good health. I shall never forget the sadness of parting with you at Calcutta until I have the pleasure of seeing you again. Seraj-ul-Millat-wa-ud-Din”.

The entente cordiale is becoming daily more firmly cemented; we have certainly gained an ally on our turbulent North-West Frontier, and this must be full of political significance and an event in our Indian history.

Tuesday, 5th March. Calcutta

The weather is getting terribly hot. Returned just in time for a meeting of the Fancy Fête committee at 6 o’clock; about 50 members present. We have now got in all the accounts and I am delighted to say we have cleared £23,000. It is a splendid result.

Wednesday, 6th March.

Held a meeting of the Patrons of the Fête and after much discussion came to a decision as to the distribution of money. The Natives were particularly cordial to me and were anxious that I should take a large sum for my nursing scheme, but I am sure we have been prudent in giving the lion’s share to the Calcutta charities.

Thursday, 7th March.

I have heard from Major Brooke, who travelled with the Amir to the frontier, that his emotion on receiving Rolly’s telegram of farewell was quite painful to witness. He drew Sir Henry McMahon aside, put on his motoring goggles to hide the tears that were coursing down his face, and was too overcome to say one word. He finally jumped on to his horse, spurred him into a gallop, and disappeared through the mountainous passes towards his barbaric kingdom. I have always forgotten to mention that the Amir became a Freemason during his visit to Calcutta, He was installed by Lord Kitchener and Sir Andrew Fraser; the latter told me that, on taking leave of him, he pressed his hand and murmured “good-bye, my brother”.

The last official report from Kabul brings the following gruesome tale:

> “Two woman attendants escaped from the Amir’s Harem, but were promptly caught and brought back. As a punishment their feet were at once cut off to ensure their never committing the same offence again. These cruelties are perpetrated by the Amir’s brother, Nasrulla Khan, the gentleman who resided for some weeks at Dorchester House a few years ago.”

After the Amir's visit and another by the Duke and Duchess of Connaught and their daughter, Princess Patricia, Mary left for England with her two elder daughters, Eileen and Ruby, and her youngest son, Esmond; returning to India in July. During her absence, her youngest daughter, Violet, 18 in May 1907, stood in as her Father's hostess. A journal of daily events was continued during this time by the Viceroy's Private Secretary, Major Dunlop Smith.

Thursday, 14th March.

We got through our preparations somehow. The things for London, Minto, and Simla have been sorted. I have had final interviews with various members of the staff. The Nursing Scheme has been "fixed up" for the present, and Mrs Davies, the Chief Lady Superintendent, is taking kindly to the work. The proposed reforms for the Dufferin Fund have been discussed with Colonel Crooke-Lawless, and the proposals drawn up to show to Lady Dufferin during my stay in England. A new system for keeping the household accounts has been gone over with the Comptroller and Military Secretary, and a proof sheet has been submitted. I have had a terribly hard fight, as India is the most conservative country in the world, and I was told the present system was drawn up by Lord Dufferin during his Viceroyalty. This gave me a good opening to suggest that this was all the more reason for adopting a new method, as poor Lord Dufferin was not a financial success. Fortunately even the Treasurer expresses approval, so now all is well. I made a final tour round the house and added to my long list of articles to be bought in England to put the necessary final touches here and there. I looked through the plans for reconstructing the Military Secretary and A.D.C.s' quarters, and I went over the Simla improvements with our Clerk of the Works, Mr Mackinnon, and look forward to making endless purchases with the liberal Government grant placed at my disposal.

Have received a most pathetic little token of farewell from the Amir, which has been brought to me by Sir Henry McMahon, who was commissioned to deliver it into my own hands. It is a charm in the shape of a tiny golden ship on which is a swallow and the words "good-bye, India." I am quite disturbed at reading the following notice in the paper, and hope this visit to India may not result in his assassination:

> THE AMIR'S VISIT.
> AFGHAN DISSATISFACTION.
> Peshawar, 13th March.
> Information has been received from Kabul that a good deal of dissatisfaction has been aroused among the more fanatical portion of the community by the visit of His Majesty the Amir to India. It is impossible to say in what form the accounts of the Amir's doings in India have reached Afghanistan, or how they have been

> interpreted, but the chief points to which exception appears to have been taken are the Amir's dining with British officers, and the friendliness he has shown towards them. His adoption of European clothes and the large purchases he has made of English articles, including the material for a bridge, and, lastly, the admission of the Amir into the Masonic fraternity during his visit to Calcutta, appear to have particularly given rise to misconception and suspicion.

By 5 o'clock even my letter of thanks to the Amir was written and all other business disposed of. It was quite hateful saying good-bye to Rolly and Violet, and I fear they will be dreadfully lonely. Violet was splendid and cheered up everyone; she and Esmond have been quite inseparable for nearly four months, and I can't think what she will do without him. Found a large number of people at the station to see us off. We left by special train at 7.30.

Have had a very interesting letter from Sven Hedin from Shigatse, telling me of his experiences crossing ranges of mountains over 19,000 feet high. The Tashi Lama has received him with great cordiality and is giving him every assistance, but the Chinese are making trouble and refuse to let him go to Gyantse, where our Commissioner, Captain O'Connor, is stationed. The reports from those parts are somewhat disquieting. It is not the policy of the present Government to assert themselves, and they cannot see the importance of playing the bold game which seems such a pity after Sir F. Younghusband's expedition.

After Luncheon at Barrackpore.
Back row: Lady Ruby, Count Wedell, Lady Violet, Capt. Fitzgerald, Miss Janet D. Smith, Countess Wedell, Col. D. Smith, Mrs Adam, Mrs Pelly, Col. Crooke-Lawless, Miss Smith, Geni, J. Maxwell, Mrs Crooke-Lawless, Major Feilding.
Middle row: Princess Patricia, Lord Kitchener, Duchess of Connaught, The Viceroy, Duke of Connaught, Her Excellency, Hon. E. Elliot, General Negriez.
Front row: Colonel Adam, Captain Mackenzie, Major Brooke, Captain Elgee, Maharaja Scindia, Captain Miles Ponsonby, Lady Eileen Elliot, Captain Webber, Captain Bulkaley.

Friday, 15th.

It has been perfectly cool all day. We are fortunate in having no sun. The wind appears to have risen, and I feel anxious as to the condition of the sea. "It is quite a large tank," the Amir remarked on first viewing the ocean at Bombay. Mr Hewett took us on board the S.S. Persia[128] on his launch. She looks quite a nice ship, and our cabins are clean and airy. The Captain will let us sit on the upper deck when we like, which will get us away from the crowd of passengers and be a great relief.

This ends the first part of my Indian journal. A great deal has happened since we first saw this harbour 16 months ago, and I hope and think that everything has gone well.

July 14th, 1907. In the Red Sea.

After a holiday of four months I feel very reluctant to pick up the threads of my journal again. Colonel Dunlop Smith has most kindly kept me au fait of all that has been going on in India and sent me a weekly diary. Very anxious times they have had with the agitation and unrest. I am glad to think things are improving a little, but Rolly has had a terribly trying time. During the three months I have spent in England I don't think I have seen the sun more than a dozen times. It has never been possible to wear summer clothes, and there has been an immense amount of rain. On arrival in England we were all more or less laid up with chills and colds. We spent a very happy four weeks at Minto during the boys' holidays till the 6th of May. Larry has become quite a grown-up boy and measures 5ft. 9ins. He has come on immensely in every respect. All our improvements at Minto are an unqualified success, the electric light being the greatest boon. The bath-rooms and servants' wing all combine to make the comfort of the house far more complete. Louisa, Ruby and I spent a very happy week with Nancy Astor at Cliveden for Ascot; Elizabeth Kenmare and the Laurence Drummonds being also of the party. The only contretemps during my stay in England has been Eileen's state of health; she was greatly run down and a succession of late hours proved too much for her and necessitated her going off to Malvern with a nurse for a fortnight. She has much improved during that time although her season has been knocked on the head.[129]

I had some very interesting interviews with Mr Morley. His relations with Rolly are most satisfactory, he spoke about him in quite affectionate terms, and nothing could be more cordial than he was with regard to Rolly's administration. Sir Arthur Godley and Mr Ritchie at the India Office have also been most complimentary, and in spite of his Radical colleagues, Mr Morley is loyally supporting Rolly's policy. I went to the House to hear his

128. The P & O liner was sunk by a German U boat in December 1915. 343 of the 519 passengers were drowned and a considerable quantity of gold and jewels lost.

129. Eileen was suffering from an unhappy love affair and the effects of the various sleeping and anti-depressant drugs of the time.

Budget Speech, and after his previous attitude with regard to Ireland it was very satisfactory to hear him saying the Viceroy had no other course open to him but to deport the leading agitators Lajpat Rai and Ajit Singh.

The Prince and Princess of Wales have been particularly kind and cordial. I have seen them several times at Marlborough House, and the Prince takes the greatest interest in everything that concerns India. Both the King and the Queen have been very nice. The King told me to tell Rolly that he had the fullest confidence in his judgement, and that he was thoroughly satisfied with his administration. I have managed to see all my friends, and have met most people who have any connection with India, such as Lord Roberts, Lord Lansdowne, St. John Brodrick, &c., and have seen Mr Buckles, Mr Moberley Bell and Mr Leo Maxse.[130] Sir Arthur Bigge[131] is always charming and ready to give many a useful side-light. I have had two meetings of the Committee of the Up-country Nursing Association, and have come to a most satisfactory understanding with them; they merge their name and become the home branch of the Indian Nursing Association, and everything points to the work being carried on in the most efficient manner.

I had a very busy time in London buying furniture for Simla, Calcutta, and Barrackpore, and must have selected quite £4,000 of goods worth for the Government; this, with my own trousseau needed for India has fully occupied my time, and I have been living almost beyond the power of human endurance as my duties as chaperone have kept me up most nights to between 2 and 3 A.M. Interviewing possible A.D.C.'s has also been another of my duties, Captain Jelf, 60th Rifles, strongly recommended by Sir E. Hutton accompanies me to India. Captain Mackenzie has been made Comptroller, and Captain Bulkeley has resigned; we shall miss him sadly, as he was most devoted to our interests, but he wishes to return to his regiment after an absence of three years. I was much surprised on opening the paper on the 28th June to find my name down for the Kaisar-i-Hind Medal given for distinguished services in India, which sounds so grand. I feel I haven't been in the country nearly long enough to deserve it, but it is extremely kind of whoever is responsible for giving it to me. I am delighted to see Colonel Crooke-Lawless and Mr Palmer have each a C.I.E.[132] They richly deserve it after all their work in connection with the fête.

My life in London has been so strenuous that without the help of a lady, Miss Hole, who came every morning to help me, it would have been impossible. She wrote the answers to all my notes, even to forging my name; paid bills; did the house books; helped even in the selection of cretonnes and did all the odd jobs I required. The electric landaulette has also been a god-send. It has been going morning, noon, and night, and the saving in time has been invaluable and quite worth the absurd charge of £95-0-0 a month, as it has done the work of six carriages. This is a very brief résumé of three strenuous months. Everyone tells

130. Eminent journalists.

131. 1st Baron Stamfordham, Private Secretary to Queen Victoria and, from 1901, to George V.

132. Commander of the Indian Empire

me I am crazy to attempt to go through the Red Sea at this time of year but the rumours of people being packed in ice and dying of heat apoplexy has not deterred me. I must hope for the best. I said goodbye to the boys very sadly on July 2nd.

Thursday, July 4th.

A good number of my friends kindly came to see me off at Victoria, Mr Morley amongst the number. The last good-byes are always trying, and one feels strangely tongue-tied. I felt very depressed and lonely leaving so many of my family in England, but it is no use regretting the inevitable.

Friday, July 5th. Marseilles.

Greeted Captain Horton and all my friends of the Persia with effusion. I have got two very nice cabins opening into each other, with a gangway just outside which will give me a good current of air. It seems quite strange to be without Dwyer, who has accompanied me on all my travels for the last nine years. I miss her dreadfully in a thousand ways, though Gould seems most tidy and attentive.

July 14th. Arrived at Aden.

And now to describe the Red Sea: I must admit that it has been anything but pleasant. The first day we bore up with fortitude. I kept saying to the Captain with a voice full of conviction: "This isn't really a bit bad," but when it came to four nights and four days of this incessant heat, sleep was impossible, as after about two minutes one felt one's pillow was a burning marsh, and oneself a saturated sheet of pink blotting paper, and one's spirit began to flag. There was a disjointed moist appearance about the passengers and crew, and when we reached Aden, where a fresh breeze was blowing, I felt I had had about enough. One night I attempted sleeping on the upper deck. The Captain gave me excellent advice. Above all things he said: "Avoid a chill and put plenty of flannels round your body." Down I went to my cabin, which registered 91°. I fortified myself with flannels and returned to the bridge, but the effort of thus dressing saturated my apparel, and the slightest breeze blew with a chill blast on my poor hot body; after about 10 minutes spent in balancing the pros and cons of risking pneumonia, I decided that the cabin without any clothes and without any chill was the soundest course to adopt, so I deserted my bed on the bridge for more private and safer precincts and tossed for another sleepless night in the stuffy steamy atmosphere.

Captain Lee, the Acting Governor, came to see me; also Captain Christian of H.M.S. Perseus; he only arrived from Bombay that morning; the funnels of his ship well whitened by the monsoon spray. The men of this ship helped during the Fancy Fête last winter, and he told me that they had been made supremely happy by receiving medals and grants of money in recognition of their services. At 3 o'clock we started to battle for five days with the monsoon. There is no doubt about it; it is an odious experience, but if one hadn't felt limp and reduced from the four days in the Red Sea I don't think it would have been so bad. Personally I was not ill, but hadn't the energy to move about much the first two days, and the stewardess was angelic in the way she looked after me. Poor Gould was dreadfully sorry for herself, her face looked whiter and her hair redder than ever, and Captain Jelf, as the saying goes, wasn't worth 8 annas. The heat isn't nearly as bad as it was in the Red Sea, and I have seen far bigger seas in the Atlantic and Pacific, although no doubt one suffers to a certain extent, people exaggerate the danger of travelling at this time of year enormously. The Captain tells me that in 30 years he has only heard of one death and that man was a drinking individual who would, probably have died anyhow on shore.

I have formed quite an affection for the Captain; he is a thorough sportsman, adores fishing and hunting, which he indulges in with the West Meath hounds whenever he gets the chance. He knows the name of every race-horse on the turf for the last 50 years, and was full of anecdotes. His caustic remarks about some of our fellow-passengers I enjoyed immensely. A certain lady, no longer young, wore a sleeveless blue gown every night with a very decollete back and front, and a skirt the length of walking tweed. "I have no patience," said the Captain, "with these old ladies dressing themselves up like this, or rather undressing themselves, they have nothing to gain by it," and one cannot but feel the force of his remark. I told him I had been very lazy and hadn't walked a yard. "That's right," said the Captain, exercise does you no good unless you enjoy it," so after that I sat contentedly in my chair with a clear conscience.

Friday, July 19th.

I had a most impressive send off from Bombay. I don't know for what reason, by the station was crowded with people, and Lord Lamington and a good many officials came to see me off.

Saturday, 20th.

Had to get out at Bhopal to have an interview with the Begum. The rains have not come; they had had 18 inches in Bombay, but there have been no rains further north, and they fear a famine. Francis had a terribly hot journey south. They said the thermometer had been 118°. This is the journey that I had been anxious to avoid, as the stifling heat of the plains has often been described to me, and no doubt people do die of it. The rains are due the middle of June, and are a month late. We made up our minds, as we left Bhopal with a cloudless sky and burning sunshine, that we must endure the heat of the journey as best we could, and hoped we should come through alive. I felt very tired and uncomfortably hot, so after breakfast I undressed and lay down on my bed to rest. I must have fallen asleep, but was roused in an hour by peals of thunder and sheets of rain beating against the windows. The monsoon had come and we continued our journey in perfect comfort. Providence had been very kind and had saved the situation, but had run it terribly fine! In Simla they were in an agony at the thoughts of our having to pass through the parched and burning plains, wondering how we should bear the ordeal. Now the people think I am the goddess of rain, for one month they have been anxiously waiting in vain, but the first day I set foot on Indian soil down it comes in torrents. It is pleasant to be associated with good omens.

Sunday, 21st.

Reached Kalka quite early, and left in a landau with Francis at 9.30 to drive to Solon, 30 miles, where Rolly and Violet were to meet me. It was a moment of great excitement, the meeting after my four months' absence. Rolly is looking wonderfully well in spite of all the worry, though I think it has told on him a little, The whole of Simla greatly regrets my return: they say Violet has been such a splendid hostess, the youngest Vicereine ever known as she took office before she was 18. Now, as Rolly says, she has been reduced to the ranks. I talked to them telling them all the news for three solid hours in the carriage, and I arrived at Simla at 5.30, exhausted with a parched throat. I found all the staff and their belongings and the wives of the Members of Council waiting to receive me. We had tea and talked of the weather, but they had great tact and soon took their departure. I then walked round the new terraces and walks with Rolly. I am perfectly enchanted with them. It seems like magic. A year ago I was drawing rough designs, and now the borders are a blaze of colour, and huge walls and balustrades stretch in broad terraces from the house to the tennis-ground, a distance of 200 yards.

Monday, August 5th. Simla

The fortnight that has elapsed since I arrived has been a very busy one. Old Sir Pertab is here staying with Colonel Dunlop. Everybody loves him. He can hardly read or write, but he is the most perfect gentleman. He does not believe the agitation has gone so very deep. He said to me: "People know Viceroy, he soldier, he two-hand man, he make people happy; every one trust two-hand man. Civilian, he only one-hand man." The following story gives an insight into Sir Pertab's character: A young English officer died while staying in Sir Pertab's house, and his brother officer went to Sir Pertab and asked him to order some sweepers to come to carry the poor boy's body to the gun-carriage. Sir Pertab wouldn't hear of sweepers, and said he would come himself. The officer remonstrated with him and reminded him that he would lose his caste if he touched a dead body; but Sir Pertab wouldn't listen, and not only assisted in carrying the boy to the gun-carriage but helped to lower him into the grave. The next morning a party of Brahmins called on Sir Pertab; they said: "A most terrible thing has occurred." "Yes, indeed," said Sir Pertab, "a young officer has died." "Far worse than that," they answered, "a great nobleman has lost his caste." "Listen to me," said Sir Pertab, "I recognize one caste alone, and that is the caste of a soldier— leave my presence, you swine," and with these words he chased away the whole party with a hunting whip.

Another story was told me by a Colonel Turner, who has been much with Sir Pertab. Early one morning he and Sir Pertab were sitting smoking in front of his house; a coolie came up wringing his hands and flung himself to the ground at Sir Pertab's feet, saying he had murdered his wife. Sir Pertab never moved, and without removing his cigarette said: "Come back at 2 o'clock." Colonel Turner asked him why he allowed the man to escape, suggesting that he would never return. Pertab merely nodded his head and said: "You'll see." At 2 o'clock back came the man, although he well knew what awaited him—he was promptly shot.

The only three original members of our staff that remain with us are Colonel Dunlop Smith, Colonel Crooke-Lawless, and Francis Scott. Captain Mackenzie makes an excellent Comptroller, knowing the language so well makes it easy for him to go into the minutest detail. We have now a Quarter-Master-Sergeant, Gough, who weighs everything that comes into the house, and our expenses have been reduced from Rs. 12 to Rs. 16 a head a day to Rs. 4, a saving of Rs. 24,000 or £2,000 in six months. When we arrived in India we took over all the stores in the house at a cost of £500. I believe there was sufficient to last for several years. The Store *baboo* had been about 30 years at Government House and naturally preferred using the new consignment of provisions, which was ordered in every six months. Consequently when he was dismissed and things were looked into, an enormous accumulation was found to have gone bad and had to be thrown away. The same sort of thing took place with regard to the stables, the headman had only to requisition for sums of money and no account of any sort was ever shown. With 50 horses and 50 syces this method cannot have been exactly economical. Colonel Victor Brooke, our Military Secretary, is full of reforms, and is putting the Barrackpore estate under an entirely different management and our farm and dairy arrangements are to be remodelled

We have two very nice extra A.D.C.s: Captain W. Cadogan, 10th Hussars, whom everyone adores, and Captain Norton, E.A., a friend of Colonel Polly Carew's. A Captain Harker, 60th Rifles, is with us now. He has had a horrid polo accident which has damaged his nose; otherwise he is extremely good looking and very efficient. Violet's governess, Miss Salberg, who when I left was not of much account in the house, has become a general favourite. The A.D.C's delight in chaffing her is only equalled by her delight in being chaffed, and everyone calls her "Saucy" in a friendly spirit. She is the greatest success in Simla society, and I am told has received proposals without end, to which so far she has turned a deaf ear.

Sunday, August 11th.

Spent a peaceful Sunday marking trees and planning improvements and rode up to see Lord K- after tea; he is always busy working at terraces and new gardens; he enjoys thinking them out but when completed he takes no further interest in them. We had quite an exciting evening as relays of animals made their appearance in the drawing room after dinner; a

Unusual forms of address!

toad; a huge spider; a centipede; and sundry gigantic moths and flying insects. I don't know whether the dogs or I minded most. We have had a great deal of gaiety lately. Colonel Brooke gave a dinner and dance at Squires Hall, which was cheery and informal. They danced the Catherine Wheel Lancers. I suddenly saw Violet whirling through the air. This is the first time I have seen this weird performance which I have often heard described. I don't think it is pretty, but fortunately the ladies' skirts seem to whirl with them and don't display the amount of ankle I should have expected. Violet is quite the grown-up young lady now—only three years ago she was driving goats at Ottawa, and six months ago she declared she would never dance; now that she is obliged to, I think the dislike is wearing off.

I am longing to get nurses established within measurable distance of the outlying posts where officers are stationed. Such a terrible thing happened the other day. Admiral Sir William May's son Hughie May, a most promising young soldier, whom we knew well as he spent most of his holidays with his aunt, at Hassendeanburn, close to Minto, fell ill with fever. He had married last year, and his wife was with him, but she could get no doctor, nurses, or medicines. They were about four days' march from any civilisation. The poor wife decided to have him carried down country in a *dooly*, but he was so weak he died during the first day. If the coolies had discovered that he was dead, they would have dropped the *dooly* and run away; so for three days she pretended he was alive, brought him food and spoke to him, and managed to bring his body to a station where she had him buried. The story haunts one with its horror. I wrote to the poor wife; her courage must have been superhuman, she told me in her answer how often he had spoken of the happy days at Minto; he wasn't quite 26, and she thought, if he had not continued to work while the fever was on him, he might have recovered. I am afraid the same spirited determination not to give way, is answerable for many precious lives in this country.

A begging letter sent me the other day has the following sentence in it: "We respectfully solicit the favour of a kind reply. Your noble and illustrious feet are the sole asylum of all our hopes." I think someone with a sense of humour must have written it.

Tuesday, 13th August.

Two foreign telegrams lay on my chota hazri tray when I was called in the morning. I opened them with a palpitating heart which palpitated a great deal more when I found they contained the great news of Ruby's engagement to Lord Errington! One's feelings are so mixed, I hardly knew at first whether to be glad or sorry. She will leave the most awful blank in our home circle but it had to come some day and they are evidently both radiant. It appears to have been settled at Killarney but it seems an eternity to have to wait three weeks before we hear any details. The whole of Simla is greatly excited. I should like them to be married in Calcutta after our trip to Burma but I imagine it would be difficult for him to get much leave. I am afraid his profession will take them to the ends of the earth but I think Ruby will like the life. I am so devoted to all the Barings that is delightful to think she is going to marry into such a nice family. Violet's remark when I told her was: "I was certain she'd go and do it".

The Amir has announced his intention of visiting England, Japan, China, and, if possible, America—all in one trip.

Tuesday, September 3rd, 1907.

I fancy that there is a general impression that I have got nothing to do here. I think a sample of one of my mornings will be quite amusing as well as instructive. Violet on leaving my room at 10 o'clock after breakfast, which was rather later than usual owing to a ball given by Colonel and Mrs Crooke-Lawless at Squires Hall the previous night—which had kept me up till 2:30 A.M.—found a string of about 10 people in the passage all waiting for interviews. This passage goes by the name of the Orderley Room, and a similar scene to the one I am about to describe takes place every morning.

Knock, enter Captain Harker to report that he is in waiting on me, and to ask at what time I require the carriage for shopping in Simla—exit.

Knock, enter Colonel Brooke with plans for a new Military Secretary's Office at Calcutta.

A statement from Ram Das that, owing to the construction of the walls, the electric light fittings will be unable to be placed in the position selected. Where shall they be hung ?

The new gardener at Barrackpore awaits my orders for the arrangement of the flower-beds, and sends a general report for my approval of the work he suggests doing in the park.

A lady writes to say, unless she obtains Rs. 4,000 this week, her husband and herself will be turned out of their dwelling, but counts upon my charity and kindness of heart in saving them in their hour of need.

A violinist asks for my patronage and presence at a concert at any date I care to name during October.

The Black Hearts intend to give a Fancy Ball at the end of September, and hope for the favour of the presence of the Viceroy and Lady Minto. Query are we to go, and can I possibly endure the trouble of designing fancy dresses for the family?—exit Colonel Brooke.

Knock, enter Lord Francis Scott. The Girls' Friendly Society are to be entertained at 5 o'clock. Are the 100 members to be seated at round tables in the dining room? And where are the lady associates to partake of tea? They number 50; the list of their names has to be mastered.

An important Colonel has arrived in Simla from Delhi for two days; Shall he be asked to luncheon today? He will only make the ninth guest; plan of table is submitted; also for our weekly dinner of 60—exit Lord Francis.

Knock, enter Captain Jelf. Letters have been received from Kishan Chand in Delhi, also from Ganeshi Lai in Agra, each claiming to have embroidered the Queen's Coronation train? Her Majesty has asked me to order her another embroidered gown to be made by the man she has employed before. As both claim this honour, further investigations are necessary to avoid any mistake.

Will Her Excellency kindly make a drawing of the Jeypore chains required for Lady Grey's Ottawa Bazaar? Tarachand of Calcutta does not quite understand the kind of necklaces required—exit Captain Jelf.

Knock, enter Colonel Dunlop Smith. Brings translation of letter received yesterday from the Amir. Should Her Excellency wish to write an answer, a messenger leaves the Foreign Office this afternoon, and can take it, otherwise the opportunity will be missed for some time—exit Colonel Dunlop.

Knock, enter Colonel Crooke-Lawless. Can Her Excellency come to inspect the site of the new Dufferin Hospital. There is considerable friction in connection with the building as to which end of Simla is the most suitable; the sites are three miles apart; will Her Excellency kindly visit both, and report on the matter as soon as possible?

Viceregal Lodge, Simla.

Lady Fraser writes to beg Lady Minto will appoint a lady to be Superintendent at one of the new nursing branches in Assam. She is a trained nurse and has recently lost her husband, who was a tea planter. The poor woman is quite a lady, has two children, and her income is £22 per annum. A Superintendent has already been appointed, but the case is deserving, and we must try and arrange the transfer of the present nurse to another station.

Colonel Crooke also brings a letter from General Scott, saying he has remitted the claim from the Ordnance Department for Rs. 1,150 for damage done to goods lent for the Minto Fancy Fête—account was only submitted six months after the Fête, and a strong remonstrance was made at their unbusinesslike procedure with this most excellent result—exit Colonel Crooke-Lawless.

Knock, enter Captain Mackenzie. The menus for the fortnight that we are to be away in the mountains have to be passed, as the provisions have to be commandeered a long time before they are needed. To think out 14 breakfasts, 14 luncheons and 14 dinners at a time is a distinct strain to the ordinary brain, not entirely engrossed with the attractions of culinary act.

The month's accounts have to be inspected and comparisons made as to present and previous expenditure, fortunately the present month brings our average to about half what it was last year—exit Captain Mackenzie.

Knock, enter Mr Mackinnon, our Head Architect, Engineer, Clerk of the Works, &c., &c. At this minute, he is superintending the decoration of the guest-rooms. The curtains in three rooms are prepared for my inspection. There is not sufficient cretonne to cover all the chairs that are required, as the *durzies* have cut up the material to waste and have not matched the patterns. The fittings for the electric lamps will not arrive for a fortnight. Will Her Excellency kindly say what is to be done in the meantime, as Sir Harold Deane, Mr Grant, and General Kitson must occupy the rooms tomorrow and Sir John, Lady, and Miss Hewett arrive next week? A way out of the difficulty must be promptly found—exit Mr Mackinnon.

Knock, enter Janki Pershad, our native second-in-command to Mr Mackinnon. The rugs that Her Excellency wished to see have been spread in the Ball-Room, about 50 in all. Could the selection for the various rooms kindly be made at once, as the Ball-Room will be needed in the afternoon for the Girls' Friendly Society? The rugs that are not required can be sent to Calcutta and Barrackpore. Janki will wait below for Her Excellency's kind decision.

A consignment of black buck heads has also arrived from Roland Ward by the order of the Maharaja of Bikaner; they are also in the anti-room to the Bail-Room. Will Her Excellency be good enough to select their position in the hall?—exit Janki.

Knock, enter Furniss, the Steward. All the silver cups and presents have arrived from London. Will Her Excellency kindly inspect them before they are put away and select those needed to take on tour?—exit Furniss.

Knock, enter Long, the Gardener. The ground at the further end of the garden has been prepared for planting with 18 inches of new soil. Will Her Excellency kindly mark out where the shrubs are to be planted, as they cannot be kept much longer without the risk of dying? The ground is of considerable extent and the shrubs run into thousands—exit Long.

Knock, enter Fryer (Valet). Does Her Excellency know what happened to the sight-protector of her new rifle, which was used at Mashobra last week to shoot at bottles? In cleaning the rifle, he has just noticed the loss. Another one should be obtained.

The last shirts sent by Hodgkinson for the Viceroy ordered by Her Excellency have the wrong shaped collars. This announcement is made in an aggrieved tone of voice and makes me feel considerably humbled. I at once apologise profusely—exit Fryer.

Dining room Viceregal Lodge.

For a few brief moments I sit at my writing table, after having flown upstairs to inspect the furniture and cretonnes, and downstairs to look at the plate. Then another knock, enter my new Jemadar, a most magnificent person, who used to be with the Princess of Wales; he talks excellent English, so when I send him for a book he won't send for 10 coolies to carry my writing table to another room as the last man did. He now brings a chit from Miss Gould saying Lady Violet is trying on a new evening dress; will I come and signify my approval before she takes it off?

Finally my late Jemadar, Rumbully, comes to bid me farewell. I give him a watch and tell him that he has looked after me very well, which isn't quite true, as he was usually half asleep from the effects of opium. By this time the luncheon gong sounds. I find Sir Louis Dane in close consultation with the Viceroy. I interrupt them, and insist on their coming to luncheon. I try to forget the petty annoyances of life, and my desire to murder the next person who dares knock at my door. I have endeavoured truthfully to describe what occurs day after day and have recounted faithfully the business transacted in one morning. The constant annoyance from the unexpected interruption about some trivial thing which of itself is of no importance is most trying, but it must be attended to, and so my days pass by. Thursday, the mail day, is always an extra rush and a scrimmage in trying to write one's home letters, but I find I can only manage to keep in touch with my family, and my friends I very seldom correspond with.

Till one has attempted to do up a house in India, no one can possibly imagine the labour it is. Patterns convey nothing to the native, consequently unless each movement is watched you find your sofa is covered with half the pattern topsy turvy—then the white margin of the material figures prominently on one's best chair, and they hack and hew in the most remorseless way, consequently the waste of the material is really cruel. One durzie might be watched, but when 20 are working, and several rooms are being done at the same time, the trial to one's temper is very great.

Wednesday, 4th September.

I have allowed my journal to lapse for several weeks. Things in the political world have been moving apace, and some of the reforms that have given Rolly a great many months of anxious work have been sanctioned by Mr Morley; *viz.*: The Councils of Notables; Enlargement of Councils. Imperial Advisory Council &c., &c. The Reuters are full of praise for his broad-mindedness and foresight, no mention being made of the Viceroy and Government of India. As a matter of fact, every suggestion has emanated from the Government of India. I might go so far as to say that all the new concessions to natives have been evolved by Rolly. I don't wish to take away any credit from Mr Morley. He has been splendid and has backed Rolly up heroically and he himself does not wish to take credit for what Rolly has done; he told me so in so many words and added: "It is curious that I should find a Viceroy appointed by a Conservative Government a greater radical than myself. We shall never carry his Council or mine as far as he would like to go; but we are moving in the right direction and what I admire in him is the way he looks ahead—a very rare quality. Most of the Civil Servants believe that things can continue as they have done during the last century; well, they can't, and Lord Minto has fully grasped the situation".

In saying it would be impossible to carry public opinion far enough, Mr Morley was alluding to the appointment of a Native Member on the Viceroy's Council which Rolly feels would be a most judicious move, and checkmate all the agitators and the Congress party who say the time has come for them to rule India. As regards the unrest in India, I find, in looking through Rollys's letters to the Secretary of State, that the first mention of an undercurrent of discontent was dated March 1907. Since then, things have moved rapidly. Several political officers have lately been down from the frontier and have given us interesting accounts of their strenuous lives. Mr Grant, Secretary to Sir Harold Deane, Chief Commissioner and Agent to the Governor General at Peshawar, said that no doubt the agitation in the Punjab had greatly affected the tribes on the frontier. They believe that the British are sowing the seed of plague and so suspicious have they become that the out-patients at the Peshawar Hosiptals, which used to number between 4 and 500 a day, have fallen to under 10. Mr Grant said they expected trouble next spring—no doubt the deportation of Lajpat Rai had been a great set-back as they did not expect the Home Government to support such strong measures.

Keir Hardie in India.

Thursday, 3rd October. Camp Saura, 8,850 FT.

Keir Hardie[133] is creating a great deal of excitement throughout India. He is going to spend a month in the country and thinks he will then have mastered all the problems for governing an eastern race. So far he says the tyranny of Government in Bengal reminds him of Armenian atrocities and that India should certainly become a self-governing colony. It is monstrous these men coming out and trying to create further agitation, especially during these critical times. I should love Keir Hardie to go and see the situation on the frontier. Allow him no guard and let him shift for himself, I don't think he would trouble us again. The tribes would soon show him how they would propose to govern India. From all the Reuters it seems that all the English papers are denouncing him.

Wednesday, 9th. Narkanda.

Keir Hardie declares that he has never said the seditious things imputed to him and blames the Indian Reuter correspondents for reporting him incorrectly. In this, I fully sympathise with him.

133. James Keir Hardie, British Labour Party leader, was on a World tour 1907-1908 that included visits to India, Southern Africa and Australia.

Monday, 14th.

Returned to Simla and began the usual round of luncheons, dinners &c. Three of the chief and oldest Viceregal retainers have left the establishment and not only will our private pockets benefit greatly but it will make a considerable difference to the Government. One gentleman who had tyranised over the servants and always insisted on receiving large

douceurs[134] from them if they wished to have a satisfactory report given of their character, was followed to the station by most of the establishment playing drums and tomtoms to express their joy at his departure. Colonel Brooke insisted on having a list of the workpeople at Barrackpore, and a statement of how each was employed. The explanations were not very satisfactory and, on it has been discovered that one man has drawn his own pay and his father's for 26 years, the said father having died in the year 1881.

28th October.

Keir Hardie arrived, dressed and looking like a respectable workman; his only peculiarity was a green cummerbund that not only appeared round his waist but had long ends protruding above and below his waistcoat. He was very respectful and didn't give vent to any seditious sentiments and listened intently to what Rolly had to say. He passed through Colonel Dunlop-Smith's room on leaving and said to him in his broad Scotch accent: "The Viceroy's alright but I don't like some of his officials." The British public appear to have been more excited about him than any other episode during the unrest. I think the press that circulate stories that are not true and magnify the extent of the agitation do far more harm.

Wednesday, 6th November. Viceregal Train.

Our train consists of 10 carriages; it is 320 yards long. There are 106 native servants, 14 personal servants, 10 clerks, and with our own party of 12 making a total of 142 people. The last few days were terribly rushed as usual, with final interviews and orders. The hall is to be repanelled. There is a most objectionable man in the Public Works Department who calls himself an architect, but cannot claim to have either taste or capacity. On arrival we found that he ranked with Brigadier-Generals in the table of precedence, so Rolly put him down 17 steps. This naturally rankled. He is now leading the Department, and his parting shot at us and his criticisms on the designs drawn out by our selected man is "that the taste shown was so execrable and the style so florid that the next tenant would be fully justified in having the whole thing pulled down again." There is something rather comic in the expression of "the next tenant." I need hardly say that the work is being proceeded with in spite of this condemnation.

I must not omit to mention that all the staff have caught the Diablo craze.[135] When it first arrived at Simla, Rolly was the only person who could manipulate it with any success, having been an expert at it in early youth; he has now been left far behind by all the A.D.C.s who rush on to the platform each time the train stops, and throw the devil towards the heavens with great success, catching it with unvarying precision. We have had to damp their ardour,

134. Literally sweeteners—bribes.

135. Juggling with a Diablo or Diabolo, otherwise known as a Chinese yo-yo, first became a craze in 1812 in France. Its popularity revived again in France in 1906 and spread to England and across the World by 1907.

Train at Ahmednagar en route to Hyderabad.

and forbid Diablo being played, as the natives, not being so up to date, gazed in amazement at their vagaries, and naturally thought the Viceroy's train contained a party of lunatics.

Monday, 11th.

We reached Hyderabad at 8.30 precisely and found a profusely decorated station and crowds of officials, including the Nizam and his son. Before the Prince of Wales's visit the Nizam had never seen a motor, but he was so delighted with the one that Shaftesbury brought to Hyderabad that he at once ordered 20. Now he has 32, of which 7 are napiers. Several of these, he has kindly put at our disposal. He has a young English Chauffeur who understands the mechanism of all his cars, and has trained all the native drivers. He is dressed in a beautiful uniform and a magnificent orange pugree, and receives £600 a year. He is quite one of the most important people in Hyderabad. Mr Brian Egerton lunched with us; he has been with the Nizam's son for seven years. This boy is now 22. He has no sporting instincts, and looks half-asleep. He lately cut out his father by marrying a lady intended for the Nizam's harem. This led to some unpleasantness which has since been patched up. Mr Egerton was formerly Bikaner's tutor, they are mutually devoted to each other and Bikaner always says he owes everything to Mr Egerton, that he has been quite a father to him.

From the Palace we have a beautiful view of Hyderabad city and, in the distance, the great lake Mir Alam stretches across the landscape. It is deep blue in colour, and makes such a fresh cool contrast to the usual arid Indian plains. We all motored out 12 miles to Bolarum, the military station beyond Secunderabad, where the celebrated Hyderabad Contingent have always been quartered. In fact this place seems a sort of Aldershot. Owing to a compact made with the Nizam we are obliged to keep a number of regiments here—we had tea in the twilight, and listened to the Hyderabad Band from whom Herr Büchner was stolen by Lord Curzon causing fearful heartburnings but another German bandmaster has kept their reputation. The star-light drive back was delicious; the wretched troops and police seem to have lined the streets since 8 A.M. They were still there at 7.30 P.M. on our return. The police have a wonderful head dress, striped orange and black made in a peculiar shape like an insect wing; altogether they look very smart.

Tuesday, 12th.

Colonel Crooke, Violet, and I went off to see two State Hospitals; everything very clean and comfortable. The maternity ward was full of minute babies with bushes of black hair, but with such fair complexions that they might easily have been Europeans. In a building

Lord Francis Scott succumbs to prevailing craze.

adjoining the Hospital, all the purdah ladies were assembled, wives of the ministers, many talking English and apparently quite well educated. They were quite delighted to meet us. One told me how much she hoped education would advance that it was all important for the welfare of India, and that she was trying to start a school. Certainly the younger generation are longing to emancipate themselves, but have many difficulties to contend with, especially in the Nizam's estates. On our return we met several Indian nobles, each with their own escort, having been to the Palace to pay a ceremonial visit to the Viceroy. There is one officer of State that I have been warned against. He goes by the name of "The Duck", as he is fat and waddles as he walks. His manners are primitive. At meals, while eating curry he takes the bones in his fingers and throws what he does not require over his shoulder. When a banquet was given to the Curzons he tried to restrain himself, and didn't toss the food about in his usual style, but he unfortunately contrived to throw his debris underneath the table. He chucked it away with such violence that most of it was found on the front of poor Mary Curzon's gown who sat opposite him. I have begged that I should be placed beyond his line of fire.

The Bishop of Madras and his wife[136] came to luncheon, he with his hair arranged a la Sir Wilfred Laurier.[137] She is quite young and very fashionable, altogether most unlike a Bishop's wife. Rolly was delighted to find that her exalted rank entitled her to sit next to him, as a rule the old and staid fall to his lot. We are gradually working off the officials and soldiers and their wives at one meal or another, but I cannot yet disentangle them.

At 5 o'clock we motored out to the grand old Fort of Golconda— dashing through villages— all too fast to appreciate the kaleidoscope of colour of the natives who were crowded at every aperture, windows, balconies, and streets being packed with them. They were rewarded by seeing a motor rush past them at 40 miles an hour and smothered in dust, but no doubt they think a Viceroy too exalted a personage to be looked at, and do not resent it. The Nizam and his son were awaiting us, and we all climbed to the summit of the fort, which we reached just as the sun was setting, and the heavens were a glowing mass of crimson. We found tea spread out in a pagoda from which we could gaze at the landmarks on every side. The country is dreadfully burnt up, but the trees are a brilliant green. The feature of this part of the world are the huge rocks of all shapes and sizes that are strewn about in all directions. There is an old saying that when the world was created the Almighty dumped down all his superfluous building material in Hyderabad, where it has lain ever since.

We had to hurry home in order to dress for the State Banquet. This took place in the Chowmahalla Palace, the quadrangle of which was lighted up with millions of little lamps and the broad pathway all round festooned with blazing arches. The Nizam sat between Rolly and me; on my other side the Resident, Mr Bayley, commonly called the Camel from

136. The Rt. Rev. Henry Whitehead. His wife was Isobel Duncan, daughter of the Rector of Calne whose wife was a kinswoman of the Dukes of Atholl.

137. Sir Wilfred, 7th Prime Minister of Canada, tall and good looking when a young man, he took meticulous care of his wavy chestnut hair which later became white and receded elegantly from his high forehead.

Golconda from palace roof.

his resemblance to that animal, especially about the neck. His guttural laugh also reminds one of the sounds that emanate from the camel but he is a very nice man, and most pleasant to talk to. I had been warned that the Nizam was impossible, but I couldn't have believed that he would never give vent to more than a monosyllable as I found to be the case. I asked him every conceivable question as to the government of the country, and even risked the purdah question but all to no purpose. Poor man, he was terribly nervous at having to propose the Viceroy's health. He can't read English characters, so his speech was written in English words with Hindustani letters. The expressions were very well chosen and rather difficult, and he shook from head to foot as he read it occasionally stumbling over the longer words. It must have been a dreadful effort for him.

We didn't remain long after dinner. I talked to Mr Egerton, it seems the wretched Heir-Apparent is not allowed any liberty at all. He may not go out for a drive, or play tennis without the permission of the Nizam. He is kept very short of money, and is absolutely terrified of his father. What strikes one more than anything is the holy awe in which the Nizam is held. No one dares speak before him. If he appears unexpectedly, his subjects fly

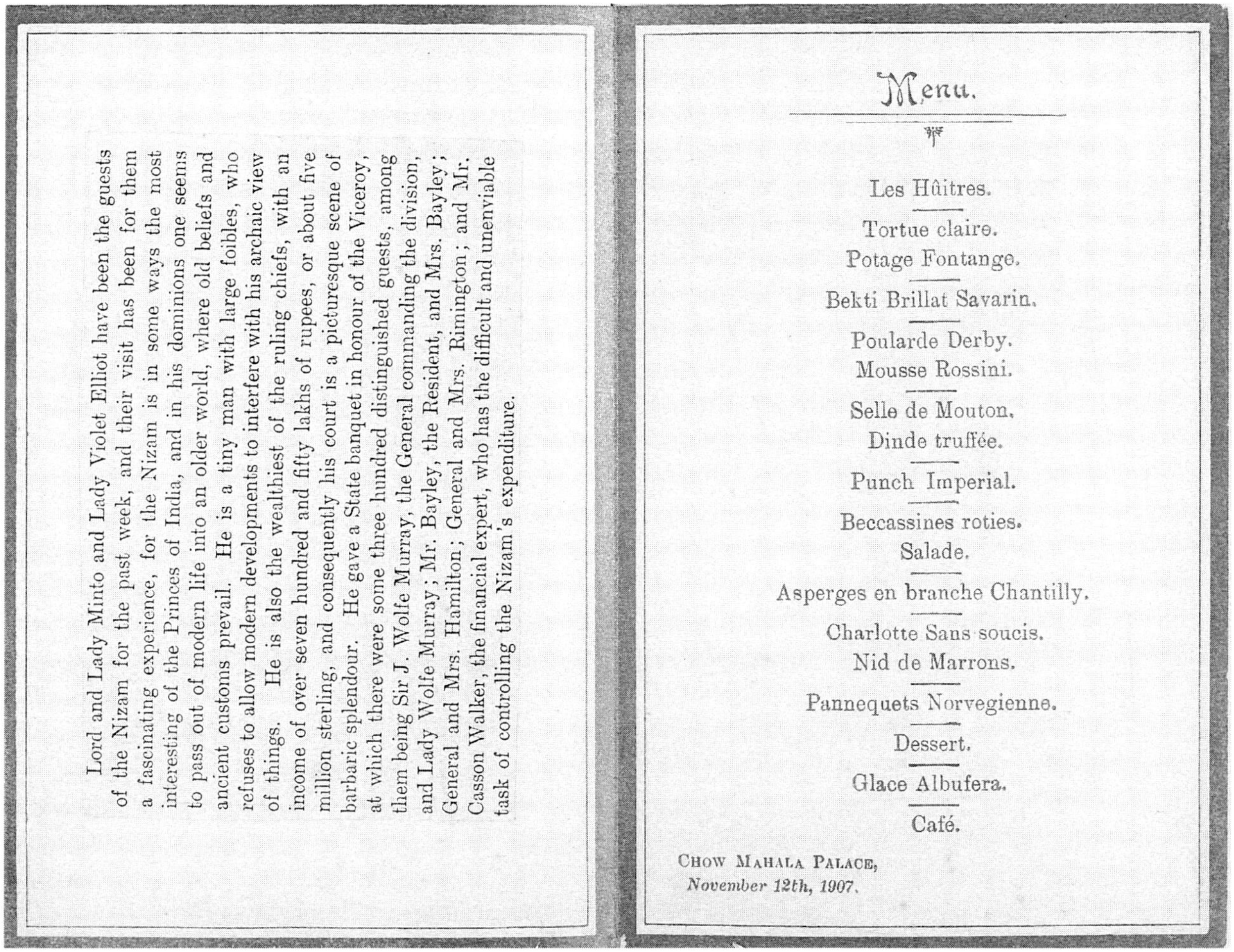

Lord and Lady Minto and Lady Violet Elliot have been the guests of the Nizam for the past week, and their visit has been for them a fascinating experience, for the Nizam is in some ways the most interesting of the Princes of India, and in his dominions one seems to pass out of modern life into an older world, where old beliefs and ancient customs prevail. He is a tiny man with large foibles, who refuses to allow modern developments to interfere with his archaic view of things. He is also the wealthiest of the ruling chiefs, with an income of over seven hundred and fifty lakhs of rupees, or about five million sterling, and consequently his court is a picturesque scene of barbaric splendour. He gave a State banquet in honour of the Viceroy, at which there were some three hundred distinguished guests, among them being Sir J. Wolfe Murray, the General commanding the division, and Lady Wolfe Murray; Mr. Bayley, the Resident, and Mrs. Bayley; General and Mrs. Hamilton; General and Mrs. Rimington; and Mr. Casson Walker, the financial expert, who has the difficult and unenviable task of controlling the Nizam's expenditure.

Menu.

Les Hûitres.

Tortue claire.
Potage Fontange.

Bekti Brillat Savarin.

Poularde Derby.
Mousse Rossini.

Selle de Mouton.
Dinde truffée.

Punch Imperial.

Beccassines roties.
Salade.

Asperges en branche Chantilly.

Charlotte Sans soucis.
Nid de Marrons.

Pannequets Norvegienne.

Dessert.

Glace Albufera.

Café.

CHOW MAHALA PALACE,
November 12th, 1907.

in all directions in order to place round their waists a golden band called bucklas, without which they cannot appear in their ruler's presence. Servants are always handy with this badge in case of emergency. Before appearing in the presence of the Nizam everyone prostrates themselves, beating their foreheads repeatedly in an attitude of servility. The Nizam's zenana is a thing which is never alluded to. None of his wives are nobly born; there are any number of them, all of low caste. They come into the zenana with a large retinue, and they say that there are about 10,000 women enclosed in the Palace grounds; when once in, even the lowest servant is not permitted to escape. The Nizam has one great quality; he never goes back on his word, he is absolutely to be relied on and fulfils all his promises. He transacts all his business in writing and hardly ever sees his Ministers, but the whole administration of the country is being put on much more satisfactory lines, and somehow he knows everything that is going on.

Nizam's banquet menu.

Wednesday 13th.

My poor old birthday.[138] I was made very happy at receiving birthday wishes from Eileen, Larry, Esmond and Louisa, and also a charming message from Ottawa. Felt very loath to rise at 6.30, but we had to start to motor 10 miles to Secunderabad to witness the review. All the world was there, and it was a very pretty sight. The Imperial Service Troops charged quite magnificently. They are under the command of a most delightful native, Colonel Afsur-ul-Mulk Bahadur, who was a champion polo player in his day. After the review, we went on to breakfast at the Secunderabad Lines—about 200 people were assembled and sat at long tables in a sort of verandah.

Thursday, 14th.

Had to rush through all my mail letters, but luckily had no function until the arrival of the Nizam for luncheon. He began decidedly to thaw, asked the names of all our staff, and produced from his pocket a lucky tiger bone, which he had shot, set with diamonds, which he begged me to accept.

He gave Violet an umbrella, the handle of which was set with rubies, and Rolly two walking sticks. I think the little man is really pleased with our visit.

Friday, 15th.

We were to embark for Rangoon at Coconada, but a hurricane has been blowing for three days and we received a wire to say that owing to a cyclone the Dufferin had gone out to sea and had not been heard of. Embarking at Coconada is always difficult, the ship has to remain five miles out at sea and the surf is invariably very high. They told us that in rough weather the only way was to ride a mussock through the surf, and then the odds were that sharks came and bit off one's legs as they dangled in the sea. It is now arranged that we embark at Madras, but we pass through the Presidency privately, as we have not yet been received there officially.

Wednesday 20th, November.

Reached Madras about 4 o'clock on Sunday. The arrangements for our vast amount of luggage were deplorable and it was past 7 o'clock before we got under way. We enjoyed a complete rest for two days on board and anchored at Hasting Point at the mouth of the Irrawaddy River about 12 o'clock. The only amusing incident that occurred during the voyage was owing to the dhobi, whom the First Officer found lighting a fire on the main

---

138. Her 49th.

deck. When he very naturally remonstrated with the man, his only answer was: "How then shall I heat my iron in order that the Lord Sahib may have his clothes smoothed to his complete satisfaction?"

We were timed to reach the wharf at Rangoon at 4 o'clock, but owing to the tides and difficulties in bringing the Dufferin alongside, it was 4.45 before we found ourselves walking towards an enclosure, filled with natives and Europeans, escorted by Sir Herbert and Lady White.[139] The Municipality presented an address of welcome and a magnificent silver ornament supporting an elaborately carved elephant's tusk. Rolly thanked them extemporarily and apologised for the inconvenience caused in our being a day late. We then proceeded to drive through the streets, where the crowd hailed us with the greatest enthusiasm. The school children in every imaginable colour were quite bewitching—small Chinese dolls they appeared to be with their close cropped hair gaily adorned with silver beads and ornaments. They frequently have a small tuft standing upright on the crown of the head tied round with ribbon. Their very narrow brilliant silk petticoats barely conceal their little legs, and their necks and arms are covered with a mass of necklaces and bangles. At each arch as we passed we were presented with bouquets, so were fairly smothered in flowers before arriving at Government House just as the shades of night began to fall. The magnificence of this building fairly took my breath away. The huge hall is beautifully proportioned with two tiers of carved arches. The staircase is a splendid specimen of massive Burmese carving in elaborate designs of dragons in that rich reddy brown pedak wood which comes from the Andaman Islands. The dining-room is all panelled with this wood, and the ball-room is white, with an elaborate ceiling and arched galleries. It is certainly by far the finest house I have seen in India. After dinner we held a reception; it was terribly hot, and the 500 hands I shook felt very moist even through my gloves. There wasn't one good-looking woman, it was quite distressing to see such an absence of beauty.

Thursday, 21st. Rangoon.

The great golden dome towers of the Shwe Dagon pagoda are a landmark for miles around. It is encircled by arcades, temples and pagodas of all sorts; figures of the Buddha loom largely on every side. The buildings are impressive enough, but what renders the picture one of the most attractive I have ever seen, is the crowd of humanity loitering in every alley—men, women, and children all grouped together in the most bewitching poses. Dense crowds clustered round the great golden images of the Buddha, and all with happy smiling faces—all eager to do one homage and often advancing with a delicious coyness that only added to their attractions while they brought us offerings of flowers which they placed at our feet. For two hours we walked amid this land of enchantment. Sometimes a band of Hpongyees, Burman priests, dressed in yellow, would be assembled at worship beneath a

139. Sir Herbert, the Lieutenant Governor, served in British Indian Burma for 38 years from 1878-1910, he wrote *A Civil Servant in Burma* among other books on the country.

Their Excellencies visit the Shwe Dagon Pagoda.

temple; in the various arcades great bowls of blue and pink and orange lotus flowers were placed for worshippers to buy and offer to the Buddha. Every now and then a mass of palm trees towered towards the sky throwing a cool shade, relieving with their green branches the dazzling gold of the temples that sparkled in the sun.

We were accompanied round by about a dozen Burmese, trustees of the Pagoda, and a charming and enlightened Chinese gentleman, Mr Chang Ko, who has taken a degree at Cambridge. Buddhists fix the date of the erection of the Shwe Dagon Pagoda at 588 B.C. In one of the shrines there is an altar which is supposed to contain eight hairs from the sacred head of Gautama. From one of the pagodas is suspended a sacred bell of enormous size. The English attempted to carry this off as a trophy after the Second Burmese War in 1840. It weighs 42 tons, and it was dropped by some accident into the Rangoon River. There it lay, as the English engineers failed to raise it. Permission later was granted to the Burmese to restore it to their Pagoda if they could do so, and the saying goes that it at once floated back with the tide, was raised with bamboo sticks and restored without difficulty to its original position. In the Pagoda grounds several English officers who were killed during the Burmese War have been buried. Their spirits are supposed to roam around, and the Burmese never like to approach near these tombs after dusk, for fear of ill luck pursuing them.

This afternoon a garden party was to take place, but just as the company were assembling a violent thunderstorm broke, with deluges of rain, and a damp crowd rushed into the house, but all the native dances called "Pwes" lost their effect in a room instead of among the picturesque surroundings of the garden. After the performances we went into a room where some of the deposed King Theebaw's[140] Queens and the Princesses of Burma were assembled. They seemed very pleased to see us, but could not talk anything but Burmese. There was also a man wearing a weird coronet poised very crooked on his head. He was supposed to be a descendant of the Kings of Delhi.[141] The storm entirely spoiled the party and I felt very sorry for the Whites.

As the rain was fortunately local, the great event of our stay at Rangoon, the illumination of the great lakes, was not damaged. After dinner we drove for four miles through a fairy scene. The golden Pagoda shone out brilliantly with lime light so cleverly managed that it seemed only to enhance the glow from the full moon. The lake was covered with boats of all sizes and shapes, decked with coloured lights. The tallest palm trees were aglow with jets of flame, and towered so high into the sky that one wondered which were lights and which were stars. Some trees had as many as 700 lights gleaming from their branches. We drove through the whole population of Rangoon round about this lovely park of liquid fire till we reached a Pagoda entirely composed of Japanese lanterns, where the State barge awaited us. This was a bower of beauty—a mixture of golden hangings, flowers and lights in which we sat between two great golden dragons with gleaming torches in their mouths and huge folded silver wings. I thought of the enchanted palace across the crystal lake in the fairy story, which the 12 Princesses nightly visited to dance through bowers of silver, gold and diamonds with the fairy Princes. I wondered if even a fairy story scene could be as beautiful as the reality at which we were gazing.

We had to be off by 7.45 to enable Rolly to open the new Port Works. The Commissioners presented him with a beautiful model in silver of a Burmese boat, and me with a very pretty

140. King Thibaw was deposed on 30th November, 1887, after the Third Anglo-Burmese war and the total annexation of Burma by the British. He was exiled to India with various members of his family and court and died in Ratnagiri, now in Maharastra, India, in 1916.

141. He probably was: Just as King Thibaw was exiled to India, the last Mughal emperor, Bahadur Shah Jafar, was exiled to Rangoon, Burma, in 1858 after the Mutiny, with a group of his surviving close relations. He died there aged 87 in 1862 but members of the family appear still to have been in Burma at the end of WWII.

bracelet with rubies and diamonds—set as all jewels are in this country with gold, but it is really very pretty.[142]

In the afternoon we attended the races—such a pretty course. There was a stand near us filled with gaily dressed Burmese ladies, their whitened complexions contrast so well with their bright silk clothes; the prevailing colour is pink. It looks so strange to see them smoking enormous cigars, much longer and fatter than any I have seen in other countries. The Burmese ponies were absurdly small, the favourite in one race was 11 hands. The gharries are drawn by these diminutive ponies; it looks cruelty to animals seeing the driver and three great men being pulled along by a pony the size of a dog. The police are also mounted on these little steeds and their long legs seem to trail on the ground. I am told the ponies are very strong, and have no mouths at all. It is therefore a common occurrence to see them running away with their riders.

This evening the Whites gave a huge ball. I must confess I looked forward to it with considerable trepidation—the thermometer in the tents at 6.30 A.M. was over 80°, so the atmosphere of a crowded ball-room filled with lights and people can easily be imagined. By refusing to move except for the first State Lancers I contrived to keep pretty cool. One gentleman, a very energetic dancer, brought four shirts and four collars with him and needed them all. My chief topic of conversation was the beauty of the ball-room. I was alluding to this in glowing terms to one Major Irwin and added: "This must be the finest room in India—Viceregal Lodge at Simla is very inadequate." "My brother built it" was his prompt rejoinder. I saved the situation by saying: "It was most unfortunate that they should have run short of funds, and spoilt the proportions of the hall by reducing it by half." I was glad he spoke when he did, as I should probably have enumerated many other deficiencies in connection with the house.

Saturday, 23rd.

I visited the Dufferin Hospital—such a nice lady doctor and 16 charming little Burmese nurses dressed in pink skirts and white jackets; all of them wore pink flowers coquettishly arranged in their hair.

Directly after luncheon the school children began to assemble at Government House. They arrived in their hundreds and sat down in companies on the grass. The Chinese children belonging to the rich merchant class were most gorgeously dressed with golden head dresses and large golden charms studded with precious stones hanging round their necks, the favorite emblem seemed to be a fish. One little boy wore three beautiful ones; they completely covered his tiny body. Some mites of children sang a delicious fan song to the tune of the Harmonious Blacksmith, but the greatest surprise awaited us when a Mr Armstrong, a Canadian Missionary, asked if his school children might sing the Maple

142. Platinum was the metal of choice for Edwardian jewellery settings.

Rowers Mandalay.

Leaf! Then began the familiar strains of "In days of yore," &c., &c., really admirably sung. It was quite a pleasure to hear it again, but it seemed so strange coming from the voices of the little dainty Burmese children, instead of the rough burly Canadians with their "Myple Leaf" accent. The only recompense the children had for coming was a holiday and many sweets distributed amongst them, but they evidently loved the outing.

We went on to the Dalhousie Park, where we witnessed canoe races, boat races and several side-shows. I longed to have a Kodak taken of me presenting the prizes to the victorious native crew. Nine great bronze figures, with magnificent chests and brawny arms, dripping wet from head to foot, knelt in a line one behind the other, the coloured scarf round their heads giving the required dash of colour. They had swept the board, beating the English team for the first time, and had to come up for three different prizes. We drove home with the crimson sun setting across the wide lake and the many coloured lotus lilies making the foreground.

Monday, 25th. Viceregal Train

Stopped for breakfast at Maymyo, the hill station for Rangoon. This is a most fertile-looking country, wooded hills in the distance, a great deal of bracken, and the gardens full of masses of poinsettia, blue convolvulus, begonia and a huge yellow shrub called the Maymyo daisy. The scenery from the train as we went on was so luxuriant, with masses of pampas grass, blue distant mountains, dense woods, and red sandstone rocks appearing here and there, and one might almost be in British Columbia. We reached the Gôkteik gorge about 2 o'clock. It lies on the oldest and most direct route connecting Burma with Southwestern China—a route which is mentioned far back in ancient chronicles as "the gold and silver road" along which Marco Polo accompanied the Chinese invading armies on their march to Mandalay. It was hoped that by building a viaduct across the gorge that trade with China would be greatly increased, but the disturbed political condition of the countries through which it passes has diverted the trades into other channels. The viaduct is 2,260 feet long, and was built by the Pennsylvania Steel Company. The rails are about 900 feet above the Choungzone stream. There is no parapet at all, consequently when our long train was crossing and our carriage came to a standstill exactly in the centre, we looked out of our windows into space and with some feeling of trepidation—knowing that our lives were depending on the same firm who were building the Quebec bridge that recently collapsed. Our pause of 10 minutes seemed an eternity; it was really caused by having to hitch on one of the big engines at the back of the train. We have usually two large ones in front and one smaller one behind, but they did not like to cross the bridge risking the immense weight of the two big engines together. We passed over eventually in safety with a considerable feeling of relief.

We have now arrived at the end of all things; the railway stops at Lashio. We are surrounded by the wildest tribes. Carriages do not exist in this part of the world. Small Burmese ponies had been provided for us, far too small to carry a lady's saddle, so we all had to mount astride. Each side of the road was lined with men and women from different tribes, dressed in the strangest costumes. A couple of hundred yards from the station was a long triumphal arch erected by the North Hsenwis. Their Chief stood in the centre of it, and greeted our arrival by doing homage. About a dozen of his tribesmen then advanced with umbrellas with long golden sticks, which they proceeded to hold over our heads as we rode along, making a long sheltered alley. These men accompanied us till we reached the second arch erected by the Mangluns. Here the umbrella-bearers were replaced by a new lot, holding white umbrellas which is the mark of royalty. In this way we proceeded for about two miles, changing umbrellas at the Tawngpeng, the South Hsenwi and Hyipas arches.

One of the Chiefs was beautifully dressed like a golden pagoda, one was like a Chinaman, the others seemed to be ordinary Burmese, one was educated at Rugby. A few years ago a schoolfellow who had entered the Political Service found this boy in prison with huge chains round his neck, arms, and legs. He seemed quite resigned to his fate, and took it as a matter of course that his father should have put him in chains. He said to his friend: "It was rather rough on the Governor. I ran away with a lady who was destined to be his wife." The Commissioner told me that he thought nothing of cheating his subjects, and confiscating their property to benefit himself. All the tribes had brought a good many of their women with them; they all had massive silver ornaments; some were covered with coins and buttons. One tribe appears to wear bath towels on their heads; another most gigantic hats. The 'Was', the tribe who collect human-heads to propitiate their gods, were the most formidable-looking savages with long matted hair, and practically no clothes at all.

Wednesday. 27th

After breakfast Rolly received all the Chiefs privately, heard their grievances, and gave them good advice. At 12 o'clock we all went to the camp where the tribes were formed up. An enormously long shed forming three sides of a square was their abode, and in the centre the wildest dances were taking place. Men with their bodies one mass of tattoo, others with terrible self-inflicted scars made to keep off the evil spirits, some with gigantic feather head-dresses, others with painted bodies and devil faces. The most fearful pandemonium supervened, each tribe seeming to attempt to outdo its neighbour in its wild antics, contortions, and outlandish noises. The scene was very remarkable, because these tribes are genuinely savage, and continually cause trouble. We told the various Commissioners to have a selection of their ornaments sent to the house for us to buy. They began by asking ridiculous prices, a pound for an 8d. hat, but I believe they at length accepted a reasonable sum for their trophies.

At 4 o'clock a wondrous procession came to fetch us for the Durbar, they brought two cushioned chairs in which Ruby and I placed ourselves. About 24 tribesmen holding umbrellas surrounded us, while a savage-looking person holding out a gigantic two-handed sword walked in front. Behind us followed a company of men, in a picturesque uniform of brown and red with beads and feathers, carrying curious old arms. In front of us marched six gigantic animals made rather like turkeys with strips of white paper—with huge dragon heads, flaming tongues and protruding eyes.

The hall was filled with people, the Chiefs sitting together in the front row. Rolly arrived on horseback in uniform with an escort, and everyone made an obeisance as he entered. One by one the Chiefs advanced were introduced and salaamed in their own native style. One old Chinaman prostrated himself three times, and bowed his head nine times to the ground, kowtowing in the orthodox fashion. Rolly made them a speech telling them that he hoped they would live peaceably and try to improve the value of their estates. This speech had been translated into Shan and was read aloud. It is the most hideous language to listen to and appeared to be composed of monosyllables. Some of the Chiefs have curious names such as Lord of the Silver Sword, Possessor of the Golden Chain, &c., &c. One old Chief brought all his kitchen utensils with him. They were arranged round his chair, I can't imagine for what reason, unless perhaps to impress us, as they were made of silver.

Friday, November 29th. Fort Dufferin, Mandalay.

This is quite the noisiest place I have ever been in. The moat which is only about 30 yards from the house is full of boats from early dawn practising for their races. There is a public holiday during our stay here, and the whole of the population must be on the opposite bank shouting with excitement. During the night the pariah dogs barked and howled, wild cats scampered about the garden, and thousands of mosquitoes invaded my room. We had an early breakfast and went to see the King's Palace. I was greatly disappointed in it as a work of art. It was very tawdry and without taste, all kinds of modern buildings having been added. One forgets how recently we took possession of Burma, King Theebaw was little more than a boy when he was deposed. I believe his favourite wife[143] was really answerable for all the acts of cruelty that have been imputed to him and used to urge him to cut off people's heads and have wholesale massacres. He is now a prisoner somewhere in the Bombay Presidency.[144] I felt rather sorry for several of the Burmese officials who were with us. They must mind so much our having usurped their land. They realise they are now secure and prosperous, and that they are governed by better laws, but I believe they rather enjoyed their intrigues. We were told many stories of the intrigues of the Palace. Mindôn Min[145] had a very large number of wives; the favourite and cleverest was called the Elephant Queen. She had three daughters, and she managed to have all three married to Theebaw. They were his half-sisters, but the Burmese royal family always intermarry. There was a young and beautiful Princess, the daughter of one of the nobles, who had been brought up with the understanding that she was to marry King Theebaw, but the Elephant Queen wished her daughters to reign supreme, so the poor girl's life was made so miserable that she ended by hanging herself. After Theebaw was imprisoned he asked to have the crown jewels returned to him but in the scrimmage they had all disappeared, and the Minister who had charge of them was supposed to have stolen most of them.

Saturday, 30th.

Rolly and I went out shopping after breakfast. We had a native policeman with us, who generally managed to get what we wanted for half the original price. The chief things in Mandalay are the brass figures and carvings. I alluded yesterday to the noise made by the multitude on the opposite shore and by the various crews competing in the boat races, but it was as nothing to what we experienced today. It was the wildest uproar in which the whole population joined. Drums were beaten, cymbals clanked, and gongs were sounded to regulate the pace of the rowers. Several Shan teams paddled with their feet as well as with their arms. These simply walked away from the ordinary paddlers. A man sat in the middle bailing out the water in time with the rowers. The heats went on the whole day. I thought I should certainly go mad if the pandemonium didn't cease for a second, but we had to endure it and get through our Christmas English Mail as best we could.

---

143. Queen Suphayalat.

144. Ratnagiri, Maharashtra.

145. Theebaw's Father.

After luncheon specimens from all the wild tribes were collected on the lawn; they didn't the least mind being kodaked and posed in a stolid way. The women belonging to the Padoung tribe are the most revolting sight. At the age of 12 they begin putting coils of metal round their necks. As the neck elongates, the coils are increased till they number 22. A woman has been known to endure 24 rings. At the base of these coils is a huge ring fixed on to their collars and standing out about six inches on their backs, making it absolutely impossible for them ever to obtain any rest. They say the husbands tie them up by means of this ring during their absence. These wretched women, in addition to their collars, have the lobes of their ears stretched till at last a long piece of metal about an inch in diameter is forced through; this ear-ring tapers off gradually and is about the length of a pencil. They all looked very ill and quite miserable. There were six men and six women from this tribe. They held hands and moved slowly round and round moaning out a most doleful dirge.

Another tribe, the Tawnpeng, bandage their women's knees above and below the joint with very thick black twine and wire. This prevents their walking with any comfort, but these people looked less miserable than the Padaungs. The lawn was dotted with jugglers, dancing girls, pwes, and so many interesting groups that the time was all too short. The last two heats of the boat races and the final were the great excitement of the day. To see this, we were taken on a magnificent golden barge towed by long war canoes to the winning post. On the opposite shore the crowd swayed like flowers blown by the breeze as they moved in their excitement to see if the Shans or the Mandalay team was winning. The Shans, with their feet-rowing, were easy victors. They say there would have been a financial crisis in the Shan district if they had lost, as every man in the tribe had backed their representatives for all he possessed. People spoke of 50,000 pounds being at stake, but it must have been rupees. The whole Burmese population are the most inveterate gamblers, and in his answers to addresses Rolly cautioned the people to resist their besetting sin.

Sunday, December 1st.

We visited the Native Bazaar, then drove on to the Queen's Monastery. The head Hpongee, clad in his orange garments with his shaven head, looked as if he lived on the fat of the land. In front of Buddha's shrine was a heap of offerings, suitable for a rubbish sale, appalling glass ornaments, fans, wisps of hair, an old bottle of pickles, and thousands of other such valuable offerings. I managed to secure a kodak of the Hpongee standing by Ruby's side. I feel sure this photo will lead to trouble. We were specially warned not to attempt to shake hands with a Hpongee. It is against all rules. I understand the Princess of Wales made a great impression on this jovial priest, and tempted him to converse with her.

The Arakan Pagoda was our next destination; inside the temple is the celebrated brass Buddha. His head dress and garments are covered with gold. The image was originally placed here about 2,300 years ago, recast and restored to its former position after it was defaced during the wars. Inside a small golden box is a tiny bone which they believe is a true relic of Buddha. We were allowed to handle it with reverent fingers. They also showed us an enormously heavy wishing stone; if on lifting it in both hands its weight does not seem excessive, your wish will be granted. I was surrounded by a crowd of people, and just to see their faces I told them I couldn't believe the stone could be so light. They looked amazed and felt confident I should obtain my heart's desire. A tank containing sacred turtles completed our morning of sight-seeing. We spent a quiet afternoon, going to church at 6 o'clock. The clergyman was most theatrical. In the middle of his sermon he suddenly struck a match. I wondered if he was going to light a cigarette, but he was only comparing our lives to the flame which was extinguished so quickly. In giving out the hymn he said: "I wish to remind the congregation that this hymn is sung in quick time." Consequently everyone sang too fast, but the choir was excellent.

Tuesday, December 3rd

We arrived at Myitkyina (pronounced Michyna) at 4.30. Here we are absolutely in an outpost of the Empire. Thirty miles away lie a range of hills; along their ridge are our forts, looking across into China. To the north is the debatable country inhabited by wild tribes. It is known as a no man's land and very frequently these Kachin tribes give trouble by raiding. Block-houses have been built right round the station, and there is a force of over 2,000 mounted police and 9 officers stationed at Myitkyina. No one can enter the grounds without a pass. The Kachins delight in committing murders. A few weeks ago a Chinaman and his Burmese wife and three children had their throats cut in the night. This was done for no apparent reason other than a blood-feud which they never forget. It bored me very much in the night hearing the sentries pacing up and down. Most of them seemed to have pneumonia from the incessant way they coughed, which was very disagreeable and disturbing to listen to.

Saturday, 7th.

We were introduced to the elite of Myitkyina, not a very exciting society. A few people dined, amongst others a Captain Pritchard. He has been in the jungle for four years away from any white people; he told me he was so afraid of becoming a savage that he tried to behave as if guests were always staying with him. He bought a gramophone, taught his servant to work it, and every night he dressed for dinner, and had a type-written programme of the music placed before him on the table. It is almost impossible to realise the intense loneliness of these jungle stations, and I think no one should be made to endure such solitude for more than a couple of years.

I hear the reason of the enormous number of sentries needed for our protection is owing to a rumour that the tribes intended to make an attempt to carry off the Viceroy. I am very thankful their idea was not carried out. A siege in Myitkyina would have been unpleasantly exciting. After dinner we went down to our little steamer to sleep on board, as we start at 6 A.M. for Bhamo. I felt quite sorry our visit has come to an end. I believe they have been making preparations for us for months past. No wonder it makes a commotion in a small station like this, when our huge party and army of servants descend like locusts and commandeer everything in the way of houses, horses, and food. It is astonishing how people rise to our requirements, although we have mainly done our own provisioning during our tour in Burma. We travel like Jacob and Esau with our flocks and herds and poultry, and kill our oxen and sheep as we need them. The '*bundobust*'[146] for a tour like this is absolutely colossal. Stores have to be ordered months beforehand, and meet us at each place at which we stay, and we have nearly come to an end of the 42 sheep we started with.

Monday, 9th. Bhamo.

Yesterday the river was very wide, with lovely mountains on each side. After Sinbo I was a little disappointed with the scenery. The Irrawaddy is brown and muddy; and having seen all the glorious waterways of Canada, one is naturally much more critical. We arrived at Bhamo at 2 o'clock and later in the afternoon went to see Kachin dances. The Chiefs were very richly dressed, most of them had elaborately embroidered Chinese coats; many of their women were covered with silver ornaments, buttons, and anklets, but their features are alarmingly repulsive and most of them have goitres. This comes from carrying loads which they fix with a strap over their brow. The men are lazy and do no work, and make their wives support them. It is quite revolting to see the lobe of their ears distorted by an enormous roll of cloth; the regular ear-ring is a long silver tube with thick cloth tassels fixed in and falling on each side of the face, but only the rich members of the community can afford so valuable an ornament. A Kachin bamboo house had been erected for our inspection; also the bamboo altars on which bullocks are sacrificed and a long pole with about 30 small baskets attached at regular intervals in which fowls are placed to propitiate the Nats (spirits). The Kachins always consult chicken bones before they dare embark on any undertaking.

We now leave our small paddle boats, and live on board a large barge fixed to a steamer on one side, and the staff's boat on the other.

Tuesday, 10th, Bhamo.

Colonel Dunlop and Sir Louis turned up in the early morning to recount their adventures. It appears that, in trying to avoid a sand bank, they were swung round by the stream, their stern becoming embedded in the sand, while the bow was swinging over a rapid. They finally drifted over their anchor and nearly ripped up the bottom of the boat. Sir Louis told us that, having exhausted all the bad language in his vocabulary, he retired to bed in the middle of the morning, while Colonel Duntop appeared in his best suit of morning clothes. He confided to Sir Louis that, if they had to take to a small boat, he preferred having his

146. Or *bandobast*—preparation.

best clothes with him. "This subterfuge," said Sir Louis "did not disguise from me what was passing through the Private Secretary's mind. In the event of being capsized, out of respect for the Viceroy, he no doubt wished to be clad in decent garments suitable for his burial." Shortly after this a plate was brought to Sir Louis with a small collection from the crew and an 8-anna[147] contribution from the Captain as an offering to their gods to save them from a watery grave. As the Captain was entirely to blame for their sorry plight, he gets off cheaply, though I expect official retribution will overtake him later. Finally a smaller boat was able to approach them and they abandoned their ship, where I suppose she will remain till the river rises. In the narrow defile the floods rise a hundred feet. We saw the marks on the bank as we passed. The officer who navigates the river and laid out all the buoys was behind us. As we went through the rapids, he told us, to his horror, he saw our skipper steering us the wrong side of a buoy. He expected us to be hurled on to rocks which are just below the surface of the water, and does not understand how we managed to escape. These native sailors are evidently most casual. I am glad that we have a European now in command of the fleet.

An old lady, called Mrs Algy,[148] dined. She is 80, but still rides most days into China, 30 miles there and back. She told me that she kept her son's polo ponies exercised when he was away. She certainly has the figure of a girl, though I cannot say the same of her face.

Saturday, 14th, Mingun.

The Royal Commission on Decentralisation, with Mr Hobhouse, under Secretary of State for India, as President, has arrived in India. Mr Hobhouse has started his campaign by offending every official he has met. He evidently is enormously impressed by his own importance; a fact which he thinks is imperfectly appreciated in India. The criticism in the Pioneer on Mr Hobhouse's opening remarks shows the feeling that has been aroused. Colonel Dunlop hopes Mr Myer, the representative of the Indian Government, and a few other outspoken officials may cause him to be in a more chastened frame of mind before we meet him in Calcutta, otherwise there will be trouble.

The following are a few extracts from speeches that have been made in Madras by a Mr Nevinson,[149] correspondent of the Daily Chronicle and other papers. He had been in the country a few days when he started his campaign. Mr Morley interviewed him before he left England and begged him to be cautious in his remarks. This shows the difficulties Rolly has to contend with. Keir Hardie, who created such excitement in England, was comparatively harmless. If this gentleman continues his seditious speeches, he will have to be treated in

147. Half a rupee—an anna was a unit of currency equivalent to 1/16 of a rupee.

148. A Mr Algy of the Civil Police appears in an account of this area of Burma in *From Edinburgh to India and Burmah*, by W.G. Burn Murdoch, George Routledge & Sons Ltd., 1908.

149. Henry Nevinson, journalist, foreign correspondent, suffragist, and author, 1856-1941.

the same way as Lajpat Rai.[150] Unfortunately being on tour Rolly only heard of his remarks some weeks after they were made.

He first of all says:

> "Mr Morley must not be judged too harshly. He succeeded Lord Curzon, who appears to have made many serious mistakes. The ship is going straight ahead. He cannot turn it round straight away. He was misinformed by his own crew. The lights were burning, everything was falsified. When we condemn him we must remember these things and his past services, and not be hard upon a fine old Liberal. I rejoice in such movements as the Swadeshi movement, the Congress movement, and above all in that sense of unity, amongst all races, languages and religions, throughout the whole of this great Peninsular. I do not believe it is possible for a nationality so different as the English to contemplate remaining for all time to be supreme leaders of another nationality so different as the Indian. I do not want to say anything seditious, but I have seen a good deal of the world, and have always found that nationality is a great principle in human conduct and life. It is the way to freedom. I do not believe that you will appeal to the English people in vain. It is true they are ignorant. We must have a liberal policy with regard to India, just as we have a liberal policy with regard to Ireland and England's own affairs at home. The arrogance with which many Anglo-Indians regard the educated Indians would be incredible to the ordinary English gentleman at home. I have a private opinion that Indians often show themselves too polite and submissive, &c., &c., &c."

This edifying doctrine is copied by all the native press, and naturally encourages and feeds the growing discontent.

We reached Pagan after luncheon where a golden barge was waiting for us, modelled in the shape of a dragon. Six canoes towed us to the shore. We walked through a reception pandal filled with kneeling Burmese, and then we all mounted ponies to visit the Ananda Temple. The building contains three rows of corridors, in which are a succession of niches with golden images representing episodes in the life of Buddha. This temple was built about 1000. It is difficult to realise that these figures have occupied the same position unchanged throughout long centuries which practically represent the history of England. Some relics were dug up yesterday; found in a sealed vase which disclosed a yellow painted box which might have been bought today at a toy shop. This contained two small Buddhas and some beads that date back 500 years, in a tiny gilded box. I took one bead as a souvenir, with the permission of our guide. Tourists apparently have been in the habit of stealing the relics, so last year they passed a law with a very heavy penalty should any looting be discovered. In one of the arcades leading to the temple some men and women were making lacquer ornaments. Each piece takes about three or four months to complete. The art is becoming

150. One of the leaders of the All-India agitation against the partition of Bengal and considered a dangerous revolutionary, Lajpat Rai was deported from India to Burma in May 1907.

extinct, and very few families work at it, even the contented Burman begins to feel that life is too short for such a tedious job.

Tuesday, 17th. Yenanyaung.

We all went out to try our luck again with the duck. They were still wilder than yesterday, and I only got four, but I was very pleased at securing a goose called nuktah, with my little gun. Some of the party walked after snipe. Some years ago Lord Curzon was shooting on this jheel. Unluckily his machan had not been built securely enough, the boards gave way and the Viceroy was precipitated into the water! The officials have never forgotten that day, and still turn pale as they talk of it. We left Paunglin at 4 o'clock. Mr Cholmondeley, the Commissioner, and his wife dined; she is such a pretty woman and very nice; the head of the oil works, Mr Findlay, a charming Scotsman and the Manager, Mr Jacob and his wife. The Jacobs are American, and I was quite glad to be told "it was a pleasure to meet me," it reminded me of old times.

Wednesday, 18th.

We started directly after breakfast in American buggies to drive five miles to the oil fields. The Burma Oil Company is an English concern, but they found it necessary to employ an American staff of drillers. They have 205 wells. The oil is found in patches, and lately the shares have been paying 30 per cent. Some wells are 1,600 feet, and they even go to 2,000; most have to be pumped. We visited their best well which flows of itself; the oil spouts some 50 feet into the air and looks like a cloud of yellow dust. This well was drilled 2¼ years ago and began to flow unexpectedly; in the first 24 hours the output was 6,000 barrels: each contains 40 gallon and a gallon is worth Rs. 3; it has realised 2,000,000 pounds sterling. The Company pay the Government a royalty of about 2 per cent, which brought in a total last year of 15 lakhs, or £106,656, to Government. They say the Mr Findlay, has already made £300,000. It was interesting to watch the primitive way the Burmese have worked these wells for the last 200 years. A small hole is dug round about 3 feet square and 300 feet deep and boarded, to prevent it falling in. With the

aid of a looking-glass one can see the oil glinting at the bottom. A man with a diver's dress and an air tube is lowered with ropes, by the aid of pulleys, worked by men and girls. He digs his small basket full of mud, and fills a 2-gallon can with oil, which is pulled to the surface by a small rope. After about an hour's work he makes his signal and emerges, the most disgusting object covered with green slime. He very soon gets rid of his garments and cleans himself by rolling in the sand. For his day's work he receives the enormous wage of a rupee a day. A native-dug well extracts about 2,500 tons of oil monthly, while the Company's output with all their modern machinery is about 3 million gallons.

We returned to the Jacobs' house and partook of a huge banquet. His eldest daughter has just returned from America, married to one of the overseers. This girl went home to complete her education; the overseer obtained leave of absence and followed her on the wings of love. They cabled to the parents: "We are married." Their answer was as follows: "We don't know whether to be mad, or glad." They evidently decided to be glad as Mr Jacob told me his son-in-law was a lovely man.

Friday, 20th, Rangoon.

We have thoroughly enjoyed our time in Burma, the natives are delightful people, wonderfully different to the Indians; they all look much richer and more contented. We found Rangoon quite cool in the early morning, and after thanking all the officials and distributing gifts we embarked on a launch which conveyed us to the R.I.M. Dufferin. I must mention one charming man who has accompanied us throughout our tour—Mr Law, Chief Police Officer. He is an encyclopaedia for Burma, and has been most useful. During his 30 years' service he only once went to England on leave, but found the country and climate so uncongenial that he returned to Burma after 3 months' absence, he hopes never to leave the country again. They say he has a Burmese wife in the recesses of the jungle, but I could never find out if this was true. The Dufferin appeared to us a palace when we boarded her—so roomy and peaceful, a perfect haven of rest after our ceaseless racket.

Sunday, 22nd.

We reached Calcutta at 4 o'clock and landed at Prinsep's Ghat. Our numerous guests are expected on Tuesday morning, leaving us only one day to prepare the house, so on arrival at Government House at 5 o'clock I at once set to work and tried to dispose of the roomful of new furniture that awaited me.

Monday, 23rd.

I started working at 9 o'clock and went on till 2 o'clock arranging the guest's rooms. None of my orders have been carried out. The electric light fittings have not been completed;

Burma oilworkers.

the Japanese flower pots are missing, apparently Japanese trade has died out with India, as they say they are not to be bought. At Barrackpore I went through all the house and bungalows, with the same loss of temper. It is absolutely heartbreaking, as I had taken so much trouble to leave everything in perfect condition last year. We did not get back till 7.30 which meant a hurried dressing for an early dinner before Albani's Concert. The Town Hall was packed. She was in very good voice, although her middle notes have nearly gone. A Mr Flint accompanies her quite beautifully, and the other performers were excellent. She was so delighted at receiving such an ovation. We went and talked to her afterwards. They say she is 61,[151] and that her husband, old Gye, has speculated and lost all her money and that is why she has to go on singing. It is very tragic—however, she sang far better than the last time I heard her 5 years ago; her high notes are still marvellously fresh and clear.

Tuesday, 24th.

Sir George and Lady M. Warrender,[152] Gerald and Cuckoo Loder,[153] Mr and Nina Russell,[154] Mr and Mrs Gordon Cunard,[155] Captain Brocklehurst[156] and Captain Elgee[157] arrived by the 6 A.M. mail. I went to see the ladies each in turn during the morning. Poor Nina has lost all her luggage. I found her in bed lying in a thick flannel dressing gown with 3 blankets, a fur coat, and a railway rug. I naturally concluded that she was suffering from a severe chill, but she tells me she always feels cold and doesn't find India hot enough. We dressed her up in Violet's clothes, and all went after luncheon for the Viceroy's Cup to the races, driving up the course in procession. I hear Calcutta is hurt at our arriving a month later than usual, so I did my best to play up to everyone I knew, and of course saw all the elite. Our guests went down to Barrackpore by special train. The house, crammed with flowers, looked very pretty, and everyone was most complimentary at the way it is done up.

Christmas Day, 1907.

Albani, Mr Gye. Mr Flint, Lord Kitchener, Colonel Birdwood,[158] and Captain Wyllie arrived during the morning to stay the night. We have of course the Smiths and Crooke-Lawlesses

---

151. Emma Albani was a highly successful Canadian opera singer, probably born in 1847. She retired with a concert at the Albert Hall in London in 1911 and died in 1930.

152. Vice-Admiral Sir George Warrender, A.D.C. to Edward VII 1907-08 and his wife Lady Maud.

153. He became 1st Baron Wakehurst, barrister, MP, and gardener, she had been Lady Louise de Vere Beauclerk, daughter of the 10th Duke of St Albans.

154. Nina had been Nina Elliot and was Rolly's niece, her two sons with Charles Russell were both killed in WWII.

155. He was the grandson of the founder of the Cunard Line and became Sir Gordon, 4th Baronet.

156. Extra A.D.C.

157. H.F. Elgee, extra A.D.C., killed WWI.

158. Commander of ANZAC during the Gallipoli campaign in 1915. C-in-C India 1925-1930, Field Marshall and Ist Baron Birdwood.

with us for Christmas, besides the rest of the staff. The Hobhouses, Mr and Mrs and Miss Blair, Colonel and Mrs Jenkyns arrived for luncheon, making us a party of 45. I didn't find Mr Hobhouse half as bad as I had been led to expect; anyhow he was quite civil to me, and Mrs Hobhouse appears to be very nice. We had a most uproarious finale to our dinner, owing to the crackers at dessert. Suitable paper caps were found for everyone, such as a jockey cap for the Viceroy, a forage cap for the Commander-in-Chief, and a sailor's cap for the Commodore. All the party have shaken up so well. I like the Warrenders and Cunards immensely. Sir George told me how surprised he was to find us on such friendly terms with Kitchener. He said I have travelled a good deal and invariably notice friction between the Civil and Military authorities, and here you find the Viceroy and Commander-in-Chief the most difficult position to hit off in the world, hobnobbing like brothers.

Friday, 27th. Calcutta.

Sir H. Risley[159] came to talk over the Victoria Memorial problem with me—not only have the foundations sunk 7 inches, but there are two large cracks across them. It is clearly impossible to add another ton and a half weight on this site. All these questions are to come up before a meeting of Trustees, but he wanted me to put Rolly au fait of the facts at some odd moment. We are practically accused of stealing some of the collection, because the Museum in which the curios are housed is under repair and a few statues and pictures have been sent to Government House, to the Lieutenant-Governor's, and Lord Kitchener's for safe keeping for a few months. Every local authority declares it is impossible to carry out the original plans. The soil cannot support a structure that is to weigh 2½ tons. Sir W. Emerson, who is only an Architect and not an Engineer,[160] will not guarantee a steel structure covered with marble which has been suggested to lighten the weight; consequently matters are at a dead-lock. The fact is that Lord Curzon and Sir W. Emerson are entirely responsible for the site and the design, and refused to listen to any local expert when they were warned that they were attempting the impossible.

A gigantic luncheon party; I hardly fathomed who all the people were. Crowds have arrived with letters of recommendation. Lady Rothschild introduced a Mr and Mrs Mocatta, swarthy-looking descendants of the tribe of Israel. Sir Henry Craik, a Conservative M.P., and Sir L. Hare sat beside me. Eastern Bengal is much upset at the attempt to murder a Deputy Commissioner, Mr Allen. All these miserable students possess fire-arms. Hare is evidently scared; he has aged considerably since his appointment as Lieutenant-Governor, and he tells me he feels the responsibility dreadfully, so I gently reminded him of the load that weighs on the Viceroy's shoulders.

159. Sir Herbert Hope Risley—long-serving Indian Civil Servant, ethnographer, Home Secretary under Curzon and member of Minto's Council.

160. Architect of Crawford Market in Bombay as well as of the Victoria Memorial.

Rolly and I attended a garden party at a new mixed club, natives and Europeans, lots of native ladies were present; great things are hoped from this venture.[161] I had to attend a charity fancy ball at the Town Hall in aid of the Women's Friendly Society. I hope my presence gave satisfaction: the entertainment didn't appeal to me, and I lost one of the small drops from my diamond necklace, so didn't feel rewarded for my kindness in going.

Sunday, 29th.

One of our usual Barrackpore Sundays sitting about and visiting the garden, &c. Sir H. Craik[162] and Mr Hitchens, who is on the Decentralising Committee, lunched. I told him we should start by cutting the cable to the India Office; that Mr Morley is the greatest centraliser, no Secretary of State having gone into detail as he has done. One question to the Viceroy is like a stone flung into the river, the ripples form and multiply, which means hours and hours of work and endless files throughout the whole machinery. How can the officials find time for each individual case and the need of sympathy which is being preached? They are driven along without a second to raise their heads from their desks. Our ancestors had a far easier time than we have. Sir L. Hare said to me I could stop sedition in Eastern Bengal in 5 minutes. I have only to deport half a dozen people and everything would quiet down, but our hands are tied; there is always the nightmare of the House of Commons which no official in England will forget.

161. The Calcutta Club.

162. Sir Henry Craik, 1st Baronet, Scottish MP, whose son Henry was Governor of the Punjab, 1938-1941.

Monday, 30th. Calcutta.

A dinner party of about 40; the house party is already so large that this did not mean a great number of other guests. I sat between Sir F. Maclean[163] and the Count Cohen d' Anvers,[164] Mrs Townshend's father, a very rich old man who has just bought the title and is really plain Cohen.

Tuesday, 31st. Calcutta.

The Maharajas of Alwar, Kishengarh, and Rutlam lunched; they all speak English admirably. We went to the Tollygunge steeple chases, patronised by the whole of Calcutta. We have such a horsey party staying with us. The Gordon Cunards and the Blairs have been thrilled by this week of festivities. All our guests have been so nice in their appreciation of everything, and I think all the arrangements have gone excellently. The last day of the year and a very eventful one it has been. There are many shoals ahead, and I only pray Rolly may keep his health and strength to steer safely through them.

163. Chief Justice of Bengal.

164. Actually Count Louis Cahen d'Anvers , a Belgian banker who bought and restored the Château de Champs. His daughter, Alice, married Major-General Sir Charles Townshend.

Barrackpore lawns.

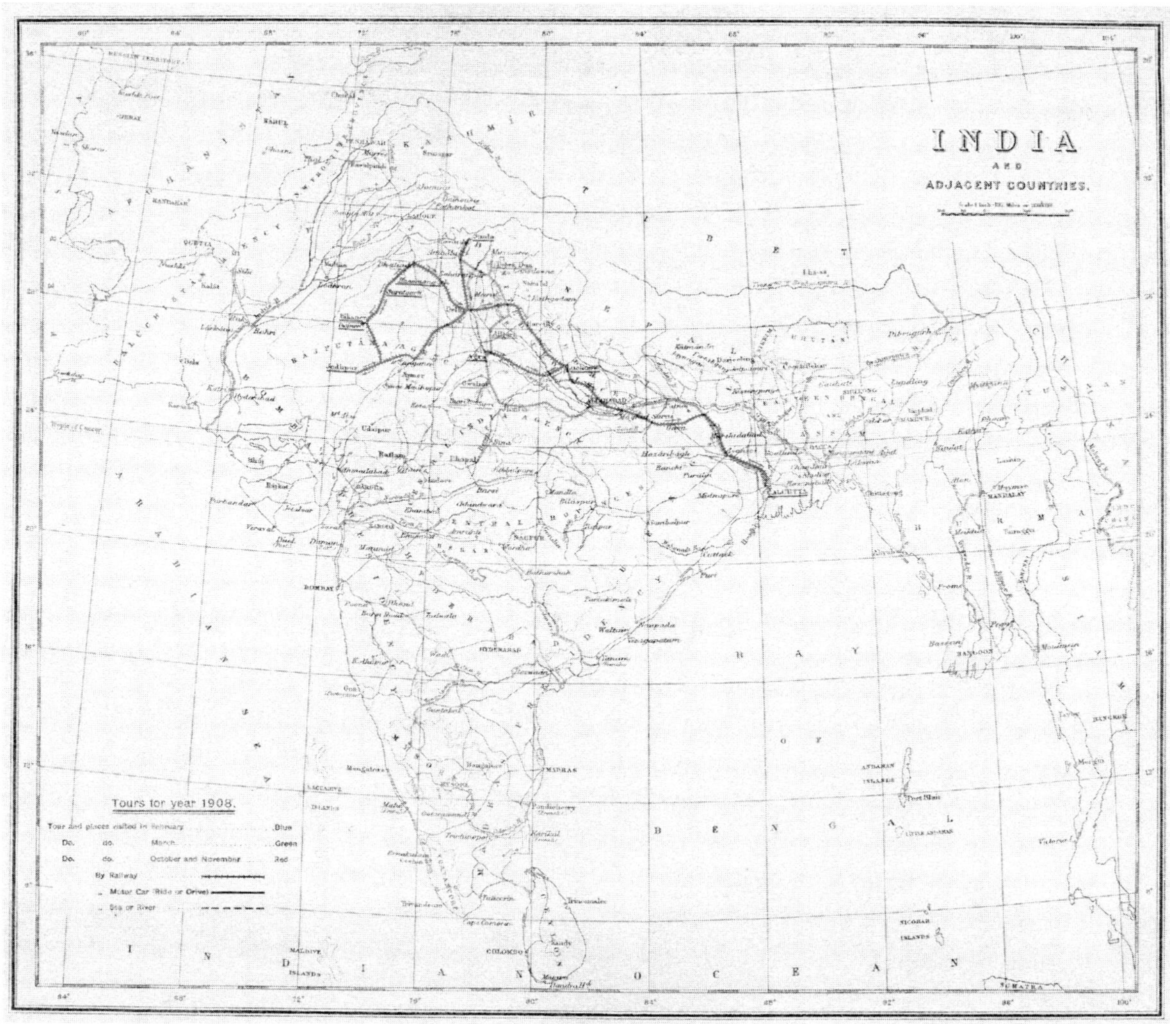

Tours 1908.

1908

Wednesday, January 1st

Drove to the Proclamation Parade with Lady Maud—there were fewer troops than usual, and in order to make the spectacular effect more striking the Viceroy's Body-guard were ordered to march past after having escorted him to the ground. The Calcutta Light Horse Volunteers, numbering 48, consisting of gentlemen chiefly of the merchant class, heard of this and imagined the Native regiment, being the Viceroy's Body-guard, would be given precedence by marching past first on parade. The Light Horse sent a message to ask Lord Kitchener to give them their usual position; this message went on to the Viceroy. Permission was at once given them to lead the parade. Meanwhile the Volunteers had taken offence, and without waiting for the reply the whole number with the exception of the Adjutant and a Sergeant marched off parade. Once a Volunteer force is on a parade ground, the men are subject to the same rules and regulations as the regular army, and not a man may leave without the General's orders. Therefore for a European corps of gentlemen to commit such an offence and show insubordination in the midst of Native regiments, during a time of political unrest before the whole of Calcutta, was a most heinous crime. The Colonel, a man called Apostolides, of Greek descent was sent for, practically under arrest. He and his 45 followers were made to sign the most abject apology. The question of having the whole corps disbanded was put before the Viceroy, and Apostolides was kept on the rack for three days, but Rolly decided the least said about the disgraceful affair the better, and every attempt has been made to hush it up. If European Volunteers walk off parade, what can we expect from Native troops? It has been a most deplorable incident.

Friday, 3rd.

Rolly had a Council Meeting and then an interview with Mr Hobhouse. The whole Decentralisation Committee has come to a dead-lock. At 9 o'clock last night Mr Hobhouse sent in 86 questions which he begged the Viceroy would consider before 12 o'clock today. He was told it was out of the question—that he was making enquiries in connection with Indian administration far beyond his powers, and that the Viceroy refused to sanction his enquiry. He was perfectly furious—demanded a private luncheon with the Viceroy in order to talk matters over. He was calmly told that His Excellency intended lunching as usual with his other guests but that he was welcome if he cared to be included in the party. He had to be brought almost by force by an A.D.C. much against his will and black with rage. He sat next to me, and cut up his food with violence, he could scarcely contain his wrath. The worse he became, the more affable and charming I was—talking across him to Sir Harvey Adamson[165] in the blandest manner. A telegram has been drafted to Mr Morley telling him he is impossible, and we must await the result. Rolly interviewed Mr Hobhouse afterwards and managed by putting on a tremendous curb on himself not to come to words. He has succeeded in rubbing up every one with whom he has come in contact.

Thursday, 9th.

Rolly, the girls, and I dined with the Bishop, to meet the members of the Synod, 12 Bishops in all—They were extremely pleasant. Rolly described them as a sporting lot. I believe Nagpur is the best judge of a horse in India, and was champion tennis player for Ireland in his day. Mrs Copleston, our hostess, has the reputation of being the vaguest woman in India. She was dining with some friends one night and suddenly lent across the table and said to the Bishop: "I think, dear, we really must change our cook." At another dinner

165. Member of the Council.

party she said to her host forgetting he wasn't her husband: "I am afraid we must consider this party as one of our failures." She upset the salt at this dinner, and at once dashed her glass of claret over it, saying how glad she was to think she had prevented the salt staining the table-cloth. A lady came one afternoon to pay Mrs Copleston a visit and remained to tea—in the middle of it Mrs Copleston got up and said: "I am afraid I must be getting home." The poor lady naturally took her leave with precipitate haste. We discussed the fancy ball after dinner. Mrs Copleston turned to me and said: "How slim Lady Fraser looked, she was personating Nell Gwyn." Lady Fraser weighs at least 18 stone, and was representing the Duchess of Devonshire in a gigantic hat, so I muttered: "Hardly slim." "Of course," she said, "I only mean by comparison." The skittish Bishop's wife, whom we met at Hyderabad, practically did the honours. She confided to me she was so thankful that only the menus had been forgotten, and not the dinner.

Friday, January 10th.

Mr Bailey, the Irish Land Commissioner, recommended by Mr Morley, is staying with us. He is a hideous little man with a crimson nose and enormous spectacles and a flow of language equal to Niagara. He sat next to me at dinner. I began at soup and asked him in acid terms if he had noticed in the Reuters that another unfortunate man had been shot at Ennis in Ireland. That set the ball rolling, and we had an animated discussion till dessert. I am glad this sort of man has been out and seen the conditions of India for himself—he has amassed an enormous amount of information and was most complimentary as to Rolly's administration. He couldn't get over the amount of work that has to be got through, and said no one in England the least realises the colossal burden that rests on one man's shoulders. He said if Mr Morley had been to India and seen what this machinery entails, he would hesitate, before asking a single unnecessary question that could add one grain to the overwhelming load. Alas Mr Morley is never likely to come to India and minute details have to be sent in connection with all departments. Lord Kitchener told me that Morley now wishes for the army returns to be sent him. These are really the routine orders of every brigade in India, and the Commander-in-Chief has never thought it necessary to go into them himself.

Sunday, 12th

Tropical rain has saved the situation and may avert severe famine in some parts of India, which is an untold blessing.

Tuesday, 21st.

Such a sad day parting with Ruby—it is an awful wrench for Rolly who cannot look forward as I do, to seeing her again in seven weeks. There is a general feeling of disappointment at the wedding not taking place in Calcutta, and no doubt it would have been a most popular move. Rowland seemed to think he couldn't get leave, but I think we ought to have agitated more about it. However, it is too late now to have any regrets, and I am glad to have the excuse of going home to see Eileen and the boys. We might possibly have followed the Queen's example when the Germans remonstrated at their future King being married in a foreign country she said: "If the great honour of marrying the Princess Royal of England falls to the lot of the Crown Prince of Germany, he must come to England to fetch her".

Friday, 24th.

A Mr and Mrs Sturgis and Mrs Stickney and Miss Ramsay, all most pronounced Americans, lunched. Mrs Stickney told me she was searching for a few handsome pearls. "Costing hundreds," I asked. "Well, thousands I presume" was her rejoinder; so the lady is evidently not short of cash in spite of the slump in the New York money market.

I have not had time to write down much of the current events that have taken place, my time has been so terribly occupied, but a few things are worthy of note. About a month ago, Sir Andrew and Lady Fraser narrowly escaped being blown up by a bomb that was placed on the line over which their train was travelling. It is a disagreeable business, but whether it has been done for pure mischief or for political motives it is difficult to say. Another important event is the split in the Indian National Congress, The Extremists and Moderates came to blows at a meeting which I hope will have a salutary effect, and help to consolidate the Moderate party and make them more willing to declare themselves in favour of the recognised official authority. Gokhale some days later had an interview with Rolly and told him he thought the Extremist's cause had received an irreparable blow at least for some time to come. Poor Sir Denzil Ibbetson has completely broken down—the operation last year was not done in time and the doctors have no hope of his recovery.[166] He has resigned and goes at once to England. The question of his successor has given Rolly many anxious moments. He has decided to appoint Sir Louis Dane, our present Foreign Minister, putting him over the heads of one or two officials, thereby causing much heart-burning, but in these strenuous times one is bound to take the best man, and private feelings cannot be taken into account. Most of the newspapers approve the choice, but Sir Louis has a certain number of enemies. Lord Curzon never forgave him for carrying out the mission to Kabul, in opposition to his views, and strongly advised Rolly to appoint a Mr Fraser as Foreign Minister. Sir Louis is extremely clever and has filled his very difficult position admirably. We shall miss him dreadfully; in the first place we see more of the Foreign Minister than any other official, and he is a charming member of the staff when we go on tour. Mr Butler, a very clever man, but not belonging to the Foreign Department, is to take his place, for the moment at any rate. This is also causing heartburnings.

---

166. Member of the Viceroy's Council, he died in London in February 1908.

Thursday, 30th.

Rolly is really rather glad a crisis has come. The raid on Peshawar by the Zakka Khels is too important to overlook. Unless we want to have the whole frontier in a blaze these raiders must be quelled with promptitude and determination. This liberal Government hates the idea of undertaking further responsibilities but if we go into the Zakka Khel's country, burn their wooden huts, which they can rebuild in a few weeks, and retire, they conclude we are too weak to hold good our position and the raiders become bolder and outrages more frequent. The only policy is to establish our rule in the country, allowing the natives to administer it themselves and gradually civilise the people. This method is working admirably in the Swat Valley and yet the Home Government hate the thoughts of assuming further responsibilities although our frontier officers know they are liable to be attacked at any moment and live in perpetual fear of their lives.

Sunday, February 2nd.

We returned from Barrackpore to go by launch to see the festival [Ardhodaya Yoga at Kalighat]. The women were mostly clad in the brightest coloured garments, and it was a very pretty sight seeing the mass of hues mingling on the steps of the bathing ghats. They were diplomatic enough, however, to remove their gayest apparel before going into the water, though all bathed in their clothes. They dipped three times in the filthy stream, spluttered and spat a great deal, and their appearance as they emerged, dripping, with their clinging garments around them was anything but a tribute to the human form divine. They certainly dried with a good deal of decency, placing their dry clothes round them before allowing their wet rags to fall at their feet. The Hobhouses joined us on the launch. We bade him farewell; he leaves Calcutta tomorrow to proceed further north with his Commission. He has really tried to be nice; he is very pleasant to talk to, and I am sure has gained much wisdom since he arrived in India. Mrs Hobhouse is extremely nice with a delightful sense of humour, and sketches beautifully.

Wednesday, 5th.

Our usual number of globe-trotters came to luncheon; amongst others a pleasant Major and Frau von Seecht,[167] recommended by Sir F. Lascelles.[168] In the afternoon I gave a native ladies' tea party to which the European ladies belonging to the Indian National Association also came. It was a tremendous success, about 70 native ladies attended. We first gave them tea in the marble hall, then showed them the house, and finally took leave of them in the garden. It was quite touching to see their appreciation; this party appears to have created a

---

167. Probably Johannes Friedrich 'Hans' von Seeckt, later de facto commander of the army of the Weimar Republic and adviser to Chiang Kai Shek in China.

168. Sir Frank Lascelles, British Ambassador to Germany. His son was married to MM's niece.

great deal of excitement throughout the native community. The papers have been full of it, and have said all manner of flattering things. That the interest taken in Hindu ladies is the beginning of a new era, and will do much to help the political situation," &c., &c.

Thursday, 13th

Mr and Mrs Gupta lunched; he goes to England to join Mr Morley's Council; she detests the thoughts of it, and, no wonder, an Indian lady is terribly out of place in London. A dinner party of 70 after which we gave a huge evening party in the garden—1,500 people. Lord K-. was in high spirits, the Zakka Khel Expedition under Sir James Willcocks starts today. Rolly considers these punitive expeditions futile.

Wednesday, 19th.

I have just been sent a wedding present to take home to Ruby from 112 Calcutta ladies. It is a wonderfully engraved agate set round with diamonds and is of historical interest, having been for many years in the possession of the Nawabs of Murshidabad. The stone at one time was worn as an armlet; it is most valuable, but unfortunately not a pretty colour. Had to work on far into the night in order to get ready for our departure tomorrow.

Thursday, 20th.

Rolly had intended leaving Calcutta this evening to inspect some volunteers and have a three days' shoot, but he received a telegram from General Willcocks stating that several Chiefs of the Afridi tribes were in treaty with him, that they promised to do their utmost to assist in bringing about a speedy termination of hostilities if the troops would remain in the disturbed country for the present, to give the loyal tribes their support and assistance by making a display of strength. This is exactly what Rolly wants, and it is beyond measure galling to have to wait for Mr Morley's sanction, who will not like a complete upset of his orders. Meanwhile now that the request comes from the Afridi themselves, he can hardly disregard it. Rolly must wait in Calcutta till everything is settled; he may be pardoned for having a secret joy at the turn affairs have taken. It almost makes up to him for having his holiday postponed.

Colonel Brooke was telling me of an interesting talk he had with the Amir last year the day before the latter left Peshawar for Kabul. They drove in a motor to some gardens, here they alighted and the Amir said: "I wish to talk with you alone." They walked to the centre of the gardens, where the Amir halted, and, with his stick, quickly traced the map of Asia on the gravel path. He drew the line of the North-West Frontier of India, and another line to show the boundary of Afghanistan, then he pointed to the narrow strip between the two countries known by the name of No Man's Land, and said: "Till the British frontier reaches the frontier of Afghanistan we never can have peace—no matter how friendly the terms between the Viceroy and the Amir, nor how loyally your Government and my Government keep their promises. So long as these tribes have not been subdued by the British there will be trouble and intrigue." There is not a thinking responsible man in India who does not share these views, and yet non-interference with the frontier is not confined to the Liberal Government. Lord George Hamilton[169] held the same views, and year after year murder and bloodshed continue, when peace and prosperity are actually within our grasp. The narrowness of the home politicians is amazing.

Violet and I left Government House at 2 o'clock, felt terribly depressed at leaving Rolly all alone. Violet has hardly ever been away from him in her life, and he will miss her too terribly, as she always insisted on his riding in the early mornings, and in spite of hard work generally contrived to make him take a little exercise. I fear when left absolutely to himself he will never leave his desk. We have Captain Jelf in attendance; Colonel and Mrs Crooke-Lawless, who come home with us; Sir Louis Dane, who is rushing home for a holiday before taking up the duties of Lieutenant-Governor of the Punjab; Hanson, the chief detective; the Mir Munshi,[170] the baggage master; Mr Huddleston, the Chief Traffic Superintendent of the Railway, and about 30 servants. We shall realise our true position when we leave our escorts and red carpets, and try to pack into two tiny cabins on board the Macedonia, which I hear is overflowing with passengers.

Wednesday, 26th.

We hope to reach Aden this evening. I shall send this Journal back to Colonel Dunlop to have printed for me, and now I look forward to having a rest from my daily chronicle, which, in the midst of my busy life, is a considerable tax on my time. There is no one exciting on board and I have sat entirely on the Captain's deck and talked to no one. Yesterday Sir Louis Dane brought up all his maps and explained minutely to me the whole of the Persian question with regard to the Russian Convention. It seems the first idea was to surrender to Russia the whole of Persia with the exception of a triangle in the south-west. This suggestion was so appalling that most vigorous opposition was cabled from the Government of India and the Home Government had entirely left out of their calculations any idea of securing the control of the Persian Gulf. Luckily the mistake was rectified before it was too late. Every English official in Persia, with the exception of the minister at Teheran, is a member of the Indian Service and through them we gain information as to everything that is taking place. The Government of India have pressed their views most strongly and, as far back as February 1906, Rolly proposed that we should enlist the support of Russia by withdrawing our opposing to her in North-West Persia and should agree to her linking up her railways via Kermanshah and Khanikin with the Baghdad Railway. The story is a very long and

169. Secretary of State for India in the Conservative Government, 1895-1903.

170. Chief Indian secretary.

complicated one—Austria, France, Germany, Turkey, and Russia all play a part. Persia was of course Lord Curzon's great hobby, and as Sir Louis Dane was Foreign Secretary through a great part of his régime, he has every position, town and island, which can be of any possible use to us, at his fingers' ends.

The weather so far has been perfect—not the least hot and the sea as smooth as glass.

Colonel Dunlop-Smith once more took up the journal of Viceragal life during The Vicereine's absence in England, keeping her in touch with events in weekly instalments through the mail.

May 17th, 1908. S.S. "Persia".

So much has happened since Violet and I embarked on the Macedonia in charge of Captain Bennet, that it will be difficult to achieve a short resumé. The passengers included 300 Australians, a vulgar rowdy lot, and the discomfort of being boxed up with nearly 600 passengers was considerable. I particularly disliked the plan on which these larger, newer P. & O. boats are constructed. Two cabins are dove-tailed into the space intended for one, to accommodate more people, leaving the cabins the size of a dog kennel. I felt greatly injured at finding one of these small boxes was the only accommodation reserved for me. The Captain was apologetic, and kindly managed to put quite a decent-sized cabin at my disposal as a sitting-room, but it was miles away on another deck, so was used chiefly to store our things. We reached Marseilles to find the whole of the warehouse strewn with charred boxes; a fire had broken out amongst the passengers' luggage in the hold of the Moldavia[171] soon after leaving Gibraltar, and the wreckage was a pitiable sight to behold. Fat old General Gubbins, Medical Inspecting Officer, was good-humouredly searching amongst the debris for some clothes fit to put on. Three brides were in tears—the whole of their trousseau being destroyed, and one poor girl, whose relations had subscribed a hundred pound to fit her out for a visit to India, had to go straight home again, not having one rag, nor any money. No one was insured, and I have since heard no one received any redress. After the discovery of the fire they steamed full speed ahead, having shut down every aperture and on reaching Marseilles poured 2,500 gallons of water through the hold, and emptied out every atom of cargo for fear of smouldering wood, so what escaped the fire was spoilt by water. Our trip across the channel was a disagreeable experience in a tempestuous sea. My salvation was in lying immovably with closed eyes and a pea-green face, but retaining sufficient interest in life to resent Violet reading her book with unconcern, deliberately cutting the pages with exasperating persistency. Towards the end of the voyage, which I just managed to endure without disgrace, I heard peals of laughter from Violet and the assurance that she didn't think I could really feel sea-sick, so had felt no sympathy for my condition.

171. Torpedoed and sunk in 1918 when serving as a troopship.

The Warrenders kindly put their house, 23, Great Cumberland Place, at our disposal, it looked most inviting, newly done up, and full of lovely flowers. The most obliging servants looked after us, even to a charming chauffeur and groom who never resented being kept out all day long on my landaulet. We somehow managed to get through the rush of trousseau and invitations with the help of Miss Hole, who came as secretary, and displayed a wonderful knowledge of the Elliot relations. The wedding was fixed for April 4th. The Frank Mildmays lent us 46 Berkeley Square for the breakfast and the presents were on view the day before. I have never seen such a magnificent array.

Ruby naturally was very nervous on her wedding day. She would hardly give us time to put the finishing touches to her wedding veil, and then, in order to give herself courage to face the ordeal, she sat studying the Daily Mail till it was time to leave the house. The whole thing went off quite splendidly, the sun shone out just as Ruby and I got into the carriage to drive to the church. The only sadness was Rolly's absence. St. Margaret's[172] was beautifully decorated and Ruby made a lovely bride. The Queen, the Dowager-Empress of Russia and Princess Victoria sat just in front of me. The Queen turned round so prettily and looked at me when Larry had to advance to give Ruby away, showing that she realised what a pang Rolly's enforced absence gave me. It was such a happiness to have all five children together under the same roof the day before the wedding after two and a half years but it accentuated Rolly's absence all the more. Spent four weeks at Minto with the family, Ruby and Rowland joining the party after 10 days' honey-moon. The only drawback was the weather which was persistently cold and raw. On the 23rd April there were 3 feet of snow in the Isle of Wight, trains were blocked throughout the country, and people were frozen to death We were fortunate in getting nothing beyond snow flurries. A week later the thermometer was 75°, and I don't regret returning to a climate that plays fewer vagaries.

I had altogether five interviews with Mr Morley generally lasting over two hours. We discussed everything; he was most charming about Rolly, saying he had never worked with any one with so much pleasure; how much he admired his absolute disregard of the personal element in trying to do his duty, whether he was praised or blamed. He told me he had implicit faith in his judgement. I told him that the tone of his (Mr Morley's) telegrams was frequently suspicious, as if he thought Rolly was anxious to get the better of him. He said: "I have never suspected the Viceroy, but I do some of his Departments." I told him that was one and the same thing, as nothing could reach him without the Viceroy's sanction. As a matter of fact, Mr Morley interferes more in Indian matters than any other Secretary of State has ever done before, and as regards appointments often puts Rolly into very difficult situations, as he rightly absolutely refuses to have as a subordinate anyone whom he does not consider the best man for the post. At our last interview Mr Morley was very bitter on this point and said he refused to have his hand forced, and that the final responsibility rested with him. This I admitted and rather brutally reminded him of two of his own appointments which have been miserable failures. He was greatly impressed at the

172. St Margaret's, Westminster.

numbers of people we have to entertain—just under 5,000 from December 25th to February 18th—it is a desperate tax on one's physical strength, and on our purse. The Viceroy is given £400 a year as entertainment allowance. Our invitation cards alone come to £170 a year, and the Lieutenant-Governor of Bengal receives for entertaining purposes £1,200 a year, three times as much as the Viceroy. People of all nationalities flock to Calcutta and all expect to be entertained. Most of them resent not being able to shoot a tiger in the garden. Mr Morley and I parted in the most friendly way, and added, as we shook hands, "I know I am swimming on a popular tide from virtues that are not my own." He feels leaving the House of Commons very much. Ruby, Louisa, and I went to see him take his seat as Viscount Morley of Blackburn introduced by Lord Esher and Lord Peel. Next morning I received a charming letter from him in which he said, "Please be sure that both on Saturday and today your kindness has done a real public service".

I have seen most of the India Office officials. Sir A. Godley, Sir Richmond Ritchie,[173] Mr Hirtzel; the two latter have evidently great influence with Mr Morley. Mr Hirtzel, his Secretary, he seems devoted to. He told me the working of the India Office was now like a happy family. Sir Richmond asked me if I intended seeing G.C. I said I meant to invite him to Ruby's wedding, but I felt the situation was a difficult one, as we had been denounced in a newspaper in a letter written by his Private Secretary for taking back from the Museum pictures and statues that belonged by rights to Government House. He also accused us of scattering a collection of treasures to the winds of heaven and practically insinuated that we were dishonest. Sir Richmond said, "G.C. frequently comes to see me." I said, "Yes, but he hasn't called you a thief;" "he has called me a traitor and a coward," he said, which seems to me as bad. Sir W. Lawrence[174] has also been very nice. I have seen Mr Balfour,[175] but have not had much talk to him. Alfred Lyttelton[176] came to say good-bye and was most charming as he always is. He tells me that he has insisted on remaining on the friendliest terms with G.C., but, as regards India, Alfred said, "he cannot be considered sane." Mr Morley did his best to get him to leave a card on me and to meet me at a luncheon party he suggested giving at Claridges, but G.C. wouldn't hear of this. I bridged the matter over by sending him an invitation to Ruby's wedding, to which he paid no attention. St. John tells me they have met on committees, and that they then speak to each other on business, but G.C. cuts him if they pass each other in the passage. St. John added "he actually puts down his wife's death to my treatment of him." Lord Ampthill asked me why the Viceroy refused to answer G.C.'s letters. I told him he had never received one; this Lord Ampthill could hardly believe—he kept on saying, but he has told me himself he has written repeatedly. I could only adhere to the truth. Lord A. tells me that, although he is a member of the Clive Memorial Committee, it has never yet met, and any letter written as coming from the Committee is simply penned

173. Born in Calcutta, he became Permanent Under Secretary of State for India in 1910 and was married to his cousin, the eldest daughter of William Makepeace Thackeray.

174. Sir Walter Lawrence, Private Secretary to the Viceroy, 1899-1903.

175. Arthur Balfour, then Leader of the Opposition.

176. Secretary of State for the Colonies, 1903-1905.

by G.C. himself. He has prepared a huge dossier which has been sent to the King in which he gives extracts from letters from all the Members of Council agreeing to his proposals and saying that Rolly is in a minority of one in refusing to sanction the attempt to raise a fund. As every member signed a most strongly worded protest in a formal despatch against a memorial being raised during this time of unrest, I can't imagine who he gets his authority from.

The King's only idea is to let the matter drop, which we are all longing to do. I have seen the Prince and Princess of Wales two or three times and have lunched and tead with them alone. The Prince is always intensely eager about Indian affairs; he is terribly bitter about G C., and this I am told G.C. puts down to my influence, although I am absolutely and entirely innocent. I dined at a big dinner at the Russian Embassy for the Queen and Dowager Empress 1 and sat between Lord Rosebery and Lord Cromer. The latter seems very happy at Rowland's marriage. Had a long talk afterwards with Sir Charles Hardinge,[177] who considers Rowland a pearl, he is devoted to him and says he is so reliable and hard working. We embarked on the Persian question and the Russian Convention as originally received by the Government of India. They practically made a free gift to Russia of the whole of Persia except the south-eastern triangle and Seistan. Russia, thinking there was something behind, hesitated and lost the opportunity. The howl from the Government of India brought alterations in the clauses. I could not get him to say more than that we should not have accepted disadvantageous terms, but as a matter of fact they were offered. However, it was very difficult to argue the point during the solos of a Russian Prima Donna.

I went to Buckingham Palace one afternoon and had an audience with the Queen and Dowager Empress.[178] Those two sisters are so enchanted at being together, and the day before I left for India I lunched with the King and Queen who were alone except for the Fife family. I had some talk with the King over the frontier troubles and these horrible bomb outrages, and the cause of the Amir's behaviour—he was exceedingly kind, and sent many messages to Rolly; begged me to tell him that he sympathised with him in all his troubles. He asked me if I had met G.C. I said "no," but I had asked him to the wedding, which, he did not attend. "What excuse did he give for not coming?" The King asked. "None," I said, "I received no answer." With great vehemence the King said "what can you expect from a man who is not a gentleman, have you ever known him do the right thing?" I was silent; I didn't wish to be considered prejudiced in any way. During luncheon the five Wales children came in, all first kissed the King's hand, and then said—how d'ye do to everyone, The tiny boy[179] is a darling and flings his arms round one's neck. They all clambered on to the Queen's knee, and seem devoted to her. None of them appear to be the least afraid of the King, and the baby amused himself in unwrapping chocolates and placing the silver paper on the King's head. They seemed such a happy family party.

---

177. Succeeded Minto as Viceroy.

178. Maria Feodorovna.

179. Prince John, born 1905.

During my visit Sir H. Campbell-Bannerman died and Mr Asquith became Prime Minister. I saw Mr Asquith before this took place at dinner at the Sassoons. Poor Margot[180] looks very ill, and bitterly lamented the cruelty of Providence that she should be too ill to enjoy what has been the summit of her ambition. I managed to see a good many plays. Tremendous excitement has been caused by a Canadian, Miss Maud Allan, who dances at the Palace; she does some Greek dances, the loveliest and most graceful things I have ever seen. Then she acts Salome, her garments are only ropes of pearls, and she dances to John the Baptist's gruesome head which to my mind spoils the whole thing; but her acting is remarkable, and the feeling and passion she puts into the tragedy of the scene is wonderful.[181] Seats are booked for weeks, in advance. Louisa and I went with Soveral[182] and Count Mensdorff.[183]

The Persia reached Bombay at 5 A.M., Friday, May 22nd. Colonel Dunlop Smith and Captain Jelf arrived for breakfast, the journey from Simla not having been as hot as they expected. I had an immense amount to hear, and I had a good two hours talk with Colonel Dunlop, who goes home tomorrow on 10 weeks' leave. I am so thankful I didn't know of all this bomb anxiety before leaving for England. About January they had intimation from the police that they knew they were being manufactured in Calcutta, but they couldn't trace them till a few weeks ago. Every time Rolly drove through the streets, Dunlop told me he was in an agony. Five times stones were thrown at the car, and once a huge brick splintered a window missing Rolly's head by an inch, and yet they didn't dare pause for fear a bomb might be placed in front of the car while they were waiting. Now the headquarters of these devils has been discovered. I trust we shall be able to sift matters thoroughly. Rolly is sending home a tremendously strong telegram saying they must enforce the same law as was introduced by the Liberal Government in 1883, saying any one discovered possessing explosives is liable to imprisonment for a term of years. Also the newspapers preaching murder must be confiscated. All the men that have been caught have confessed that it is the press that have goaded them on to attempt these outrages. Lord Morley won't like these strong measures, but if he doesn't accept them there will be trouble.

I was rather dismayed at hearing from Everard Baring that he and Mouche once travelled from Simla in May, and he wondered if they would live through the journey—he said "I really thought we were going to die the heat was so appalling." I started however full of courage, my carriage fitted up with tatties—matting windows—through which the water trickles, making a cool air as the train goes on. I had three huge baths filled with ice in each of my two rooms and electric fans in full play. The first night was quite cool going through the Ghats.

180. Margot Asquith 1864-1945, 2nd wife of the Prime Minister.

181. Maud Allan was a sensation around whom rumours swirled. She was reputed to be the mistress of Edward VII and the lesbian lover of Margot Asquith and lost a famous libel case in 1918 when she was accused, with Margot and Herbert Asquith among 47,000 others, of being part of a group of 'sexual perverts' in high places, who were being blackmailed by the German Secret Service

182. Marquis Louis de Soveral, Portuguses Ambassador, known as the 'Blue Monkey' and a fixture of Edwardian society.

183. Count Albert von Mensdorff–Pouilly-Dietrichstein, Austro-Hungarian Ambassador.

Wednesday, 27th May

The next morning at 10 o'clock it began to warm up, every window and shutter was shut to exclude every particle of air. I sat in darkness reading by the aid of an electric lamp. I began to feel as if I was being enclosed in an oven. Once I opened the door for a second, but was almost knocked down by the flood of sunlight and scorching air that choked me and beat against my face with fury. I tried going into the dining saloon for luncheon, but I couldn't face it, and the *khidmatgars* just opening the door to bring in a tray with food made the carriage appear unbearable. A second seemed long enough to allow a cruel blast of fiery heat into the carriage which seemed to swallow up the pyramids of ice which were frequently replenished throughout the day. At 4 o'clock we arrived at Gwalior. The Maharaja came to my carriage. I received him in semi-darkness. When he proposed that I should come and have tea in a shamiana at the station, I couldn't help remonstrating. How could I face going out into a burning fiery furnace? He said the Maharani had come to see me so of course I had to accept his proposal and putting on my sun-hat jumped on to the platform and rushed through the 20 yards of cruel heat that separated my carriage from the shamiana. Instead of entering a furnace, as I anticipated, I found myself in a gloriously cool bower of flowers. It seems these shamianas are composed of matting and an army of coolies pour water over them the entire time, consequently as there was a wind it blows only the cool air from the water through the room making a perfect temperature The Maharani is a tiny little woman, rather pretty, dressed in most gorgeous embroideries. Her dress was cut low and her neck was entirely covered by a marvellous necklace of about 10 rows of single diamonds, each one about the size of a sixpenny bit, worth millions. Scindia was charming—He is terribly upset at this bomb development, and spoke strongly of not losing a moment in enforcing the most stringent penalties.

Returning to the train was like entering an overheated oven; the door of my sitting-room had been left open for a few-minutes, and everything in it felt red hot. I went into my bedroom and undressed. Having lived through it I am glad to know what people mean when they speak of the heat of the plains. I hadn't the faintest notion anything but the infernal regions could be so cruelly hot. My body felt dry and parched, and my eyes like coals of fire. If one touched a metal object, one felt one's skin must be blistered. The sides of the carriage felt so thin as if one was only protected by paper from the rays of the sun. I couldn't read. The covers of the books were all curled up from the heat, and for three hours I sat trying to touch as few objects as possible. I had a bath; the water against the boiling earthenware sides felt cool, but the towels were so overheated that they undid any benefit one had derived from the cool water. At 8.30 we dined. The air was still intolerable, but the absence of sun made the whole difference, and our spirits rose. The thermometer in the train was 119°. In the dining car I think it must have been more, as no attempt had been made to shut out the air. At Delhi at 9.30 the Resident came down to pay his respects and to see if we were alive. We had struck the hottest day of the year. I have written all this as I think it is an interesting experience. There was I, surrounded by every luxury, fresh ice at every station, servants at hand to bring me cooling drinks, as one's thirst was indescribable. Every modern invention was arranged in my carriage to mitigate the heat, and yet I felt I couldn't have endured it much longer. How can anyone attempt to cross the plains in an ordinary railway carriage? I realise now that it is impossible without courting death. There can be no exaggeration of the terror of an Indian sun that turns the earth into a fierce cauldron, eager to seize upon poor victims, for there can be no escape from the pitiless devouring breath that sweeps over human beings with tongues of fire.

My first days at Simla have been very busy. I hadn't much zeal to do anything very active, as suddenly living at a height of 7,000 feet makes one dead tired, and no doubt the intense heat of the journey affected one more than one realised. The Mir Munshi waxed eloquent to Colonel Victor over his sufferings, and told him we had only just escaped with our lives. I hardly go so far as that but the heat must have been very excessive, as a box of chocolate tablets I had in my bag became liquid, and my cold cream absolutely ran away. Ointments or creams somehow evaporated and vanished into thin air, even in jars that had not been opened and we all felt the effects of our roasting for some days.

Lord Kitchener is naturally delighted at the way our frontier troubles have been overcome, never before has there been such splendid organisation. In reply to remonstrances from the Government of India, the Amir has at last been roused to a sense of his responsibility and has used his influence to recall the priestly disturbers of the frontier. He has written Rolly most friendly letters and says he has forbidden his subjects to side with the tribes on penalty of having their feet cut off. It is a great question how much power he has, or whether Nasrullah,[184] who is extremely anti-English, has undermined his authority. He explains the difficulties of his position and regrets the non-receipt of earlier news on the subject of the rising.

Tuesday, 2nd June.

Mr Morley has agreed to Mr Baker's appointment to be Lieutenant-Governor of Bengal, when Sir Andrew leaser's time expires in November. I feel rather triumphant, as during my last interview with Mr Morley he declared he would not have Mr Baker forced on him. I told him straight out it was Rolly's appointment; this he would not admit, saying the final responsibility of submitting the name to the King rested with him. I didn't wish to argue as to that, knowing that he puts a different interpretation, on the powers he possesses to any previous Secretary of State but I said Rolly must have the people he could trust, especially in Bengal, where all the agitation was resulting in these vile anarchical plots. We had rather a stormy interview, but the next day I received a most charming letter from him saying he feared he had been rather bearish, and that he would do his best to fall in with the Viceroy's views.

184. The Amir's brother and Crown Prince of Afghanistan.

Friday, 5th

The State Ball took place in the evening. A thousand guests came. We began with a State Lancers. Lord K-. was my *vis-à-vis*. I asked him if he wasn't impressed by our alterations; he said he was so struck by my gown that he hadn't had time to look at anything else. I was wearing rather wonderful gold and pink brocade presented to me by the Maharaja of Patiala, but a compliment about clothes was the last thing I expected from Lord K-. Sir Louis Dane made his first appearance as Lieutenant-Governor and very magnificent he looked in his gold coat with his Afghan Order that one mistakes for the Bath. Everyone seemed to enjoy themselves, and we have since heard that people were delighted at being able to move about freely instead of being packed like sardines in door-ways. Fryer has managed so well; it is the greatest comfort having got rid of furnace, and Captain Mackenzie has done wonders. About half the amount of champagne was drunk than at previous State Balls as he discovered that the greater part was carried away. This year it was placed under police protection with the most satisfactory results. Captain Mackenzie was congratulating himself that he had not had a single complaint from the guests, but as he stood on the steps of our splendid new cloak rooms, he overheard a man remark to his friend: "I don't think much of the Viceregal cigars." Captain Mackenzie couldn't resist looking round and saying: "Why smoke them? Have a cigarette instead".

Poor Sir Harold Deane, Chief Commissioner at Peshawar, has completely broken down from anxiety and worry, and has been ordered to start at once for England.[185] Rolly has appointed Colonel Roos-Keppel to act for him; he has done splendidly during the recent fights and has immense influence with the tribes. The whole frontier needs reorganisation; hitherto everyone has been pulling different ways, and the tribes began to look upon Peshawar as a happy hunting ground, as they always managed to get off scot free. Lord K-. is delighted at this selection. It has caused consternation in the Political Civil Service millieu, as Colonel Roos-Keppel is rather junior and has gone over a great many people's heads.

Saturday, 6th.

Colonel Roos-Keppel arrived to talk the future over with Rolly. Captain Holden also returned from the front; they both look rather thin and as if they had not found the bully beef very nourishing.

Saturday, 13th.

Colonel Roos-Keppel is still with us; he is taking many hints for his new duties at Peshawar. He had a most exceptional education. He went to school very young, and was always so insubordinate that he sampled several schools, always spending his holidays with his family

185. Died 1908.

in Normandy or Brittany; he consequently talks French perfectly. When he was 13 his father told him he could go abroad and shift for himself. He went to a family in Germany, where he remained till his father sent him enough money to pay his keep and move on. He worked his way somehow from place to place and visited every country in Europe. At 18 he went to Sandhurst with the knowledge and experience of a man of 30. Rather a risky system, but in Colonel Roos-Keppel's case it has answered. I asked him if he hadn't felt desperately lonely; he said no, that he had always succeeded to make friends, and somehow managed to fall on his feet.

Sunday, 15th.

It is rather amusing that the Times should accuse the Government of India of inaction, and express a hope that they will not go to sleep again. It is not altogether probable that the people who are affected by the bombs and outrages should have any desire to fall asleep! It is easy to criticise from a distance of 5,000 miles. I hear Chirol[186] has been ill, and is *hors de combat* at present. It is unlucky that the Times have taken on as Indian correspondent a man called Fraser who used to be on the staff of the Times of India; he got into trouble owing to drink and was dismissed; he also wrote for the National Review; he is very clever with his pen. He is a tremendous partisan, and I suppose because we were succeeding Lord Curzon he began to write spiteful articles before we reached India; these continued from time to time; then he made a most violent attack on me about the Nursing Scheme, saying I had simply made use of Lady Curzon's work, &c., &c. It is rather strange to think of the power a man like this has, and that the British public accept as Gospel truth whatever views the most wrong-headed correspondent chooses to give vent to.

Lord Windsor is making a very good and most attentive A.D.C.; he is a particularly nice boy. He has been in South Africa with the Selbornes[187] for a year and a half. The society there was of the most weird description, chiefly shopkeepers. At Johannesburg 3,000 people were invited to a garden party. He used to write all the invitations himself without any assistance. He has just sent me the following extract from a letter he has received from his Grandmother, Lady Paget.

> "I knew Lady Minto when she was quite young and her charming sister, the Duchess of St Albans. I also knew General Grey intimately and have many delightful amusing letters of his in my possession. He had, I think, more grasp of the political situation than any of those about the Queen after Prince Albert's death, and he was the only one who had the pluck to stand up to the Queen sometimes."

186. Ignatius Valentine Chirol, Times journalist and author.
187. Earl and Countess of Selborne. He was High Commissioner to South Africa, 1905-1910.

Saturday, 20th.

We rode to Mashobra in the evening and spent Sunday and Monday there, returning to Simla in time for dinner. Met Mr Buck, Reuter's Agent, riding back; he owns a house above the "Retreat" in the Mashobra woods. He asked me if I had seen a Reuter which appeared in most of the English papers of June 3rd. I told him I had seen it in the Morning Post. The message was as follows:

> "One of the most important features of the present campaign was the manner in which such clans as the Afridis, the Dir and Swat people were kept in check by the firmness and tact of our frontier officers, which prevented a general rising like that of 1897, in spite of the preaching of the Mullas. This satisfactory result was largely due to the encouragement given by the Earl of Minto, who sent commendations to the Khans of Dir and Swat. Emanating immediately from the Viceroy, this message appealed directly to the sense of personal loyalty, and in acknowledging it they replied that it increased their ability three-fold to check the incursions of Afghans and Bajauris."

Mr Buck told me that the Times had only put in half of this message; he added: "In all the years that I have been Reuter's Agent this is only the second time a message has been mutilated, and although I was loathe to believe it, I think there can be little doubt that the Times intentionally omits any mention of the Viceroy." It is almost amusing to have this direct proof of Fraser's unfriendliness, within a week of my mentioning that the Indian news was under his control. The tribes alluded to are those we met two years ago in the Malakand.

The following excerpt from a letter from leading Bengali magnates to the Lieutenant-Governor is most significant:

> "It is not only with feelings of regret, but anxiety and horror, that we have heard and read about the anarchism that has been brought to light in the Province of Bengal. There cannot be the slightest doubt that amongst the anarchists many have been led to such violence by reading inflammatory articles in the press. A press free to a certain extent all educated men will approve and desire as it is better to know the feelings of the people to a certain extent frankly than to allow everything to be suppressed, which would mean the voluminous publications of secret and seditious literature, but nevertheless we are of opinion, Sir, that a limit should be put to this unbridled license to slander, which has had a great deal to do in bringing these nihilistic ideas into our peaceful country. So our earnest prayer is that Your Honour's Government kindly forward our representation to His Excellency the Viceroy and urge the Indian Government to (1) bring in some press legislation which will be able to deal efficaciously with irresponsible press men; and (2) to hound out all the anarchist centres in India, for from the result in Bengal one wonders what the state of things may be in other provinces."

It is curious that this letter should have been written in Calcutta on the very day that the Acts dealing with explosives and the seditious press should have been passed in Simla. The Yugantar newspaper[188] has now been suppressed, but inflammatory pamphlets are still being circulated secretly. Far more criminal that the vernacular press is the sedition that is actually preached by Englishmen in newspapers printed in England. A paper called Justice is the chief offender and although its circulation is prohibited in India, extracts are freely circulated and translated into every dialect. I hear that some years ago there was an article in Justice advising Indians to murder Lord Curzon. The matter was taken up, and the Attorney-General was asked what could be done to put a stop to this incitement to crime, he however refused to take action. This was of course during the Conservative Administration. There have been meetings held recently in some place in London to celebrate the anniversary of the mutiny and honour the memory of Nana Sahib. It seems hopeless irony for the Government of India to attempt to deal adequately with the situation when such proceedings are permitted in the British Isles and men like Hyndman, Nevinson, Cotton and Keir Hardie declare themselves in sympathy with the men who preach rebellion and murder. Another paper called the Indian Sociologist preaches a violent crusade against British rule. The editor, Shyamaji Krishna Varma,[189] is a very clever man and holds extreme views but he has the excuse of belonging to the conquered race.

Friday, 26th.

There have been some most interesting disclosures within the last few days from a man who was arrested in connection with the bomb outrages who has turned King's evidence. He has given the names of many of the conspirators, and has related a most circumstantial story of the attempt to blow up the Lieutenant-Governor's train. I sincerely trust this may lead to further arrests. Meanwhile there has been another bomb thrown into a railway carriage near Barrackpore. One poor man has been most severely injured. I long to proclaim martial law and hang the culprits at once, to show that these miscreants will be dealt with summarily, and get their deserts; having the power to appeal and prolong the trials indefinitely, encourages the natives in the idea that they will eventually get off. The law of the land is quite inadequate to deal with these emergencies, but it is very difficult to get any special measures sanctioned.

A State Dinner was held in honour of the King's Birthday. The one long table looked very impressive covered with sweet peas and masses of silver.

Tuesday, 30th.

Captain Mackenzie's wedding in the afternoon was a most impressive ceremony owing to the Indian fashion of all soldiers wearing uniform. Miss Massey, I am certain, felt she was

188. Revolutionary paper, Yugantar meaning New Era, published from 1906.

189. Founder of India House in London and the Indian Home Rule Society.

the central person on the stage and performed a sort of *pas de quatre* coming down the aisle. She swayed her head first to one side and then to the other and hardly behaved like a bashful bride.

Wednesday, July 1st.

Reuters have given us a tolerably full account of the Indian Debate in the House of Lords; it is of course the absorbing topic of conversation here. It is very difficult from the abridged summary to follow exactly what was said, but Lord Curzon amongst other things seems to have stated that India could not be ruled by the House of Commons, and I am sure we all most heartily agree with him. Two of his assertions have amazed Indian officials. In speaking of the frontier war he said that he hoped they would hear nothing more of the schemes for advancing and driving railways through tribal territory. On becoming Viceroy one of the first things he made Lord Kitchener do, was to go along the frontier, and report on the proposed Kabul River Railway, without which he considered the safety of India was at stake. All his notes, kept in the office, point systematically to this line of policy. The other statement is still more unaccountable. He puts the responsibility of the partition of Bengal on Lord Ampthill, who had nothing whatever to do with it, and although Lord Curzon was in England when the clauses were drawn up, his directions were minutely followed. On his return he went through the papers most carefully, and spent one entire day with Sir Herbert Risley correcting and altering the proofs. All the notes in his hand-writing are still in the office, and he has copies of the papers with him; so there is no excuse for this deliberate misrepresentation, which he has made more astonishing by a letter to the Times to the same effect.

Lord Morley was evidently greatly nettled by Lord Curzon's speech, and gave him several hard hits. All reforms, all legislation, whether commercial, political, social, or religious, must emanate from India from the man on the spot, and the Secretary of State can alter or veto any suggestion he thinks fit, but it is impossible to govern India in England, and if only the cable could be cut for six months, I have little doubt that all agitation and unrest could be put down, and a more prosperous and contented India would be evolved. The native is accustomed to be ruled by force, and our methods of prolonged trials which justice demands in England is put down here to fear. There is considerable uneasiness out here at the remark he made in connection with the Amir and the Russian Convention. He speaks of "being about to put pressure on the Amir." If he wishes to do away with all possibility of coming to terms he has most effectually done so. The Amir is a touchy conceited man and certainly will not appreciate the idea that anyone can attempt to put pressure on him; he at least can frustrate their intentions and he most assuredly will.

It is too amusing to see the mistakes some of the papers make in connection with the Fuller incident. They give vent to the wildest theories, and mix up Bengal and Eastern Bengal and the various officials, and what they are supposed to have said in a hopeless pot pourri. Sir Bampfylde is the hero of the hour. The papers are full of his injuries, and if his advice had been followed, all agitation would have ceased, &c., &c., &c. This is all moonshine. It must be remembered that the world at home is only hearing one side of the story. In India Sir Bampfylde is almost as universally condemned, as he is praised in England. He is a clever, pleasant, plausible man, but hysterical, and tactless, the very last person to rely on to act with caution and decision in an emergency. Unless people know the rights of the case, I quite understand the public thinking him an injured individual. I have met several people who know him well, to whom he has admitted that in resigning he had made a gigantic mistake. He went so far as to say to an official: "I played a game of bluff, and lost".

Sunday, 5th July

The condition of Persia has been very critical for the last weeks and telegrams lately received announce that the British Legation is full of refugees and surrounded by Cossacks. The Shah is only able to hold his own due to Russian intervention. The Government have demanded an ample apology or else strong measures will be taken. I suppose this means sending some of the East India Squadron to occupy a Persian port. It is curious to think of the Russians playing this game while the King and the Tzar are cementing the *entente cordiale* at Reval.[190] I have heard from both Louisa and Rowland from Reval; everything seems to have gone off most successfully; no one was allowed to land for fear of anarchists. Rowland tells me he is returning with spoils; an M.V.O. and a second class order of St. Anne, both of which he has to wear round his neck on state occasions; a pin from the Tzar and a photograph from the Queen. Louisa doesn't mention her loot.

We have received most interesting letters from Dunlop; he has certainly made the most of his time in seeing people; he is so struck by the ignorance of the public of what has happened, and of what is happening at present in India. I remember meeting Lord Curzon when I was home from Canada, and he from India, at the time of the Coronation, he said exactly the same thing he told me that even the people whose business it was to know, took no interest, and that it was most disheartening. I don't see how this can be avoided, unless people are on the spot, how can they understand all the under-currents that are swelling the stream of events?

Colonel Dunlop tells me Ruby's house is quite lovely, and that she gave him an excellent luncheon. I have heard rumours of a drunken parlour maid being ejected by Kitty Drummond and Sargent,[191] the artist; certainly no better person could have been selected than Kitty for this necessary display of strength. I have not yet ascertained how she arrived on the scene at the psychological moment. Colonel Crooke writes that he and Mrs Crooke have been down to see Eileen at Camberley, and he has never seen her look so well. Violet writes from

190. A port on the Baltic where the two monarchs met to rubber stamp the Anglo-Russian agreement of 1907 that settled their countries' colonial disputes in Afghanistan, Tibet and, Persia and brought the Victorian period of the Great Game to an end.

191. John Singer Sargent.

Cliveden, where she was spending Ascot week. Esmond tells me he looks a dream in specs which he has to wear at present for reading, as the oculist says he has stigmatism, and Larry also gives a good account of himself; so I am reassured this week about the family.

Thursday, 9th.

Simla society has been convulsed by a formal complaint having been made in the newspaper by a member of the A. D. C. as to the conduct at the theatre of certain young ladies. No names are mentioned but everyone knows that the girls referred to, are Mary DuCane-Smythe, and Lorna Hewett, who with their party were occupying the Stage box at a performance of the "Hook of Holland." Simla is divided into two factions, for and against Mary DuCane. As she is really quite a nice girl and decidedly pretty, I think the balance weighs in her favour, and it is rather mean to complain publicly about her, although no doubt she richly deserved it and needs correction. Our little Simla scandals become rather insignificant when one hears rumours of Lord Charles Beresford[192] addressing a strongly worded memorandum to the Admiralty stating that the fleet at his command is inadequate and that he is unable to guarantee the security of the United Kingdom against Foreign attack! This promises to expand into a really big row.

Monday, July 13th.

Since I last wrote my journal, we have had daily luncheon parties. There has been another shower of horse hair near Rangoon! People are getting quite accustomed to it. The papers are full of the Suffragette procession in London. I think it is positively humiliating that ladies such as Lady Francis Balfour and Mrs Alfred Lyttelton should walk through the streets of London waving banners, followed by 10,000 infuriated women.

Tuesday, 21st.

There is great jubilation over Tilak's sentence of transportation for six years and a fine of Rs. 1,000. Tilak is about the cleverest man in India, he has had a most disastrous influence on the youth of India, preaching sedition to them in a most subtle way.[193] At last he gave vent to so violent an article in his paper that he was arrested; the trial continued for a long time. Tilak's own speech in which he tried to vindicate himself lasted over four days. When the crowd found out he had been removed to prison for this long term of years, there was a riot, which for some reason is connected with the mills, as they have all gone on strike, and soldiers were needed to restore order; about a dozen people were killed and 30 wounded.

---

192. Admiral and Commander of the Channel Fleet.

193. Lokmanya Tilak, Indian nationalist and independence fighter. He was held in Mandalay prison until 1914.

I received a few days ago a most charming letter from the Maharaja of Bikaner; he says:

> "What horrible deeds have been perpetrated in the last few months! Though shocking, it must be some consolation to His Excellency to know that all the people of India of any importance are practically to a man with him and the Government, and that we all admire his great courage and coolness in grappling with these difficulties. What a cruel irony of fate that there should be such a legacy left to a Viceroy of such a sympathetic and kindly nature! While on the subject I hope to be pardoned for mentioning here that I have lately been upset by some alarming rumours which have reached us of His Excellency's threatened resignation over some alleged difference of opinion with Lord Morley about Mr Baker's successor. If this were to turn out true, it will be a dire calamity for India, and as for myself I would honestly regard it as the greatest misfortune that could possibly happen, and so both for public and private reasons I sincerely hope and pray that all this may turn out to be false and groundless. The rumour seems to be spreading, and there will be, I am sure, a decided relief when it is contradicted. To show our active co-operation and sympathy with the Government, we passed the Explosive Substances Act on the 10th July to have effect throughout Bikaner State at once."

Friday, 24th.

On Thursday we had a very pleasant dinner, and the band played a delightful programme till quite late. Sir James Willcocks was very interesting; he told me a good deal about the two campaigns; he was so amused at a letter Lord Morley wrote him; it was couched in very complimentary terms, and added: "I must congratulate you on having carried out my orders so efficiently and for having brought the expedition to so successful an issue." General Willcocks said: "I really believe Lord Morley imagines he commanded the Army." He went on to tell me that Rolly had got an immense influence with the natives as well as the Europeans in the country. He said he travelled about a great deal, and that he heard it on all sides, and that the feeling was very genuine. The natives lay the greatest stress on what they call a real "Sahib", and that is how they describe the Viceroy. Mr Crump, the Waziristan Agent, came to see us on his way through Simla en-route to England on 16 months' leave. After living for four years in daily dread of his life, what a blissful change to be a free man, and roam at will without fear of assassination! His native servant, who had been his devoted follower for seven years, was brutally murdered this spring by some Waziris, simply because he was serving Mr Crump.

Went round to see the wives of our bandsmen, with Colonel Victor; they have all got such comfortable houses. The new unmarried quarters are just built, and are quite charming. The men were playing tennis on an excellent court with about four little boys to pick up their balls. Fancy what luxury for the ordinary Tommy. No wonder when they join our band they guarantee to remain on for their 21 years of service. One gentleman was insubordinate the other day, so was packed off at once; he loses his pension, and has to serve his time in a regimental band, a salutary warning for the others.

Tuesday, 28th. Dehra Dun Circuit House.

It is actually our silver-wedding day. I can hardly believe 25 years of our married life have passed; the time has flown, but it has anyhow been very full of incident, and I am more than thankful to have had a share in Rolly's wonderfully interesting career. Our life in Canada and India has given me endless opportunities, which an ordinary home life would never have brought me. I still hope to be able to develop one or two schemes in which I am interested before we leave India. Our mail brought us several interesting items of news, one being Ruby's visit to Esher where she met Lord Curzon, who appears to have been charming in every way. He alluded in a most appreciative manner to the improvements we have made at Barrackpore and Simla, &c., &c. I forgot to mention when alluding to Tilak's trial that the Judge was a Parsee; his original jury were composed of nine men: five Europeans, two Parsees and two Hindus. Tilak himself objected to the two natives; consequently two Europeans were substituted. It is interesting to note that no Indian will ever trust his own kith and kin and invariably prefers to depend on the honour and justice of the Englishman.

Sunday, August 9th. Simla

The London papers are full of the Indian Budget debate. Mr Buchanan seems to have made an excellent speech, and almost every one alluded to the present difficulties which the Viceroy and the Government of India have to contend with. The Old Age Pensions makes another very serious rock ahead; Lord Rosebery, Lord Cromer and Lord Lansdowne made speeches denouncing it, but it seems the Lords did not think it politic to throw it out. It will lead us into untold and ever-increasing expenditure, which will fall very little short of ten millions a year. Every drunkard and good-for-nothing loafer can now count on his 5 shillings a week at the age of 70.

Thursday, 13th.

Colonel Godfrey, who lives in the Malakand, tells me that in every bazaar in the Swat Valley the tribesmen were discussing the Secretary of State's threat that pressure was to be put on the Amir to make him sign the Russian Convention. These Pathans thoroughly understand our methods of government. They did not take exception to anything Lord Curzon said, knowing him to belong to the Opposition, but realised Lord Morley's remarks were much more significant. There are signs which point to a religious rising. If this really means war with Afghanistan and the frontier tribes join in, reinforcements would have to be sent from England. We hear they haven't a man they can spare and yet Winston Churchill is meddling at the War Office recommending that the army should be further reduced. This does not inspire one with confidence in the Government as Germany meanwhile goes on gradually strengthening her army and navy in spite of the King's friendly visits.

Sunday, August 16th.

Colonel Dunlop arrived from England and dined upstairs with Rolly and me, so that we might have an opportunity of hearing all his news. He has seen so many people that it is impossible to give an adequate resume of his impressions. Altogether Lord Morley was most friendly, the jealousy with which he guards what he considers his rights is almost unbelievable; he actually did not allow Colonel Dunlop to have an interview with Sir Edward Grey, although the latter through Lord Morley suggested an appointment with Colonel Dunlop three times. In each case Colonel Dunlop received the message too late to avail himself of it. Morley also implied to Dunlop that he would not allow any discussions with Members of his Council. Dunlop told him that some of his greatest friends were amongst them and that they must meet in society. It seems Asquith even, had to manoeuvre before asking Colonel Dunlop to luncheon, and Mr Nash, Asquith's Private Secretary, told Colonel Dunlop that it had taken a fortnight to arrange the interview. Colonel Dunlop had a long interview with Lord Curzon, who had evidently prepared his statement. Colonel Dunlop attempted to interrupt him in order to correct an inaccuracy; he waved him aside, saying "your time to speak will come later." However, Lord Curzon spoke on till 5 minutes to 12, and as he then had another engagement, Colonel Dunlop had no opportunity of saying a single word, so nothing was achieved and no misunderstandings smoothed over.

Tuesday, 18th.

I have only just discovered that it is the custom for the Viceroy's wife to call on Members of Council's wives, so they have all been expecting my visit for nearly three years. Have changed our day for entertainments from Thursday to Tuesday. As the mail leaves at 8 P.M., Thursday evening, it was the day of all others that Rolly felt least inclined to play up to two strange ladies at dinner. However, it had always been done, and for nearly three years we have meekly acquiesced in this very bad arrangement. We recently discovered that the mail in old days left Calcutta and Simla on Wednesday, hence the reason for Thursday being considered a Government House night, and hitherto everyone has been too conservative to make any alteration in this custom.

Thursday, 20th.

Attended a lecture given by Professor Wragge:[194] "The Majesty of Creation, the Romance of the Earth, the Solar System"; having already attended "A Voyage through the Universe" I was

194. Clement Lindley Wragge, Meteorologist and Theosophist.

very disappointed to find so much repetition. Some wonderful photographs were shown of the moon, all the mountains and craters coming out with amazing distinctness. We also saw Mars with all the canals which Wragge declared were made artificially by the inhabitants for irrigation purposes, to prolong their existence, now that Mars has commenced the process of cooling, it will soon dry up in the same way as the moon has done, and become uninhabitable. Some information was extremely interesting, but the whole thing was spoilt by Wragge's appalling delivery, at his attempt to be facetious, and also by his mistaken endeavour to improve our morals. After a marvellous photo of myriads of suns in the universe, it was provoking to be shown a slug on a leaf, then an ugly fat baby, and to be told that one and all belonged to the marvels of creation; however, as half the proceeds of his four lectures are to be given to my Nursing Fund, I have naturally had zealously to support old Wragge.

Sunday, 23rd.

We are having anxious times now in connection with Afghanistan. The Amir does not wish to have trade relations with Russia forced upon him, nor does he want any intercourse between his own frontier officers and those of Russia, so in spite of many letters from Rolly he has persistently ignored the Convention. Then came Lord Morley's unfortunate speech in the House of Lords, June 1908, on the Curzon debate, saying they were on the verge of "using pressure." Pressure to the understanding of the Afghan means force of arms; rifles have been distributed throughout Afghanistan. The Amir has made a statement saying he does not wish to bring the misery of war upon his country but if he is bullied by a neighbouring State he will defend himself and leave the issue in God's hands. The Amir's idea is that Russia and England intend to divide Afghanistan between them. Meanwhile, if we force him to accept our terms there would be a strong feeling in his favour throughout India and a conviction that England had been answerable for bringing an unjust war. The whole Mahommedan population will be in sympathy with the Amir, and the Hindus naturally would encourage any idea of hostilities as it would enable them to embarrass us by breaking out into further seditions. It is altogether exactly the situation that Rolly predicted, and Lord Morley still goes on saying the Amir must be made to fall in with our views. Morley says: "If the Convention breaks down it must leave a most ugly, embarrassing and dangerous ragged edge, Russia will be sore; her military party jubilant; her frontier machinations will start afresh in fuller blast than ever. The Afghan will feel, and with good reason, that he has scored against us, and our disaffected Indians will know this too. We shall be discredited in Europe. The Germans will be delighted beyond words." One cannot exaggerate the disastrous effect any hostilities would have on the Indian population, but one must hope for the best. I don't think Morley seems to anticipate the possibility of the Amir fighting us and yet we hear through our agent, that in Afghanistan they are thinking of nothing else

For two years Rolly has been thinking over a scheme to create a native regiment, which would be an outlet for the Cadet Corps, who when formed were promised Commissions by Lord Curzon. They were grievously disappointed, to find that they received different

Afghan soldiers, 1906.

Commissions from English officers, and were not entitled to be promoted higher than an English Subaltern. There are many more difficulties in connection with the forming of this regiment than would at first appear, one of the chief obstacles being that the officers themselves might object, owing to religious scruples, to take orders from a superior officer belonging to a lower caste. Rolly has discussed the questions with numbers of soldiers, and thinks it would be possible gradually to form a regiment which would in course of time have a native in command. This regiment would be directly under the command of the Viceroy. Lord K-. is opposed to the scheme, and says it will not work, but Rolly doesn't agree with him and has frequently told Morley of his project which he wishes to announce with other reforms on the 1st January 1909. Colonel Dunlop, from Lord Morley's reticence in discussing Rolly's proposed reforms with him, thinks it likely the credit may be taken at home for suggestions which are emanated from India, and, for this reason, he wishes me to chronicle what suggestions have been made, which may or may not be adopted, and which possibly may be wholly at variance with Morley's views.

Sunday, August 30th.

The frontier officials are doing what they can to restore confidence amongst the tribes, who have been unsettled by rumours emanating from Afghanistan. Rolly is writing privately to the Amir assuring him that we have the welfare of his country at heart, and that we have no thoughts of using armed pressure. I hope this may allay the feeling of distrust as to

England's intentions, which no doubt has been rapidly gaining ground, which feeling the anti-British party have been careful to foster.

A most interesting Minute has been found in the office written by Lord Curzon, which was sent home in 1902. In spite of the unanswerable arguments it met with no favour from the Secretary of State. The Memorandum states the financial position of the Viceroy very clearly, and is a most interesting record to keep. Captain Mackenzie is making out a statement of comparative prices which shows an enormous rise during the last few years. It is not yet completed so cannot be inserted this mail. It is clearly not right that a Viceroy should receive absolutely no remuneration for toiling harder than any public servant in the Empire during his regime, and in a climate that must tell on his constitution.

Tuesday, September 1st.

Gave our usual dinner party. Found Mr Meston very entertaining; he is Acting Financial Member of Council. I had some talk after dinner with Mr Pagan, the Presbyterian Minister;[195] he has made a great reputation for himself by giving some lectures, which I hear were quite excellent. He is also a first-rate preacher, but Mashobra interferes greatly with our church attendance. Another most interesting person was Mr Marshall,[196] the archaeologist. Dancing went on as usual after dinner, and I really enjoyed the evening; if only we could perpetually entertain the clever, interesting people, it would be such a comfort, instead of having to get through the tread-mill of the inevitable visitors that flock to Simla from all parts of India, and have to be entertained.

Wednesday, 2nd.

During the week we entertained Madame Isabelle Massieu at luncheon; she is a marvellous old lady of about 60, has travelled all over the world, having no knowledge of any language except French. In spite of this she has been all over India without any companion, having only natives to look after her.[197] She is fat and unwieldy and yet last year she rode on a man's saddle 200 miles in Macedonia, accompanied by four officers, doing 40 miles a day. She boasted to me that at the end of the journey she was in better condition than the men, and felt no fatigue whatsoever. She has travelled from Pekin to Burma and has been up to Lhasa, and enjoys these solitary journeys. Sven Hedin will be at Simla next Thursday; he has made wonderful discoveries: new ranges of mountains, &c., &c. For three days he is going to be in hiding at Colonel Dunlop's house, getting a new outfit, as his civilised clothes have been lost, and he is dressed like a Thibetan.

---

195. Gavin Laing Pagan: After a year in Simla became Minister of St George's Edinburgh and joined up as a private in the Royal Scots Regiment aged 41 early in WWI. Captain Pagan was killed in action in the Arras offensive in 1917 after preaching a final sermon to his men.

196. (Sir) John Marshall, Director General of the Archaeological Survey of India, 1902-1928.

197. Author of *Népal et Pays Himalayen*.

Monday, September 14th.

Sven Hedin has arrived safe and sound; he has been away two and a quarter years. Since he left us in May 1906, he has never slept in a bed, nor indulged in a blanket, and has only used a fur-lined bag. His feet were benumbed from cold for two months; he had no feeling whatever in them. He could stick needles into them without any sensation, and was quite unable to walk. I can't understand why they did not mortify, but when the weather became

Sitting room Viceregal Lodge

less intensely cold the circulation gradually returned. Otherwise he has not had one day's illness and presented the Tashi Lama at Lhasa with all his medical stores, chiefly in the shape of tabloids. He advised the Tashi Lama not to swallow any of them without consulting an English doctor, but I hardly think it was a kind present to bestow on an ignorant man and only wonder that we have not heard of the Tashi Lama's demise. He was so grateful for the assistance Rolly gave him before he started on his travels, although he absolutely failed to get Morley's permission for Sven Hedin to enter Thibet and he had to go round by Chinese territory. The Times have given him £200 for a telegram of 3,000 words. He has written 9,000 pages, descriptive of the country he has passed through. In his telegram he says he wishes "with the Viceroy's permission" to call the new range of mountains over which he passed "The Trans-Himalyan". Dunlop pointed out to him that the mountains are not in the Viceroy's jurisdiction, and that no permission from him was needed. Sven Hedin responded—"I don't care; I will not send my telegram without those words, it should annoy Lord Morley".

Monday, September 21st.

On our return from the play at 1.30 A.M. I saw two telegrams lying on the table addressed to Rolly, but as he gets dozens daily, I did not anticipate their containing anything of special interest. Imagine my surprise when Rolly rushed into my room with the news that Violet was engaged to Charlie Fitzmaurice. For some time past I have realised that this would probably happen some day, and I felt rather anxious when we heard that after Charlie had spent three days at Minto he had persuaded Violet to go to Dereen[198] with Larry. We have already received several letters on the subject from Lord Lansdowne and Maud, and they both told us they feared that Violet had no intention of accepting Charlie at present. The telegram we received expressed unbounded satisfaction now that she has relented. I own that my first feelings were entirely selfish: we shall miss Violet too desperately, and I don't know what Rolly will do without her, but she certainly could not have selected a more delightful person and it is everything knowing him and his family so well. It is curious that she should have become engaged in Co. Kerry, Ruby having also selected that county for the scene of her engagement last year. Colonel Crooke is very excited about it, as he hails from that part of Ireland; and says it has evidently a disastrous effect on the family. I must certainly prevent Eileen running the risk of going there for some time to come, unless I wish to be robbed of all my daughters.

198. The Lansdowne's house in Co. Kerry, Ireland.

Tuesday, 22nd.

We only told the most intimate members of the Staff of Violet's engagement, as I felt it was impossible to cope for a day or two with the flood of congratulations which would naturally flow in.

Violet is such a favourite in Simla, they were all greatly impressed at the way she acted hostess last year during my absence in England. She was so attentive and courteous to the old ladies at the dinner parties, that they all love her, and I quite realised how much they regretted the change when I returned, and Violet was dethroned. We can make no plans for the future at present, but I am sure Rolly won't allow Violet to go to England to be married; he will never consent to the ceremony taking place in his absence.

Thursday, 24th.

Sven Hedin happened to tell me today that he had met an Indian medical man at Gartok in Tibet, who was the first person to tell him of the unrest in India, of the throwing of bombs and the risk which Europeans were running. He exaggerated the situation a good deal but when Sven Hedin asked him if the Viceroy was not in great danger he said: "Oh no, no one will try to do him an injury, first because the people believe in him and they know he has their good at heart, and secondly because they consider his predecessor largely responsible for the unrest, and they recognise that Lord Minto has had nothing to do with it." I only trust what these men say may be true; anyhow it is a satisfaction to know what is in the minds of some of the people. Sven Hedin delivered a lecture at Viceregal Lodge after dinner, and got so carried away, pointing out the places of interest on a huge map that he has been busy drawing for the last week that he entirely forgot time and his surroundings and thought he was again in the unexplored regions of Tibet. He went on speaking for two and a half hours, instead of for an hour and a half. Fortunately he is not only an explorer, but an artist, and his drawings of the inhabitants are marvellous, clearly showing the various types of the most degraded-looking and barbaric inhabitants of the earth.

Sunday, 27th.

Rolly has received a very nice private letter from the Amir. It contains so many allusions to "friends" that it appears to be almost a joke. It is however quite a triumph, as it shows that his visit to India has stood us in good stead, as he evidently thinks that Rolly is to be trusted. The official document that accompanies the letter is 54 pages long, and is full of common sense, bringing excellent reasons forward why certain clauses in the Anglo-Russian Convention would not be beneficial to the interests of Afghanistan. Curiously enough, Rolly has himself argued these very points with Lord Morley. It is very satisfactory to see that the Amir is inclined to be friendly; he has a very difficult part to play with his anti-English subjects

Sven Hedin with retainers.

Wednesday, 30th.

The Maharaja of Alwar has arrived on a two days' visit; he wears European dress in the day-time, but wrecks his appearance by leaving off his pughree, especially as he wears emerald ear-rings and hideous little side-whiskers. He speaks perfect English, much better than Scindia. He is immensely interested in the native regiment that Rolly is so anxious to start. Lord Kitchener will not view it in a favourable light, which is most unfortunate, but Rolly hopes to start it directly under himself and the Foreign Department, who are the only officials who are in touch with the Native States and can ascertain who would make the best recruits.

Friday, October 2nd.

This evening the Black Heart's fancy ball took place. A Mrs Wilson, a lady who has had a great deal to do with theatrical costumes, very kindly undertook to evolve my costume. I was supposed to be Margaret of Valois, wife of Henry IV of France about 1410. The whole thing was manufactured by *durzies* in Mrs Wilson's house. I only tried the dress on once, and it was really a most magnificent production. Gold tissue, embroidered with pearls and marvellous precious stones. A blue velvet cloak edged with ermine, and a magnificent head-gear surmounted by a small crown. It was most regal, although I do not think it was exceptionally becoming. The whole thing cost a tenth of what would have been charged for it in England. Mrs Wilson managed to find all the materials in the bazaar here. I am so afraid the gold tissue will tarnish; otherwise the dress might almost become an heir-loom. The ball was wonderfully pretty, the costumes exceptionally good. There were three most startling ones that created some excitement. One a directoire which opened up on one side of the skirt, showing white breeches and a black garter when the lady moved; another was supposed to be a fencing costume, and the lady evidently thought it easier to dispense with a skirt, as she had only an apology for one, very few inches long. The third was Mrs Maddox who appeared to have put on her night-gown. I believe she thought she was empire, but it wasn't pretty.

Monday, October 5th.

Guests came to luncheon and I had to go to a musical recital given by a poor man called Edgar whose brother has just committed suicide, owing to their failure to make money by giving concerts. This poor creature looks as if he might shortly follow his brother's example. I finished showing Doctor Sven Hedin my scrap books in which he took the liveliest interest. The expression he used about them was that he wouldn't miss seeing them for anything this side of the moon. He returns to Sweden via Japan and the Siberian Railway. I think he is privately most anxious to succumb to the charms of some fair lady, now that he has accomplished what he felt to be his great mission in life. Having travelled four times across Tibet, he has no other important country left to explore.

Friday, 23rd.

Had a few people to dinner—amongst others Sir George Roos-Keppel and General Drummond. The latter has just returned from England, where he has been interviewed by Lord Morley about Rolly's scheme for a native regiment. General Drummond told Morley how keen all the Native Princes were about this regiment, and that it was a great thing to have the support of the Maharaja of Udaipore, the first Ruling Chief in Rajputana. Morley asked if he was a Mahommedan. I suppose to anyone who has not been to India it is a most intricate puzzle to understand, but everyone here knows that Udaipore is a great Rajput

Chief of the Hindu faith, and that during the conquest by the Moghuls in 1561, 300 of their women committed suicide sooner than risk the fear of falling into the hands of the Mahommedans. Sir George Roos-Keppel told me that his Zakka Khel servant, who is six-foot six, and who accompanied him when he stayed with us a couple of months ago, turned up his nose dreadfully when he saw that Government House at Peshawar was not as big as Viceregal Lodge. He didn't take long to become fastidious, as he had never before seen anything beyond a mud hovel. What impressed him most of all was the Band. He said he didn't know that even a Viceroy would have only Sahibs playing in his Band; any one in uniform appeared to him to be of equal rank, so no doubt he imagined the 40 Bandsmen were all Generals.

Sunday, October 25th.

Immensely excited at the thought of Violet's arrival. We had planned to go and meet her after luncheon, but a telegram saying she and Francis were leaving Kalka at 7.30 A.M., only gave me time to drive a few miles down the hill, before her landau, with galloping ponies and clouds of dust came in sight. I never saw any one looking so well, or in better spirits. She seems radiantly happy and full of zeal as to Charlie's future career. We reached Viceregal Lodge about 2.30 amidst general rejoicing at her return.

Tuesday, 27th.

Guests came to luncheon and we also gave a small dinner party. Lord Kitchener sat between Violet and me, and was in most tremendous form. He is very anxious Charlie should go up for the examination for the Indian Staff College which takes place next month, and the poor wretch is to be greeted with this news on his arrival at Bombay, November 5th. I told Lord Kitchener that when he wrote to me last year when I was in England telling me how well Violet was doing hostess, and that she was more than equal to filling my place, I had fully expected to receive a telegram telling me that he was going to become my son-in-law! He roared with laughter, and expressed great regret at having been supplanted. Lord Kitchener loves being chaffed, chiefly because people as a rule are afraid of him and rarely have the courage to contradict him.

Sunday, November 1st. Jodhpur.

We reached Jodhpur at 5.30 and were received by the Maharaja, his 10-year old son, and a splendid guard of honour of Imperial Service Troops. The drive of three miles from the station to the Palace was about the most picturesque scene I have ever beheld. It was exactly as if we have gone back 500 centuries at least. The entire route was lined on each side with the Thakurs[199] and their retainers, each band of men having their distinctive pugrees. The medley of animals and men was remarkable, about 8,000 in all. On either side of the road there were caparisoned horses with marvellous trappings, long flowing draperies covering their heads, richly embroidered with gold and silver, all wearing the thick gold bracelet above the right knee, pawing the ground, and arching their necks as they are all taught to do. Elephants completely covered with velvet embroideries, and massive silver ornaments. Camels galore; some carrying antediluvian guns which look as if they could never have done much execution, so heavy and cumbersome did they appear. Mounted men covered from head to foot with chain armour, wearing the identical suits of mail used in battle at the time of the early Moghul Emperors. The horses were covered by four plates of looking-glass which stood out like petticoats and which in the old days was supposed to sparkle and flash in the sunlight as they galloped here and there, thereby dazzling and disconcerting the enemy. To the left of us the grand old fort stood out darkly in bold relief against the clear lemon-coloured sky. The glow of the setting sun enormously enhanced the beauty of the scene. I must not forget to mention the many groups of dancing figures that pirouetted about here and there. Their costume dated back many centuries and consisted of voluminous skirts made out of over 50 yards of white material. A kind of girdle held them in place below the waist, but they flew out in all directions as they rapidly revolved. These dancers are called Yamas. The Palace is quite an imposing building of red sand-stone with a great deal of ornamentation; from an open balcony we overlook a forest of tents, where the staff and guests are accommodated. We were thankful enough to dine alone and go early to bed, after the heat and fatigue of the day.

Monday, 2nd.

I started early with Violet, Colonel Crooke, and Colonel MacWatt to visit the Zenana Hospital. The patients all looked clean and well-cared for. They inhabit quite a fine palace with wide courtyards and carvings, and the Maharaja gives them as much money as they require to support it. Walked on about 50 yards to a native school, rather a pathetic establishment with an old fashioned and apparently incompetent teacher. Our way wound in and out of the old paved city, with narrow streets overshadowed by tall houses with overlapping carved balconies, all beautifully executed in red sand-stone. Every alley and niche was filled with a motley crowd dressed in varied hues. They gazed at us as we passed with stolid apathy. The air was pleasant enough when cooled by the shade of the houses, making the contrast all the greater with the burning heat of the sun which devoured the open spaces, glaring savagely on the whitened walls that stood out in acute relief against the deepest of blue skies.

By 10.30 we found ourselves in the great Durbar tent which was filled with Thakurs and their followers. November 1st, the 50th Anniversary since Queen Victoria took over the

199. Holders of a feudal title literally meaning lord.

Jodhpur Group
Top row: Mr Guise, Lord F. Scott, Lord Windsor, Capt. Gibbs, Mr Gabriel, Col. Mac Walters, Capt. Sowter, Capt. Jelf.
Front row: Col. Dunlop Smith, Col. Crooke Lawless, Col. Pinhey, Mr Butler, Lady Violet Elliot, His Excellency, H.H. The Maharaja, Her Excellency, Mr Colvin, Genl. Drummond, Col. Brooke.

government of India from the East India Company, being a Sunday, Monday 2nd was fixed upon for the message of good-will from the King to the Princes and people of India, sent to them through the Viceroy. Rolly and his staff arrived, heralded with a flourish of trumpets, dressed in full uniform. After investing the Maharaja with the K.C.S.I., Rolly made a few introductory remarks, and then read the King's message. The material for the letter had been submitted from India, but considering it was drafted by one of our greatest literateurs, I think the language distinctly disappointing. It was an opportunity which might have inspired high-flown eloquence, but I felt no thrill of emotion, and was left absolutely cold and unmoved. All the Thakurs then came up to make their obeisance, after which we returned to the Palace, where we were left in peace till 4 o'clock. We then started in motors through the desert, 11 miles to Mandore, a kind of oasis, full of flowers, trees and streams where the Maharaja's ancestors have been buried in sundry cenotaphs. There is a long gallery with gods and goddesses carved out of the solid rock, more curious than beautiful,

as the figures are covered with plaster and painted in the most vivid hues. On our return we stopped at Balsamand, which is a Palace built on a large lake, with a broad terrace up to the water's edge. Here we had tea, which was very welcome after our dusty drive. The garden was a mass of red and pink oleander and bougainvillaea, and flowering shrubs. We had planned to visit the wonderful old fort at the bewitching hour of sunset. To get us there in time the Maharaja, who was driving us, literally, flew along the newly restored roads which were in perfect condition, the rains and floods of this year having destroyed roads and villages alike.

I find it is quite impossible to describe this wonderful structure; it is surpassingly beautiful. The natural grandeur of the rock, surmounted as it is by this huge pile of masonry, with its exquisite gate-ways, arches and carvings. As we reached the long court-yard the shadows fell almost black across the pavement, while, in the rays of the setting sun, a host of retainers stood in a blaze of light shining on a kaleidoscope of colour from their gay-coloured garments. Rows of men with dandies waited to carry us up the steep ascent, passed the cruel-looking gates with the long spikes to keep off the attacks of elephants, up to the dwelling part of the fort where the two Maharanis and their numerous suite are still lodged. Leaving our dandies we mounted up flights and flights of tortuous steps, till at last we reached the platform on the roof. The city lay below us, bathed in a golden glow, with mauve shadows melting in the mysterious darkness of the desert that appeared like a sea of opal in the fading light. I shall never forget the impression that this great building made on me, towering so grandly towards the heavens, so silent, so full of secrets that will never be divulged, a monument of innumerable intrigues and crime. Although times have changed, the women lead the same life as they have for centuries past, buried within those walls, and even now there are heart-burnings and questions as to who will be the next heir. The Maharaja has three charming little boys of 10, 4, and 18 months, even the youngest can lisp out his "How do you do?" and gives orders as if he expected to be obeyed. This year the Maharaja has married a second wife, a daughter of the ruling family of Udaipur. The law is that should she have a son, he must become the Maharaja on the death of his father, and one wonders what will become of these three attractive boys.

Tuesday, November 3rd.

Felt very loth to leave my bed at 5.30 A.M., but I was anxious to see the pigsticking, Jodhpur being the finest country in India for this sport. The Maharaja drove Rolly, Violet and me out to the ground in a motor. We then mounted Arabs—such beautiful ones—and rode to a hill nearby. I was dreadfully disappointed at not being allowed to follow the riders, but there was some idea of its being dangerous, as there is an off chance of a wounded pig turning, and making for one of the horses. A man on a camel beats up the pig, then four riders start off galloping for all they are worth, and there is immense competition as to who secures the first spear. We saw Colonel Victor get two pigs, Francis one, and three more were killed after we left, so it, was a good morning's sport. At 4.30 a gymkhana took place and I did my duty by talking to the elite of Jodhpur. These Rajputs are wonderful riders, and are put on ponies almost before they can walk, so it did Francis great credit winning one event, and also Colonel Victor, who was either first or second in five different competitions. The Maharaja had most of his horses brought out for Rolly's inspection—he has 400 of the most perfect ones that can be bought. They are broken in a wonderful way; all have excellent mouths.

One Arab he rides in a bridle without any bit. The crowds round the gymkhana ground were enough alone on which to feast one's eyes.

This is the country of the Rathores; the ruling family of Jodhpur are probably bracketed with one or two other Rajput stocks as the most noble house in the world and their pedigree begins with the beginning of time. The present Maharaja is terribly delicate, he has tuberculosis and entertaining us was evidently a great effort to him; he really does not look as if he could live long. Previous to our departure he dined quietly with us; also the Pinheys, Mr Gabriell, the Commissioner, and General Drummond. Immediately after dinner, we motored to one of the palaces in the city. From a platform on the roof we gazed at a town of liquid fire. The fort and every principal building was outlined by myriads of tiny lamps, while masses of rockets and balloons were despatched into the sky and fountains of flame sprung up in all directions. It was really a unique sight, and the perfect temperature with a balmy breeze made the evening most enjoyable. We reached the station at 11 A.M., and bade farewell to Jodhpur, our visit having been accomplished with complete success.

Friday, 13th. Bikaner.

Everyone seemed to know it was my birthday. Rolly gave me a lovely Jaipore chain; the girls books; the Maharaja some embroideries. There was a banquet in the evening, but no speeches, as our official visit took place two years ago. Went during the afternoon to see all the zenana ladies; the Maharaja's mother seems to be the moving spirit, and the first wife's nose has been put out of joint by the little new wife whom he married last May. She is very small, but has quite nice features, and I believe he is very fond of her. The two children, who are not the least shy, made some diversion, but these purdah ladies seem terribly timid and ill at ease with strangers. The Maharaja is so European himself he refuses to follow all the old customs. He tells me a man is not supposed to address his wife or children in the presence of his parents; in fact, he has to obtain their leave before seeing her.

Saturday, 14th

Left Bikaner for Gujner after luncheon. I went with Arthur Guise and Colonel Victor and photographed the pig in the forest while they were being fed. They are supposed to be wild, but appeared to be very greedy and extremely tame.

Tuesday, 17th.

We had all the Maharaja's A.D.C.s in after dinner to give them presents. Everyone has looked after us in the most wonderful way and I have never seen such an excellent host as Bikaner himself. I wish all Indians were like these Rajputs, they are such a splendid race. We all felt dreadfully sorry to say good-bye to them.

Mehrangarh Fort, Jodhpur.

Thursday, 19th. Lucknow.

Arrived at Lucknow at 8.30 A.M.; a public arrival and an address of welcome at the station after which we drove to Government House. In the evening we went to the Talukdar Fête, which was quite lovely. The garlands they presented to Rolly and me are worth about £20.00 a piece; every person was given a small one, even the two sentries from the Royals, who stood on each side of our chairs, had garlands round their necks. Imagine a Tommy's feelings on being thus decorated.

Saturday, 21st.

Visited the Dufferin and the Kinnaird Hospitals in the morning. The Dufferin is greatly improved since I saw it two years ago. The other is an American Methodist Hospital, and the number of patients attended to by four women is quite extraordinary. They must be worked to death. The lady doctor told me how interesting it was getting to know something of these native women's lives. She told me there is an invariable strain of melancholy amongst the Mahommedans. They never know how long their husbands will look upon them with favour. Often without any warning they find they have been supplanted by another wife. The Hindus have a much greater hold on their husbands, and have altogether a happier existence. Hindus often object to going to a hospital, as their religion necessitates their dying in their own homes.

We started at 2.45 for the races. Rolly and I drove up the course in State, escorted by the Royals, which caused us to swallow cart-loads of dust. There was a good deal of heart-burning over the Army Cup which was won by an outsider. The excitement of the day now commenced for me. We expected Eileen and Larry to arrive at 6.30. To our intense disappointment we heard that the train was three hours late. We dined upstairs, and sat ready dressed for the reception awaiting them. They arrived five minutes before we had to go downstairs. They were naturally extremely tired, but both seemed to be very well, and they had had an excellent journey, but horrible food on the "Egypt".

Monday, 23rd,

Had a very exhausting morning interviewing the Maharani Sahiba Gaekwar of Baroda. She remained quite half an hour discussing the political situation. I tried to be as nice as I could to her as she has the reputation of being very anti-British. I afterwards interviewed three other Ranis. One of them told me that she knew we looked down on Indians, and only considered them half-educated, and although she acknowledged that we wanted to be kind and sympathetic she said: "You must be still kinder and you must try and understand us better." I told her how much I regretted not speaking the language. She said: "If you will only learn it, the people will be pleased and know that you think it worthwhile." She told me she had been born under an unlucky star, and that everything had always gone wrong with her through life. She had been to England, and spoke English quite well. She was extremely interesting, and I only wish I could get in touch with these Indian ladies, as they influence their husbands so enormously.

Saturday, 28th

Had a peaceful four days at Agra. Rolly had to give up all thoughts of coming; there is so much to do in connection with this new legislation and his presence in Calcutta gives confidence. I have hastened my departure and leave with the family for Calcutta on Saturday night. It creates a great deal of disappointment as our visits to Benares and Pusa have been cancelled. The only contretemps is Lord Windsor being laid up with a sharp attack of fever; he has felt ill for some days. Mr and Mrs Crooke remain to look after him.

Friday, 4th December. Calcutta.

The body-guard have not yet arrived from Dehra Dun, consequently we are being guarded by a regiment of Hodson's Horse. The men are wild-looking Afridis, with long hair, and the man who stands outside my door, with a huge curved drawn sword, appears to me to look much more alarming than any Bengalee who might possibly attempt to attack me. We are so distressed to hear from Colonel Crooke and Major Birdwood that they pronounce Lord Windsor's fever to be enteric;[200] so far there are no bad symptoms but it will be such a terrible anxiety for his people so far away.

Friday, 12th.

The Viceroy's Legislative Council assembled to pass a Bill to "provide for the more speedy trial of certain offences and for the prohibition of the associations dangerous to the public peace." The Council met in the Throne Room at Government House, to which access was only given on presentation of special pass issued for the occasion. The support the Bill received was practically unanimous from Natives as well as Europeans. Dr Rash Behari Ghose was the only Member who was anxious to introduce amendments and even he appeared to be dissenting more from party reasons than from conviction. He is extremely eloquent, and though an Extremist is on very friendly terms with Rolly. The measure was made law after a short speech by Rolly closing the proceedings. Mr Perceval Landon[201] told me he considered this was the most important act that has been passed since the Mutiny. Two days after passing the new law, terror was struck into the heart of the Bengalis by the deportation without trial of 10 men. We hear that this has made a profound sensation; no one knows

200. Typhoid.

201. International journalist, special correspondent of The Times and friend of Rudyard Kipling.

who may be the next to be arrested, arms and ammunitions have been thrown in the river, and in outlying villages the Zamindars,[202] instead of assuming an insulting attitude, have offered their services to assist in restoring law and order.

The last attempt on Sir Andrew Fraser's life facilitated matters enormously, but the absurd articles that have been appearing in the Times and Daily Mail saying how unfortunate it is that the Viceroy does not seem, to be aware of the serious state of affairs, only makes one laugh at the hopeless ignorance of the writers, who unluckily take in the British public. Rolly has had to fight the apathy of a certain class of officials, and also to avoid being carried away by the hysterical nervousness of another section of the community, and no doubt his calmness regarding his own personal safety has inspired confidence in others. Mr Halliday, the Head of the Police, told me everyone knows the Viceroy never even asks what precautions are being taken for his safety, and this makes them, all the keener in looking after him. Half the police are not in uniform, and in driving through narrow streets they are now posted alternately facing first the crowd and then the street. It stands to reason that it is much better to look at the crowd than to have one's back turned to them. Of course Rolly thoroughly realises that it would be madness not to be careful or to run the slightest unnecessary risk.

Lord Windsor's enteric is running the normal course; he has two splendid nurses. Colonel Crooke and Major Birdwood are looking after him, and I pray all may go well.

Tuesday, 15th.

The levee took place in the evening; 1,732 people attended; the newspapers chose to remark that natives were conspicuous by their absence; but as a matter of fact there were 25 per cent, more than usual, and hundreds applied to come who were not eligible. Every man who came had to be vouched for by a person on the Government House list, and a great deal of extra care was taken to avoid the possibility of any undesirable person getting access into the house.

We are terribly distressed at getting a much more alarming telegram as to Lord Windsor's condition, and this keeps me in perpetual anxiety and dread. Evie Gibbs has gone up to Agra with Colonel Crookes.

Saturday, I9th.

Dr Stein lunched.[203] He has just returned after two years and eight months' exploration in Turkestan and China. The very last night that he was in the mountains his foot became

---

202. Hereditary landowners.

203. Aurel Stein, archaeologist and explorer.

frost-bitten and he has had to have his toes amputated. He is very lame and fears that another operation may be necessary. He has discovered the most wonderful manuscripts, and showed us specimens of a great many. He came upon a village near the old Chinese wall which owing to the water having receded is now practically deserted. Here they had recently discovered an old temple almost buried in sand. Dr Stein was able to make friends with the priest, and by a series of curious coincidences he was able to persuade the priest that he had been brought there owing to the guidance of the priest's particular patron saint. He was eventually allowed to carry off an enormous number of their priceless relics.

He had numberless small blocks of two pieces of wood tied together with string, and sealed with a white sort of clay, dating back to about 200 A.D. He made Rolly open one of these blocks and I another, the ink inside was as black and fresh as if it had been written yesterday. There was a beautiful engraving taken from a wood cut about 800 A.D., which shows how much further advanced the Chinese were in their civilisation, as we had no printing presses till about 600 years later. All these manuscripts are chiefly Buddhist writings; they are going to be deciphered at the British Museum, and then the collection is divided, some being sent to various museums in India, such as Calcutta, Lahore, &c., &c. Dr Stein thinks this is simple vandalism, as the whole collection is by far more interesting altogether.

Wednesday, 23rd.Calcutta

Lord Windsor has had a most serious relapse. Throughout the morning the telegrams became more critical, and during the afternoon we received the tragic news of his death. It is too terribly sad. For the past week Colonel Crooke has kept him alive after every collapse with injections of strychnine and oxygen, and on Monday they thought he had turned the corner. He has had very little delirium, and was a most wonderful patient, so calm and placid, always inclined to take interest in what was going on, and always cheery and uncomplaining. On Monday he rallied for 24 hours, and then the temperature rushed up again, his lungs became affected and he was unable to struggle any more with the violence of the fever; it was then the 32nd day of it. I have never met anyone with a more charming disposition; he was so keen to learn all he could about India and was so intelligent. Everyone was devoted to him, he was an absolutely ideal eldest son and I am haunted by the misery of his poor family, it will break his mother's heart. He was treated for enteric from the first appearance of fever, and everything that was possible was done which is my one consolation and no one was ever nursed more devotedly. It is a great trial having this huge Christmas party in the house, but it can't be obviated.

Thursday, 31st December, 1908. Calcutta

The last day of a terribly full year. During the past three weeks a wonderful change has taken place in Bengal. Two days after passing the Anarchist Bill, nine men were deported.

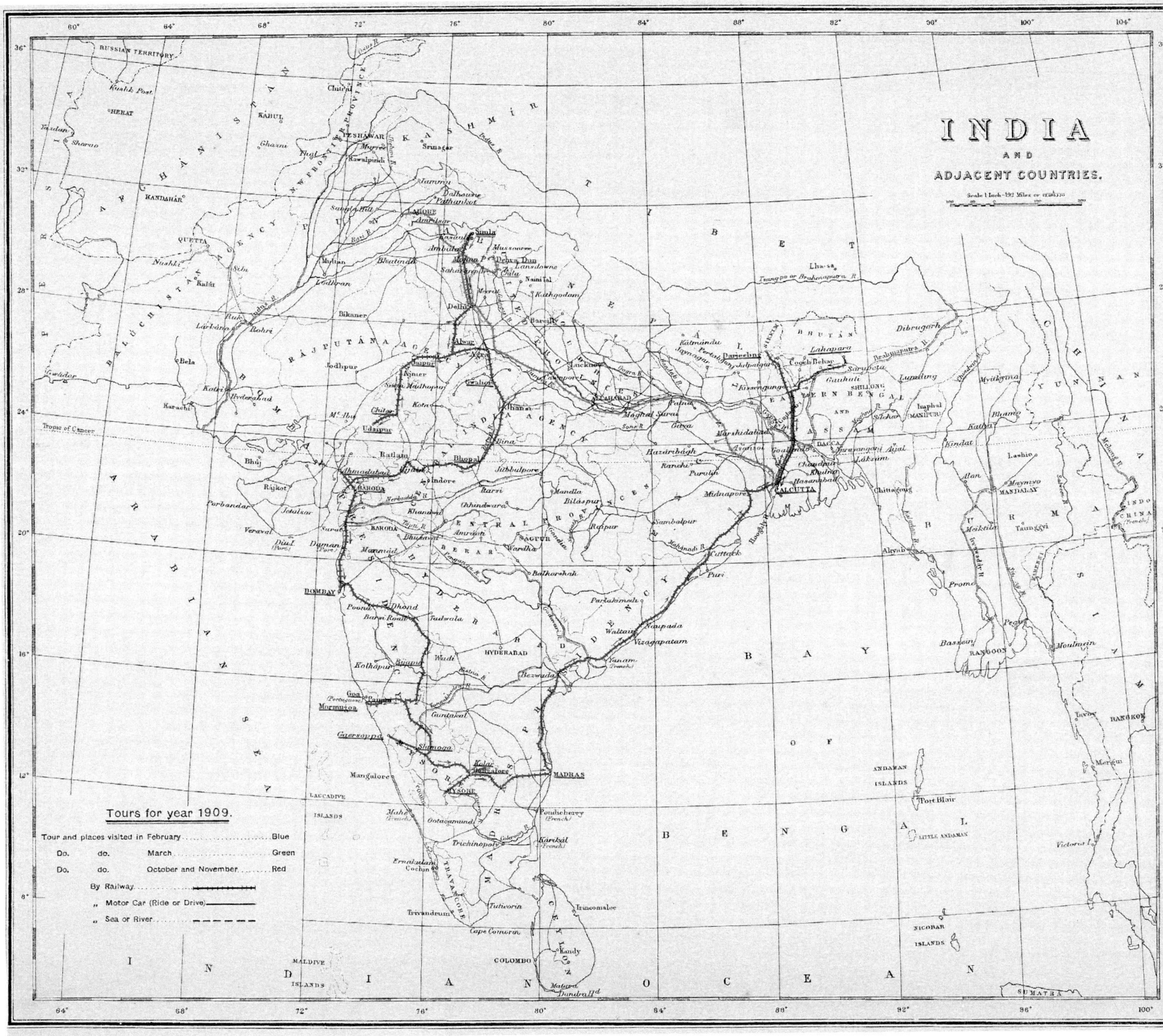

INDIA
AND
ADJACENT COUNTRIES.
Tours for year 1909.
Tour and places visited in February .... Blue
Do. do. March .... Green
Do. do. October and November .... Red
By Railway
„ Motor Car (Ride or Drive)
„ Sea or River

Then came the announcement of the Reforms which Rolly has been working at for the last two years with his Council. The details are too voluminous to record, but any one reading them must see that the entire work has been carried out by the Government of India and that Rolly has throughout adhered to the opinion he expressed two years ago to Lord Morley when he suggested that the Reforms must emanate entirely from India and that the Natives must not think a radical Government had forced the Government of India to agree to concessions they were unwilling to accept. The Reforms have been received in India with a chorus of approval. They are far more liberal than anyone anticipated. A few days after the announcement of the Reforms, Rolly received a most remarkable and representative deputation composed of all sorts of different political opinions, but all unanimous in supporting him.

1909

Friday, January 15th.

Maud Lansdowne arrived from Lucknow with Lord Freddy Hamilton.[204] Charlie has got a chill, and was not well enough to come with her. Maud remembers many of the old servants and notices every tiny change in the house. After dinner Rolly and I went to a party at the Museum to celebrate the 125th Anniversary of the Asiatic Society. We saw so many remarkable things that I can't attempt to describe them, from gigantic flat fish caught in the Bay of Bengal that contain in their bodies 80lb. of oil, to specimens of the minutest mosquitoes, some harmless, other spreading malarial germs. There were wonderful specimens of prehistoric documents, such as Buddha's farewell to his father; embroideries which were several hundred years old in William the Conqueror's time; and samples of clay that look like stones which the natives eat during the time of famine. This habit becomes incurable, and they crave for this sort of food as if it was a drug.

Monday, 18th.

Charlie Fitzmaurice arrived, still feeling very seedy. Colonel de Lisle during manoeuvres makes them swim the Gumtee on their horses; they then remain out all day in their wet clothes; it is therefore not surprising that fever should be rather prevalent. At 4 o'clock we went to the Cathedral and heard the rehearsal of some of the music. Government House is overflowing with guests. We gave a dinner party of 109 people at 10 round tables. It all went off admirably. Violet's table was decorated with violets. Afterwards we went up into the ball-room, where the presents were on view. There was a certain amount of dancing and I think everyone enjoyed themselves.

204. Former A.D.C. to Lord Lansdowne in Canada, where he introduced skiing as a sport, and India, author of the memoir *The Days before Yesterday*.

Map of tours, 1909.

Wednesday, 20th.

Arthur Guise and Mr Landon have returned from Burma. The Maharaja of Gwalior has also come to attend the wedding. The presents have all been arranged in the marble hall, and make the most splendid display. I have never seen any one calmer than Violet was, quite undismayed at the thoughts of the ceremony in which she had to act the chief part. We were kept busy the whole morning long with countless trifles, and just as I thought we should have ample time to array ourselves leisurely for the wedding, Violet's bouquet was brought for my inspection. Our own *malis*[205] had been most anxious to make it, and having seen all the flowers in the early morning and described exactly how I wanted it arranged, I did not anticipate their producing a small compact conical-shaped village bouquet of the most appalling description. There was nothing for it but to re-make it myself. Stiff wire and more flowers were somehow procured, rows of agitated *malis* handed me the sprays, and in 10 minutes we produced quite a passable bouquet with long trails of ferns and orange blossom, which Gould tied up with white ribbons. The day unfortunately was exceptionally hot which made any exertion an effort. I managed to toss on my clothes, and rush round to Violet's room to adjust her wedding veil, which was the same one as Ruby wore. She looked the greatest darling, really an ideal bride with her fair hair.

Charlie was fortunately a good deal better, but he has been a greatly pulled down by his illness, and dreaded the thoughts of the inevitable function. The ceremony passed off without a hitch of any kind. The Cathedral was beautifully decorated, but the smell of tuberoses was a trifle overpowering. The procession up the aisle was impressive. Rolly in full uniform and the best man supporting Charlie, standing on each side of the bride and bridegroom, made an effective group at the steps of the chancel. The three tiny pale blue bridesmaids, each holding a bunch of violets, played their part to perfection, and carried out their instructions with soldierly precision. The return procession through the lined streets was quite impressive, and the crowds seem thoroughly sympathetic and friendly. Violet only remained a short time in the marble-hall receiving congratulations; then Eileen and I helped her to change into a most becoming going away frock, and we all went into a huge shamiana together, in the centre of which stood the gigantic cake. After Violet had cut the first slice with a great deal of assistance, their health was proposed by Lord Kitchener and they drove off to Barrackpore leaving us very sad and lonely but thankful that everything had passed off so well.

Tuesday, 26th.

We gave a purdah tea party, which went off successfully. The ladies were delighted to have an opportunity of meeting Maud Lansdowne. The red servants were hidden away, and the bandsmen's wives made indifferent substitutes in dispensing the tea. Kitty Jones sang several songs to them. Then the Indian ladies wished to show their proficiency in the

Rhino shooting cartoons.

205. Gardeners.

musical line, and a long and dreary ditty went droning on for a considerable time. The only contretemps was due to the leg of a chair giving way, and one of the chief ladies being hurled to the ground with some violence. This naturally upset her considerably and her dignity was greatly wounded. She required a lot of soothing before the hysterical element passed off.

Thursday, February 11th. Camp Lahapara

We have had three thrilling days after rhino; it is a much more dangerous game than I realised, the result being that poor Colonel Victor is returning with a broken arm. The first day we went after a tiger. Rolly declared he was certain to break into the open in front of me, and sure enough a little in advance of the line of beating elephants, Rajee, who was in the howdah with me, pointed to the jungle grass moving mysteriously in our direction. I can't describe how one's heart beats with excitement and how long the seconds of anticipation seem before anything is visible. At last a flash of yellow appeared amongst the tall grass, I fired with a paradox, saw the tiger's white chest as he raised himself and then with a wild bound he dashed past our elephant into the jungle beyond us. I thought I had missed him; however every one else said he was hit, and with marvellous rapidity the line of elephants was formed up, surrounding the jungle, where Cooch Behar thought he was lying. Very soon we were made aware of his presence, as with a fearful growl he came out of a thick patch of grass, and made for Captain Jelf's elephant, smiting at his trunk with his mighty paw in passing. Then he made a desperate spring on to the hind leg of the next elephant. It is delicate work killing a tiger when he is hanging on to an elephant, however, Captain Jelf covered himself with glory and shot him through the heart and he fell down absolutely stone dead. My shot had gone right through his shoulder, so it seems extraordinary that any animal could go on as he did with such a huge bullet wound in a vital spot. There was a great deal of excitement, as the tiger had shown such fight. It was a tigress, not very big, about 8 feet 10. One of the Native clerks happened to be in a howdah with Major Herbert in the thick of the fray; he was heard to ejaculate from time to time: "My God, my God, but this is a dangerous sport." On being asked another day if he wished to accompany the shooting party, he said: "My God, no, what I have seen, I have seen".

Friday, March 12th.

Returned to Calcutta to see Violet off; it is too horrid to think it will be a year and a half before we can hope to meet again. I am thankful she is not going to lead the ordinary life of a soldier's wife in India, they have such difficulties to cope with and the account she gave of Charlie's quarters at Lucknow was not alluring; cupboards raised on bottles to defeat the inroads of white-ants and a general appearance of desolation, which, after the luxuries she has been accustomed to, would not have been easy to be enthusiastic about.

Rolly is greatly amused at receiving a telegram from Lord Morley asking about the status of women in harems in Native States; in reply Rolly tells him that he has imposed upon him a somewhat difficult duty and adds: "I will do my best! I think I told you that Scindia's Maharani sang: "Coming thro the rye to me from behind the purdah, but as yet I have not looked into the Zenana!"

We have just received the English papers with the account in the House of Lords of the Debate on the Indian Bill; it is too deep and complicated to go into. Lord Lansdowne and most of the old Indian peers greatly dislike the suggestion of a Native Member on the Viceroy's Council. St. John Brodrick made an excellent speech, and Lord Cromer appears to have accepted the idea of the Native Member. A friend, who is greatly interested in Indian matters, wrote to me by this mail and said that, "Lord Morley had not been astute about the Bill, having included the Executive Councils without Indian support. He plastered George Curzon with compliments and George Curzon then proceeded to tear the Bill to pieces".

Sunday, March 21st. Barrackpore.

England is in a state of agitation over our Navy, which is supposed to be totally inadequate. A German invasion is spoken of not only as possible but probable; a great deal of discussion is going on in the House as to the number of Dreadnoughts we require. We always seem to rush to extremes at once, but they say 200,000 German spies have employment in England, ready to take up arms at a moment's notice.

Wednesday, 24th.

The following announcement in the morning papers makes a landmark in Indian history: "It was officially notified in Calcutta on Tuesday evening that His Majesty the King-Emperor has been pleased to approve of the appointment of the Hon'ble Mr S.P. Sinha, Barrister-at-law, Advocate-General of Bengal, to be Legal Member of the Governor General's Council, in place of the Hon'ble Sir Erie Richards, who vacates that appointment in April." Mr Sinha is a most able man and has immense practice at the bar. He is making £20,000 a year; so it is most patriotic of him to give up this income in order to become a Member of Council on £5,000, but it shows what importance is attached to the prestige of this new departure.

Sunday, 28th.

Have been learning to drive the motor, and have been out for half an hour for the last three evenings with Thomas, who stands beside me on the step. There is a good deal of traffic on all the roads, so I find it quite exciting. Thomas keeps on assuring me that in a 40-horsepower I am travelling faster than I realise; no one except Eileen has so far shown any desire to accompany me.

All the staff and their belongings dined, and we had a biograph afterwards showing the wedding procession; it is very good, and it was quite amusing to watch oneself walking down the main stairs and getting into the carriage and driving off with the body-guard.

Thursday, 1st April.

We arrived at Amritsar at 8 A.M., and found an elaborately decorated station, the Commissioner, Mr Younghusband, and all the members of the Municipality to receive us. We started off in a magnificent blue and silver carriage, the property of the Maharaja of Kapurthala, who had kindly lent it for the occasion. The postillions were dressed in resplendent livery and the carriage was drawn by four enormous grey horses which Rolly declares are a French breed called Percheron. No doubt this splendid conveyance was evolved to do honour to the new beautiful Spanish Maharani whom Kapurthala[206] recently married and for whom a gorgeous French palace has been built. This Spanish wife accompanies him wherever he goes, for the simple reason that, if she were left at Kapurthala without his protection, she would in all probability be poisoned. We drove about two miles out of the town through avenues of Shesham trees to the Khalsa College. They gave us a most hearty reception in spite of rumours that this college had not escaped the wave of unrest which has recently swept over the majority of the educational institutions in this country. We then drove back to the city through narrow streets of the most picturesque

206. Anita Delgado Briones became the 5th wife of Jagatjit Singh of Kapurthala and was known as Prem Kaur.

description towards the golden temple. It is impossible to paint in adequate colours the bewildering beauty of these tortuous streets, the carved balconies and tall houses packed from pavement to roof with a tangled mass of enquiring humanity. What struck us most was the genuine smile of welcome which accompanied their salaams as we drove past, each one seemed anxious to receive a look of recognition, and the smile broadened and assumed a look of proud satisfaction if they felt that they had obtained a personal acknowledgment.

We alighted at the marble steps at the entrance to the tank, in the centre of which the golden temple is built. In an alcove with gold and silver chairs bowing attendants removed our desecrating shoes and replaced them with beautifully embroidered velvet slippers, suited to the gorgeous times of the Emperor Akbar. We walked round the tank over the marble causeway with hundreds of golden lamps, to the sacred temple in which rests the sacred Granth. Before it sat a young priest dressed in blue and silver, two satellites stood behind him and waved away the flies with yaks' tails. Inside the elaborately decorated temple all the priests sat round and prayed. Then the book was reverently opened, and the young high priest chanted out a few verses of the sacred words, while the other priests bowed their heads in prayer. The Viceroy's offering of a 1,000 rupees was given into the hands of one of the holy men, and he presented it before the Granth, chanting a verse in rhythm, while tiny silver bells tinkled, rose leaves were scattered all over us from the golden balcony above and the holy pigeons came flying around, cooing their soft accompaniment to the prayers of the priests. It was a unique sight, and one felt the charm of the old Eastern world and the fascination that belongs to bygone centuries. In those days there was time to worship and meditate, and any idea of Western customs forcing themselves with feverish rush and hurry upon the holy traditions of the past seemed sacrilege. I realised that we in our modern dresses were strangely out of place.

At another shrine we witnessed two boys going through the ceremony of initiation in order to become Sikhs. They stood below a highly carved balcony, while a priest, in crimson garments and black pughree with splendid features and a flowing white beard, chanted words to which they reverently responded. All the while he dropped water on them from a bowl. Finally they drank up what remained of the holy water, and demolished an amazing quantity of a sticky sugar concoction, and so they proudly took upon themselves the vows and became Sikhs. I felt sad at resuming the ordinary task of daily life which was inevitable when my own shoes were restored to me, and we turned our backs on the sacred precincts.

We spent 10 minutes in a carpet factory; it is most interesting seeing how the patterns are worked and the rapidity with which they manipulate the hundreds of strings, seemed most confusing. One man shouts out the orders for the stitches to the corresponding worker and describes the colour and the other follows his directions, while others read off their instructions from slips of paper. We had to leave Amritsar at 12 o'clock as we were due to arrive at Lahore at 1 o'clock. Our first official visit to the capital of the-Punjab means a big tamasha, and so it indeed proved to be.

Friday, 2nd.

At 8.30 we drove to the entrance of the city, and Rolly and I mounted a resplendent elephant with the most magnificent trappings, and a mahout clad in cloth of gold. Mahommed Khan and Taker Das, our Jemadars between them held a gorgeous red embroidered umbrella over our heads. There were not more than 10 elephants in all, but the procession was made far more imposing by an escort from various regiments. Rolly and I were sandwiched in between a large detachment of troops. We saw the old city of Lahore at its best, teeming with life and colour and for two hours we marched, bowing continuously to the right and to the left in response to the amazing outburst of enthusiasm with which we were greeted on all sides. Never before in India have we experienced anything like it. Sir Louis had received hundreds of letters begging him not to take the responsibility of allowing the Viceroy to risk going through the Native Bazaars, no Viceroy having ever done so before. Certainly at times we could almost touch the walls of the houses with our hands, and the balconies full of smiling little ladies were exactly on a level with our heads as we sat in the howdah. If they had wished to attempt an outrage nothing would have been easier, but the natives were evidently anxious to show that they knew Rolly was in sympathy with them, and that they were grateful. Hardly a house was without some welcoming token and thousands of

Arrival Lahore.

mottoes were stretched across the streets; on one was written: "Ripon,[207] Minto, Morley, England's greatest three, India sing their praises till eternity." We passed altogether 38 schools; here the cheering was deafening and the waving of flags enough to terrify both elephants and horses, but it was all most gratifying as there was undoubted proof of the good-will of the people. I have never enjoyed a two hours' ride more, and how I wished I could have photographed some of the effects and impressed them for ever on my brain.

At 5 o'clock we motored to the Aitchison College and saw all the boys drawn up in the big hall. Then we went on to the Shalimar Gardens for a garden party given by the Punjab Chiefs' Association. We received the inevitable address, most loyally worded, bringing in about the reforms, and the better feeling that now existed in the country. In replying Rolly said that when the air had been so full of political discussion together with anxieties as to the peaceful administration of the country, it was very encouraging to recognise in the Punjab Chiefs' Association a common effort on the part of those who are the natural leaders of the people of the province and who have the greatest stake in its prosperity to unite together in the representations of interests, which not only affect themselves, but the population amongst whom they live. Rolly then presented a Kaisar-i-Hind Medal to Faqir S. Qamr-ud-din, an old man of 93, whose father had been foreign minister to Ranjit Singh. His joy at receiving this honour from the Viceroy was quite touching.

Saturday, April 3rd, Lahore.

This is the exact moment to see Lahore; the fresh spring green only lasts about three weeks, so no doubt we are getting a most favourable impression. From the Fort we went to see the Badshahi Masjid, which is a splendid building with a magnificent hall decorated with marble and painted stucco, which is kept in excellent repair.[208] Then we visited Ranjit Singh's tomb which is enclosed in a raised marble edifice in another garden. We motored over the Ravi River on a bridge-of-boats, and drove through the most lovely palm avenues to the Shahdera, where Jahangir's tomb rests in a beautiful garden. The white marble is inlaid with many coloured stones and agates and remains in wonderful repair. The heat was getting excessive by this time, as it was past 11 o'clock, and I was beginning to get very weary and hungry. Nur Jahan, Light of the World, Jahangir's brilliant wife, who really ruled India for many years, is also buried in this garden. Her brother, who assisted her in the government, has also a mausoleum, the dome of which was covered with brilliant yellow tiles, but most of them have fallen off and the Government find it is too expensive to replace them while the art of producing these vivid colours has been lost.

---

207. 1st Marquess of Ripon, Liberal politician, Viceroy 1880-1884, Instigated reforms in education, land rights, local government. His regime is notable particularly for the Ilbert Bill, introduced to create equality between races under the law and for the repeal of the Vernacular Press Act that curtailed the freedom of the native Indian press.

208. Built by Emperor Aurangzeb and the largest mosque in the World until 1986.

To luncheon came Sirdar Ayub Khan,[209] the Amir's first cousin; he is marvellously like him in appearance. Should anything happen to the Amir, this man is next in succession. He seemed a quiet, modest man, shy about speaking English although he talks it fluently. He has 4 wives, 12 sons and 16 daughters. He has a cousin who rivals Solomon in the number of his wives and family; 74 daughters and 56 sons. The number would rather cripple most estates with the present death duties in addition to portions for the younger children of several generations.

General Sir O'Moore Creagh[210] has been appointed Commander-in-Chief when Lord Kitchener retires in September. We don't know him personally. Some people swear by him, others say he is a wild Irishman and cannot be taken seriously.

Sunday, 4th

The first anniversary of Ruby's wedding day. Cabled our congratulations and received an answer quite quickly; it is always a joy to feel we are in touch with the family by getting news the same day although 7,000 miles apart. It was such a relief to have a quiet morning after our strenuous days. Did nothing till we went to the Museum and School of Art at 4 o'clock; the former has a most interesting collection; amongst other things some admirably modelled figures done by Rudyard Kipling's father, who lived at Lahore. Princess Bamba Dulip Singh[211] came to have tea with me, she is supposed to be a very seditious lady, and has never called upon the Danes; her reputation is none of the best, but as she suggested coming we thought it better to propitiate her. We kept off all dangerous subjects; she has quite an attractive personality. Her brother, Prince Victor Dulip Singh, arrived at Bombay this year, and a great fuss was made with him. Rolly, however, refused him permission to go to the Punjab, as he might be a dangerous element at this moment. Old Sir Pertab Singh, who is the most popular native in India, happened to be in Bombay with his polo-team at the time. In his strange expressive English he said of Prince Victor: "Me no liking him, him looking like buffalo." Our visit came to an end after dinner

Tuesday, 13th April. Chila Camp

Captain Mackenzie and I left by special for Chila at 3 o'clock. Captain Keighley and the police officer, Mr Straight, met us at the station, and we rode to the camp on elephants, which we had to change en route as we crossed a very wide part of the Ganges by boat.

209. Victor of Battle of Maiwand in 1880 in the 2nd Anglo-Afghan War, beaten later that year by General Roberts at Kandahar.

210. General Sir Garrett O'Moore Creagh VC, C-in-C 1909-1914.

211. Daughter of Maharaja Duleep Singh, last Maharaja of Lahore, and granddaughter of the Lion of the Punjab, Ranjit Singh.

There is a place four miles down the river, from here called Hardwar, where the Hindus hold their great melas or fairs. Thousands of pilgrims come from all parts of India to bathe in the sacred river. Three big festivals have taken place in the last six weeks, one only occurs every 14 years,[212] another every 8, so it is curious that they should all have fallen so close together. At this moment 300,000 pilgrims are at Hardwar encamped all over the place. From 30 to 40 special trains bring a daily influx of pilgrims, and as a natural consequence from such numbers, cholera has begun. As I rode past the river en route to the camp, I saw three large smouldering fires, consuming the charred remains of the dead. Beside one fire, a corpse was lying all bound up in yellow cotton; a man was anointing it with holy water before flinging it upon the pile. A most disagreeable smell pervaded the place where this gruesome work was going on; the fires were being racked together by sundry attendants, and occasionally broke out into flames.

Saturday, 17th. Chila Camp.

The beat was eight miles off. The elephants were sent on early, and the whole party started off riding. I reminded Rolly that I was a novice on a man's saddle, and begged him to have some consideration for me. The grassy glade I suppose was too much temptation for him, the going was excellent and after looking round once or twice to see if I was still in the saddle, he started off at a gallop, and we did over eight miles in three quarters of an hour! The sun was intensely hot, the day very close and oppressive. I had taken the precaution of bringing a thin cotton shikari suit to change into, and we started on elephants for the beat. During luncheon the hills became hidden by ominous black clouds, and our long line of elephants was proceeding across a huge plateau when the storm burst with all its fury. A hurricane of wind blew, a veritable deluge descended, and in every direction huge streaks of forked lightning seemed to be striking the earth. I got off my pad elephant, into a howdah with Captain Mackenzie; we were all holding our rifles loaded with cordite

Cartridges, and we might as well have held lightning conductors, but even without the rifles the howdahs have so much iron that the danger wasn't greatly accentuated. I wasn't much reassured by being told that during a storm in Simla, Captain Mackenzie had come upon two people lying dead in the road, having been struck by lightning. The noise was deafening and besides the forks of flame, flashes of light seemed to break out in all directions. The shed where the ponies were was fortunately barely half a mile away, and at last we reached it in safety. It belonged to professional cattle-lifters called Gujjars; inside there were several men and children, and a woman sitting by a fire, her arms covered with silver bangles. Cows were chewing grass, cocks and hens strutted about, pariah dogs sniffed at us, syces with some of our horses, and several of the body-guard were huddled together inside the shed.

212. The Kumbh Mela pilgrimage is celebrated at each of 4 locations, Hardwar, Allahabad, Ujjain, and Nasik, every 3 years, returning to each after 12 years. An Ardh (half) Kumbh takes place in each location every 6 years.

We crowded under the shelter of the thatched roof, the most sorry-looking company I have ever seen.

Rolly said I should die if I tried to ride home in my saturated clothes. My change was produced from a dripping bag that had been in my howdah; but how was it possible to change before such a crowd of people? With marvellous ingenuity two charpoys (beds) were seized and placed in an upright position, while my friend, the native officer, held a blanket across them as a screen. Behind this I was to disrobe. I still hesitated, there was a space of about three feet showing from the ground, but the cattle-stealer's wife threw herself into the breach and came and stood before me. I wonder what nationality she thought I belonged to. All the dye had come off my lower garments and had stained my legs green, my clothes couldn't have been wetter if I had fallen into the river, and I never was so grateful for anything as when I was arrayed comparatively dry in my riding things. The storm had by this time abated, and we enjoyed the ride home; I went to bed till dinner, but to my amazement was hardly at all stiff, which after galloping 16 miles was very surprising.

It was very amusing when our dangers were a thing of the past, discussing what our feelings had been in the moment of peril. We all agreed that as long as the Viceroy held on to his rifle, the rest of the party were in duty bound to follow suit. Rolly declared that he would have given a thousand pounds to get rid of it, but his *izzat*[213] forbade his taking such a course. The police officer was heard to mutter, "Oh dear, oh dear, I know this wetting will bring on a bilious attack," and so I was told it had, but that he had cured it with a large glass of kummel in the early hours of the morning! Captain Jelf, who is careful to take precautions against a chill which might bring on fever, had brought a little woollen jacket with him, in spite of the great heat when we started. This unfortunately was of no use to him, as it was saturated before he had time to put it on. Great anxiety was felt regarding his health, but on his return to camp he imbibed so much whisky and hot water that he couldn't remember if he was in

213. Honour.

Surnais on ganges.

the 60th or the body-guard by the end of the evening. We saw a most wonderful shooting star as we were sitting out after dinner. It started with a long red tail, and ended in about a dozen large green balls of flame. It was more like a superior Crystal Palace rocket than a star. I have never seen anything to approach it before.

Sunday, 18th.

We pic-nicked on an island, and after luncheon floated down the river on mussacks. It is a very primitive way of locomotion. A charpoy is tied to two inflated bullocks. Two men lie across two other mussacks, holding them together, their legs revolve round which form the paddles, and so we proceeded five miles down-stream, the occasional rapids making it quite a pleasant experience. We returned to Dehra after a very pleasant week in the jungle, and found Eileen, Xandra and Tiger all eager to hear our experiences. In Europe there seems to be nothing but rumours of wars, and in Turkey a civil war seems to be raging.

Wednesday, 21st.

We were all to have gone to Mohand camp today, but there have been such a succession of storms that we have had to put off our departure. On Monday night it was so cold we had fires. On Tuesday at luncheon time the heat necessitated punkhas, and by tea time we were all putting on thick tweed suits. The temperature is 20 degrees lower than usual at this time of year throughout India. In Lucknow they had five inches of rain in a few hours. It looks as if the rains had commenced two months too soon. We have passed the time riding, motoring and playing golf. Goold was very upset at seeing a funeral procession coming from a tiny native hut in the compound not 20 yards from her tent. We made enquiries and found that the wife of the sweeper who remains on the place had died 10 days after the birth of her sixth baby. It seems so awful that we should have known nothing of it till she was dead, with a doctor at her door who probably could have saved her life, but it is impossible to force assistance on a native, as they have no belief in our methods. Captain Mackenzie found out that the husband was earning Rs. 6 a month, which doesn't sound riches to clothe and feed himself and six children. We gave him Rs. 30, nearly half a year's pay, so the poor widower has now become a *parti*.[214]

Wednesday 28th. Dehra Dun. Circuit House.

There has been a remarkable demonstration in favour of Mr Sinha throughout India; his appointment as Member of the Viceroy's Council is a turning point in Indian history, which most people at home contemplate with dismay. It may be interesting to look back to in after

Rolls Royce Dehra Dun.

214. A good marriage prospect.

years, when we have the means of knowing if the majority of Anglo-Indians now in India are right in being sanguine as to the result of the reforms, or if they have been attended with disaster as the home press and the British public, who take their tone from the man in the street, without any real knowledge, predicts. I am afraid Rolly will continue to have an anxious time. Morley cannot realise that be knows nothing of Indian conditions and is trying to work out the detail of the reforms at home. Mr Hobhouse has already made several misleading statements in the House implying that the Government of India approve of certain proposals which they have so far not even considered. The regulations of the Bill will have to be carefully thought out by the Government of India, and if the House of Commons interferes, chaos can be the only result.

Thursday, 29th.

When this house was built by an English officer a few years ago, the grounds were supposed to be haunted by the spirit of a holy man who is said to be buried under a tree in the garden, the place being marked by a white stone. It seems that all the servants think the fakir's spirit walks about appearing to people and they firmly believe that the ghost has appeared to the Viceroy. Today at sunset all the Mahommedan servants flocked round the fakir's tomb, burnt sandalwood, intoned chants, and prostrated themselves repeatedly before the stone. Colonel Dunlop discussed the performance with his old bearer while dressing for dinner, and asked if they were praying for the peace of the soul of the holy man, and invoking blessings upon themselves. The old bearer is rather a character, and answered: "Some may

have been praying as the Sahib suggests, all I know is, that I hurried to the spot to see what was going on, and heard three Khidmatgars praying for an increase of their wages." I had been so impressed by the solemnity of the ceremony which I had watched with interest and the worldly aspect thus thrown upon it certainly detracts from the genuine motives of the religious enthusiasts.

Tuesday, 11th May.Simla

Rolly and I were going for a walk on Friday before tea, with the three dogs Dandy, Dehra, and Tashi when a little fox-terrier appeared on the lawn and suddenly made for Tashi, who was standing just in front of us, he rolled her over, and tried to bite her. Rolly belaboured him with his stick and the dog made off. We both examined Tashi; there was a good deal of saliva on her sides, but we found no wounds. I had gloves on, Rolly of course had not. We neither of us had ever seen the dog before, but the chaprassies told us he belonged to Olivier, the Chef. We consequently thought no more about it and continued our walk, after which we played tennis. It gave me rather a turn on our return, from Annandale late on Saturday evening, to meet Olivier's dog, heavily chained and raving mad, being taken along by several men to execution. It seems Olivier thought the dog was behaving curiously on Friday morning, but he ran away and never re-appeared till we met him on the lawn. He bit Eileen's Ayah and a chaprassie before Olivier could catch him and was then sent to the dispensary, chained up and watched. He was found to be in an advanced stage of rabies, so he had to be killed. Meanwhile Colonel Crooke insisted that the head of the Kasauli Pasteur Institute should be sent for to pronounce if there was any risk to Rolly, who had had his hand covered from the saliva when he was examining Tashi. The doctor, Captain Carter, quite a young man, arrived on Monday morning, and said there was no question it was essential that we should both undergo the treatment. He says that if the poison dries on one's hand or glove, and that one unconsciously touches one's eyes or mouth, that one can be infected. He asked me if I could guarantee that I had not put my hand to my face, which of course was impossible. They have reduced the treatment to a fine art and as far as I can gather we shall not be much inconvenienced.

We had our first injection on Monday afternoon, three incisions just above the waist, nothing very awful, although it leaves a feeling of tenderness. Our only restrictions are no violent exercise or alcohol. The Chef is also undergoing the treatment, the dog having scratched the back of his hand with his teeth. Tashi also is being treated. The Ayah and chaprassie have gone to Kasauli. The Ayah adores dogs; she always fondles every one she meets. The other day Eileen seeing her with Tashi in her arms remarked on her love of animals, upon which Phyllis answered: "Oh yes, my lady, my stomach is full of them." Captain Carter has many blood-curdling anecdotes of people getting hydrophobia who have not undergone the treatment. Last year two sisters in Simla had a cat who went mad, one was bitten and went to Kasauli, the other was only scratched and refused to have the treatment. She was at a tennis party six months afterwards and had played six sets, when this awful rabies came on, and she died in agony. There is a far larger percentage of rabies in Simla than in any other part of India, the jackals bite the pariah dogs and they spread it around. Captain Carter tells me he was treating an old lady of 84 and a baby of 18 months at Kasauli when he left.

Thursday, 20th.

Poor Lady Duff is most terribly upset at her husband not being selected as Commander-in-Chief. She wears deep mourning as a proof of her sorrow, and goes nowhere except to church. She sits looking tragic in Lord Kitchener's pew and admits that she attends so regularly in order to pray for Sir O'Moore Creagh's death. The subject that excites the military circles in Simla at this moment is the appointment of Major Wilson to be Military Secretary to Sir O'Moore Creagh. We don't know him personally, his nick-name of "Scatter"[215] is said to describe him; he is a junior Major in the Army and all the Generals and Colonels are pulling long faces, as an enormous amount of power rests with the Military Secretary and no one appreciates the prospect of having to go to Major Wilson's office hat in hand. Those who know him say he has brains, but has never done a stroke of work and has never taken anything seriously in his life. He married Babara Lister, who came out to India for a short time, two years ago, but always hated it and declared it was a country unfit for white men to live in, so I hardly think she will accompany him.

We have just completed our second course of treatment, but we still have to guard against cold, and Colonel Crooke kept following me urging me to "keep off the grass"; it sounded like a joke and in any case it was almost an impossibility to stick to strips of red carpet. I was explaining to a Mrs Irvine, why Colonel Crooke was showing so much anxiety on my account, and she said with a beaming smile: "Of course, you are undergoing the Pasteur treatment, do you like it ?" I felt my glance was withering and my tone icy, as I pointed out that it would be curious for anyone to enjoy going through such an ordeal.

Our family at home have evidently not been in throes of anguish over our condition. We have had crowds of telegrams from Indian Princes and officials, including one from Chang from the Chinese Legation, whose identity we have had difficulty in ascertaining. Morley was greatly fussed lest the current of work should he suspended for a few days. It is extraordinary how tactless people are in enlarging on the horrors of their experiences of innoculation. Sir Fleetwood Wilson[216] regaled Rolly with every sort of symptom which

---

215. Scatters' was apparently so-called because of his habit of carelessly leaving money about a room. Cynthia Asquith described him as a "funny, ebullient bounder" and Lady Diana Cooper "a dashing soldier" who, as a child, she had found "funnier than any of the clowns" and who in later life "could still keep the table of all ages in a roar." He was a bad judge of horseflesh and of business and the lover of the 2nd Lady Curzon among others. After Curzon's death Gracie was ably assisted by Scatters in running through the money she had been left by her husband. His youngest son, Peter, was expelled from Eton for breaking bounds while 'associating' with Tallulah Bankhead—he later became chairman of Sotheby's.

216. Financial Member of the Council, author of *Letters to Nobody* and *Letters to Somebody*, died in 1940 aged 90.

he had gone through while being treated in Paris. His depression he said was so great, that he narrowly escaped committing suicide, and even decided that flinging himself under a train would be an easy and effectual method of terminating life. Another man told me of two friends of his who went on a shooting expedition to Kashmir after going through the treatment, one became covered with boils and the other had fits! Meanwhile for two days Rolly was sunk in an abyss of despondency, and declared his constitution was ruined, but he has become quite cheerful again, and looks forward with hope to the future, although we have got to be more or less careful for another fortnight. It's an ill wind, and no doubt good will come out of our adventure, as stringent orders have been issued to have the pariah dogs and jackals killed down, and many suggestions are being made to enforce a stricter supervision of all dogs.

Sunday, 23rd.

England is plunged in despair over the Budget. The taxes in order to raise the 16 millions deficit seems chiefly to hit the landowners and the brewers. The Duke writes to Francis that he will have to give up the hounds.[217] There is to be an extra 20 per cent on land and such appalling death duties that no one in future will be able to live on their properties. I still hope that we may be able to open a corner of Minto when we get home but the outlook is anything but rosy. Lord Morley, writing on April 7th, in alluding to the Budget, says:

> "You own land, so I must bid you tremble a little. But then you don't derive profits, I surmise, from public houses, nor restaurants, not grocers' licenses, so you will not turn a hair at the fates of those interests."

Louisa is at Malta with the King and Queen; the former is still very depressed about the Native Member.

Monday, May 24th.

An Agent from Kabul arrived, bringing Rolly an extremely nice gold cigar-case from the Amir; it is quite plain and in the best possible taste, with the accompanying letter:

> Ark, Kabul, 5th May 1909.
>
> MY DEAR AND ESTEEMED FRIEND LORD MINTO,
>
> It is long since I have not the pleasure of perusing neither of my friend's nor Her Excellency Lady Minto's private letters; therefore I have the pleasure to send this letter as reminding and a set of cigar gold case as remembrance.

217. Francis' Father, the Duke of Buccleuch refused to pay the guinea subscription to his local football club on grounds of the impact of the new land taxes.

If my friend wants to know about me, I am sorry to say that it is four months and six days since I am suffering from gout. It is in such a state that, if I get better for two days and walk, the other ten days I lay in bed. In every case we must hope in God. I hope it will be convenient to my friend to tell my salaams to Her Excellency Lady Minto and ask her on my side about her good health.

Your friend,

SIRAJ-UL MILLATI-WADDIN.

It is hard to believe that this man is the barbarian which, if the reports that come from Kabul are true, they prove him to be.

Tuesday, 25th.

Gave a dinner of 60. Mr Sinha, the new Member of Council, took me in. He is extremely pleasant, and might be an Englishman from the way he reviews the whole situation in India. He is intensely broad-minded and discussed the impossibility of any Indian rule without British protection. "If the English left India in a body," he said, "we should have to telegraph to Aden and get them to return as fast as they could, India would be in a state of chaos in a couple of days." He discussed the tremendous mistake Lord Morley has made in suggesting electoral colleges. He said: "If only they had left things alone in England, and accepted His Excellency's proposals, the Mahommedans were prepared to be perfectly satisfied. Now all these questions have been raised in England, and Lord Minto will be expected to get them out of the scrape. All Indians have such a thorough belief in him, that no doubt he may be able to save the situation." It is annoying for Rolly having these difficulties made for him. I think he means to send for the leading Mahommedans in order to have a consultation, but they are asking for many more concessions now than they at first expected.

Wednesday 26th.

The Reverend J. Bateson came to luncheon to say good-bye before leaving India. He will be a terrible loss; he has done wonders with the Army, and has raised the total of teetotallers to 45 per cent. He has worked so hard, his health has quite broken down, so he is obliged to go home.

Had a long talk to Captain Patterson, Political Agent at Wano in Waziristan, who is here for a week's holiday. Wano is the home of the Mahsuds; they are the most troublesome tribes on the frontier. It must be terribly trying having to depend for protection on a guard raised from tribesmen who may at any minute turn and shoot you. The officers play tennis surrounded by soldiers, and whereas 15 years ago a couple of *sowars* were sufficient protection in going from one station to another, Captain Patterson had an escort of 200 men on leaving Wano. The number of rifles they have obtained is most alarming; 10 years ago they had about 30 in the district, now they have 10,000 of the most modern description, in fact they have better arms than our militia. Everyone thinks that sooner or later there must be a fearful blow up. People who know the frontier say we are courting disaster by refusing to accept our responsibilities in not making roads and forts. Captain Patterson told me the natives have often asked him when the British were going to leave the country; he answered that they meant to stay. "Then why don't you rule it?" they ask.

Friday, 28th

Opened a Sale of Work at the Town Hall for the benefit of the Salvation Army. Commissioner Booth Tucker received me looking appalling in a kind of native costume of salmon colour and red.[218] Lord Kitchener came to tea with me; we discussed the situation in India and England for about two hours. He was in his most charming mood. I think he will be sad at leaving India, although he feels that he has been here long enough. He is going to travel home quite alone via China, Japan, and America. He means to grow a beard and fondly imagines no one will recognise him. He has had A.D.C.s looking after him for the last seven years, during which time he has never had one farthing of money in his pocket, so I think there is every likelihood of his being arrested for not being able to pay his cabs. We formulated a scheme for him to start a bank in Switzerland where income taxes do not exist, through this means he thinks we shall be able to invest our money, and escape the wholesale robbery of the new duties proposed in the Budget.

Rolly and I have completed our Pasteur course, for which we are supremely thankful. We have overwhelmed Captain Carter with thanks, and presented him with a large silver token of our gratitude. He tells us that we have been excellent patients, neither of us being afflicted with nerves. It certainly pulls one down a good deal, and takes away all desire to exert oneself.

Sunday, 30th, Whitsunday, Mashobra

The King's horse Minoru has won the Derby: a Sergeant Penn in the 12th Lancers has won the Calcutta Derby Sweep. Major Crawley tells me he is a charming man, almost a gentleman; he advised him when he drew the favourite to sell a certain amount, which he did. He has however realised £25,000, and is leaving the Army. He has given about 100 pounds to the regiment in treating the men. Violet Crawley heard from the wife yesterday saying that, in spite of this, there was so much jealousy she almost regretted having won the money. They are going home at once and mean to give their two little boys a good education.

218. Frederick Tucker was in the ICS until he joined the Salvation Army in 1881. His 2nd wife was Emma Booth, daughter of the founder, William Booth, whose name he added to his own and with his fellow Salvationists in India adopted Indian dress and an Indian name, Fakir Singh.

Sunday, 6th

The King writes to Rolly in the most depressed frame of mind on account of the Native Member of Council; he seems to think that it means the downfall of the Empire, and he says the letter of explanation written by Rolly going into the whole question has not convinced him. The Prince of Wales writes in the same strain, but in a less despondent spirit. He says that Charlie is making a most efficient equerry and that he is very glad to have him with him. Louisa writes from Athens, where she is with the Queen. She says the heat is terrific and she was not enjoying herself, the novelty has now worn off as she has been there several times before, and this year the number of royalties assembled has been overpowering.

Sunday, 13th.

Received a very satisfactory mail from England. Francis heard a most delightful story about Antrim. A Salvation Army enthusiast went up to him and asked him if he was saved. This question was received with a volley of violent oaths. The Salvationist asked Antrim what he objected to in his religion, upon which he responded, "It isn't you religion I object to but your d----d vulgarity and your dirty hands".

We rode towards Naldera and paid a visit to old Sir Alfred Mackenzie. He has got a house on a ridge with a wonderful view of both ranges of mountains. The house itself was a terrible chamber of horrors with an exceptionally nice picture here and there. His strawberries, however, were quite beyond criticism.

Monday, 14th.

The whole of our party dined with Lord Kitchener, a dinner of 50. The Birdwoods brought in a few people afterwards, and we danced. Lord K- was in the most tremendous spirits. A delightful valse was being played, so I went up to him and asked him to have a turn; he declared his damaged leg would give way, but on my pressing him he said: "All right, I'll try, if you will take the risk," upon which we flew round the room. I shall never forget the look of amazement on the faces of his staff, Colonel Birdwood told me he had been with the Chief for nine years and had never seen him dance before. We had two turns, and the next valse I made him dance with Eileen, but that rather ended in disaster. Captain Fisher got his spur through Eileen's skirt, which he tore to ribands. Lord Kitchener remained erect as a tower supporting Eileen, but Captain Fisher, I imagine, from terror at having cannoned into the C-in-C, let his partner, Mrs Wingfield, fall with some violence on the floor! After this Lord K- insisted on my dancing a Kitchen Lancers and from his behaviour last night I have no doubt he will frequent every London ball-room in the future.

Sunday, 20th.

The Political Officer from Bhopal is staying in Simla. He met Captain Mackenzie and was discussing our programme during our visit to Bhopal. "One afternoon", he said, "the Begum suggests giving up to shooting." "Really", said Captain Mackenzie, "what sort of shooting is it?"

"Clay pigeons," answered Mr Bailey. "The Begum has purchased a gun; she has ordered 4,000 cartridges, and wishes to have a shooting match with Her Excellency. She has had an enclosure made which is strictly purdah." This information was rather a shock to me; in the first place I never can hit a clay pigeon, and if the Begum is beginning now to dispose of her 4,000 cartridges by practising every day, I shall not have much chance against her. I think the only sound thing will be to leave my gun behind. The Begum is a most determined person, and will probably insist on practising till she rivals Lord de Grey,[219] but I expect there will be several vacancies in her suite before she gets accustomed to handling a gun.

Reuter telegraphs from London that there are rumours in the lobby of the House of Commons that Lord Minto has asked to be allowed to resign owing to stress of work, the newspapers out here have all written very indignant articles that a reliable news agency should publish disquieting statements without the slightest foundation. A short time ago a canard was started that Winston Churchill was going to succeed us. This brought forth a torrent of abusive language from all the newspapers, which showed that he would not be received with open arms in India. It would be interesting to know who starts these rumours, and for what reason it is done. Sir Lawrence Jenkins has taken up his appointment of Chief Justice in Calcutta, and so far has rather startled everyone with his extreme partisanship for the native. He is remitting sentences and is making the position of the police extremely difficult, they have a most difficult part to play; as they are nearly all native, and if they give information run the risk of assassination.

Monday, 28th.

The leading Mahommedans have been in Simla and have been meeting the members of the Reform Committee. Rolly interviewed the three principal ones yesterday. The discussion was most amicable, and the result extremely satisfactory. The full text of their decision will not be published for three weeks, as they have to meet their colleagues in consultation. It will be a tremendous triumph for Rolly if he gets the 60 million Mahommedans in India to agree to his proposals, and it will be such a snub for the little handful of Moslems in England and the Aga Khan, who have made trouble with Morley. They all realize out here that the scheme has been nearly wrecked by Morley's suggestion of electoral colleges which he has

219. Earl de Grey, 2nd Marquess of Ripon, one of the greatest game shots of all time. Shooting at Sandringham with Edward VII he shot 28 pheasants in 60 seconds and dropped dead in his butt on 22nd September 1923 after shooting 51 grouse in 1 drive.

now withdrawn, but this caused them to raise many objections which had not occurred to them before. However, if everything goes well now the success will be all the greater.

Tuesday, 29th June.

Ever since we landed in India we have been well aware that there is an organised campaign on the part of a certain clique, connected with the Times, and several other papers, to write down the present Indian administration. They have been watching keenly for the slightest slip, hoping to make capital out of it, and they have continually wilfully misrepresented the policy of the Indian Government. If some successful measure cannot be overlooked, they ignore the Viceroy, and give the credit to an official, either at home or in India, who has had nothing whatever to do with it.

The frontier causes trouble, but it always has and always will, till we take upon ourselves a civilising influence and accept our responsibilities, but here the Home Government ties our hands, and no attempt is made to improve the condition of things. Sir George Roos-Keppel says that before we can really obtain much influence over the tribes we shall have to give them a good hammering, and prove our superiority. Hitherto we have always walked out of the country as soon as hostilities cease, which the tribesmen interpret as a sign of weakness.

Quite the most difficult task Rolly has had, has been to keep in harmony with the Secretary of State, to put forcibly before him the conditions and requirements of the country, and to convince him as to the necessity of certain measures, often wholely distasteful to his radical mind and the liberal views of the free-born Englishman. When history comes to be written, the letters that have passed between the Unionist Viceroy and the Radical Secretary of State will reveal quite an unexpected condition of things. The courtesy of their correspondence is remarkable. By degrees the Secretary of State has begun to realise the immense difficulties attached to the office of Viceroy, and the dictatorial tone has greatly decreased. Indignation is expressed at the Socialist Members of Parliament who attack the necessary action of the Government, while an almost pathetic note of regret creeps in that so little sympathy and understanding is shown by old political colleagues. The letters will some day be very interesting reading, and I wish they could be published before we are all dead.

The debate on the Indian military administration took place in the House of Commons. Lord Curzon made his attack. The contention is that the Commander-in-Chief being the sole Military Member of Council, he becomes an autocrat, that the scheme is not working, that there is a great congestion of business, that the Commander-in-Chief cannot possibly carry out satisfactorily the enormous work put upon him and that it will be impossible for him to acquaint himself, as he should do, with Native troops. As a matter of fact, the machinery has worked perfectly during this past year. All the heads of the various military departments have done their work most efficiently and Lord Kitchener says himself that he has less work to do than he had under the old system. Anyhow he rarely works after 12 noon, so the labours are not so incessant. He was rather amusing about Lord Curzon's accusation that the C-in-C must become an autocrat. "How is it possible," he said, "when every important file has to be submitted by the Military Member for the sanction of the Viceroy? What about the Viceroy being an autocrat?" This fact did not seem to endanger the Empire in Lord Curzon's eyes when he held the reins of office.

Friday, July 2nd.

Horrified at the terrible crime that has been perpetrated in London. Colonel Dunlop was a great personal friend of Sir Curzon-Wyllie's and is terribly upset at this ghastly outrage.[220] It is curious that, after devoting his life to improving the status of the Indians, Sir Curzon should himself fall a victim to their vile anarchical plots. It will be very interesting to see what effect this will have in England. Morley remained very calm during the Muzafferpore murders, and the three attempts on Sir Andrew Fraser's life, and the various police assassinations which have taken place in India, which made us realise that we were in the forefront of the battle out here. Now this crime perpetrated in London will bring it home to them, and I daresay will simplify the prosecution of justice, and make the role of Mackerness, Cotton & Co.[221] less popular in the House of Commons. Rolly has met both Dhingra's bothers who live in India; they are exceedingly well-to-do, clever people, one is a doctor at Amritsar and recently wrote a book which he dedicated to Rolly. Poor man! He has telegraphed in most terrible distress at his brother's awful crime.

Friday, 9th.

Rolly's birthday; he has not been at all well for a fortnight and has at last been persuaded to take a day off in bed, which I am sure will do him good. It is quite a relief to see him reading "The Man from Snowy River"[222], which Eileen has given him as a birthday present, instead of grinding over his inexhaustible files.

Friday, 16th.

The meeting of the Viceroy's Council commenced at 11 o'clock. There was a tremendous discussion about the Mahommedan representation. Lord Kitchener was very anxious to

220. Sir William Curzon-Wyllie, former Indian Army officer and government administrator, mainly in Rajputana, was Political A.D.C. to the Secretary of State for India and closely involved with Indian nationals in England. He was assassinated by the student, Madanlal Dhingra, at the Imperial Institute while attending an event organised by the National Indian Association on 1st July, 1909.

221. Liberal MPs and Indian Civil Rights campaigners.

222. 1890 poem by Australian, Banjo Paterson.

give the Mahommedans 8 seats on the Legislative Council, Rolly will only consent to 6 but they have the option of standing for election and the Viceroy has the power of nominating 2, which they will be given to understand he will do if they fail to obtain any seats on the general electorates. This anyhow gives them 8 seats and a possibility of 11. Rolly thinks this a more diplomatic way of giving them fair representation and with less likelihood of offending the Hindus, and if only the Home Government don't interfere, he thinks he has satisfied both Hindus and Mahommedans, although one never knows what stumbling blocks may arise. The final suggestions of the reform scheme are now going home to receive the sanction of the Secretary of State.

Wednesday, 21st.

Rolly at last seems to be quite well again; he is much thinner and only weighs 10.6. He had a couple of sets of tennis today; he has not played for quite a month.

Friday, 23rd.

Sir George Roos-Keppel very strongly advised my going to an American dentist, called Smith, in preference to our usual English dentist named Jones, as he considered the former more up to date; they live within 20 yards of each other. Having a tooth that needed stopping and chaperoned by Colonel Crooke, I went to Smith and gave myself up to his tender mercies. Without looking at my teeth, he advanced with the horrid whirling foot machine, which he rammed into my mouth. I immediately realised to my dismay that his hands were shaking as if he had the palsy, and that he was trying to steady them by my jaw. I managed to make him remove the instrument before the wheel had done serious damage. Before I had time to make any remark he said, "I am terribly disappointed I can do no work today, but I fell against a bit of furniture just before you arrived and hurt my arm which I am now unable to keep steady." I expressed regret rather coldly, as the left hand was shaking just as much as the right and I have since heard that Smith is drunk six days out of seven. I was unlucky in not striking the seventh day. I beat a hurried retreat and he no doubt saw the carriage drive up to Mr Jones's, who did what was required with a perfectly steady hand much to my relief.

Sunday, 25th.

Colonel Dunlop has received such a wonderfully touching letter from poor Lady Curzon Wyllie, marvellously brave and only wishing to be worthy of her husband. She says she was gratified at receiving a cable from the Resident at Mount Abu saying "all Rajputana mourn with you," and every Chief telegraphed to her individually. Poor woman, she says she never can forget the awful sight and adds: "Thank God I have been kept from bitter thoughts, he died for the India he loved." One of Eileen's letters contained the following rather amusing story: "An American lady given to the study of philosophy was introduced to the King at Ascot, and told him that she had been living on Schopenhauer for the last four months. "R—really," said the King," some new pr—repar—ration I suppose, like gr—rape nuts."

I have advanced in the social scale recently. I received two letters the same day—one addressed to—Her Majesty the Countess of Minto; the other to—Her Royal Honour Lady Minto.

Saturday, August 7th.

Mr Marshall came to luncheon and brought the embossed casket containing Buddha's bones for us to see. It is beautiful in detail and in excellent preservation. On it is engraved in some old world dialect "Assisting Engineer to Kanishka" and the date about 2,000 years ago. Some other words are not decipherable. The crystal jar was unsealed for our benefit, and we all touched Buddha's bones, thereby no doubt gaining much merit, indeed they are said to have the power of expiating passed sins. It is encouraging to think we can begin life again with a clean sheet.

Sunday 15th.

The picture papers are full of Bleriot's air-ship flying over the Channel. It is sad for the poor Englishman Latham having fallen with his aeroplane into the sea when a third of the way had been accomplished. I suppose in a few years, we shall fly about in aeroplanes, with as much confidence as we now drive in motors.

Friday, 20th.

The Nawabs of Maler Kotla and of Loharu lunched today. The Nawab of Maler Kotla is an insignificant little man without much personality. The Nawab of Loharu, on the contrary, is very imposing and was beautifully dressed in golden brocade. He is extremely cultivated, and pleasant to talk to. He told me that he lived 35 miles from the railway across the desert. The distance having to be traversed either on a camel or an elephant, as the sand made a carriage impracticable. I told him he would shortly be using a flying machine which would avoid the difficulties presented by the sandy desert. He was quite up to date in his ideas with the exception of the way he considered malefactors should be dealt with. The Dhingra family, he said, should be exterminated. "But", argued Rolly, "Dhingra's father and brothers are most loyal, respectable members of society, and they are not responsible for the action of one member of their family." Loharu raised both hands to his face, and said, "That cannot be helped. It is their misfortune; they must suffer as an example to the public. This is the will of God." No oriental can understand our views of justice; it all seems contrary to the customs of their race to show mercy and pity.

Friday, 20th.

During the week I have paid frequent visits to Mr Jones, the dentist, as it was necessary to kill a nerve, hardly a pleasant experience, which the idiotic dentist in Calcutta failed to discover.

Saturday, 21st.

The farewell dinner to Lord Kitchener took place yesterday at the Club. Every one I have met has told me how admirably Rolly spoke, and I think the knowledge he displayed of the various campaigns surprised the soldiers. Lord K-'s speech reads extremely well, but it was disappointing at the time. Colonel Birdwood (who by the way has now become a General) told me he was dreadfully distressed that Lord K- did not even attempt to make the most of his speech. I fancy he was rather disconcerted at Rolly having spoken without any reference to his notes, became nervous, and consequently put on his specs and held the paper in front of his eyes, reading as fast as he could, leaving out words here and there and giving the impression that he was only anxious to get his lesson over as soon as possible.

Friday, 27th.

There was a sort of semi-dressed rehearsal of Truth this evening, to which a few people who are leaving Simla tomorrow came. Rolly and I had to go to the Volunteer Ball, so were not present. Captain Mackenzie gave me the most killing account of Scindia, who insisted on seeing the play. He was sitting at the end of a row next to Captain Mackenzie. Fryer was standing near him also looking on. In the second act, there is a great scene between Eileen and her husband, when he suspects her of carrying on a flirtation. Captain Mackenzie saw Scindia turn to Fryer and ask for a glass of soda water, which he drank; this evidently did not give him relief for more than a few minutes, and again he asked for another glass of soda water. Very shortly after this, he removed his pughree and brushed the tears away with the embroidered end Then Captain Mackenzie heard three convulsive sobs, after which he bolted from the room. As soon as the act was over, Captain Mackenzie went out and found him sitting sadly on one of the sofas in the hall, crying quietly to himself. "That telephone scene was too much for me" was all he vouchsafed to say. Colonel Hobday, who is a skilled artist,[223] has done the most excellent picture of Scindia dashing from the room in floods of tears, followed by an anxious attendant, and a *chaprassie* moping the floor.

223. Colonel E A P Hobday, Royal Artillery, amateur actor, director, artist and songwriter, author of *Sketches on Service, 1897 Indian Frontier Campaigns*.

Sunday, September 4th. Simla.

About six weeks ago Lord Morley offered Colonel Dunlop Sir W. Curzon Wyllie's position at the India Office. Colonel Dunlop hates leaving Rolly before he has completed his term of office, but this appointment means £800 a year for life beside his pension of a £1,000. We shall miss him terribly; he has worked his heart out on Rolly's behalf, and would any day lay down his life for him. I am trying not to dwell on his departure yet, as I am glad to say he remains with us till February. It will be almost impossible to replace him, but fortunately it will only be for a short time. Kitchener is furious at having Malta forced upon him, and tells us frankly that he means to make things as nasty for the Government as possible. On his return home he means to let it be known that on the day that the Government appoints any one else to India, he will resign the command at Malta, consequently they must either appoint him Viceroy, or acknowledge that the Malta command was a fraud, created to get rid of the Duke of Connaught. Kitchener has got a very strong position, and he intends to make full use of it. I have discussed the probability of his succeeding us for hours with him, and on the whole I don't think a better man could be found. He has a great knowledge of India; he recognises the importance of a continuity of Government during the initiation of the reforms. The tribes are frightened of him, and the Amir likes him. I don't think for one moment he realises what the work is, he has always been very clever in getting other people to work for him, but in the case of the Viceroy this is really impossible. We have also discussed the necessity of his having a wife if he came here; he realises this to the full. I asked him what age he considered suitable; he suggested 45, which I told him was certainly 10 years too old. Lord K- said, "You speak as if the whole thing were settled, and excite me by all the plans you are making for me." I told him I knew Rolly would do all he could to further his wishes, and I would keep him informed as to what we heard. In saying goodbye I said, "Au revoir till we meet in 14 months' time on the steps of Government House, Calcutta." What the future is to bring forth, must for the present remain a mystery in the lap of the gods, but I own to feeling greatly interested. Lord Kitchener once said to me, "If such an unlikely thing as my succeeding you should come about, I am certain Lord Curzon would have a stroke of apoplexy".

Tuesday, 7th.

The Maharaja of Bikaner has come to stay with us for a week, and the Cooch Behar family lunched. Bikaner is of course like a European to talk to. He told me he had heard that people in England criticised the Native Member on the Viceroy's Council and that they went so far as to say that Native Princes would not consort with a man of inferior caste. Both Bikaner and Gwalior went to call on Mr Sinha the first day they were in Simla. Bikaner also dined with him, so all anxiety on that score can be set at rest. Bikaner is building a terrace and garden in front of his old historical fort; this he is calling the Minto Park. One of the entrance gates is named after the Princess of Wales, the other after me. He showed us all his designs; they are excellent, beautiful drawings of iron work and carved marble

With Maharaja Ganga Singh.

balustrades, principally copied from illustrations in Country Life. The Maharani Cooch Behar tells me that no doubt the young women in Bengal are terribly anti-English, but she says the interest we have taken in giving purdah parties has decidedly done good, and that they have no feeling against us personally; in fact, she told me one of the leading agitators had told her himself that Rolly had actually saved them from a mutiny.

Monday, 13th

Sir O'Moore Creagh arrived in Simla on Sunday, and came today to pay Rolly his official visit. I happened to meet him on the stairs and certainly there can be no mistake as to the country he springs from. Rolly liked him; he was most straightforward and outspoken. He was not loud in his praise of the organisation of the India Office; he said they had no telephones, and that the one and only messenger-boy was usually impossible to get hold of. He thought they carried on the work in a conservative manner.

Tuesday, September 14th.

Gave a ball asking about 400 guests. Sir O'Moore Creagh made his first appearance in public. He hasn't got Lord Kitchener's presence and has only three medals and no clasps, one however is the V. C. He was totally ignorant of the lancers, but I managed somehow to drag him through. He is very pleasant to talk to and with a decided twinkle in his eye. The ball was a great success.

Friday, 17th.

In the afternoon attended a theatrical performance at the Loreto Convent. Some of the children acted admirably, one of the nuns was stage manager, and had painted all the scenery. All I can say is that her early career must have been spent on the boards of the Gaiety Theatre.

Tuesday, 21st September, Chail.

The cricket match ended before luncheon. Patiala had to follow their innings, and only saved being defeated in one innings by 25 runs; he is the proud father of a daughter a fortnight old. He has quite a big black beard and is six months younger than Larry. Francis did splendidly bowling or catching most of the Eleven. The Maharaja was so surprised and

annoyed at being beaten, having defeated the Simla eleven so easily this spring, that they have arranged to have a return match in Simla the first week in October. The huge luncheons of innumerable courses we have had to endure both days have been rather a trial. Major Thompson tells me, that this is only the second time the Maharaja has eaten European food, he certainly did full justice to it. He had twice of every course, and I was rather staggered to see four quails at one time on his plate, although no doubt he did not consider them a serious item. I am greatly impressed with this young Maharaja, he is most sensible to talk to, and thoroughly realises how many pitfalls beset his path and how difficult his position is, having succeeded so young. He is devoted to his uncle the Kunwar Sahib and is most anxious to keep clear of both English and Indian toadies. He spoke a great deal of the folly of the agitators and used curiously high-flown language in speaking of the obligation Indians are under to the English, who have shown them what truth and justice means, and who by the grace of God have kept India from the horrors of civil war and blood-shed. I was quite touched by his wonderful courtesy.

After the cricket was over, we went to some very pretty gardens where excellent tennis-courts have just been made. The Maharaja fancies himself a great deal, but was handsomely beaten by Major Campbell, who is certainly an excellent player, in both a man's set and in a four where I was Major Campbell's partner. The staff think the Maharaja is inclined to swagger about games, so were desperately anxious he should be beaten both at cricket and tennis. However, he took his defeat with perfect good humour.

Sunday, 26th. Narkanda.

Rolly writes to me that the whole of Simla is in the throes of excitement discussing Lord Kitchener's farewell speech. How the extraordinary similarity in the phrases (in the farewell speeches of Lord K- and Lord Curzon) came about is not easy to explain. It has been an open secret that Sir Beauchamp Duff has often been Lord K-'s scribe. Lady Duff was careful that we should all hear that he had written Lord Kitchener's farewell speech, but in any case it almost appears as if this must have been done with malice prepence and the story will grow into something colossal. For the present Lord K-, I think, had better remain at sea. The world will assume that he wrote his own speech, in which case he cribbed from Lord Curzon, whilst if it is found out that Sir Beauchamp wrote it, it ceases to be Lord Kitchener's composition and he will be shown up as getting other people to do his work. I really think it must have been devilment on Sir Beauchamp's part putting Lord Curzon's words into Lord K-'s mouth, as being a clever man, I cannot imagine his doing anything so idiotic by mistake. No doubt Duff is feeling intensely sore at not having been selected as Lord K-'s successor. The situation is intensely comic. I can imagine Lord K's utter disgust and Lord Curzon's smile of triumph at this sequel to their desperate encounter which led to Lord Curzon's defeat and resignation.

Cricket, Chail, 1909.

Thursday, 30th. Simla.

Stories are flying about "Scatters" galore; he is said to be always quoting "Henry Asquith", and informed a friend at the club that the last time he played Bridge with "Alice Keppel" she won £75. He talks about "Eddy" and "Hugh" to these ladies, who naturally have never heard of Lord Derby, or Lord Lonsdale's existence, and look at him blankly. There is also a rumour that when he dined with us, seeing a lady, who was totally unknown to him, looking at him across the dinner table, that he raised his glass at her and winked, the said lady was naturally greatly annoyed.

Tuesday, October 5th.

The Patiala eleven played cricket against Francis's eleven today, and only made about a hundred in the first innings to our 240. Gave a dinner party to which the Maharaja came; he is quite delighted at having been given his powers. I congratulated him at dinner, and he said he would endeavour to be worthy of the confidence the Viceroy had placed in him. He really presented a most imposing appearance. Major Thompson told me he was wearing £700,000 worth of jewels, one of his pearl ropes alone being valued at £60,000, Colonel Dunlop reproved him for not putting on the wonderful Sanci diamond and Empress Eugénie's famous necklace; he answered quite naively, "I didn't think I had room for any more." It was rather a terrible dinner with crowds of unknown Railway people.

Wednesday, 6th.

The Maharani of Cooch Behar lunched, bringing her girl "Pretty" I like the Maharani so much; she sat with me for a long time after luncheon discussing her children's future. She is greatly exercised over Pretty's prospects, as she is so absolutely European in all her views.[224] The eldest daughter has married a Bengalee and is very unhappy. Pretty has many admirers, and several Englishmen amongst others; but the Maharani very naturally fears a marriage of mixed races would not turn out happily, and to me it seems out of the question to contemplate such a thing.

Friday, 8th.

The Envoy from Kabul lunched with us; he has been in Afghanistan for over two years. He told me he was kept practically as a prisoner and was not allowed free intercourse with anyone. Had it been discovered how much information he was sending, his life would not have been worth a minute's purchase. He says the Amir has deteriorated, and takes no

224. Pretty, Princess Prativa Devi, married Miles Mander, a British character actor, in 1912 and was divorced in 1922, dying a year later.

interest in the government of his country; he spends his time in his harem and in cooking and photographing! The Amir sent most affectionate messages of friendship to Rolly and me, but it appears as if he had become thoroughly demoralised. I asked the Envoy if he was returning to Kabul, he said with a look of resignation: "It is my duty, my word has been given to the Viceroy, that I will undertake this work, and my life is in his hands." As a matter of fact, Rolly does not intend to allow him to return, he would in all probability be assassinated, as they must realise that he knows too much.

Tuesday, 19th.

A red-letter day; historical owing to Louisa's arrival.[225] She came up in the Dane's motor and reached Viceregal Lodge at 11-30. I can hardly realise that she is really here and naturally we spent the entire day in talking. Unfortunately this season has been an abnormally hot one in the Red Sea and she is extremely tired, and consequently feels bewildered. It is the greatest happiness getting her here at last, and she has told me a thousand things about the family that I was dying to hear.

Friday, 22nd.

Mr Sinha lunched and had a good deal of conversation with Louisa; he is extremely pleasant, and she was very favourably impressed by him. Mr Halliday, chief of the Police in Calcutta, is here for a short holiday and tells me he thinks things are really quieter in Calcutta. This morning the Legislative Council was held under the old conditions that have existed since 1862. The questions discussed were not interesting, but it is historical as closing an epoch in the history of the Government of India. Mr Ramsay MacDonald, the Labour Member who is travelling about India, attended; he has a very nice face and hates Lloyd George, so he may have promising characteristics; anyhow he is better than Keir Hardie.

Monday, October 25th.

The whole party started at 9 o'clock driving in landaus to Kalka, lunching at Solon en route. I am really sorry to leave Simla this year. The weather has been perfect, and I don't feel Louisa has had sufficient time to enjoy it.

Tuesday, 26th.

Reached Alwar at 8-30. The Maharaja was at the station with Mr Colvin, Agent to the Governor General of Rajputana, other officials and a most imposing guard of Imperial

---

225. MM's sister Louisa Antrim.

Service Troops. Rolly drove with the Maharaja. I followed with Mr Colvin. The Lansdowne Palace, Lord Lansdowne having laid the foundation stone, stands on the top of a hill and the road takes so many turns round and round that the approach appears much further than it really is. The furniture as usual is appalling, a highly decorated dressing table placed for no rhyme or reason in the reception hall, and everything intensely ornate. Louisa already is enormously impressed, although as far as native pageants go, this is a very insignificant show. The heat here is cruel. The Palace stands on a huge rock which radiates heat all around, and the house, totally without accessories, such as blinds or shutters, becomes stoked up to a temperature of the infernal regions. No doubt we feel it more after the Simla breezes, but with the exception of Rangoon this is certainly the hottest experience I have had in India.

The Maharaja amused me by telling me that when Lord Elgin was here he expressed a wish to see the gaol and the Manager in his eagerness to show respect to the Viceroy put up in huge letters over the door: "Welcome to the gaol." No one saw the humour of it, so it did not signify. Alwar's personal body-guard wear the most lovely uniform. A very bright rose du barri coat, with the palest grey blue pughree and sash, the combination with their curved swords and golden belts is perfectly irresistible. The men are magnificent and most of them have extremely handsome figures.

Very sorry to see poor Ito has been assassinated; he showed profound contempt for me when I met him in Yokohama at the legation and refused to enlarge on my attempts at conversation, but it is a cruel ending for a man with such great qualities.[226]

Alwar group—Tiger, H.E., Maharaja of Alwar, M.M., Louisa, Col. Victor, Xandra.

226. Moderniser and Japanese statesman, 1st and 4 times Prime Minister of Japan, Resident-General of Korea after Russo-Japanese War when Korea became a Japanese Protectorate, shot by Korean nationalist An Jung-geun.

The Maharaja took us to the station, and saw us off at 10. Nothing can have been more attentive and charming than he has been to us throughout the visit. He has the reputation of being a man of moods, people say he cannot be relied on and that he is anti-English at heart, but to us he has been a perfect host. During the State Banquet I had a most interesting conversation with him. We discussed the condition of the country, and then he said if he was permitted to speak perfectly frankly that he would like to tell me how much the Indian Princes felt they owed to Rolly. He said: "I consider the present state of unrest is due entirely to Lord Curzon, it is not so much what he did, but the way he did it which alienated the whole community, and Lord Minto did not arrive a day too soon in India." In saying this he added:

> "I have no personal dislike to Lord Curzon, he was always extremely kind to me and I admire his brilliant qualities, but officially I hated him. He was fearfully overbearing and could never realise that it was possible that people could hold different views to his own, and gradually he became a positive danger to the country, and did more harm in India than any previous Viceroy. Lord Minto has not in the four years he has been here made as many public utterances as Lord Curzon did in one year, and yet it is known through the length and breadth of India what he has achieved, it is not only that he has gained the respect and confidence of the people, but they have a feeling of genuine affection for him."

I told him that there was a regular conspiracy in England to try and belittle his administration amongst a certain clique of newspapers, such as the Times, Chronicle, Daily Mail—all in fact under the Harmsworth influence, who was a strong supporter of Lord Curzon's. As the General Election was approaching, Rolly received daily telegrams trying to make him agree to concessions, either in connection with the deportees, or else with the Mahommedan electorates, simply to pander to the ignorant class at home and to make a bid for popularity with the advanced Socialist. Rolly has firmly declined to consider any of their proposals, and has told them that he does not think the condition of the country would justify him in risking experiments which would be put down to weakness.

In talking of the agitation and how far it affected the safety of the Viceroy, Alwar said that of course police protection was necessary for appearances sake, but that he would guarantee that Rolly personally would be perfectly safe driving alone through every Native State in India. Of course there might be fanatics in any community, but he was only describing the feeling that he knew existed. He added: "I think after this tour is over, Your Excellency will acknowledge that I am right." I was immensely interested in this conversation, because the substance of it was the same as Colonel Wilson had told me in Simla. This made me realise that the Maharaja is really genuine; he naturally had no idea that I could possibly have already been made acquainted with his views by chance in a casual after-dinner conversation.

Tiger Hunt Jaipur.

Thursday, 28th. Jaipur

The reception here was one of the most picturesque receptions I have ever seen. The route to the Residency extending for three miles was lined with elephants, camels, and horses and riders in all sorts of costumes; old men with fierce white beards parted in the centre, dressed in every sort of gorgeous raiment, sitting erect in their saddles as if they and their caparisoned horses were one.

After breakfast we repaired to a tent in which were displayed a marvellous selection of jewellery, brasses, enamels, and swords. The heat was intense and the struggle to select the prettiest article before any one else had pounced upon it, added to one's agitation.

At 2.30 the Maharaja paid his official visit to the Viceroy which was returned at 3.30. Poor man, it must be a- great effort attending these functions, as his favourite wife is dangerously and I fear hopelessly ill. We all drove to the Durbar Hall and were conducted to a gallery which overlooked the hall. The mottoes along our route through the city were very comic: "We meet in glory here today", "Oh I this joyful day", "Truce to thee Minto, Thrive this blessed time."

It was a magnificent sight, seeing rows and rows of splendidly attired individuals, all wearing the old costume of three and four hundred years ago. Gorgeously embroidered coats, with stiff white petticoats over white wrinkled trousers, and golden head dresses with cross bars of jewelled bands and plastered with every sort of precious stones. As Rolly entered to the strains of "God save the King", everyone rose and salaamed with profound respect. It was a most impressive sight, and I am glad Louisa and the girls should have seen such a truly typical Eastern pageant.

Saturday, 30th.

A good many of us left at 8 o'clock in carriages for Amber, the old capital and palace of the Princes of Jaipur. We had to get into tongas for the ascent of a steep hill, and for the latter part we were conveyed in dandies by an army of red men; through tortuous paved passages with high walls, while some of the party rode on elephants. This palace is beautiful, although the architecture varies in style a good deal. What struck me so much was the amount of verdure here, which adds enormously to the place. I should have found it very hard to leave all these surroundings, and take up my abode in the new pink city of Jaipur, which is laid out in wide streets quite unlike an Indian town. The whole population emigrated in one day and having outgrown Amber occupied the newly built city. An old Scotch missionary, called Mr McAllister, came with us to show us all the places of interest; he adores the Maharaja and speaks of him as "Our King." After dinner the head Minister brought a lovely embroidered gold and white coat for me as a present from the Maharani; it will make a beautiful tea gown. I at once put it on and drove to the station in it. We are all sorry to leave Jaipur and nothing could have gone off better than this visit.

Sunday, October 31st. Udaipur.

The Maharana was awaiting us at the station. When he came to see Rolly at Dehra Dun, his beard was coal black, today it was beautifully brushed and combed, but nearly white. I have since heard that he spent a day in dyeing it before his visit to Dehra. Anyhow Rolly was terribly confused and didn't think he could be the same man. The drive from the station was over three miles. It was not nearly such a pretty sight as Jaipur, because this Maharaja likes all his people to wear white and only their sashes and pughrees give any coloured relief. The Residency is a charming house, and beautifully done up. Everything spic and span, very pretty china, lovely chintzes, wonderful embroidered sheets, with pale blue ribbands run through them, lace mosquito nets, and even rose du barri bath blankets.

Monday, November 1st.

Did nothing till 4.30 when we went in a steam launch on Pichola Lake to Yagmandir Island, where tea was waiting for us in arched recesses, on a marble terrace, overlooking the lake towards the big palace. It was really like a scene on the stage, the setting sun gave a pink glow on the huge expanse of white palace, and the outlines of minarets and domes stood out against the sky. Further up the lake, visited another island where the Raj Kumar received us. This Prince is the only surviving son of the Maharana and he is a cripple. He has a very nice face, talks English and is most intelligent, he is 25 years old. It is sad to see with what difficulty he moves. Many years ago some Princess was poisoned by this Mewar reigning family and the tradition is that they were then cursed for seven generations, and that no Maharana should have a son or be succeeded in the direct line. Strangely enough this prophecy has come true. This Maharana finishes the seventh generation, and the curse will perhaps die out. We drove home round the lake and through the palace gardens, a really beautiful drive.

Wednesday, 3rd.

We started for the State Banquet at 7.45, drove to the Padre Ghâut and went in a huge State boat through the upper part of the lake, which was quite enveloped in darkness, as the moon had not risen, and it is divided from the upper lake by a big wall and one arch-way through which we could see gleams of light appearing. On passing through the arch-way a dazzling scene of glowing fairy palaces was disclosed. On the left the towering walls and minarets of the palace glittering with light, illumined the lake, and we seemed to be gliding through a sea of liquid fire, while thousands of sparkling diamonds fell from the oars of the 10 rowers. We landed at the palace ghât, finding armies of red men with golden inlaid dandies in which

to carry us up the steep incline to the entrance of the palace. Here the Maharana met us and conducted us to the banqueting hall. After dinner the Maharana returned and his speech was read by Mr. Holme. Rolly's answer is so important as a message to the Princes of India; Udaipur was selected in which to make this speech, as it is the most influential Hindu State and probably the oldest in the world. The dynasty dates back 2,500 years, and the Princes of Udaipur claim to be descended from the Sun. This Maharana is most simple in his ideas and refuses very rightly to allow motor cars and other modern inventions, which would attract tourists, to desecrate the peaceful beauty of his State. He is, of course, held in the deepest reverence, and when any subject speaks to him they place a towel over the mouth in order that their breath should not come near him. He dresses in plain satin coats, opening on the left side over a coloured waistcoat and wears hardly any jewels. The palace is a wretched building, a labyrinth of small, inadequate rooms. After dinner we mounted to the roof by a narrow staircase of immensely steep steps. Here we looked on at fire-works which to my mind rather spoilt the peaceful beauty of the illuminations.

Friday, 5th.

We have had to give up our visit to Ajmer on account of the plague, and so we remain in the hot little train till 9 o'clock tomorrow evening when we get on to the broad-gauge line at Agra.

Saturday, 6th November. Gwalior.

I have not had one moment to chronicle anything. The Maharaja has had bad fever and appears very much pulled down, but he is looking after us quite splendidly. The palace is huge, marble court-yards, and sentries everywhere, but relentless sunshine which it is difficult in any way to modify. Louisa and the girls are in the guest-house, with apparently about a 100 other guests as well. The State Banquet took place in the evening—120 guests sitting at three tables in a long narrow room; it was quite well done, and was not at all hot; in fact, so many electric fans were playing they absolutely blew us away, and one after another had to be stopped. The excitement at dessert was a small silver train which runs by electricity round the table carrying wine, sugar plums, cigarettes, &c., &c. The Maharaja can press a button under the table and stop the train, and the fact of lifting off a bottle also brings it to a standstill. It caused a great diversion, and no doubt assisted conversation.

Monday, 8th.

Started by motor at 8 A.M. to see the review of Scindia's troops. There were 5,000 of them on parade, and he may well be proud of them. He has a far larger army than any other Indian Prince and 3,000 Imperial Service Troops. Men and horses looked splendid; the

Udaipur.

elephant corps were most impressive, also the transport drawn by Bhils. When one sees a force like this and recognises the power Scindia has, it maddens one to think how absolutely wrong-headed people become at home when they speak of the necessity of trying to propitiate only the Mahommedans, ignoring the far greater number of Hindus and the multiplicity of other sects. We had some of the people belonging to the place to dine with us. There is an Italian colony here of Feloses who have been in Gwalior for many generations.[227] One of them was the architect who designed the big drawing-room which is really a very fine, well-proportioned room.

Louisa and I went yesterday to see the two Maharanis, the wife and mother. They were so charming and cordial that they begged us to return and see them again, which we did at 10 o'clock after bidding our other guests goodnight. The little Maharani, the wife, is the most fascinating creature; she is the tiniest grown-up mortal I have ever set eyes on; she was covered from head to foot with the most wonderful jewellery which must have been quite heavy for her tiny body to support. We explored all their rooms. They are done up in European style of the worst hotel-taste possible; they have had an inferior English lady with little individuality to look after them, hence the want of taste. We went into the Maharani's dressing-room; all her sarees are neatly folded and piled in heaps on ledges round the room; a selection of priceless embroideries, which reminded me of Haynes's shop. Her jewels could be counted by the thousand; boxes of bracelets, glass-cases of pearls and necklaces of precious stones. Her dressing table was a mass of gold bottles, combs, scents, &c., &c.—all in bewildering profusion. Her bath-room was unique. A large silver slab was placed in a marble basin; on this she sits and has water poured over her out of silver chatties, of which there are countless numbers. The most divine little jackets of soft muslin and lace, which look as if they had been made for a child of three, of every shade and colour were spread out on shelves so that she may select the variety and hue she prefers. Her bed in another room stands on four silver bells; it is wide and has hard pillows for the head and two resting on each side. The most fascinating sight of all were the rows and rows of tiny dolls shoes that she gets from Paris and which look as if they could fit no human foot. Some of her sarees were covered with sequins made by Marshall & Snelgrove, these she seemed to like better than the priceless gold and silver embroideries of Benares. We were then taken to see some of the embroidered Chandari muslins and she seemed to take delight in loading both Eileen and me with presents, saying so prettily: "It is nothing; it is your kindness in taking them." The mother cannot speak

H.H. the Maharaja of Gwalior with M.M.

227. Descendants of Jean-Baptiste de la Fontaine Filoze 1775-1840 who commanded Scindia's troops in the Anglo-Mahratta wars in the early 19th century.

English; she and the Maharaja are dittos. I have never seen a mother and son so alike; she is a very clever woman and acts as Regent in the Maharaja's absence. They seem to be such a happy family. The little Maharani swims, rides, drives, bikes, plays tennis, and even the old mother has killed three tigers, and can use a '450 rifle. They are full of the joie de vivre, such an unusual sight in a zenana.

Tuesday, 9th.

The King has sent me the Crown of India, the Order which hitherto all Viceroys' wives have had on their husbands' appointment. When we came out, the Prince of Wales told me that he much regretted that the King had decided to stop the Order in future. In England it naturally does not signify, but in India natives set an enormous store by these things, and it was considered a pity that the Viceroy's wife should not have the Order that many Indian ladies possess. Some one evidently has contrived to make the King change his mind. Rolly invested me in the drawing-room before dinner. Scindia was so nice and cordial about it; he came up and told me how glad he was that I should have received this honour while I was his guest. He told me that the Princes had resented my not having been given it before, especially as it was not the King who had thought of stopping it, but Lord Curzon who had advised his doing so. I don't quite understand why or for what reason he should have wished Lady Curzon to be the last recipient of the C.I.

Wednesday, 10th. Bhopal.

Found the Begum at the station to receive us with her three sons. We stayed at the guest-house, which has been done up quite charmingly; everything absolutely new, with priceless carpets, and fresh chintzes. The garden is a blaze of colour, poinsettias, morning glory, and masses and masses of chrysanthemums, which are banked up from the road to the verandah, and carpet the whole space round the house. At the foot of the hill there is a lovely wide expanse of water, and the camp is most artistically arranged, with rose-beds and flowering shrubs, and the tents have been lavishly furnished. I am told the Begum spent four hours yesterday in superintending everything, and seeing to all the final arrangements herself.

The Begum's two sons have married two sisters; these appeared clad in Jodhpur breeches made of cloth of gold, over which a very thin transparent gauze petticoat fell to the knee. They were covered with ropes of pearls and rubies, and I was thrilled by their appearance, very straight, well-cut features, glorious eyes, and charming expressions. They are by far the prettiest Indian women I have ever seen, and I consequently fell a victim at once. Between them they have five boys and one girl—all beautiful children; all the boys down to the two-year old were dressed in the uniform of the body-guard. The heir-apparent is betrothed to his cousin, which seems a mistake as they are first-cousins twice over. Another very handsome Afghan girl of 10 also appeared; she was married last year to the Begum's 16-year old son, but the Begum means to keep her under her eye and educate her until she is 18, which she considers the correct age for a girl to begin the cares of a household. After the usual attar and pan I was simply overwhelmed with presents. Needle-work done by the various princesses assumed every shape and form. Cushion-covers, table-cloths, doyleys, bags, screens, a tea-cosy with Gilbert John Murray Kynynmound encircling it embroidered in golden thread. Then an enormous silver centrepiece was produced and presented to me, with elephants and wild animals at the four corners and a box containing a lucky fossil fish. It was most embarrassing to receive so many gifts, especially as an enormous amount of loot was also prepared for Eileen and Louisa, who had not come with me.

In the afternoon we went to see a gymkhana. I sat on a sofa surrounded by the five tiny boys whom the Begum declared were acting as my body-guard. Duty compelled us to invite some of the guests to dine; one lady I thought had found the champagne too good, anyhow she insisted on disclosing secrets about a certain bishop, whom she declared had some unfortunate little failings. I asked in which direction the faults lay, and discovered that they were neither drink nor flirtations, but an irresistible impulse to cheat at games which very naturally infuriated his congregation.

Thursday, 11th.

A terribly strenuous day. I met the Begum at 8.30 at the Lady Lansdowne Hospital. Wonders have been done here, all owing to Her Highness's energy; she has built a proper operating theatre, providing all modern equipment. A bungalow for the European Matron has also been added. The Begum had up all the hereditary *dhais*[228] and lectured them on the advantages of modern treatment. A class of 30 has been formed. Her Highness gives them a monthly allowance and one trained Nurse goes to each confinement case with them, and the European Matron visits each case on the third day. Since the class was started in July of this year 222 cases have been reported upon. We then motored on to the Sultana Girls' School where a wonderful address was presented to me. I suddenly realised that I was expected to answer, and that a rough draft of what I should say had been given me in Simla which I had never even looked at. I got through pretty well, as it was quite easy to praise the pupils and to tell them what a wonderful ruler they had, which was duly translated to them. But much worse awaited me. We drove on to the Ladies' Club, and under a huge shamiana were sitting in rows all the purdah elite of the State of Bhopal. When duly ensconced on a raised dais a lady in beautiful clothes advanced and began reading an address in Urdu. I was at my wit's end, not having a notion what it was about.

To my intense relief the interpreter, who was standing by me, presented me with a copy of the translation. This I glanced at hurriedly. I discovered I was to open this Ladies' Club, and

228. Traditional midwives.

in my reply found myself talking of our late Queen Victoria and the interest she took in her Indian subjects and how fortunate they were in having a ruler who was so progressive and anxious to improve the status of women, &c., &c. Fortunately the lady interpreter was far more eloquent than I was and evidently made them a suitable oration. As neither Louisa nor Eileen noticed my agitation, I must have concealed it better than I should have thought possible. I was of course sent the answers later which I should have made, and no doubt they will appear in the newspapers and no one will be any the wiser.

In the afternoon I went with Rolly to open the Alexandra College and a museum, so the Begum is answerable for five excellent institutions, all started by her initiative. She is a most remarkable woman and a tremendous power in her State. She has her petticoats very short for fear of tripping over them and wears a very coarse sort of shooting stockings, with ugly flat shoes, and cotton gloves in all shades—red, black or white. All her cloaks look very old and creased, but if not a good dresser, she is a splendid ruler, and one feels

Bhopal group.

Welcome message Bhopal.

irresistibly drawn towards this little Begum with her determination and her wonderful power of organisation.

Friday, 12th.

Louisa and I with Colonel Crooke, Captain Jelf, the police officer, Mr Straight, and a Captain Luard, who has run the camp here and who is an encyclopaedia on ancient history, went an hour's run by train to Sanchi, to see some marvellous old Buddhist remains, 150 B.C. We rode up to the top on a splendid elephant, with a silver howdah and a golden cover over his head; the sun was terribly hot. These are the most perfectly preserved Buddhist monuments in India. Four gate-ways with marvellous carvings representing episodes in the life of Buddha, so well preserved that the expression on the faces remains perfectly clearly outlined, and the pose of the figures is wonderfully graceful. It was these carved reliefs that the French Emperor tried so hard to get for the Louvre, but fortunately he was frustrated in his wishes.

We got back at 3 o'clock and had rather a rush to be ready in time to distribute our presents to many people who have taken trouble in connection with our visit, before starting for a garden party at the palace. We then repaired to a rifle range, and I shot a match with the Begum. I knew nothing of the rifle, so shot very badly, but not quite so badly as she did, upon which she presented me with a brooch, saying I had won the prize. I think she probably missed the target on purpose. She and Rolly drove off together in a motor. It was quite amusing seeing him eloping with a lady in a bourka. I felt really sorry to leave Bhopal; it is a lovely place, and there is a genuine ring about it all which was very refreshing. No expense has been spared in connection with our visit, but the Begum has made permanent improvements—electric light, new roads, new buildings, &c., &c., all of which will benefit her State.

Saturday, November 13th. Baroda.

My birthday, which proved to be a day very full of incident. Our train was an hour late in arriving at Ahmedabad, an intensely hot place which they say runs Jacobabad[229] very close. We got out at 12 o'clock, and received a deputation from the Mahommedans. The crowd was very dense, and the police arrangements were very inadequate. As we were only to be two hours in Ahmedabad, the escort was a much smaller one than usual. Rolly had the head of the carriage put down in spite of the heat, as he thought it would disappoint the people if they were not able to see us. I was looking very attentively at the crowd, and contrasting the countenances of the people very unfavourably with the Rajputana natives. I was sitting

229. Jacobabad, Sindh – now in Pakistan - was known for having most consistently the highest temperature in South Asia.

as usual on the left side of the carriage, and saw a boy standing in the front row of a crowd of people with two round white balls in his hands about the size of a turnip. He was holding them so openly, that it never occurred to me that they could be bombs. I saw him raise his right arm and throw something at us as hard as he could; this bounded off the hilt of the Sergeant's sword. Then I saw the boy put the other ball he was holding in his right hand and throw again. This my own Jemadar Thakar Das flung back with his left arm, slightly cutting his wrist from the force of the blow. It seems Thakar Das thought from the first it was a bomb, although I personally did not feel the least alarmed.

Ahmedabad bomb.

The curious thing is that, for the first time on any official occasion, we were without a member of our own staff in the carriage. Mr Barrow, the Commissioner, was with us on account of pointing out places of interest as we drove round. Had the missiles not been stopped by the Sergeant and Thakar Das, I think from the direction in which we were going that one would have hit Mr Barrow, who was sitting opposite me on the back seat of the carriage, and the other would have grazed passed the back of my head and hit Rolly. I have never seen two better shots. Mr Barrow did nothing, though Colonel Dunlop on being told of the incident sent a policeman back, but it was of course much too late. We paid little attention to the episode and drove on to the Rani Sipari's mosque, the Jumma Musjid and the mosque near the Daskroi cutchery. We gave luncheon in the train at the station to Mr Barrow, Mr Cousins and Mr and Mrs Sladen, the latter is a cousin of our Mr Sladen at Ottawa.

A poor man has since died. He was a *bheestie*[230] and, it appears he hammered a coconut on the edge of a cart before it exploded; it was the ordinary bomb that they make in India, a detonator, picric acid and nails. We cannot be thankful enough that the bomb was minus the bit of lead which it needs to make it explode easily; had it been otherwise the results would have been very different, but it does not do to dwell on these things, we have got to play our part, and we must take the fortunes of war, but I recognise what a narrow escape we have had with an intensely thankful heart.

The annoying part of the whole thing is that the boy has been allowed to escape. The staff are all indignant that Mr Barrow did not at once spring from, the carriage, and collar the boy, he was so close to us; even had it not been a bomb he should have been arrested for throwing anything at our carriage, but the whole thing happened in such a second and we were all taken so unawares, it was difficult to act on the spur of the moment, and I know Rolly would never have allowed the procession to stop. A bomb is hardly a suitable birthday present, and November 13th will always be associated with this unpleasant incident. It brings possibilities home to one, seeing that the poor chief of police and his secretary have both been killed by a bomb in Buenos Ayres.

We arrived at Baroda at 5 o'clock and were greeted by the Gaekwar, covered with ribbons and chains, and Orders of his own invention; he drove with Rolly, I followed with Louisa, The Gaekwar has no Imperial Service Troops, and no Viceroy has been here since Lord Elgin, so Rolly ordered a full Viceroy's escort to come from Mhow to make an impression, which no doubt they did.

Monday, 15th.

Louisa and I went at 12.30 to return the Maharani's visit. She told me many causes for discontent always returning to the fact that Lord Curzon had interfered with them, and

---

230. Water carrier.

had taken away their rights. The Gaekwar's son has no official rank, and this his mother chafes at. It seems to me that he ought to have it, and it would do us no harm at all. One feels in this State there is an atmosphere of discontent. Rolly and I are sparing no pains to dispel it. The Gaekwar is an extremely pleasant man, and he made a most loyal speech at the banquet.[231] After dinner we went up and sat with the Maharani and looked at fire-works. She has a most evil-looking son of 17, who, I am sure, would not be averse to committing any crime. We didn't get to bed till 1 A.M.

Gaekwar Baroda.

Tuesday, 16th.

Sat with the Maharani at the review of the troops. She really pays very little attention to purdah, and only does it at all on account of the feeling there is in the State. The Gaekwar appeared in a very shabby old riding suit. I exclaimed to the Maharani on seeing him that I thought he ought to be in uniform at the head of the troops. I said it as a joke, but I thought it as well she should know that he has no business to appear in those clothes before the Viceroy, who was as usual in uniform. I believe the relations between the two are not extremely friendly, as he finds her terribly difficult to manage. At 4 o'clock we went to see the state jewels. Outside the house there were three golden guns drawn by bullocks with horns encased in gold, and magnificent draperies hanging over their bodies; also golden carriages with horses covered in wonderful harness. Upstairs in glass-cases the display of jewels was bewildering; pearls by the thousand, single earrings of colossal size, each pearl the price of a king's ransom. One necklace had six rows of such huge pearls that they were almost vulgar, but their value must be several million pounds. There were also a variety of gorgeous diamond necklaces, one centre diamond which must run the Koh-i-noor very close, and strings and ropes of emeralds and rubies, all beautifully cut and set. These gems have not been valued for 30 years, and then must have amounted to at least 50 million pounds, so a small idea can be formed of the boundless treasures the Gaekwar possesses and was no doubt originally loot taken in battle, when a pearl the size of a pigeon's egg was of no account.

We dined quietly with the Gaekwar and his family at his palace—he has an excellent French cook, and the most imposing English butler. Everything was extremely well done. He is an excessively pleasant man, and we parted with mutual expressions of regard; how much this means I do not know. I fear from all I hear his word cannot be very reliable. It is rather curious that on the very day on which Morley did his best to force Rolly to release the deportees, putting such powerful pressure as I think few men would have resisted, that the proof of the sedition that has been preached by the deportees should have resulted in this bomb outrage on ourselves. It would indeed have been the irony of fate if, in the same newspaper that announced the attempt on the Viceroy's life, a full and free pardon had been

231. The Gaekwar was a supporter of the Indian National Congress. In 1911 he created a furore when he appeared not to show due deference to the King Emperor George V at the Coronation Durbar in Delhi.

extended to the men who have preached both sedition and violence. After this evidence of the condition of the country, they can hardly attempt to force Rolly's hand again, or try and induce him to agree to a policy which he considers would be a danger to the peace.

Thursday, 18th. Bombay.

This bomb business has resulted in so many kind enquiries from all parts of the world. Hundreds of telegrams and letters have been received and every spare minute that I have not been sightseeing or at a function, I have spent at my writing table. What this means to Rolly, no words can say. He has to make careful answers to all his addresses, he interviewed 14 Native Chiefs, one after another the morning of his arrival, he has his usual work to get through, his weekly letter to Morley, and letters also to the King, Prince of Wales, &c., about this wretched outrage. Admiral Slade[232] told me that he realises what a terrible strain this touring must be; he said he was quite surprised to see me get out of the train at Bombay Station at 8 A.M., looking fresh, clean, and untired. I told him I was glad I had succeeded in taking him in, as I was feeling dirty, jaded, and extremely hot.

The banquet took place in a huge shamiana. There was a long pause before dinner commenced; we heard later this was owing to the soup being stopped by the sentries with fixed bayonets. The Tommies said they had their orders, and that no one should come that way without a pass. The Steward in despair vainly remonstrated, at last he said he would fetch the Military Secretary, a name he had always hitherto conjured by. "If you bring the General himself," said the sentry, "I intend to obey my orders." The officer of the guard at last appeared on the scene and the soup, rather cold and nasty, was allowed a free passage into the dining tent. After dinner we held a reception, for grotesque beings the most marvellous I have ever seen, Jews, Turks, Infidels and Heretics, all congregated together, many blazing with jewels. Some hurried past salaaming without looking our way; others lingered, and had a real good look at us until coerced into moving on. No doubt the bomb outrage has shed a halo round our heads, and Bombay turned out in their hundreds to do us honour. Louisa thoroughly enjoyed herself, standing back to the right of the throne, looking most dignified, with a granite face. I could not resist an occasional eye-meet when a more than usually abnormal apparition glided by.

Louisa fills us all with the deepest admiration; she is always ready, always dressed to perfection for the occasion, never fussed, never hot, and this with only a quarter of the train accommodation that I have. Spacious apartments are always provided for me, I have countless servants to attend to my wants, and yet I am conscious of always being in a hurry, always having to send back at the last minute for a handkerchief, a motoring veil, or a kodak, which needless to say I have forgotten. I suppose long practice of travelling with the Queen has brought her to this stage of perfection, which thrills Rolly and I fear he is making

Ladies party, Bombay.

232. Admiral Slade's daughter Madeleine became one of Mohandas Gandhi's greatest supporters, known as Mirabehn.

most unflattering comparisons between us, although I claim that he has never had to wait for me in his life, but on this point he refuses to agree, and although the staff privately know I am truthful, they are too diplomatic to announce it openly.

Friday, 19th.

Louisa, Eileen and I went to a purdah party given by the Begum of Junagadh. This was quite an historical event, as it is the first time anything of the sort has been given before. Outside in the garden a British band was playing, inside the purdah was strictly maintained. The Begum herself was beautifully dressed in pink brocade with huge pearls in her nose and ears. She speaks no English and hitherto the Commissioner's wife is the only European she has seen. About two hundred ladies in gorgeous costumes were introduced to me before we repaired to the verandah where refreshments were served; champagne, hock, &c., being offered, and a great commotion ensuing when I asked for tea. The Aga Khan's wife was there, a colossal lady starting in rolls of fat from her eyes downwards, and with a curly

auburn wig. I really felt I couldn't blame him for deserting her, but I hear she is a very good sort and feels terribly self-conscious, realising what her appearance is. It is so ludicrous to read in huge letters extracts from the Times, which publishes the Aga Khan's views on the Reforms as if he were an oracle. In India he is absolutely discredited and Sir George Clarke tells me he doesn't think he would dare land in Bombay for fear of being assassinated. He belongs to the Bhora[233] sect of Mahommedans, they are a very murderous community and I fancy his life would not be worth many days' purchase out here, which no doubt he well knows.

Saturday, 20th.

The head of the Criminal Investigation brought two boys who have been arrested in connection with the bomb outrage for me to see, in case I could identify them. They were brought into the verandah one at a time. They had a very low caste of countenance, but I am sure neither of them was the thrower of the bomb; I think the culprit was more of the student class. The police are disappointed as they hoped they had a clue.

In the Times of India of November 18th an article appeared on Rolly's administration. The first part was very complimentary, the second part was very much the reverse, saying that as soon as Lord Curzon's strong hand left the helm, that things had fallen back into the same old grooves, the same fatal mistakes were being made that had needed nearly seven years of Lord Curzon's brilliant statesmanship to get rid of, &c., &c. Everyone was furious about this article, as it was obviously in extremely bad taste to publish it on the occasion of the Viceroy's visit when the whole of Bombay society seemed anxious to vie with each other to do him honour. Criticism at any other time would not have mattered, but this paper has always been Lord Curzon's special mouthpiece.

Louisa and I went to a Gymkhana Club. The membership is open to all creeds and races; it has only been started 10 months and is doing very well. The whole thing is being managed by ladies and it is wonderful to see Mahommedans, Hindus, Parsees, and Europeans all mixing. They had a bridge room; about five games were going on; three badminton courts; three excellent tennis courts and a croquet ground. The club is open two days a week for purdah ladies, two days for non-purdah ladies, and two days for both men and women. I think it ought to do good in bringing the various communities together. We were photographed sitting at tea with a mixed company of ladies in gorgeous costumes.

We had to leave immediately after dinner. Sir George and his Staff all seemed equally pleased and surprised at receiving presents; they have been most kind and have spared no pains in looking after our comfort. I believe the number of police employed has been double what they had during the Prince of Wales's visit, but that was before the days of sedition. All the sentries at night round our bungalow wore tennis shoes in order not to disturb us.

233. Bohra.

Friday, 26th November. Mysore.

Rolly and I went with the Maharaja and the Yuvaraj[234] to see the Maharani Girls' School. There were a great number of child widows amongst the pupils; it seems so awful to think they can have no future whatsoever. They have passed a law that a child must be eight years of age before they can be legally bound by a marriage contract; this is supposed to be a wonderful concession. They live with their husbands from the age of 10 or 11. Many of the widows we saw will take up teaching as a profession. I asked the school mistress why they didn't go in for nursing, as these poor girls are really outcasts having no one to look after them, but they don't seem to care for the medical profession. If a girl has any sort of love affair, her parents at once turn her out of the house, so it seems as if everything combines to prevent her having a chance at all.

Saturday, 21st

After dinner we drove to the palace; the Maharaja met us on arrival and as we entered, about 12 servants sounded trumpets, and shouted out his titles, as they walked before him. We looked on first at a dance performed by some men called Golams in the courtyard. They are the chief men in certain villages belonging to a particular caste, and are very well-to-do. There is a story that the Chief once told one of the men to climb to the top of a tree overhanging a precipice. "Now let go," said the leader. The man fell 300 feet and was dashed to pieces. He turned to an Englishman standing near and said: "Would your people obey you like that?"

After listening to the wild discordant tones of the long silver horned instruments and tom toms it was a surprising change to go to an up-to-date French drawing-room, and listen to the most divine organ, beautifully played by an organist from Madras. To find this Louis XVI room in the centre of an ultra-Hindu palace seemed strangely incongruous. The programme of the music was arranged entirely by the Maharaja himself. It was a really excellent concert with violin and cello. The lady who played the piano was the Maharaja's former music mistress; she told me that he had the most marvellous ear and can himself play a variety of instruments, one can see how immensely music appeals to him, his choice was from Gounod, Mendelssohn and Chopin.

Sunday, 28th. Kheddah Camp.

We passed hundreds of natives, grouped all along the route to the Kheddah Camp, a drive of 45 miles. We were often reminded of views of Surrey, as we travelled through avenues of magnificent trees with beautiful flowering shrubs on either side. The camp is a town of canvas; the guests include one lady who impressed the staff very much. She has red hair,

234. Crown Prince.

and bright red nails to match and so shiny they are like looking-glasses. We started at 5 o'clock and motored five miles, walked for a short distance through bamboo glades to a platform overlooking the river with open jungle beyond. The beat had commenced and a herd of wild elephants that has been watched day and night for many weeks was driven down towards the river. Shades of night had already begun to fall, when a line of dark objects appeared and plunged into the river. The beaters lighted bamboo faggots behind them, which added an uncanny appearance to the scene. The elephants had followed their usual run which led them into a cleverly devised enclosure and a heavy gate was dropped over the opening, imprisoning eleven animals, large and small. This enclosure was encircled by a high platform, to which we climbed, and looked down on the poor elephants who have said good-bye to freedom for ever. It was curious to see the systematic way they formed a line and hurled their combined weight against the sides of the zereba. It needed to be strong to resist such a force, and we left them straining every nerve to demolish their prison walls, and returned only just in time for dinner.

Monday, 29th.

Watched the Kheddah operations during the whole morning. The eleven elephants include two tiny ones who sought protection from the swaying mass under their mothers' bodies had during the night trampled the ground into a sea of black mud. The gate was again raised and seven large tuskers ridden by mahouts entered the enclosure. There was now hardly room to move, and it was a long operation surrounding an elephant, tying his hind legs firmly together, and then with a huge cable fastening him to the side of the enclosure. It was rather pathetic to see the great beast gather up his force and pull with all his might till he fell down in his fruitless attempts to free himself, rest for a space and then resume again. By degrees all the elephants were roped with huge cables round their necks, each one being chained to a tusker. The ropes got hopelessly entangled, the elephants fought, and the whole thing took hours to accomplish. At last the gate was raised, three elephants were left tied in the Kheddah, the others in great confusion were led forth, and we walked to the edge of the river and witnessed a wonderful sight. The poor brutes miss the want of water more than anything; consequently as they emerged from the wood and saw the river flowing below them, they rushed towards it trumpetting with trunk up-lifted, straining at the rope controlled by the sedate old tusker, who in spite of himself was forced to hurry his ponderous footsteps. Into the river the two plunged, captor and captive, and already the work of taming seemed to have begun. Each elephant is led through the river and chained firmly to a forest tree, and in eight days the little ones become tame, though it takes from four to six months before an old elephant can be trusted. It is necessary to have these Kheddahs as if the herds increase too much they do great damage. The last Kheddah was four years ago, when the Prince of Wales was here; before that there had not been one for 10 years. It costs, as a rule, about £5,000 even after the elephants have been well sold. People apply for them from all parts of India. For four months previous to a Kheddah they are guarded and surrounded by 3,000 men, as they must be kept in a certain locality. The

Keddah camp group.

Maharaja tells me it is so interesting to watch these elephants in their wild state. They are very kind in helping each other with the young ones. The elephants always assist in carrying the baby elephants across the rivers. A crowd of people were looking on, massed together round the enclosure opposite us.

Thursday, 2nd.

Motored to the Kheddah to see the elephants driven into the stockade. It was a lovely morning, the sun shining through the bamboo glades and crowds of natives loitering about in picturesque groups. They are really little better than animals, they live in the jungle, eat roots and wear hardly any clothes at all. Their dishevelled hair testifies to the fact that they have been guiltless of combs and brushes. There were about 40 elephants and it took a long time before they could be driven into the enclosure. Great excitement was caused by one huge old elephant being in the herd, such a splendid animal, but marred by one of his tusks having been broken off. The difficulty was that being so much bigger than any of the tame elephants they naturally did not like facing him. Ten tame elephants were placed in the stockade in a line with their tails to the wild elephants. The first time a tame tusker

turned, the huge wild elephant made for him at once, the mahout was off his back and had climbed on to the platform in a second, and there was almost a panic among the elephants. It was altogether a pitiful sight the capture of that splendid old tusker who had enjoyed the freedom of the forest for at least 60 years. I hate even to think of it. It took the whole day to get him secured. The Maharaja says he will be tamed in six months. I only hope this is true, and that we shall not hear he has died of a broken heart. His value is about Rs. 8,000.

In this State wherever we have been the trees on each side of the road have had white and brown rings of paint round them. The Maharaja says this is done partly to keep insects from climbing up the trunks, but chiefly to avert the evil eye and to keep bogies off the road. In the elephant districts the mile stones are black with white letterings; it is useless putting down white ones, as the elephants tear them up. Several of the tame tuskers employed in the stockade were only caught four years ago in the Prince of Wales's Kheddah. I wonder if they recollected the misery of it, they evidently had no compassion, as they seemed to enjoy prodding the new poor victims with their tusks, and behaved altogether in a very heartless manner.

Friday, 3rd.

We motored 8 miles to Seringapatam. The water from the Cauvery River makes everything look green and fertile, and irrigating canals make the growth luxuriant. Rolly was specially interested in the place, as his grandfather, Sir Thomas Hislop, was present at the storming of the fort. We visited Tippoo Sultan's tomb; he is lying beside his father Haidar Ali in a pretty mosque surrounded by a well-kept garden. We then visited the summer palace, the outside walls are decorated with frescoes of battles between the French and English, with Tippoo always leading his troops to victory. The whole palace is a mass of colour with elaborate designs in gold, green and red, a sort of Persian effect of decoration, very pretty to see once, but impossible to endure for long. The Duke of Wellington lived here for two years. We went on to the fort; saw the breach in the wall and the various points of attack. This is a most fascinating spot, and I felt quite sorry to resume our travels. We arrived at Bangalore at 5 o'clock. The most enormous crowds were collected along the route to the Residency. Mr Fraser told me there had been double the number of tickets issued for admission to the station than for the Prince's visit. I am sure the bomb episode has made us objects of interest.

Saturday, 4th December. Bangalore.

Rolly, Colonel Victor and I motored at a furious pace for the 66 miles to the Kolar Gold Fields. We did the distance in 2 hours and 10 minutes, including a great many stops to be garlanded, and touch fruit. The Manager of one of the mines, Mr Richards, met us on arrival at Kolar. After the fertile valley with the great stretches of water that we had been passing through, this barren rocky soil looked very bleak and parched. It was hot work motoring

Bangalore raft.

from place to place to see the crushing, smelting, &c., &c. Some mines are being worked at a depth of 3,500 feet. The electric light is brought from a power house over 40 miles away. It was rather alarming to see live wires with a voltage up to 2,000. I most enjoyed seeing the liquid gold being poured into a mould which was cooled down in water into a brick worth £3,400 in an incredibly short time. We were given a gigantic champagne luncheon, to which the whole of the English population were invited. It was extremely well done, and they were a very nice lot of people. We returned by train, and got back to Bangalore at 6 P.M.

Thursday, 9th. Madras.

Lady Lawley has done up Government House quite charmingly, she found a lot of nice furniture in godowns,[235] and even some beautiful red silk which now covers all the furniture in the big central hall, where they have some very nice pictures. There is a view of the sea through the trees of the park, and a delicious breeze which makes the heat quite bearable. Luncheon is in a huge outer verandah; everything is most soigné and well done. The servants wear long full starched white petticoats like the pictures of Akbar's attendants; they all talk English. Altogether there is an old-world feeling in Madras very different to the bustle of Bombay with its growing commerce, and huge harbour. Madras itself extends over an area of 40 miles which is the same as Paris.

Friday, 10th.

There was a men's banquet in the evening. Rolly tells me the officials seem to be very superior to the ones it is our fate usually to meet.

Saturday, 11th.

Interviewed native ladies from 11 A.M. till nearly 2 o'clock in the banqueting hall. The conversation was terribly difficult, carried on through an interpreter, a charming old lady, called Mrs Frith; she has lived all her life in Madras, and interpreted for our present King when he was in India 33 years ago. He was talking through the purdah to a Native Princess whom he had been told was very pretty. They tried to arrange looking-glasses so that he might have the satisfaction of seeing her. She was at last induced to shake hands with the Prince through the curtain; he rose to the occasion and placed a ring on her finger as a memento of his visit. Perhaps Mrs Frith's imagination has grown during these long years, but she was very amusing in relating these reminiscences. She has an orphans' home, which she supports entirely with the aid of voluntary contributions. She prides herself in never having asked for a farthing in her life, her finances have been reduced as low as Rs.2, which she gave to a poor beggar woman and was rewarded next morning by receiving cheques

235. Warehouses/storerooms.

in letter to the amount of Rs.500 from various friends. She has a hundred girls, clothes and feeds them and teaches them practical things to enable them to become good housekeepers. Their work is exquisite; she presented me with a beautifully embroidered baby's robe for my future grandchild. I stopped in the motor on our way to Guindy and saw all the orphans. They seem contented and happy and it was a joy to be able to remove all anxiety with regard to their expenses, any rate for some weeks to come.

Wednesday, December 15th.

Arrived at Calcutta at 4 o'clock after 42 hours in the train from Madras. It feels quite cool after the intense heat of the South. The streets were thronged with people, but their undemonstrative silence struck us immensely after the enthusiasm we have met with everywhere on tour. The officials and soldiers all greeted us very warmly at Government House, and my heart sinks at the prospect of having to plunge at once into a round of society. I had of course to show Louisa part of the house; she is naturally appalled at its size, and its want of accommodation. The great excitement of the evening was unpacking piles of boxes containing a trousseau which Ruby has kindly chosen for me, chiefly from Reville and Rossiter.[236] In spite of having to arrange my sitting-room, I managed to have time to try on four dinner gowns, three smart day and two lace gowns, besides an evening cloak and a coat and skirt. They fit me beautifully and I am delighted with them all. Ruby deserves a medal for having made such an extraordinarily pretty selection. I shan't like it so much when the bills come in.

Thursday, 16th.

My one morning in Calcutta was rather a nightmare. Thousands of things had to be seen to on arrival, officials, tradesmen, staff, &c., &c., all clamouring for interviews. I sat up till 1.30 last night trying to get through my English mail, and part of my morning was occupied with the milliner, who has been to Paris, and brought me a huge assortment of head gear, worthy of my new clothes. I am horrified to find that most of the smart hats cost at least £10. Louisa tells me in Paris they ask £30 and 40 for each hat and that people are wicked enough to buy them! We drove to the station in our new Rolls Royce landaulette; it is a real beauty, runs quite noiselessly and was their exhibition car. I was very glad to see Thomas, our chauffeur again; he was very nearly killed in that awful motor accident with Lord Lonsdale;[237] the latter was driving a new 150h.p. machine and going at about 100 miles an hour. He realised too late there were two sharp turns at the foot of a steep hill and in his anxiety to slow down and quickly use the brake, he by mistake put on the accelerator. The car dashed forward at

---

236. Reville and Rossiter was appointed Court Dressmaker to Queen Mary in 1910.

237. 5th Earl of Lonsdale, 1856-1944, the famous 'Yellow Earl'. Founder and 1st President of the AA, described by Edwar VII as "almost an emperor, not quite a gentleman".

a terrific speed and carried away 25 feet of stone-wall. Lord Lonsdale, as one would expect, got off without a scratch. Thomas was many weeks in hospital with a fractured skull and injuries to his leg, but he says he is all right again now.

Wednesday, 22nd. Calcutta.

There has been another horrid murder, a Collector, Mr Jackson, who was just leaving India for good, was invited to go and see a native play somewhere in the Bombay Presidency, he was shot dead by a boy of 18 as he entered the theatre. Owing to this Rolly will not be able to discharge any of the deportees, and I expect this will greatly annoy the authorities in England, as unless the deportees are released the Government will lose many of the labour votes.

Louisa and I motored to Barrackpore with Captain Mackenzie; she was delighted with the beauty of the place. As usual most of the furniture has disappeared. Louisa was so amused at the violence of my temper! Considering I have arranged the furniture in these bungalows scores of times I certainly had provocation. My wrath anyhow had the desired effect, as during tea we saw 24 coolies in a long line hurrying past the shamiana each with a table on his back!

Christmas Day.

It is hard to believe that this is our fifth Christmas in India. I intended giving no presents, but it ended in my sending small tokens to each of the permanent staff and the family. Everyone has been extremely cheerful and they have amused themselves with tennis, golf, croquet or riding. I played golf with 'Scatters' against Tiger and Captain Fisher and we won our match.

Friday, 31st December, 1909. Calcutta.

Most of the party went to a ball at the Unceremonials[238] to dance the New Year in. Personally, I had not the zeal to sit up and heard the clock chime out the magic hour from my bed.

Old Sir Pertab Singh wired some time ago to Colonel Dunlop telling him he was arriving on such and such a day in Calcutta. Colonel Dunlop telegraphed asking him what his address would be, the answer came back: "I am staying with you." Consequently he has been living in a tent in the garden for three weeks, and he lunches or dines with us, whenever he chooses. He talks the most marvellous jargon, but all he says is much to the point. Speaking of a man arrested for sedition he said: "Not waiting try man—much chili—then hanging." Chili he suggests putting into a man's eyes in order to obtain information. He made a speech at the Polo dinner which delighted everyone: "Me thinking it good thing Englishman winning polo match—Rajputs and Englishmen all brothers—no damned Bengallee Babu." When Evie

238. The Unceremonials Club.

Tennis players, Simla
Capt. Harker, M.M. Capt. Tod.

Gibbs introduced him to his brother who has just arrived from England saying: "This is my brother Maharaja Sahib," the old man answered: "Not your brother: my brother." Another time he went up to a man in a crowd and said: "You Bengalee Babu; you teaching me making bombs, but when I making bombs not killing Englishman, I killing you." In speaking of Rolly's ancestors he said: "Viceroy he good pedigree: why for sending man no pedigree—not buying horse no pedigree, not buying dog no pedigree, not buying buffalo no pedigree, why for man no pedigree?" His own pedigree dates back for thousands of years. The following are a few of the many hundred telegrams and letters we received, congratulating us on our escape from the Ahmedabad outrage:

H.M. the King-Emperor to Viceroy. Telegram, Windsor Castle, 15th November 1909. Sincere congratulations on escaping from the dastardly attempt on your life. Trust Lady Minto has not suffered from the shock.

Chief of Bhor to Viceroy, Baroda. Telegram, Bombay, 15th November 1909.
I feel extremely delighted to know from Times of India that by the grace of the Almighty God Your Excellency was miraculously saved from the mischievous deed of miscreants of hurling bombs at Ahmedabad, and I pray that the Almighty God may always be with Your Excellency to protect Your Lordship and Lady Minto.

Comtesse Pierreford (The Empress Eugenie) to Countess of Minto.
Telegram, Farnboro, 15th November 1909.
Shocked at news; rejoice escape.

H.H. Nizam of Hyderabad to Viceroy, Telegram, Hyderabd, 15th November 1909
Just heard shocking attempt made at Ahmedabad on the lives of Your Excellency and Lady Minto. Kindly accept my most sincered congratulations on your providential escape. I admire Your Excellencies' coolness and courage in going on as if nothing happened.

The Hon. the Maharaja of Burdwan to Viceroy. Telegram, Burdwau, 16th November 1909.
Horrified to hear of dastardly attempt. Thank Providence for miraculous escape of Your Excellencies. Don't lose heart. You have real India at your back.

W. Hyslop, Esq., and others of Toronto, Canada, to His Excellency the Viceroy.
Letter, dated Taj Mahal Hotel, Bombay, 17th November 1909.
We, Canadians, travelling on the S. S. Cleveland, on Clarks Tour of the World, were horrified and shocked at the dastardly attempt on your life, and that of your wife, Lady Minto, in which we know the whole of Canada joins. Permit us then, on our own behalf and that of the land of the Maple Leaf, to extend to you our sincere congratulations, that both of you have been miraculously saved from the assassins' bomb, and for which we thank God, and that both of you may be long spared in your sphere of usefulness, and to happy old age is the wish of the undersigned, we may say every Canadian, and we believe, outside of a few assassins, the people of India.

Sirdar Amrik Singh to Private Secy, to Viceroy.
Letter, dated Lahore, 30th November 1909.

Viceregal staff, 1909.

I was filled with rage on reading in the papers that a useless wretch had offered injury to the exalted Viceroy and to Lady Minto. When I heard this I was ill and in the Doctor's hands. As I have eaten the salt of Government, the news gave me great pain. My heartfelt wish is to come to you and offer my services in connection with this, but I had to postpone my purpose until I am well. I am now well and must I show my loyalty in any part of India you may choose. These times are more difficult than those in which I won distinction, but I still long to serve the Sirdar. I hope so to come and see Your Honour in Calcutta.

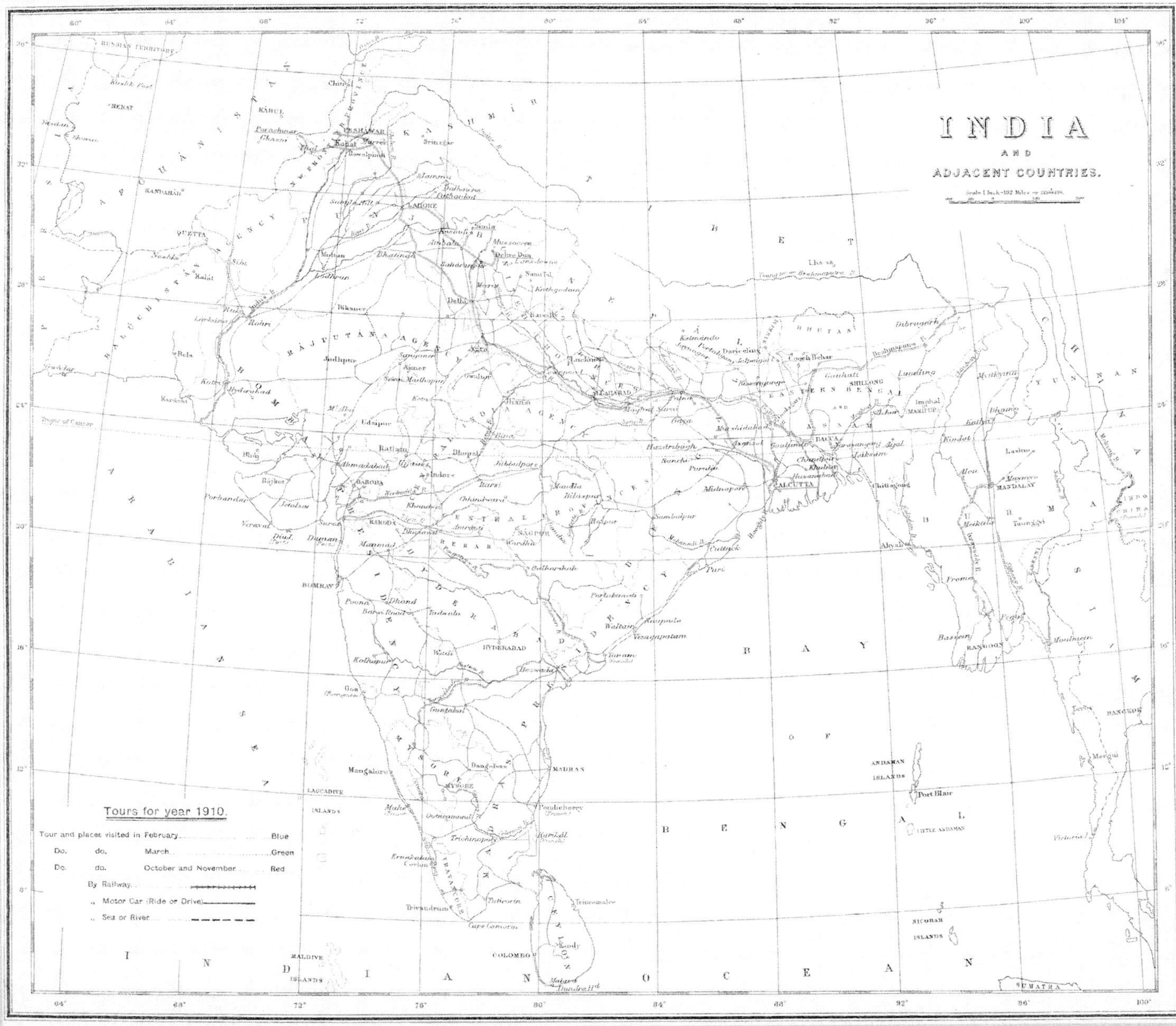
INDIA
AND
ADJACENT COUNTRIES.
Tours for year 1910.
Tour and places visited in February .... Blue
Do. do. March .... Green
Do. do. October and November .... Red
By Railway
,, Motor Car (Ride or Drive)
,, Sea or River
BAY OF BENGAL
ARABIAN SEA
INDIAN OCEAN
CALCUTTA
BOMBAY
MADRAS
HYDERABAD
MYSORE
LAHORE
PESHAWAR
QUETTA
KARACHI
RANGOON
MANDALAY
COLOMBO
ANDAMAN ISLANDS
NICOBAR ISLANDS
LACCADIVE ISLANDS
MALDIVE ISLANDS

1910

January 1st, Calcutta.

It seems incredible that we are beginning the final year of our regime here, and that we attended our fifth and last proclamation parade this morning. The whole party turned out in force and were photographed in a huge group on our return. Rolly was then taken alone with his staff, and poor old blind Dandy occupied the same place at his feet as he did five years ago. He is now rather a pathetic relic of old times.

Thursday, 6th.

Gave a huge dinner party. The investiture took place first. Rolly made the two first people Members of the Indian Empire instead of Star of India, but as they have their ribbons to vouch for them, it didn't signify, and I don't think many people noticed the slip. Dear Dunlop knelt and arose Sir Dunlop. I hate to think he is leaving us in a month's time, and he himself cannot speak of it without emotion. The Maharaja of Jodhpur received the G.C.S.I.,[239] and his two darling little boys came to see the ceremony. The Maharaja told me they were going on to the Circus, and that they had had a splendid time shopping in Calcutta. I sat between the Maharaja and Sir Lawrence Jenkins[240] at dinner. The Maharaja was exceptionally nice and told me how all the Princes longed to speak out on Rolly's behalf, but that there was always the risk of Lord Curzon being able to influence the Government at home against them, if they said what they felt. He told me that he had never been to Government House in Lord Curzon's time and had only seen him at the Delhi Durbar.

I was very brave with Sir Lawrence Jenkins, and plunged into a discussion on the danger of the trials of criminals being so prolonged. I rather surprised him by saying I thought it a pity we had not followed the same course as the Dutch who have one code of laws for themselves and another for natives. This information I had only gleaned on the previous day from Mr Allen, who has just visited Java, but it greatly impressed the Chief Justice with my knowledge of the law! Sir Lawrence quite agreed that it would be far better to have more summary punishment, which would impress the natives who at present despise our dilatory investigations, but we have to abide by the law of the land, although Rolly is working hard trying to get more stringent measures enforced.

The dinner was a great success and the table looked very pretty covered with roses from Barrackpore.

Wednesday, 12th.

Louisa and I motored down to Barrackpore after luncheon in order to have a completely undisturbed afternoon. I can never be grateful enough for having had such a delightful time

239. Knight Grand Commander of the Star of India.

240. Former Chief Justice of Bombay and member of the Viceroy's Council.

with her. She has enjoyed every minute and has taken the deepest interest in all she has seen and heard. She has mastered the political situation in a wonderful way, and goes home primed by all the authorities here.

Thursday, 13th.

Such a sad day of parting. Xandra and Tiger have been with us for nearly 10 months. They both say this has been the happiest time of their lives, and they are genuinely upset at leaving. Felt too unhappy to do more than dog Louisa's footsteps during the morning, and went with her to the station immediately after an early luncheon. They have very comfortable carriages and a large retinue of servants, so they will not feel they have fallen from their high estate until they get on board the S.S. India[241] at Bombay. Returned with a feeling of overwhelming depression which I found impossible to shake off. This is also felt by Rolly, Eileen, and all the Staff, so I meet real sympathy on all sides, but the blank Louisa leaves seems paralysing.

Friday, 14th.

The Staff gave a ball in the Town Hall. It was really the best done thing I have ever seen. The whole of the building was draped in blue and white material with palms and flowers, and the three supper rooms were beautifully decorated. The menus were a work of art, and quickly disappeared as the guests stole them as souvenirs. The older people recalled a ball given in the eighties by the Buffs which is still quoted as the most brilliant function in the memory of Calcutta; this ball in future will be bracketed with it. We didn't get home till nearly 3 A.M. after a thoroughly enjoyable evening. Captain Mackenzie tells me that seven miles of blue material was used in draping the rooms. This gives one some idea of the size of the building and the magnitude of the undertaking.

Saturday, 15th.

Felt cheered by getting the dearest letter from Louisa. She tells me that she, Xandra, and Tiger felt terribly depressed and are quite satisfactorily sad at having left us.

Sunday, 16th.

Such a peaceful Sunday, the first real rest I have had since we left Simla. Rolly is trying hard to get further Acts passed to deal with the present unrest. We have known for some days past that the Jat Regiment was not absolutely to be relied on. There has been a conspiracy

---

241. Used as an armed merchant cruiser in WWI, torpedoed and sunk off Norway in 1915.

to encourage the soldiers to become members of seditious associations. The men have been given money by the agitators. It sounds very serious once they begin tampering with the Army, but in some ways it strengthens the hands of the Government of India and will enable them to take much stronger measures.

Tuesday, 18th.

The Maharaja of Bikaner arrived; he is my favourite of all the Princes, and I look upon him as a real friend. I found myself at supper next to Mr Justice Fletcher; he is the Judge who, for some unaccountable reason, acquitted a native who had murdered a planter in Assam. The whole English community are so furious with him that they make their dislike very evident when he appears in the Bengal Club. I launched out in my most innocent manner on the iniquity of long trials which do so much in India to lessen our authority, and told Mr Fletcher that instead of allowing a known murderer three appeals, I would hang him and all his accomplices in public on the Maidan. The idea seemed to shock him greatly, and he was evidently uncertain if my remarks were accidental or specially aimed at himself. He kept on disclaiming any responsibility in the recent trials and I disarmed him by assuring him that I realised how much he must disapprove of the 14 conspirators in the Manicktollah Garden case having got off.[242] He was terribly flurried, to my great satisfaction, and did not know what to say.

Wednesday, 19th.

We dined with the Chief Justice and Lady Jenkins. Mr Fletcher was also there, and he told me that my blood-thirsty views as to hanging people had given him a sleepless night. I told him I was glad of it and hoped he would realise the importance of following my advice. Lady Jenkins is a splendid hostess; she says the unexpected thing in a most amusing manner. After dinner we found two Native Judges, Mr Mookerjee, a great friend of Rolly's, Vice-Chancellor of the University, and a Mr Chatterjee, awaiting us. Lady Jenkins went up to them; assured them she had forgotten all about them, as owing to some tiresome caste rules they could not dine with us. Then she added: "How long have you been alone in this room? What have you stolen? Let me look at your pockets?" They were quite unaccustomed to this sort of chaff, but enjoyed it thoroughly. After the late Chief Justice's wife, Lady Maclean, who thought herself too great a lady to do more than patronise me, it is a great relief to have some one who views life from a cheery aspect.

---

242. This was the Alipore Bomb Case in which, among others, the Nationalist leader, Sri Aurobindo, was acquitted. Arms and explosives were discovered by the police at a house belonging to him in Manicktollah Road in the suburbs of Calcutta. His time in gaol before the case was heard appears to have marked the start of his spiritual journey. Justice Fletcher had form, he had additionally made himself extremely unpopular with the British authorities in 1909 by awarding damages against the *Englishman* newspaper to Lala Lajpat Rai, the deported activist.

Thursday, 20th.

A native gentleman sent me during the afternoon a cheque for Rs. 2,000 for my nursing scheme, as a sort of parting present to me; he was at Herr Büchner's concert arrayed in all his glory, so I had an opportunity of thanking him. The Indians have been so good in helping me, but we have never asked them for subscriptions, as these nurses do not in any way benefit them.

Friday, 21st.

We dined with the Lieutenant-Governor. I sat between my host and General Kitson; everything was very well done. The Bakers' servants have blossomed out in a crop of Royal Crowns that look ill at ease resting over a plain ugly B on the breasts of the *khidmatgars*. Crowns and B's adorn their glass and china, the menus, and appear on every available spot. I don't believe he has any right to them, which is rather pathetic. There was quite a good dance after dinner. I created a sensation by falling flat on my back during the lancers. I was dancing with Sir Edward. Eileen implored little Baker to swing me round, and in his endeavours to revolve with speed, he trampled on my tail, which somehow twisted itself round my feet, and I found myself hurled to ground with great violence. My combs flew in all directions, but I was up in a moment. I have evidently profited by long practice in falling on the ice, as every one said it was quite a stage fall. Eileen declares Lady Baker came up, peered through her lorgnette and said in an agitated voice: "I don't think you have lost any hair, Your Excellency!" Curiously enough once my combs were replaced I was little the worse except for a bruised hip, and a good deal of skin off my elbow. Lady Baker insisted on boracic ointment being applied to avoid blood poisoning. Countless people came up to me and expressed horror at the catastrophe, so Lady Jenkins' remark was rather refreshing; she flew up to me and said: "Oh Your Excellency! I am so grieved at having missed the sight of the evening; unfortunately I wasn't in the room." She has a story of poor Mary Curzon, who once had the misfortune to fall. An A.D.C. not seeing who had been knocked over screamed out: "Sit on her head." Needless to say that particular A.D.C.'s services were not required any longer at Government House.

Tuesday, 25th.

At 11 o'clock the new Legislative Council assembled. It was a very historical day, and Rolly might well feel gratified in seeing the fulfilment of his hopes. At the last moment he had to change part of: his speech on account of the horrible murder that was perpetrated the night before. The native police have shown such wonderful pluck in following up information in spite of the risks they run. This poor man was their very best Inspector.[243] The Council

Legislative Council of His Excellency the Governor General 1910.

243. The Deputy Superintendent of Police, Samsul Alam, had been assassinated by Biren Datta-Gupta.

Room was packed with people, and the solemnity of the occasion seemed to impress itself on every one; Rolly commenced his speech amid perfect silence. He spoke gradually with more and more emphasis, and, as he announced that whether for good or ill he alone was responsible for the reforms, his strength and determination quite carried his audience with him and they broke out into an enthusiastic burst of applause, a thing unheard of in the Council Chamber. I looked up and saw the picture of Rolly's great grandfather listening, as it were, to the measures introduced by his descendant just a hundred years after he himself had held the reins of government and wondered if he was following the trend of affairs and the aspirations of the Eastern community from an unseen world..

Thursday, 27th.

I heard from Sir Sven Hedin by the last mail. He is very proud of having received the K.C.I.E., for which Rolly recommended him. In return he has got his King to give Dunlop a K.C. of the North Star and Victor a Swedish Military Order. He says that the fact that King Gustave has decorated both Rolly's secretaries is meant to be an act of gratitude to the Viceroy.

Monday, 31st.

Having enjoyed the Paperchase so much last Tuesday I determined to go out again. For some unknown reason both Rolly and Eileen were much averse to this excess of zeal on my part and both implied that I should certainly kill myself if I attempted to ride round the course. This was naturally very upsetting, but at the same time these predictions are hardly ever fulfilled. The course was a very twisty one and I had great difficulty in getting Waitress over rather a large mud-wall surmounted by palm leaves. After about half a dozen determined refusals, I managed to get her over. She jumped the top twig, which was so high that I thought we were never going to land on the earth again. All went well for a couple more fences, and although Waitress seemed inclined to refuse, I got her safely over another fence and a small mud-wall. We then pursued a circuitous jungle path for a bit, and on coming out into the open the paper led towards a high mud-wall. Thinking I would not give her an opportunity of swerving, I galloped at it pretty fast. Captain Muir, who was riding behind me, says that he thinks she never had any intention of jumping and we were going too fast to enable her to stop. Anyhow she never rose an inch, and the next thing I knew was that we had turned a complete somersault over the wall, luckily falling on the right side, which enabled me to get free of her. We came down a fearful smash. I was conscious of a very sore head, hand, shoulder and leg, but got up at once, as luckily no bones were broken and Waitress stood quite still and I didn't let go of her. Mrs Buck, who was just in front of me, saw the whole thing and thought I must be killed; she and Captain Muir came and picked up the pieces, very relieved to find that I was still alive. It evidently was a horrible fall to watch. I got on Waitress again who was none the worse, and rode back to the starting point. I felt very crestfallen and my hand was badly sprained and hurt horribly. On arriving home Dr Clarke came and overhauled me and found no bones broken, but my hand will have to be tied up for some days and writing will be impossible. Eileen telephoned to Rolly, who was still at Barrackpore, to break the news to him in a diplomatic way. He naturally says he expected some such thing to happen, and that grandmothers are not supposed to go over a paperchase course. I was obliged to pull myself together, and with my hand in a sling and a terribly stiff leg, had to appear at the garden party; 2,300 people were invited and my hand of course made the topic of the afternoon. Eileen has developed a rash and Colonel Crooke fears measles, such a terrible trial, just as we are playing up for our final Calcutta fling. A quarantine of three weeks will be a serious calamity.

Tuesday, 1st February.

So terribly sore and stiff that I remained in my bed. Eileen has measles alas, I am so sorry for her.

Wednesday, 2nd

I gave a purdah party in the afternoon to about 80 Indian ladies and a good many English ladies came to assist in looking after the guests. The little Rani of Vizianagram told me that this was the first party she had ever been to in her life but she was quite at her ease, very dignified and gave everyone the impression that she considered herself superior to everybody else. However, she made friends with Lady Creagh and arranged to call on her before leaving Calcutta next week. They all consumed an enormous number of sugar plums and chocolates and we had quite a difficulty in getting them to leave the house after a visit of nearly two hours. Apparently these purdah parties are quite an innovation and nobody realised how popular they would be.

Friday, 4th.

My hand continues to be very painful, so I went with Colonel Crooke to have it X-rayed at the Lady Minto Annexe that I recently opened. It evidently brought very bad luck my having said in my speech that I should not have another opportunity of visiting the hospital, as in the following week I had to return there as a patient. The new apparatus brought out the bones of my hand with wonderful distinctness and showed a break straight across the bone of my little finger slightly below the knuckle joint. It is a great nuisance, as I shall have to keep it in splints for a few weeks, and it makes writing practically impossible. Colonel Bird modelled a zinc splint on my hand which is not unwieldy and has the merit of being tolerably comfortable. It was impossible to detect the break in my hand owing to its being so fearfully swollen, but the fact of not keeping it perfectly still the first few days has rather increased the inflammation and certainly made it more painful.

Several people came to luncheon, amongst others the Consul for the Argentine, Monsieur de Basaldua. He has an intense admiration for Rolly. His French is very difficult to understand, but as far as I could gather he desires to collect a pice from each of the 300,000,000 natives in India, in order to strike a medal to commemorate his rule. I am afraid the 300,000,000 are not likely to fall in with his views.

Sunday, 6th February.

Just as we were going to bed a telegram arrived from Charlie announcing the arrival of a daughter. It was a great relief to get good news of Violet and the baby, but I suppose a boy would have been still more welcome.

Tuesday, 8th.

The Legislative Council assembled at 11 A.M. in order to pass the Press Act. The proceedings were opened by a very fine speech by Gokhale. He wanted a few amendments to the Bill, but in the main he agreed with it and paid a gratifying tribute to Rolly. It was an historical assembly and one could not help being astonished at hearing so many different natives speaking with such a command of the English language and in such broad-minded terms. I did not return at once after luncheon and unfortunately missed hearing a most eloquent speech of Sinha's which I believe was entirely unprepared. I returned to the Council-room after tea and heard the end of the amendments, the Bill was passed practically unanimously.

Rolly has considered the pros and cons of letting out the deportees, and has come to the conclusion that it will be impossible to keep political prisoners deported for an indefinite time. He consequently felt that the moment was a propitious one to let them out, as we are now armed with the Press Act and the Crimes Act which will make it much easier to arrest suspicious characters. The announcement of the release came as a complete surprise to everyone, with the exception of his Executive Council and one and all imagined that he had given way to undue pressure from home. Although Morley has never ceased agitating about the deportees for the past year, he himself did not know that this moment had been selected to release them. Rolly is quite certain that he has done the right thing from a political point of view. The deportees will be under police surveillance. This act of clemency will propitiate an enormous number of the native population, who will consequently be more inclined to assist in giving information as to the secret conspiracy, and if the Labour Party had raised a hue and cry in the House of Commons on the assembly of Parliament making martyrs of the deportees, their utterances would have been greatly exaggerated in India and copied into every vernacular paper which does an incalculable amount of harm. Whatever may happen in the future and however stringent the measures that may have to be taken, Rolly will undoubtedly be in a far stronger position to cope with them, beginning as he does now with a clean sheet.

We attended a Go-Lightly dance in the evening, the first we have ever been to. It was very well done and very cheery, although I am told that all the commercial community in Calcutta are perfectly furious, and are certain that the release of the deportees will cause a rising. I fancy they all expect to be murdered in their beds. Of course to us they were very reticent and did not express these views, but the Staff, who naturally did not know all the reasons that have influenced Rolly, returned in an absurdly depressed frame of mind.

Wednesday, 9th.

Dunlop came to say good-bye to me just before luncheon. It is too tragic having to part with him, and we both disliked saying good-bye equally, All the Staff went to see him off at the station.

The Maharani of Cooch Behar came up to see my sitting room after the tennis party was over. She appears to be intensely grateful to me for having started purdah parties. She declares that the fact of asking these ladies to meet at Government House has brought the different sections of the Indian community much closer together, as they have not been in the habit of visiting each other. She told me that she saw very strict purdah people drinking tea here, while they would not touch a drop of water in her house. The curious thing is that now these ladies have found out that it is quite pleasant to go into society, they prefer going to a European lady and asking her to make the arrangements for them to visit a native house, as they feel shyer of Indians of different caste than they do of English people. The Maharani attaches enormous importance to the feeling of friendliness that these parties create, and hopes that it may benefit the whole political situation. She is an extremely nice woman and I am sure her feelings of gratitude are genuine, although I personally realise that they have been earned very easily.

Sir Thomas Lipton arrived yesterday. I have not seen him for 11 years since we went on board the Erin during the time of the race of the 1st Shamrock for the American Cup.[244] He was full of conversation at dinner, did not conceal in any way that he had begun life as a grocer and confessed complete ignorance of what he called 'Viceregal Etiquette'. He certainly sampled a good many titles in addressing me. He called me Madam or Ma'am, my Lady, Your Ladyship, Your Grace and Your Excellency all in turn. He told me his father and mother were Irish and lived on a small farm in Scotland. His mother saved £80 with which they purchased a tiny shop in Glasgow. Everything he put his hand to prospered and he has recently sold his English business for £2½ million. He now owns half of Ceylon and has an enormous business in India but his trade in America brings him in the largest part of his fortune. He was very amusing in telling me how the whole of the Royal family were continually yachting with him. He seems to have been in the confidence of Princess Ena before she became Queen of Spain and thoroughly discussed what chances she had in captivating Alfonso. He asked her if she wanted to marry him, she replied tha she hadn't a cent and that of course she was most anxious to become a Queen. She told him there would be great opposition to her changing her religion and he advised her to turn Buddhist if the need arose.

The Aga Khan arrived to stay with us today. I found him most pleasant at dinner; evidently all the stories we heard about him in Bombay cannot be true, as he seems to have had a triumphal progress through India amongst the Moslems. He told me that the only way to appeal to the feelings of a native is through the superstition of his religion, and consequently he has told the priests in every mosque to issue a decree that, if any Mahommedans are found inciting rebellion and preaching sedition, they will be eternally damned. He suggested that the Hindus should issue a similar kind of manifesto, as they have no regard for this world's advantages, but would mind intensely if doubts were thrown on their prospects of happiness in a future state, but I am afraid there are too many various beliefs to make this feasible.

244. The Erin was Lipton's yacht—he also had several racing yachts names Shamrock.

Friday, February 11th.

Sir Thomas Lipton is very full of anecdotes, he apparently calls most of the leading ladies in London society by their Christian names. I confess he amuses me greatly. He is impressed by the amount of work the Viceroy has to do, and told me that he had had up the young men of his firm, expressly to tell them that Lord Minto was so busy he had not only been unable to come to luncheon, but he had also had to return to his work immediately after dinner. He added "those fellows don't realise what an easy time they have got." At breakfast, Fryer, who was pouring out his tea, asked him if he liked it strong or weak. "Strong," replied Sir Thomas, "it is good for trade"—he never loses an opportunity of alluding to his business.

Saturday, 12th.

We were to start for Barrackpore at 1 o'clock, and on going to Rolly's room to ask him if he was ready, I found him fuming with indignation at the whole of his morning having been wasted. Apparently the Chief telephoned directly after breakfast saying the matter was so urgent that he must see the Viceroy at once. He came round in mufti in a great state of excitement, having received a telegram from General Wodehouse, saying that a party of ladies had been missing on the frontier for 24 hours, that he feared the worst, that he found great difficulty in restraining the garrison and was anxious for orders as to what steps he should take. Mr Butler was sent for, the telegraph lines were cleared and all other business was suspended for about three hours, till information could be obtained. The Chief was anxious to telegraph to order every Afridi on the frontier to be arrested, but when Rolly discovered that the telegram had been sent en clair he began to be doubtful as to it being authentic, as no General could possibly have sent such an alarming message for every telegraph clerk to read. Imagine the indignation of the official world when a telegram was received from Lorna Hewett[245] saying "I hope the hoax Miss Johnston[246] and I have sent you has not caused you much inconvenience. Please forgive us, as we telegraphed in ignorance of what the consequences might be." It is such a criminal thing to have done with India in its present condition, that one is simply staggered at the effrontery of these girls, and all Rolly could think of doing at the moment was to order them out of the Frontier Province.

Sunday, 13th. Calcutta.

Telegrams are still coming and going in connection with Lorna Hewett's hoax. She seems to realise the enormity that she has committed. Forging General Wodehouse's name brings her under the Crimes Act with a penalty of five years' penal servitude. However, everyone has calmed down now and Rolly has sent a telegram forgiving her, but it is the greatest

---

245. Daughter of Sir John Hewett, Lieutenant-Governor of the United Provinces.

246. Her friend Sibell Vanden Bempde-Johnston who had come to India on a visit (the Editor's great grandmother).

mercy that the newspapers did not get hold of it and that a disturbance on the frontier was not reutered home to England.

Tuesday, 15th.

A totally different complexion has now been put on the Lorna Hewett episode. It seems when Sir O'Moore was recently in Lucknow, a great deal of chaff went on about these girls going to the Frontier, and the Chief cautioned them not to be taken prisoners. They asked him if he would send an expedition to rescue them, and he said he would command it in person, so they told him to expect a telegram. The telegram they sent him was signed "Wood Louse" I suppose the result of more chaff, and an officious clerk changed this into Woodhouse, as from the first it was noticed that the name was not correctly spelt, it should be Wodehouse. How this can have escaped the Chief's memory I fail to understand, but Sir O'Moore declared that he hardly knew either of the ladies. The ease with which the Commander-in-Chief has been taken in, and his excitement under the circumstances makes one wonder what the outcome of his regime will be as regards the efficiency of the Army. One cannot imagine anyone, however intimate, sending a ragging telegram to Lord Kitchener.

Wednesday, 10th.

Went with Miss Sorabji and Colonel Victor to see the Kali temple. It is a most squalid, miserable place and with nothing at all fine in the way of architecture. I believe on Tuesdays, the day the goats are sacrficed it is running with blood and crowded with worshippers. Today there was nothing special going on and one could only be disgusted at these revolting fakirs who are supposed to be holy men and sit covered with ashes, paint and dirt for days and days in the same attitude, occasionally allowing a worshipper to take a whiff from an opium pipe, on payment of a pice. We could see the image of Kali with the three red eyes and the golden tongue through an open door-way. No one but the priests is allowed inside the sacred precincts. One fakir sat motionless with head bent, and arms and legs folded in the position of a Buddha. He was under the effect of narcotics, and would probably remain in the same position meditating for six weeks at a time. Disciples then come and minister to his wants, and gratify his slightest wish. Parents never demur if Kali demands their best-loved child; they dare not refuse the sacrifice. It is too tragic to see these poor miserable little girls sitting about in groups. They are called "Temple Children". It is almost inconceivable to think that educated people can come and prostrate themselves at the various shrines before these images and smear themselves with mud, but Miss Sorabji tells me that many Hindus whom we consort with, conform to all the observances that the worship of Kali exacts, perhaps even more strictly for having allowed themselves to be influenced in any way by European ideas. The priests have the most extraordinary power over the people and no doubt have a great deal to say to the sedition that is being preached, for if Kali orders a man to murder his best friend feels bound to submit to the will of the gods.

Tuesday, March 1st.

Have had 10 days of nearly unbroken quiet at Barrackpore, which has done us all an immense amount of good. The Leo Rothschilds' third son and a young Guest[247] are staying here for a few days; they are travelling round the world together; they both seem very nice boys. An old friend of Rolly's has appeared on the scene, called Tottenham. He is extremely pompous, has a lame foot and is travelling round the world with only a hand-grip, so his appearance is not very aristocratic. He firmly refuses to have a bearer—how long his determination will last I don't know. He will be unable to obtain a bath or food if he adheres to his determination to refuse all outside assistance. A Major Bell lunched with us on Sunday. He brought with him a marvellous collection of medals and rather startled me at luncheon by asking me if I had not been at school in Pimlico in charge of the Clewer sisters. A sister of his had informed him that she had known me there. The thought of finding myself in that milieu seemed so intensely comic that I could only with difficulty conceal my amusement but I answered him as gravely as I could and told him my education had been neglected as I had never received any instruction Pimlico from the Clewer Sisters.[248]

A great deal of excitement has been caused by the crisis in Tibet. The Dalai Lama is now on his way to Calcutta and is to live at Hastings House.

London, February 23rd.

Reuter's Agency learns that some 25,000 troops, trained on the Japanese system, are being pushed into Tibet from Szechuan. They are equipped with an installation of wireless telegraphy and quantities of machine guns and mountain guns. The force is under the command of the vigorous and enlightened brother of the Viceroy of Szechuan.[249] The intention, apparently, is to establish Chinese domination over Tibet, to remodel conditions on the frontier, and to encourage Chinese settlement.

We hear from England (not from official circles) that Lord Kitchener and Sir Charles Hardinge are the two favourites in the betting as our successor. The latter, our informant states, finds the labours of the Foreign Office rather trying, and would appreciate the

---

247. Anthony Rothschild and Oscar Guest, son of 1st Baron Wimborne.

248. The Clewer sisters were the Sisters of St John the Baptist, their founder, Thomas Thellusson Carter was Rector of Clewer in Windsor for 36 years. Their main work, including at St Barnabas Mission and other houses in Pimlico, was with 'fallen women', 'higher class penitents' and in the training of orphans for service.

249. Chao Erh-Feng (Zhao Erfeng), known in Tibet as 'Butcher Feng'. His brother, the Viceroy, was Chao Erh-Hsun (Zhao Erxun).

change. I wonder after a year in India if he will find the work of the Viceroy the rest-cure he anticipates. The only new name I have heard suggested lately is Lord Balfour of Burleigh.[250]

Wednesday, 2nd.

Two years ago I received a letter from Mrs Cotes, who was formerly Marie Halboister, the Laurence Drummond's Governess, begging me to make acquaintance with a certain Miss Noble who was living in Calcutta, and had adopted the Indian mode of life. Her letter was so interesting that it is worth quoting an extract from it:

> "It is 10 years since I last saw Vivekananda, and he died in 1902, but no day passes without my thinking of him and few without my speaking of him. You very likely know of him and of his work as a reformer, of his scheme of establishing temples where all religions would get a hearing with the one limitation of not belittling other beliefs. I hear that you are keenly interested in the welfare of Hindu women, yet you must find it difficult to really get at them. Now there is in India a woman, an English woman, who has become one of them. She is a woman of education, who now and again has books published all referring to Hindu creeds, some of them translations from the Sanskrit. She was a Miss Noble, but gave up everything to help the Swamy in his work, and is now known by the name of Sister Nivedita. I believe she will tell you more about what you might wish to know concerning the way of Hindus than anyone else, at any rate of the Hindu women. I would love you to be the one Vicereine who really got at the heart of the Hindu woman problem, and I believe you will".

I received this letter just as I was leaving Calcutta for England so could not act upon it at the time. Last year I again made enquiries about Miss Noble, but found that she had gone to England. I kept the letter, as I still hoped to have an opportunity of making her acquaintance. Mrs Phillipson, while sitting next to Colonel Brooke at a dinner party, happened to tell him how interested she was in the condition of Indian women. Curiously enough I had given him Mrs Cotes' letter to read on the previous day, telling him to try and find out whether Sister Nivedita was still living in Calcutta, as I was anxious to meet her. Thinking this was rather a curious coincidence, Colonel Victor told Mrs Phillipson all he knew of Sister Nivedita, and advised her to seek her out. She went off the next day to the address he gave her, found Sister Nivedita, had a long talk to her, and realised at once what an interesting woman she was, with a genuine knowledge of the inner life of the Hindus. She lives in the heart of the native city in a tiny house in a back alley, and considering the present unrest I knew I should never be allowed to go to that quarter of the town without special police protection, if people knew I was going. I consequently begged Mrs Phillipson to say nothing about it to anyone, but simply to ask Sister Nivedita if she might bring a friend to see her, which she gladly agreed to. Having obtained Rolly's permission, I walked

250. Secretary of State for Scotland 1895-1903.

across to Thacker Spink's with Colonel Victor, where we met Mrs Phillipson and got into her very dilapidated motor to the intense surprise of my jemadar, whom I left standing on the pavement. How Mrs Phillipson ever discovered the house I am at a loss to conceive. We had to climb up a sort of outside ladder and were greeted by Sister Nivedita, who has a most charming face with a bright intelligent expression. Mrs Phillipson at once told her who I was, and when she had recovered from her surprise, we sat down and had a most interesting conversation.

She looks at everything from an Indian stand point, but she spoke most gratefully of the reforms and the sympathetic treatment natives had received during our regime.[251] She has a small school of about 100 girls which she took me round. She tells me the people amongst whom she lives are quite high caste, but intensely poor and very proud. I think she idealises their virtues, but she quite recognises all the difficulties Government have to contend with, and was evidently much delighted at my having taken the trouble to come and visit her. She has studied the question of religions which date back thousands of years and maintains that philosophy and knowledge originated in India, and not in Greece. I returned safely to Government House, having quite enjoyed my escapade and having planned to visit one of the temples with Sister Nivedita at some future date.

Friday, 4th.

I went in the afternoon with Captain Jelf to the St Mary's Home for Old Women, which has recently been repaired and enlarged. One little room was inhabited by an old lady whom I had told I had met before when I visited the Home four years ago. She must have been quite 80 years old, extremely fat with a short crop of white hair, but with rather an intelligent expression. As I entered, she was busily reading a periodical, which I took up to see what kind of literature she was interested in. Imagine my surprise to find that the article in question was entitled: Is flirtation legitimate?" I was immensely amused at the zeal of this old lady, in thinking it worth while to glean information on such a subject. I however told her that I felt sure it was quite legitimate, and at once called Captain Jelf, who was waiting for me in the hall, to discuss the subject with her, which he did, while I inspected the rest of the building. He no doubt made her supremely happy.

Gave our last Calcutta dinner party.

Tuesday, 8th. Calcutta

At 4.30 started in the motor with Colonel Victor to pick up Sister Nivedita who had arranged to take us to the big Hindu temple on the banks of the river. She insisted on

251. Sister Nivedita was a nationalist who had been blacklisted by the authorities; her school was something of a centre for nationalists and revolutionaries. She encouraged Sri Aurobindo to take refuge in Pondicherry after his release by the British

my seeing some wonderful copies of frescoes taken from Indian temples painted by a Mrs Herrington, who apparently is a well-known copyist of the Italian school. We then drove on to the temple, left the motor outside the garden gates and walked in, first passing a Neem tree which is supposed to be sacred and where Mahommedan women come and worship, leaving curious little mis-shapen clay horses at the foot of the tree as an offering to the gods. We walked on till we came to a stone terrace which faces the Hughli.[252] Under a tree on this terrace Vivekananda meditated for 12 years till he was satisfied that he had discovered the meaning of "Truth". The spot was well chosen for such meditation, looking peaceful and beautiful in the setting sun. We were joined here by a Swamy who escorted us to the cloister that surrounds the court-yard of the temple. We were not allowed to penetrate further, but looked through the arches towards the building in which the image of Kali dwells. Priests were walking backwards and forwards and tiny naked children were playing about the steps. This wonderful temple seemed to breathe peace and contentment; it was scrupulously clean and was a marked contrast to the Kali Ghat. Pilgrims came along with bunches of flowers as offerings, which were to be laid at the foot of Vivekananda's holy tree. They had branches of a particular tree with a small kind of magnolia flower that has the most delicious perfume. One of the pilgrims overheard me say how much I liked the smell, and at once gave me two of his branches. I found out afterwards that the name of the tree is Pterospermum acerifolium; it is the most fragrant tree I know.[253]

We were taken to see Vivekananda's little bedroom which is considered so holy that we were obliged to remove our shoes before entering. It was a curious mixture of squalor and comfort. The bed with mosquito curtains seemed quite luxurious; the walls were hung with a curious medley of pictures, gods and goddesses next to one of our Lord saving Peter from drowning. This little room seemed to fill Sister Nivedita's mind with holy thoughts, but to me it was the only jarring note in the otherwise beautiful surroundings. We walked down the flight of steps to the river, and got into a little native boat rowed by three men, who sat diagonally in the bows, while one man steered in the stern. I never thought that I should be able to take a trip incog. in one of these little native boats.

Sister Nivedita's friend, Sister Christine, was sitting in the boat awaiting us. They provided cushions for me to sit on and they then proceeded to make some tea as we were rowed down the river. I took the precaution of saying that I preferred my tea without milk, as visions of typhoid passed through my mind. It had an extremely good flavour and I think must have been the best orange pekoe, but they told us every thing was Swadeshi, biscuits, tea, sugar, cups and saucers, &c., &c. I thoroughly enjoyed our half-hour's row to a landing stage, a mile or so down the river where the motor had been sent to await us. Of course no one recognised me during the afternoon and the four boatmen who really displayed an unwonted amount of energy in rowing us to our goal were overwhelmed with surprise on receiving

252. Hooghly.

253. The Bayur or dinner-plate tree.

far more than a month's pay in *backsheesh*. I found the afternoon extremely interesting and Sister Nivedita was charming to talk to, she sees beauty in all her surroundings and has a wonderful knack of quoting old Persian poems that seem applicable to the subject of conversation, reciting in. a curiously pitched voice of reverent devotion.

Wednesday, 9th.

Started at 10 o'clock on another expedition with Miss Sorabji, which compared very unfavourably with yesterday afternoon. We were anxious to visit the Jain Temple, but a great many of the roads are under repair and we drove round about for ages before we were able to find our way. The temple itself is the most appalling erection of stucco and coloured glass joined together in mozaic fashion. After passing through many intricate lanes we came to another little temple, an off-shoot of what we had seen yesterday, but immensely inferior in every way. This was where Vivekananda had taught his pupils, and Miss Sorabji and I were much amused at the extraordinary mixture of English civilisation amongst Hindu surroundings. The most amazing feature was a European lavatory, which is quite unorthodox, and against all caste prejudices. The priests were having their mid-day meal when we arrived, amongst them was a European who looked strangely out of place with his white face and closely cropped fair hair. He was a Dutchman and had been converted by Vivekananda in America. He told me that he found the mid-day sun most trying without a hat; my only wonder is that he is alive. Everything was scrupulously clean and the priests evidently preferred English beds to the ordinary Indian charpoy. I at once detected the same priest who showed us round the temple on the previous day and he equally recognised me, so if he finds out who I am—and I think he had become suspicious, he will imagine that I am about to embrace the Hindu religion. Miss Sorabji tried to make the priests talk politics but in this she absolutely failed. They said they were holy men and politics were beyond their sphere.

After tea we went to St John's Church to attend the christening of Mrs Parsons' baby. Rolly is godfather. The baby behaved like an angel, he barely cried enough for luck. After the christening we remained for the evening service, at the conclusion of which Rolly unveiled a bust of his great-grandfather to replace the one smashed in the earthquake of 1897 on the pedestal remaining with Lord Minto's name on it. Rolly has had a beautiful marble bust made by a man called Jenings who took the likeness from the picture of Lord Minto in the Council Room.

Thursday, 10th.

Prince Liechtenstein, Duc de Mouchy and Count Potocki have arrived to stay. They brought letters from Lord Knollys,[254] Horace Farquahar[255] and Count Mensdorff. Mr Price Collier, author of "England and the English" has also arrived.[256] The three foreigners all seem very pleasant. I remember dancing with Count Potocki's Father at Grosvenor House in the dark ages. He was very good looking and I believe rather a *vaut rien*.[257]

Monday, 14th. Calcutta

At 11 o'clock the Dalai Lama paid Rolly an official visit, he only had a few followers with him and in his hasty flight he did not bring any of the ponies and weirdly dressed retainers that made the Tashi Lama's arrival in Calcutta so picturesque. A lot of people came to view the Dalai Lama from the balcony; he is quite a young man, with a pleasant expression; he and his suite mounted the steps with the ungainly gait unavoidable in walking in Tibetan boots. In the afternoon he had a long private talk with Rolly; he wants to be sure of British protection. It is curious that five years ago he fled to China to avoid the English; now things are reversed, and he seeks shelter in English territory from the Chinese.

Tuesday, 15th.

Arrived at Benares at 11 o'clock. The Maharaja and his son were at the station to receive us. Mr Lovett, the Commissioner, and his wife motored us at once to the brass bazaar; we walked through tiny lanes of shops shining with brasses of all shapes and sizes. We struggled to select a variety of objects, and then walked on to the celebrated embroiderer Hari Das. Here we saw the most dazzling brocades of gold and silver. I resisted buying many priceless tissues with great difficulty but even now I fear my account will be an unpleasant surprise when I receive it. The walk through the tiny narrow streets was like a series of brilliant pictures glowing with colour. I made a school of diminutive boys happy by asking for a holiday for them; they were sitting demurely in rows before a shop, being instructed by a Munshi. My request was greeted by a hymn of praise.

It was too late and too hot to go on to any temples that morning, so we returned to the guest-house, where the Maharaja entertains us. At 4 o'clock we started for the Maharaja's palace (Rarapur), which is 10 miles away. Here we were received with all due honour—

254. Private Secretary to the King.

255. Liberal Unionist politician and Lord in Waiting to the King

256. Price Collier wrote *England and the English from an American Point of View* published in 1909, also *Germany and the Germans* etc.

257. Worthless person.

elephants and trappings, guards of honour, &c., and the Maharaja himself awaiting us at the entrance. He conducted us through red carpeted passages lined with soldiers to the Durbar Hall. We watched a nautch for some time, then he took us to be photographed, and finally we looked at his armoury. On our return to the guest-house the Maharaja's Secretary brought Eileen and me two beautiful white silk coats with golden embroidery which will make lovely wraps for the evening.

We felt exhausted by dinner time, but had to sit through the most enormous meal provided by the Maharaja. The menu was as follows, which was rather over-powering for five people.

Hors d'Oeuvre
Fresh Oyster
Soup
Julienne
Fish
Fresh Pomfret, Maitre d'Hotel
Sauce
Entrée
Pintade à là Volail
Mutton Cutlets à là Champignons
Joint
Roast Turkey and boiled ham
Roast Saddle Mutton
2nd Course
Roast Quail
Asparagus, Butter and Vinegar Sauce
Sweet
Cherry Tart and Cream
Maraschino Jelly
Cheese and Biscuits
Strawberry Ice-crem
Desert Coffee

Wednesday, 16th

We were ready by 7 A.M. and motored to the river, where the Maharaja's barge awaited us, rowed by 20 men. In this we glided down the stream. There were not very many bathers, but the scene was extremely picturesque. Aurangzeb's two great towers and mosque stand up high above the town, the river is clear and blue, and the palaces with turrets and pillars make a splendid façade. We passed the burning ghats, and saw a poor corpse being hurried towards them by four bearers who were singing the usual dirge, *Ram Ram sath hai.*[258] I am told that, when the present Czar was at Benares, he expressed a hope that he would see some corpses actually burning; he was told that by his benign desire there would be an abundance of corpses. Three hundred were awaiting cremation in the morning, whether they had died a natural death or had been assisted out of the world for the occasion was doubtful.

258. The name of Ram is truth.

The Viceroy at Benares.

From the Temple of Vishwanath we proceeded to the temple of the Saraswati, goddess of plenty; where we were allowed to enter the court-yard and a chair was placed for me in the centre facing the open door of the temple in which the image of the goddess was being worshipped. I have never witnessed a more interesting scene. Tree would make thousands if he could reproduce it at His Majesty's.[259] A marvellous hymn was chanted without ceasing, lamps of sacred fire were waved and the altar was continually dusted with tails of yaks that were constantly swept across it. In the centre a raised platform was railed off, this was surrounded by carved pillars and was crowded with worshippers, some lay with their foreheads on the ground as they presented their offerings, others in attitudes of devotion were reciting prayers with intense reverence. Petals of marigolds strewed the floor, but the faces of the people were the most interesting study of all. A square colonnade surrounded the temple, and in almost every niche sat a fakir, quite covered with ashes, his face besmeared with paint, and his hair falling in matted ropes. A very old man, who sat just behind me blew an occasional blast on a marvellously shaped shell, this seemed to give him untold pleasure, and his withered old features relaxed into a smile as he accomplished this feat. By this time I had four garlands round my neck; they were damp and a terrible weight to carry. I was impressed by the kindly expressions of the crowd, a tall bare-headed man stood amongst them, and I could not help noticing that he was continually looking my way. I pointed him out to Mr Straight who told me he was one of his best Bengali detectives. I gazed passed the crowd clad in every coloured garment to the inner recess of the temple from which one caught glimpses of gold and silver, images, flames of fire, and priests in orange garments. The air was pervaded by an aromatic scent of incense and flowers. We sat in the comparative cool on the shady side of the temple, but just beyond us the sun beat down with cruel force, baking the stones of the court-yard like an oven. I hated leaving but every step we took along the tiny streets seemed to bring another brilliant picture before one. The native policeman preceded us, and all the natives rose and salaamed as we passed. The alleys are so narrow that no ray of sunshine penetrates, and this makes them astonishingly cool. Our next place of interest was the observatory, from whence the old astronomers could watch the signs in the heavens and foretell events. The heat was so great here that we hurried to the shelter of the motor, and were refreshed by the quick motion through the air as we returned home after a really thrilling morning. I have enjoyed my visit to the full and feel I have seen a greater variety of the religious side of Eastern life than ever before.

Thursday, 17th. Calcutta.

The Dalai Lama sent a small deputation with an offering of silk for me and Eileen. My roll of white brocaded silk is beautiful, but looks more as if it came from Lyons than China. Eileen's is a piece of genuine soft dark blue Chinese silk. Prince Antoine of Orleans has arrived for a few days. He has a cynical manner which is not at all prepossessing and evidently prides

259. Sir Herbert Beerbohm Tree, Actor Manager and owner of His Majesty's Theatre, Haymarket.

himself on saying sarcastic things. Mr Gladstone has also arrived for one night. He is the owner of Hawarden and I believe was a celebrated oar at Oxford.[260]

Friday, 18th.

I went to a purdah party at Woodlands given by the Maharanis of Cooch Behar, Moharbanj, Burdwan, and the Rani of Vizianagram as a farewell to me. The Maharani of Cooch Behar had already told me that, as the party was in my honour, I must consent to fall in with her wishes. I then found that she was bent on dressing me up as an Indian bride and had taken the precaution of asking me to put on a white gown, which would harmonize with an Eastern dress. I was taken to her bed-room and was arrayed by Princess Pretty in the most gorgeous gold and silver dress which she swathed round me in their clever style. A beautiful crimson and gold saree was draped about my head and I was then informed I was in the orthodox bridal costume, and that I must consent to go through the bridal ceremony for luck. I made anxious enquiries about the husband, but fortunately his presence had not been included in the programme. I pointed out that as a grandmother I made a most unsuitable bride, but the Maharani would not be denied. I was conducted to a platform in the centre of a large conservatory, round which fantastic designs had been painted. The Maharani then led a procession walking round and round me, some carrying lights, others flowers, others cakes and sweets. As each procession started the Maharani made passes over my head, placed leaves round my feet and finally held a tray of lighted lamps before me, passed her hand through the flame and touched my head and body with the sacred fire, which is supposed to bring good luck and send away any evil element. We then repaired to another room where the marriage cakes were presented. I was told that I must keep the marriage garments as a souvenir of the occasion; I believe the Indian ladies were really delighted to see me dressed up and I returned home in my gorgeous costume to be duly admired by Rolly. He knew that I was going through some sort of ceremony that afternoon and was rather relieved to hear that the husband had not put in an appearance.

Tuesday, 22nd. Calcutta

Had a very busy day sorting and arranging what things should be sent direct to England. It is astonishing how everything accumulates and I am at a loss to conceive where our huge collection will be stored at Minto. We must have hundreds of caskets of all sizes and descriptions and as we have been sending them home by degrees the number will be quite overwhelming.

---

260. William Glynne Charles Gladstone, grandson of the Prime Minister was the owner of Hawarden, killed in action 1915. His cousin Albert was the rower: he rowed in the Oxford team in the Boat Race 4 times and in the Leander eight that won gold in the 1908 Olympics.

At 5.30 I received a deputation of ladies who have subscribed towards a farewell present for me. It is an extremely pretty jewel made by Hamilton of Calcutta in the shape of a diamond Lotus.[261] What chiefly gratifies me in this presentation is that so many Indian ladies have subscribed and they all made a special effort to come to Government House today, 195 English and 179 Indian ladies. I am told that this is the first time that they have joined a movement of this kind. I was very sorry to say good-bye to the Maharani of Cooch Behar who leaves for England next month. She has been a real friend out here. She and her sister, the Maharani of Mourbhanj, the Maharani of Burdwan and the Rani of Vizianagram have combined to give me an ornament for the dinner table in the shape of a silver lotus, as a little extra farewell present. They have one and all been most charming in expressing their regret at our approaching departure. Motored back to Barrackpore in time for dinner.

Saturday, 26th. Barrackpore.

Mrs Besant came to see me and we had an interesting talk of an hour. She tells me that she considers the political situation certainly more satisfactory. The success of Rolly's policy she considers has already been proved. She herself has an extraordinary influence over the students in Benares; there are about a thousand boys at the College. She added that anything she could do or say to express the admiration she felt for the Viceroy was simply the desire to offer a small tribute of flowers, as a respectful token before a shrine which she venerated. She was so interested to hear that I had met Sister Nivedita and some of the Hindu swamies. All these enthusiasts are immensely pleased at my having shown interest in the complex question of castes and religion. After each visit I have invariably received some book in which they are specially interested; I am consequently collecting a large library on the various religions of the country.

On our way to Barrackpore Rolly and I stopped to see the art gallery of a well known Indian, Kumar Nagendro Mullick. He has got the most enormous palace in the heart of the city. The great Holi festival having taken place this week, half the population are dyed the most brilliant hues of orange and red which often includes their hair and faces, and gives the weirdest effect possible to the crowds in the streets. Mullick has evidently a passion for birds, as sacred peacocks were flying all over the place and in the courtyard there were crowds of parrots with the most brilliant plumage. We had not told him that Rolly was going to accompany me until the last moment, and his excitement

261. Hamilton & Co were known as the Garrard of India, the company, started by Robert Hamilton in 1808, invented the Toffee Pot, a coffee pot that could also be used for tea.

MM dressed as an Indian bride.

at receiving the Viceroy knew no bounds. His house is the most extraordinary mixture of marbles, bronzes, fine pictures and rubbish. He has two Gainsboroughs and a Rubens. Mullick has the reputation of being the richest man in Calcutta; he is very philanthropic and feeds a thousand poor people every day. We left covered with garlands and with masses of orchids. I am sure it pleases people that in spite of sedition we are not afraid to motor through these narrow streets and although one never can be sure that some fanatic may not commit an outrage, I think that the feeling of the people themselves is more friendly than it was when we arrived in Calcutta three months ago.

Monday, 28th.

Motored with the Sutherlands, Longes and Captain Muir about 7 miles beyond Barrackpore to see a Jute Mill. It has only been running fourteen years. Sir George Sutherland[262] himself decided where the jungle should be cut away, and the factory built, and it now appears to be a huge town. They employ 5,000 hands, and one building alone covers two acres. One machine drives the whole plant; it is a gigantic wheel with 2,000 horse power. We saw the whole process from the raw jute to the making and packing of the sacks, 150 miles of material is made every day, In one department tiny children were placing large empty reels on pins and carrying away filled ones; they evidently looked upon it as the greatest fun and there was much rivalry as to who worked the quickest. They did not look more than six or seven and I hated seeing their tiny figures so near the relentless machinery. Several babies were peacefully sleeping on heaps of rags under the wheel of a machine at which its mother was working. The noise was deafening and the fluff from the jute covered us from head to foot. The women were extremely smart, hung all over with silver bangles and rings and showed the greatest delight at my admiring their trinkets.

This is our last day at Barrackpore. No words can say how sorry I am to leave this ideal spot. As a final effort I have planned a new bit of garden at the commencement of the pergola. A great many small rose beds are to be removed, which gave it rather the appearance of a nursery garden, the whole space will be laid down in grass, with clumps of palms and lovely flowering shrubs. They have promised to have it completed by November, so I shall hope just to see it before leaving.

Tuesday, 29th.

Rolly went to Calcutta early for the final Council meeting; I followed later and listened to the speeches for a bit, but they were intensely dull. A good many of the Members lunched, also Miss Sorabji. She always has satisfactory things to tell one. She told me a tiny Raj Kumar who happened to be with his mother when she was visiting her said "Why is the

---

262. President Calcutta Chamber of Commerce, 1900-01.

Laut Sahib going to leave us? Is it because he wants the gods to let him live on a great stone horse on the Maidan like I see other Laut Sahibs, so as to watch over the people. The great Queen asked the gods to let her come to India too which was very kind of her, and she sits and watches over them from a chair".

Wednesday, March 30th.

Went at 10 A.M. to see the new Home which has just been started for the Minto Nurses. The Bengal Government have rented a very nice house in Camac Street. It is most satisfactory to think that we have been able to establish branches in every province in India with the exception of Bombay and Madras, where they have their separate organisations. We have now seven nurses in Calcutta, the rooms are charmingly furnished; fresh flowers are sent there daily from Belvedere. We are giving pictures to decorate the walls, and quite a nice little library has been started, so the house has got already quite a home-like appearance.

Went to the Council to hear the conclusion of the Budget Debate. All the Native Members concluded their speeches by thanking the Viceroy for the inestimable boon which the possibility of debate has given to the enlarged Councils. Already they notice the benefit that has arisen not only from a wider scope for discussion, which before rested in the hands of a small number of officials but also from the personal contact of the various Members who meet from all parts of India and who have now the opportunity of talking over questions of interest in a friendly spirit. Rolly may justly feel proud of being the author of this new Legislation which has been more successful than our most sanguine hopes allowed us to expect.

Thursday, 31st.

All our things have already been packed for England. I suppose we shall only return to Calcutta for about a week in November before leaving for good. It is a satisfaction to think that every single room has been done up, and that the new-comers will find a house replete with every comfort, instead of the barrack which we found on arrival, with its mustard coloured walls and an entire absence of anything attractive and homelike.

We drove to the station with a full escort of the Bodyguard. There were dense crowds in the street, and the difference in the feeling of the people to that which existed three months ago on our arrival in Calcutta, was most striking. The countenances had lost their sinister expression and everyone salaamed with effusion. One can only conclude that the people have realised that a genuine movement has been made to give the Indians a share in the government of their country, and I think they know that we both take a sincere interest in their welfare. This was certainly quite a differently disposed Calcutta crowd to any that has previously greeted us. The sentences in the Nasik murder trial have given universal satisfaction. Three men are to be hanged, three transported for life and one has two years rigorous imprisonment. Officials think there is no doubt that this gang were responsible for the bombs they threw at us at Ahmedabad.[263]

Rolly is quite pleased with the following announcement. The Anglo-Indian until our arrival drove to see his lady friends in his tum-tum, wearing his solar topee. At the door his top-hat was produced from under the seat, invariably brushed the wrong way; with this in his hand he made an imposing entry into the drawing-room.

> "If we are to accept the view of a Calcutta sporting newspaper, the greatest achievement of Lord Minto has been his discouragement of the top-hat! This is hardly the kind of distinction which we may expect in due course to find graven on brass or marble, but there is no doubt about it that by banning the top-hat whenever possible the Viceroy added greatly to the comfort of a large number of most estimable people. Anglo-India and modernised India will remember him in her prayers! It has been a pleasant relief, and it is no small thing to have accomplished, for custom dies hard in India and the furry, insanitary, uncomfortable and oft-times sadly ill-conditioned and undipped top-hat was never meant for torrid climes!"

Friday, 1st April. On the Train.

I think Cawnpore is the saddest place I have seen in India, far worse than Lucknow, where anyhow there were more troops and the Europeans were able to make a more systematic resistance. Seeing the various places where ghastly atrocities took place, made one's blood boil, and one realised more than one had ever done before what these unfortunate people must have suffered, not only from the tortures they were put to, but by being exposed day after day to the merciless rays of a June sun. We motored for about five miles out of Cawnpore to a place called the "Retreat" which Mr Allen has turned into the most delightful abode. I felt as if I had been suddenly transported to a backwater on the Thames, especially as Mr Allen took me in a punt where I lay at my ease on soft cushions. We landed in a flower garden with a green sloping lawn, where tea was awaiting us and, after tea, went with Mr Allen up another channel. A coolie tried to propel the punt with very moderate success, running first into one bank and then into another. I felt that Rolly would not long resist the longing to take the paddle; this he very soon did, and brought us back to the shore in the proficient style for which he was so famed in Canada, to the great surprise of the coolie, who evidently thought the Laut Sahib must be demented in undertaking so laborious a task for his own pleasure. Sir Alexander McRobert, the Cawnpore Woollen Mill owner, met us here.

263. The Collector of Nasik (now Maharashtra), AMT Jackson, a popular ICS officer sympathetic to Indian nationalist aspirations and a student of Sanskrit, had been shot dead by the student, Anant Kanhere, at the theatre at Nasik during the performance of a Marathi play. There was a view amongst a group of extreme nationalists at the time that good officers presented greater danger to their goals than obvious hardliners. The police investigation into the murder found evidence of a widespread conspiracy to overthrow British government in India through force.

His mills were burnt down last week. Damage to the amount of 11 lakhs has been done and his insurance only covers four. However he seemed quite cheerful and expects to resume work again immediately.[264]

Tuesday, 5th. Delhi.

The house here is much larger and more commodious than at Agra; it has electric fans which obviate the nuisance of having a punkah-wallah sitting day and night outside one's room. They are the most irritating race, always dropping off to sleep and snoring loudly, then awaking suddenly they pull the punkha with such violence that one is nearly blown from one's bed. They all evidently suffer from lung trouble, as one is deafened by a series of coughs and chokes, which no amount of abuse seems able to control.

Visited the Jumma Masjid after tea, and went on to the Fort. The Peacock Throne has been entirely repaired with Pietra Dura work. It has been magnificently restored and is now absolutely complete with the exception of one panel which was smashed purposely by one of the Fort attendants who had been discharged for bad conduct. His revenge cost him dear, as he was given five years' imprisonment.

Wednesday, 6th.

Rolly visited all the places of interest in connection with the Mutiny, accompanied by a native who was with the Commissariat during the siege. He was 22 at the time and remembered everything with wonderful distinctness.

At 4 o'clock we started for the Kutab,[265] motoring round by the old fort at Tuglakabad, which was built in the 10th century. The whole place is now in ruins; it extends over a large area and must have been well nigh impregnable, judging from the enormous thickness and height of the walls. We drove past the Kutub and visited parts of old Delhi, walking amongst ruins and finding unexpected alleys leading to fine old marble tombs with elaborate carvings and arches. There is a curious well here, 80 feet deep, at the bottom of which is nine feet of water. On the wall of this well six old figures were sitting. They at once proposed to jump down for our benefit. The well was so narrow that I thought it must be extremely dangerous. However they one after another precipitated themselves feet foremost to the bottom and emerged by a flight of steps unscathed on the other side. I suppose long practice has made them perfect, for they were all old men with bald heads and grey beards,

Diving well at Nizamuddin.

264. In 1911 Sir Alexander married Rachel Workman who was 30 years younger than him, the daughter of an American explorer whose wife was a mountaineer. They had 3 sons, the eldest killed flying in 1938, the younger 2 killed in action flying for the RAF in 1941. Lady McRobert gave a donation of £25,000 to the RAF to buy a Stirling bomber to be named "McRoberts Reply" and, in 1942, a further donation to buy 4 Hurricane fighters named after her 3 sons and herself. The McRoberts were, it seems, made of stern stuff

265. Qutab Minar.

looking far too decrepit to perform such an athletic feat. I asked if they were not afraid of hurting themselves against the sides of the well, but they said no, that no accident had ever happened as they first prayed to their saint and he protected them as they plunged into the holy water. We returned to the Kutab and walked up to the first platform which is about 100 feet high where the most gorgeous view is visible. It comprises new Delhi and a series of old Delhis, which were built one after another by the various Emperors, they occupy an area of 45 square miles. We seemed to be overlooking a sea of ruins consisting of minarets and tombs interspersed with fields and trees in their garb of fresh spring green.

Thursday, 7th.

We motored round the site of the Delhi Durbar before breakfast; only an enormous flat expanse of land. Lord Curzon was very anxious to erect a memorial of the Durbar but the scheme proved a failure as the country is flooded each year by the Jumna, making any permanent memorial impossible to build.

We then motored up and down Chandni Chauk, the celebrated Delhi bazaar where the mass of humanity must exceed any other in the World. A marvellous variety of vehicles move about the narrow streets; besides the regular bullock carts, there are weird shaped trolleys drawn by camels. Most people use ekkas, some are made with smart backs of cross bars of shining brass; they cannot be comfortable as they jiggle fearfully as the pony trots along. Whole families travel in long wagons drawn by fat bullocks with crimson curtains half hiding the women folk from view. Where this crowd of beings can be trekking, I am at a loss to conceive. We got out of the motor at the end, and walked down the very narrow Daria Bazaar, packed thick as sardines with people. This is the first time that Rolly has walked unattended in a native quarter and I believe was freely commented on. We walked to the end of the street to the celebrated ivory shop where we examined wonderful carvings. We quite thought we had not been recognised, but as we left, the shop man with many salaams begged for a letter of appointment, so they evidently had little doubt as to our identity.

Saturday, April 9th. Parachinar.

Arrived during the night at Kohat. The order to march was for 9.30 and our allowance of kit was very meagre, as the baggage had to be conveyed the 116 miles by motor car. The party consists of Rolly and me, Eileen, Colonels Pinhey, Crooke, Brooke, Captain Jelf, Francis and Mr Butler. Mr Merk, who is Acting Chief Commissioner for the North-West Frontier Province during Sir George Roos-Keppel's absence on leave, met us with his Assistant, Mr Griffiths. Never before has the Kurram seen such a procession of motor cars, 15 in all. The road has been carefully repaired by a regiment of Sappers. It has very steep inclines and sharp corners. A wild-looking native stood waving a red flag at all the dangerous turns, and wherever an indentation occurred in the road two white lines were painted across it to warn the chauffeur to go slowly. The road appeared to be so level that without this warning it would have been impossible to drive smoothly. Only in India would this acme of luxury be possible, but the Viceroy must not be inconvenienced by a single jolt during his drive, and Europeans and Natives have worked alike to arrive at this state of perfection for his comfort. I couldn't help thinking as we drove along this wild frontier road in comfort, of the pit falls in Sussex Street, when we first arrived in Canada in 1898.[266] They broke the springs of the carriages and dislocated all the bones of one's body.

Our first halt was at Thal, 60 miles from Kohat; where triumphal arches had been erected, and the wild men of the district came down to have a look at the Viceroy. Mr Pears, the Political Agent met us, also another smart young Political Officer, called Garstin, and Mr Ross of the Sappers who was responsible for the white lines on the roads. This wild frontier existence, where every man practically carries his life in his hand, develops these young men wonderfully; one feels that one could rely upon them in any emergency and the prestige and honour of the Empire can be entrusted to them with confidence. How different they are to the miserable double-faced politician, who contrives to control the country at home and is ready to tell any lie, in order to remain in power.

The country is surrounded by great bare hills and Mr Merk pointed out all the places of interest as we passed. The post where a company of Sikhs were killed close to Fort Lockhart during the Tirah Campaign, and, beyond, Dargai, where the boy piper continued to play "The Cock of the North" after being hit through the ankle. London rang with his fame, but I fear his heroism was spoilt by his consenting to appear at various music halls on his return home. Tremendous storms of wind and dust suddenly arise in these parts, and we encountered a really bad one about 20 miles from Parachinar. I thought we should be blown over, as clouds of dust obscured the road and I had hard work to hold on my hat in spite of numberless pins and four motoring veils. We arrived at a dear little bungalow at Parachinar about 4 o'clock and, after trying to get rid of some of the layers of dust, Mrs Merk gave us some very refreshing tea. Rolly and I walked up a pathway towards the mountains, followed by a stalwart Zakka Khel, dressed in crimson, with a large revolver strapped to his waist. Such a splendid specimen; 6 feet 8 inches in height and correspondingly broad; he is the man Sir George Roos-Keppel brought to Simla two years ago straight from the wilds. He says his father is a head taller than himself and he has a sister 6 feet 10 inches.

Sunday, 10th.

It was delicious waking up in this fresh pure air blowing straight from the mountains, but one needed warm clothes, and a wood fire was very pleasant. At 11 o'clock there was a jirga; about 1,000 Turis who have always been faithful to us in war assembled inside an enclosure, while outside there were about 2,000 more. Such splendid-looking men, some were quite fair with blue or grey eyes. They were told they might tell the Viceroy if they

266. Sussex Drive in Ottawa, the main ceremonial route where the Governor General's residence, Rideau Hall, stands.

had any grievances. One man after another spoke with amazing fluency and they made their requests. Mr Merk speaks Pushtu remarkably well; it is a very pretty soft language to listen to. He translated both the Turis' remarks and Rolly's answer in a flow of wonderful sounding words. They were evidently enormously pleased and flattered at Rolly having called them old friends and all grinned from ear to ear. We admired their coats, and one and all expressed great eagerness to lay their own particular garment at the feet of the Viceroy for his acceptance.

Jirga at Parachinar, April 12th 1910.

Only last night there was a murder in the bazaar here. One man killed another with whom his family had had a blood-feud for years, and so it goes on for generations. Whether in time civilisation will put a stop to this practice remains to be proved, at present to belong to a family with a blood-feud shows that you are of some social standing. A murder is taken as a matter of course, and at any moment the assassin may be killed in his turn. No one is safe even from the hand of a brother, so there is always a certain amount of excitement in living on the frontier. The ambition of every man is first to own a rifle, then a wife. We saw one man whom we were told had been ruined; he had bought four wives hoping to recoup himself in time by selling his daughters, but all four ladies died childless, and he had no more capital to invest. A girl costs about Rs. 300, but if she is very beautiful or belongs to a good family the price goes up to Rs, 1,500. The women work for the men. Mr Merk tells me when he was a young assistant on the frontier, a Pathan offered him his daughter for Rs. 1,500, and told him she could beat all the other girls in the village, as she could carry double as much as any other woman, so he considered her a splendid bargain. A woman carries from 80 to 100 Ibs. on her head. A man with a large family is looked on as specially favoured by Providence. The sons fight for the honour of the house, the daughters with any luck will be good-looking enough to fetch long prices.

In the afternoon some of the party rode out to a village called Shalozan, which Rolly was anxious to see again. The beauty of the ladies in the village is celebrated; the Amir's father is supposed to have got all his ladies from there. When Rolly rode into the village, a great stalwart man advanced on horseback and said he would show them the places of interest. The features of the man seemed familiar and Rolly told Mr Merk to ask him if he knew if a man was still alive who had acted as a guide 31 years ago during the Afghan war. The guide was a boy at the time, but Rolly remembered as he ran along he had a trick of brushing his ankles with the chaplies (sandals) till at last he inflicted serious wounds on them. This boy also was supposed to have a most beautiful sister whom all the officers vainly attempted to see; this no doubt made him a special object of interest. As soon as Mr Merk told the Pathan that the Viceroy was asking after a man who had been his guide and who used in running to make his ankles bleed, the man flung himself off his horse in the greatest excitement, kicked off his boots showing the old scars on his ankles, and with delight seized Rolly's hands and declared that he himself was the man. He said he had continued the habit of hitting his ankles to the age of 25, and that since then he had always worn boots.

That Rolly should have recognised him is perfectly remarkable, he was only a boy of 16 at the time and the coincidence that he should have by chance met the riding party today is also very extraordinary. Rolly went to his house and partook of tea; after which they swore eternal friendship. I motored out to join the others for tea in a sort of orchard, a piece of land that was bought by Lord Roberts in 1878. Rolly was shadowed by his friend Gulam Khan, who employed his time in picking wild flowers and presenting them to us. After dinner we looked on at very good sword-dancing round the bonfire and at excellent fire-works, they were let off with lavish rapidity, and were very creditable having been made in the wilds of Dera Ismail Khan.

Tuesday, 12th.

Felt very sorry to be leaving this fascinating part of the world. Our programme was to travel the 160 miles by motor, which, seemed quite a formidable undertaking, and it speaks well for our Rolls Royce car that we arrived in Peshawar punctual to the moment. We started at 3.45 on the last stage of our journey, 40 miles into Peshawar, straight over the Kohat Pass, which is 2,800 feet above sea level. We drove along a blood-curdling road up a desperate incline. Thomas took us at a frantic pace. No doubt it may be easier for the car, but it was a great strain on our nerves. We got safely to the summit, where a guard of honour stood presenting arms, and we stopped to gaze at the beautiful wide valley below with range upon

Kurram valley.

range of mountains. Amongst them are the salt mountains, which, alas, we have never seen, and which I believe are most interesting, with caves full of glittering stalactites of salt. We rushed down the hill and seemed to reach the foot of the Pass in a few minutes. Here, drawn up in a large square, the Afridis were waiting to receive us with painted goats, flowers, fruit, and long skewers on which was strung small round pieces of sheep's fat. The natives are all Pathans, but are called by the name of their tribe, of which there are any number. The two tribes drawn up facing each other quite peacefully had only last week had a desperate fight, one tribe having killed 13 of the other, and they each know that before long vengeance must be taken. Today in honour of the Viceroy's visit the hatchet was buried, and they all appeared to be on the most friendly terms. Every single man was armed, mostly with Martini-Henri rifles, but some had Mausers and the old Snider, while others carried rifles most cleverly made in the valley. Mrs Merk received us at Government House. They are both extremely pleasant people and have made us most comfortable. They have got a lovely collection of brass curios. We sent back the Rolls Royce to pick up any passengers who might have come to grief, as almost every car, except our own, had some casualty during the journey. Thomas drove close on 200 miles that day, without a single contretemps, a record for this wild part of the world.

Friday, 29th. Simla.

Reached Kalka early in the morning, and reached Simla about 12.45. Thomas was promised £25 by the Rolls Royce Company if we could give him a certificate to say that he had driven the car throughout the season without a single mishap. The car has covered 7,100 miles without any contretemps of any kind or sort. The two front tyres are the same that came out from England, and I do not believe Thomas has had more than three or four punctures the entire time and fortunately never with either Rolly or I so we can give both the car and Thomas a clean chit with a clear conscience. The following is an extract from the Kabul Diary:

> "His Excellency's visit has created a great impression among the Jajis, where the Viceregal motor is described as being 'two yards high and much swifter than the wind.'"

Saturday, 7th May.

Rolly came to my room very early in the morning with the terribly sad news of the King's death. It seems so sudden and unexpected, and one can hardly grasp at once all it may mean. Personally after reading yesterday's telegrams I felt things were as critical as they could be, as I was sure they would have suppressed bad news as long as possible. The curious thing is that for a week past the native servants have predicted that something was going to happen on the 6th of May. We all rather imagined that they were thinking of an earthquake, as I am told that they were equally correct in their prophecy at the time of the big earthquake on the 4th of April 1905. It was therefore rather a relief to read in the Reuters that there had been one in Costa Rica in which 500 people had lost their lives, and I felt that for this time we had escaped the predictions of the birds of ill-omen. I hear that in India a comet is supposed to foreshadow the death of Princes; the natives are very superstitious about this, so now that the King has died, besides several Indian potentates this year, their belief in the signs of the heavens will be more implicit than ever.[267] I am afraid the King's death happening at this terribly critical time will make things more difficult politically than ever in England, as no doubt his influence on Foreign Powers was very great indeed. We spent the morning in putting off all our social functions and in trying to order a suitable outfit to meet the demands of the long mourning.

Sunday, 8th.

It is interesting to hear that the 30 people accused of conspiracy in the Nasik murder case, were most anxious to send a message of sympathy to the Queen, and were greatly surprised when the prison authorities would not allow them to do so. Rolly attended service at Christ Church. I was unable to accompany him, as my mourning did not arrive in time. It was a special service with allusions to the King throughout. I got up at 4 A.M., went out on the verandah, and had the most splendid view of the comet, its tail was stretching across the sky like a great search-light, and just to the right of it Venus was shining with magnificent brilliancy. The last comet I saw was in 1883 from Weston, the Bradford's place, but this one was by far finer, and has a much longer tail.

Monday, 16th.

I have received a photograph from the Dalai Lama which will be an interesting memento of his visit to Calcutta. The following words are written across the photo in most beautifully neat Tibetan characters:

> "He who follows the precepts of the Lord Buddha, the Mighty, 13th Dalai Lama, Immutable, Holder of the Sacred Thunder bolt, Powerful Ruler."

Below the writing there is an impression of the great seal in red ink. This is an interesting souvenir, as there was a good deal of agitation at the time of the Dalai Lama's flight, because he had carried away with him the sacred seals of State.

Friday, 20th.

This is the day that has been set apart as one of public mourning and on which the King's funeral takes place. The Memorial Service was held in Simla at noon, which all officials

267. Halley's comet made one of its appearances during 1910.

attended in full uniform. Rolly rode to Christ Church with his Staff and escort. The feeling shown by the natives has been remarkable. All our Mahommedan servants gathered together and had a service of their own on the lawn. It is most touching to see what feeling has been shown by every Indian community. As we drove into Simla to attend the service, everyone seemed anxious to show sympathy and respect for the King's memory and Europeans were dressed in black. The tolling of the bell and the booming of the guns added to the solemnity of the occasion. The 68 guns which were fired as the final tribute to the King were timed to cease as the sun set. Rolly and I watched the flash at Jutogh from the summer house in the garden, this was followed a few seconds later by the boom of the gun and the echo which took almost a minute to reach the mountains beyond. We felt quite sad as we sat in a bower of luxuriant roses watching the sun sinking lower and lower and finally dipping behind the glorious range of mountains, as we knew that, as he sank to rest, the last token of respect had been paid to Edward VII and that a new order of things was commencing.

Sunday, May 22nd.

The mail has brought us interesting letters. Morley, after declaring that he would sooner resign than appoint Lord Kitchener, is evidently coming round to the idea of his succeeding us; his chief objection is that, by appointing Lord K-, it would appear to the public to be an admission that the reforms and the conciliatory policy had failed, and that we now intended to try force. As a matter of fact, no one would be more anxious than Lord K- to follow the existing policy; this he told us very decidedly before leaving India. It would however take the public some time before they understood the situation. No one is more intimate with the conditions of India than Lord K-. As to its being a popular appointment, I have grave doubts. I am not certain that either the Anglo-Indians or the Native Princes would approve, chiefly because he is a reserved man and they do not understand him, and I am afraid they might think him hard and unsympathetic. I am very conscious of having encouraged him in the idea of his becoming Viceroy; in fact, I believe that I was the first person who made him consider it seriously.

It is hard to understand why the Secretary of State dislikes the severe sentences that have recently been passed on several seditionists. His protégé at this moment is Arobindo Ghose, whom he hopes will not be convicted! As he is responsible for the murder of the two poor women at Muzzafferpur, and is certainly the most dangerous man in India, one can hardly accept the Secretary of State's reasoning or reconcile it with a desire to stamp out sedition. There is a warrant out against Arobindo, he is consequently living at Pondicherry, beyond the reach of English law, and I hear he is waiting there for a French ship to take him to France. Once in Paris he will no doubt be busy concocting fresh anarchical plots. Mr Jenkins, the Home Member, who has recently come from Bombay, told me that the arrest of an Indian, on board one of the P. and O.'s with a Browning pistol and voluminous receipts for making bombs, was followed by a flood of telegrams from the India Offices asking if they were sure the man was really guilty. As he had himself confessed that his accomplices at home had wanted him to bring out 30 pistols; that he had not liked to take so great a risk, but had helped them as far as he was able by bringing one; there can be little doubt that the man deserved the sentence he received.

Sunday, 29th.

Lord Morley tells us that by the time his letter reaches us the decision will have been made. He says that it rests between two great civil men. These, I hear from other sources, must mean Sir Charles Hardinge and Sir George Murray. If the latter is in any way celebrated, we must all be intensely ignorant, for hardly any one here has ever heard of him. However Whitaker tells us that he is Permanent Secretary to the Treasury, has been Gladstone's Private Secretary as well as Lord Rosebery's. He is no doubt a most admirable official, but if they send out a man who has been saturated all his life by official red-tapeism, I cannot think that he will have sufficiently broadminded views to make a good Viceroy, nor do I think would he find it easy to cope with the social requirements, which, properly handled, go far towards the popularity of a Viceroy. Rolly remembers that Sir G. Murray was connected with the post office when we were in Canada, and during the time of the inauguration of the penny postage between the two countries he was found to hold the most hopelessly retrograde views.

Saturday, 11th June. Simla.

Sir Charles Hardinge's appointment has been officially announced this morning. Personally I am very glad and think that by far the best selection has been made. I am sure they will both do it admirably, and I think Lady Hardinge is sure to carry on all the charities in which I have been interested, and I hope they will appreciate all that has been done to the various houses and gardens. I am afraid Lord Kitchener will be much disappointed. He has no doubt been very badly treated, as he was practically promised the post.

Sunday, 19th.

The mail brought us some interesting letters. Lord Kitchener, I hear, has been most outspoken, and announced that, if he was not appointed to India, he would shake the dust off his feet on England and go and travel in Persia. I hear he was at some official luncheon recently, had just sat down and was saying how-d'ye-do over his shoulder to one or two men as they passed him, when he realised that he was shaking hands with Lord Curzon, who said: "How are you Kitchener? Well, I hope." So the meeting that Lord K- dreaded so much, passed off more calmly than could have been anticipated. Lord K- was asked by a friend if he would like Egypt if he did not get India. He replied that he was a man of one idea, and if he was not appointed to India, he would go nowhere.

Everyone has been greatly exercised by Mr Roosevelt's speech at the Guildhall in connection with Egypt. After his shooting expedition in Africa, Roosevelt visited some of the European Courts where he was received with Imperial honours. His son gave a friend of mine a very amusing description of him. He said: "I don't think my father has enjoyed King Edward's funeral ceremonies very much. He does not understand not being the central figure when he attends a function. If he goes to a wedding, he would like to be the bride; if he goes to a funeral, he thinks he ought to be the corpse." There was a very amusing cartoon in Punch recently in connection with Roosevelt's visit. The stone lions of Trafalgar Square were represented surrounded by police with a placard on them "Not to be shot".

Sir Arthur Bigge[268] has sent me all the information I begged for in connection with the entertainments we may give and the mourning that is to be worn. I am glad to say that, in view of the climate, people will be allowed to come to Government House in half mourning from the 1st July.

268. Private Secretary to George V.

Wednesday, June 22nd.

An official who has been in Kabul lately gave rather a gruesome account of his visit there. He said he was walking in the street and his companion meeting a friend introduced him as one of the prominent men in Kabul. When they walked on the officer said: "Did I understand that your friend was a doctor?" "Oh no," said the guide, "he is not a doctor, only the taker out of eyes." I am afraid from all one hears that this man is kept fully occupied.

An interesting man, called Captain Shuttleworth,[269] and his wife lunched. He has recently been acting as our Consul at Kashgar and has had a most interesting journey, returning to England through Central Asia. He says that Tashkend,[270] in Russian Turkestan, is a town as up to date as Bombay, with electric lights, trams and equipped with all modern improvements. The Russians have lately opened a strategic railway from Orenburg to Tashkend in addition to the already existing Trans-Caspian Railway.

---

269. Captain A.R.B. Shuttleworth, generally described as one of the players in the Great Game but about whom not a great deal appears to be known.

270. Tashkent.

Simla, 1908.

Friday, July 1st.

After luncheon I interviewed a Mrs Currie, who is Lady Superintendent of the Pilgrims Department in Bombay. She was quite an interesting person to talk to. She tells me that she saw off 26,000 pilgrims during 1909. It takes them about eight months to get to Mecca and back, including their devotions there. The purdah women are the difficult ones to deal with and all have the greatest objection to being medically inspected for plague. Before we came to India 10 days' quarantine was enforced on the pilgrims. Rolly has had this reduced to three, and as accommodation for pilgrims in Bombay is limited, they are intensely grateful to him for having mitigated their sufferings. She told me that the Mahommedans had only recently begun to realise that the agitation the Hindus were advocating against British rule was intended only to benefit themselves. Mrs Currie said that many Mahommedans had told her that they had nearly fallen into the trap, but had realised the position in time which had accentuated their loyalty to the British Raj. She thinks a great deal of the present difficulties have arisen owing to the fact that education has been advanced too much on Western lines which does not suit the Eastern mind. She seems to have a thorough knowledge of their character, as she has lived entirely in this country, which her father, grandfather and great grandfather have done before her.

Sunday, 3rd.

The mail contained more interesting news than usual. Sir Harold Stuart, who has recently arrived in England, tells me he is surprised to find a very general belief at home that India is on the verge of mutiny, or anyhow tending rapidly in that direction, that the Government of India was little more than the obedient creature of Lord Morley, and that the only remedy was Lord Kitchener!! Sir Dunlop continues to fight the good fight against the hopeless misconception of the existing situation, but it is hard for any one to make a stand against Lord Morley, who for nearly five years has undoubtedly led people to believe that he is not only Secretary of State, but combines the powers of the House of Commons, the King-Emperor and the Viceroy. His sympathy with seditionists is inexplicable, and he not only expresses the hope that Arobindo Ghose will not be convicted, but professes horror at the severity with which the seditious Jat Regiment[271] has been treated. Luckily he has not power to interfere with the sentences that are passed in India, and an enormous number of people have been convicted and imprisoned without his knowledge.

We hear that Lord Stafford is still paying the greatest attention to Princess Priti Cooch Behar in England, and she gives out that she is engaged to him. She is an extremely nice girl, but I sincerely hope such a marriage will not be allowed, as it could lead to nothing but disaster.

271. The 10th Jat Regiment based at Fort William had been encouraged to revolt as part of the Nationalist rebellion but the action did not really take off.

Thursday, 7th.

Faqir Sayad Iftikhar-ud-din, the Envoy from Kabul, has just arrived in Simla having vacated his post in Afghanistan. I am so glad he has returned alive to this country. He lunched with us and gave us lurid accounts of all that goes on in Afghanistan. He was in such a hurry to get away that he rode the first 30 miles on leaving Kabul in record time and his horse died from exhaustion at the 27th mile en route to Peshawar.

The following is an extract from his diary, June 15th:

> "On the night of the 10th instant, 15 out of 18 prisoners escaped from the black well. Three could not move on account of weakness. The soldier on guard also made away with the rifle he had with him. On the following morning three companies of the Kotwali battalion, with Colonel Daud Shah Khan at their head, were sent out to search for the prisoners. One was found after about half-an-hour's search. He was lying in some grass about half-a-mile from the prison. His statement before the Sardar was that he was in the well for over twelve or thirteen years. He was very weak, and could neither walk nor recognize anything in the world. He was carried on the back of one of the prisoners for some distance, and then left, where he was caught. He is kept in jail. The rest have not been apprehended. The sergeant of the guard has been punished by having his eyes gouged out."

Tuesday, 19th.

Gave our usual big dinner party. I sat between Mr Sinha and the Bishop of Lahore. The latter told me that undoubtedly a more friendly spirit had arisen between the Indian and the Englishman, that he had heard far fewer complaints of rough treatment of the native in railway carriages than in former years. He alluded to a well known story of a young officer who tried to insist on an Indian gentleman getting out of his railway carriage, and on his refusing to do so, locking him up by force in the lavatory. On arriving at his destination it was discovered that he had unwittingly imprisoned the Raja who was to act as his host, and who had kindly consented to make all the arrangements for a shooting expedition in his State. Mr Sinha has made up his mind to resign his appointment on the same day as our term comes to an end. He told me of the financial sacrifices that he had made in order to become the first Indian Member of Council; they are quite enormous—between £12,000 and £15,000 a year. He fully recognises the political significance of his appointment, and told me that, if Rolly had been staying on another year or even two, he would have remained with him, but he is not prepared to make the same sacrifice for any one else.

Saturday, 30th.

A damp atmosphere pervades the house, everything smells musty, and the food has a mouldy taste. I had some conversation with Mrs Charlton. She is the daughter of Lord

Abinger and gave vent to the most astounding sentiments. She is crazy about animals and declares that goats are flayed alive in order to procure long kid gloves, as a live goat's skin stretches more than skin taken from a dead body. She is indignant at the thoughts of any animal being hunted, and regards it inhuman to slaughter animals even for the purpose of sustaining life. On the other hand, she looks on with indifference at human suffering; says she would enjoy sticking pins into her *jhampanis* and regards children with inveterate hatred. She declared that her only daughter had married and had a baby simply to spite her. She told a lady I know who happens to have five brilliantly clever sons, who have all obtained scholarships, that she considered her an extremely wicked woman for being responsible for such an increase in the population. She is so genuinely mad that my conversation with her amused me very much.

Captain Annesley[272] told us an extraordinary story in connection with animals the other day. The 10th Hussars had a hyena that became so tame that it wandered about their camp doing no harm. He grew very devoted to Captain Annesley who made a special pet of him, and he would follow him about like a dog. Unfortunately the children belonging to the soldiers were terrified of the hyena; consequently he was presented to the Zoo. Three years afterwards Captain Annesley visited the Zoo and passed a hyena's cage which bore the inscription: "Presented by the 10th Hussars." He at once recognised his old friend and asked the keeper if he might go into his cage and speak to him. The keeper declared that the hyena was dangerous and extremely fierce, and that it would be as much, as his life was worth to allow any one to approach him. The hyena was lying asleep at the end of his cage with his back to the passers-by, but the instant Captain Annesley called him by his old familiar name, he raised his head, listened and rushed to the bars of the cage in a state of wild excitement. The keeper at last permitted Captain Annesley to put in his hand and the hyena allowed himself to be patted and fondled and showed the greatest delight at meeting his old friend whom he had not seen for three years. Captain Annesley begged hard to be permitted to take him for a walk as he used to do, but the keeper said it was against all rules and would not allow him to take the risk, and the poor hyena died shortly afterwards. It seems almost incredible that an animal should recognise a human voice after being in captivity for three years.

Thursday, 4th August.

A good many of the Members of the Legislative Council have recently come up to Simla to attend Rolly's last Council. We have had most of them to lunch with us. Probably the most interesting of them is Gokhale, who has been staying with Sir Guy Fleetwood Wilson, who has found him a most interesting companion. Sir Guy quite realises the importance of keeping in touch with these clever Indians. Gokhale tells me that he recognises the change

---

272. Captain the Hon. Arthur Annesley, killed Ypres, 1914.

of feeling that has come over a large section of the Indian community and his gratitude to Rolly is very genuine for the consideration that he has shown towards the Indian Members and his desire that they should participate in the government of their country. He added: "it makes us all very anxious as to the future, as it is impossible for us to know what attitude the new Viceroy will assume, and unless we can feel the same confidence in him as we do in Lord Minto the situation will at once become strained". Sirdar Pertab Singh of Kapurthala told me that India had undergone the most remarkable change in the last five years; that the emancipation of the women was advancing with giant's strides, and he thought that in 20 years time purdah would no longer exist.

Friday, 5th.

Lady Dane came to see me with regard to a present some of the Indian and European ladies intend to give me. They have been wonderfully kind and generous and have collected quite a large sum. Lady Dane suggests that the present should take the form of a few really good pearls. This I should appreciate much more than anything else, especially as a barbaric Indian ornament which some of the ladies might wish to give me, would really be of very little use.

Tuesday, 9th.

I hear that Lady Warwick's wreath for King Edward was made of daisies and forget-me-nots with the inscription: "In certain hope of eternal reunion." This seems hardly possible, but I am told it is true.[273]

Dunlop writes to say that Mr Montagu's Budget speech was of the most priggish type, a pedagogue lecturing to a set of schoolboys. The interference from home is becoming absolutely intolerable. Lord Morley has caused consternation amongst the members of the Government Railway Board by making contracts which affect the management and financial aspect of all the railways throughout India without asking the advice of a single person in the country. He is totally ignorant of the conditions and has made so serious a mistake that he will be forced in some way to reconsider his agreement, but the mischief is done. The full text of Mr Montagu's Budget speech has only just reached us. It is very clever, and excellent as regards the review of the condition of the country, but he ignores the Government of India and says: "Lord Morley and his Council, working through the agency of Lord Minto, have accomplished much;" this is positively insulting. I suppose it is hard for people in England to realise that out of the 3,000,000 Indians few know that there is a Secretary of State at all. It is the Viceroy that the people look to as their ruler, because they know that he represents the King, which is the most powerful factor in their

273. Daisy Warwick had been one of the King's mistresses.

eyes, and they look upon him as ruling over them by divine right with all the picturesque beliefs of prehistoric ages. As one of the Indian Members of Lord Morley's Council recently said to a friend: "The Secretary of State himself carries his bag and travels by underground, how can he understand the magnificence and pomp that must necessarily attend, not only the Viceroy, but Governors and Members of Council. To lessen the respect for the Viceroy, and to leave this vast country with its complex questions to be dealt with by Members of Parliament, must mean the beginning of the end."

Reuter: The death is announced of Miss Florence Nightingale. The King and Queen have telegraphed to the relations of Florence Nightingale deeply regretting sad news of death. Her untiring and devoted services to British soldiers in Crimea will never be forgotten. To her striking example we practically owe our present splendid organisation of trained nurses.

Saturday, 13th August.

The Indian newspapers have been as indignant as one could wish at the reference to the Viceroy being the Agent of the Secretary of State. Rolly had an interesting letter from the King criticising the speech on the same lines and also referring with annoyance to the fact that no mention has been made to King Edward's death nor to the Indian Army nor to the Indian Princes. We have heard from other sources that Sir Herbert Risley has been weeks in getting up the speech for Mr Montagu. No doubt the reference to the power of the Secretary of State has been thought out very carefully by Lord Morley, and especially the term 'Agent' which was applied to the Viceroy with the evident desire to clip the wings of the Government of India for ever. Rolly has written him a most dignified remonstrance and a despatch is being framed in such strong terms that I fancy it will not be very palatable to him, but there is no doubt that this is the time to fight for the rights of the Viceroy and Indian Government which hitherto have never been questioned. That Risley, who was two and a half years drafting every detail of the reforms under Rolly, should turn such a traitor is simply unbelievable. I suppose a leopard cannot change its spots, and Risley is only living up to his reputation. I shall not spare him when we meet, and look forward to giving him a really uncomfortable half hour.[274]

Tuesday, 16th.

Six Indian gentlemen were present at dinner which is an evidence of the way people have advanced. I am told before our regime no Indians were invited to dine with the Viceroy and Bikaner himself told me on the occasion of Lord Curzon's last official visit to Bikaner he as the host was advised not to dine at the State Banquet.

---

274. Risley retired from the ICS in early 1910 and became Permanent Secretary of the Judicial Department of the India Office and President of The Royal Anthropological Society, he became ill and died in 1911.

Friday, 26th.

The Children's Fancy Dress Ball this afternoon was a huge success. The Begum of Bhopal, her three sons and four little grandchildren accepted our invitation to attend and were a great addition to the party. I think most of the children thought the Begum in her white Borkha was a ghost but her presence did not inspire the same terror as the masked clown last year. Towards the end of the entertainment all the children were made to sit in a circle round the room, and Rolly and I went round giving each a medal and a present which greatly delighted them. The two little Princes in the Tower were a charming couple and a little mite of four gorgeously attired as Pharaoh's daughter with a shining green serpent encircling her waist, was adorable. The satisfaction of most of the children at their own appearance was delightfully naive. I told a tiny boy that he looked beautiful as a cavalier. He promptly answered: "Yes, I know I do." The anxious mothers rather spoilt the effect of the children, by standing in the centre of the ball-room to admire their progeny. Mrs Biddulph and Mrs Atkinson, the two biggest women in Asia, constantly obliterated the view in this manner, and no persuasions on the part of the A.D.C.s had any effect in moving them on.

Wednesday, 31st.

Mrs Earle gave a very select purdah party for the Begum which I had promised to attend. I received a message in the morning begging me to adorn myself with a blaze of jewels, as the Indian purdah ladies did not understand the reason of our modest taste in dress. I refused to drive down the Mall with my tiara round my hat, but I put on the Crown of India, and the Coronation Medal, and as many brooches and necklaces as I could find room for. Apparently the ladies greatly appreciated my smarter appearance, they had evidently commented unfavourably on my dowdy get up at Barnes Court, and Mrs Earle, in writing to thank me for joining her party, told me that the little ladies had talked of nothing else but my Orders and jewels after I had left, and said that they had not known before that English ladies ever possessed any jewels at all. Of course they never go out at night and consequently have no opportunity of seeing any.

The Maharaja of Scindia has arrived to stay with us for a couple of days. We had a most amusing dinner with him and Sir Pertab. The latter declared "that all Maharajas crying when Viceroy leaving." Rolly said: "Viceroy will be also crying," to which he responded " when Viceroy crying all Maharajas going with him to Aden".

Thursday, 1st September.

The Maharawal of Dungarpur has arrived to stay with Colonel Pinhey at Observatory House. He is young and rather good-looking, but seems a little inclined to give himself airs which I think is really due to shyness. Old Pertab is his uncle on his maternal side and at once, noticed that his manner was a little off-hand, so he went up to him and said: "If you going Eton, although you being Prince you staying downstairs blacking Sahibs' boots, this good teaching for you." Poor Dungarpur was rather taken aback. I am very glad he said it, although his description of Eton is hardly accurate!!

Saturday, 3rd.

The Begum came to pay her farewell visit to Rolly; we have not taken leave of her for good, as she intends coming to Bombay to see us off. All our Maharajas have left us, but Scindia and Pertab are coming to the Bhurtpore[275] shoot in November when we halt at Agra en route to Calcutta.

Friday, September 16th.

The Indian community gave a farewell Garden Party at Annandale in our honour. Several thousand people were present and the hill sides were covered with gaily dressed natives I believe it is the first time that such a gathering has assembled in Simla to bid farewell to a Viceroy, and there was evidently a great deal of enthusiasm and good feeling which was very gratifying.

Sunday, 18th.

Spent the morning in sorting things for England instead of going to church. An appeal has appeared in the Times of India about the Calcutta Memorial. I have reason to believe that this letter was written by Scindia. He and Bikaner, I know, have been in correspondence with Sir Edward Baker about the memorial to be raised in Calcutta by the European and Indian communities combined, and I see by an Indian telegram that the Calcutta people are falling in with his suggestions. If a statue of Rolly is put up, I sincerely hope that it will be an equestrian one, on his unrivalled Arab, Newminister, as the horse and rider would make a perfect picture. Such a statue would certainly be an addition to the Calcutta Memorials, and one of which I should justly be proud. Newminister is the most beautiful Arab I have ever seen and shows, by his arched neck and proud demeanour, that he is fully conscious of his beauty.[276]

MM with Simla guards.

275. Bharatpur.

276. The equestrian statue of Lord Minto by Sir William Goscombe John was considered (rightly) by his daughter Ruby in 1915 to be "a little disappointing" but mainly on account of the bas-relief panels on the pedestal which were later removed and donated to the Victoria Memorial by MM. The rather stunted statue rests now in the gardens of Flagstaff House, Barrackpore, beside those of other notables of British India.

Wednesday, 21st.

A Dr Budding, a German, has arrived to stay for a few days. He is studying the political administration of India and is a Member of the Prussian Parliament. He informed Captain Tod, who met him at the station that he hoped to remain for three weeks. Captain Tod hastily told him that we were leaving for a camp at Naldera on Sunday, and that Viceregal Lodge, would be shut up, so nipped his intentions at once in the bud. He is quite pleasant, but a little of him goes a long way as he is thirsting for information and asks such ceaseless questions that we suspect him of being a spy. He is probably laying in information to enable the Germans to carry on the government of the country when they have wrested India from us. I hear what he misses chiefly in India is a manicure and does not know how he will get on for six months without one, which rather damns him in our eyes.

Sunday, 25th.

Have sat up for the last three nights till 2 A.M., arranging all my things, and sorting cupboards and drawers. Five years' accumulation assumes alarming proportions. Fryer will pack everything while we are away at Naldera, and it will be a great relief to feel that this herculean task is accomplished. We brought out far too many of our own possessions, especially in the way of books; there is a splendid Viceregal Library, so we really have not required them and the climate has damaged them considerably.

Friday, 30th. Naldera Camp.

We have thoroughly enjoyed our time here. The camp was admirably arranged, and there has not been a drawback of any kind. We have played a lot of golf, have practised shooting at clay pigeons and have ridden our mountain' tats down the paths towards the Sutlej, which we could see shining below us. A great deal of fresh snow has fallen on the far off mountains on the horizon, which has added much to the beauty of the view, and the sun-sets over Simla with range upon range of mountains beyond, fading in the golden mist, have been glorious. A great many people come to Naldera to play golf. The Haigs have a small encampment on the top of the hill. Lady Haig has my old Ayah, Polly, with her. She was altogether 12 years at Viceregal Lodge and became rather too intimate with the ways of the establishment, so we thought it was wiser to make a change. Lady Haig likes her very much and I was quite glad to see her again, although my present Ayah, Christine, is really more efficient. These Ayahs are excellent when they look after one entirely, and are most attentive, but they all resent the supervision of a maid. I can't bear the thoughts of saying good-bye to my personal servants. The attention and devotion with which my head Jemedar and *Khitmagar*, Thakur Das and Budhou, have looked after me is quite touching. They anticipate my wishes, and I feel I shall be parting with real friends when I leave India All my other attendants are also exceptionally obliging, and I realise how different it will be when I get home. No one will care if my coffee is not exactly to my liking, nor if my special biscuits are not forthcoming, and the rebellious spirit of the footman who says "let them ring" will be a sad change after the instant appearance of the silent and respectful messenger who flies on willing feet to carry out one's orders. The establishment is much more economically run than in the old days, but we have still a goodly array of servants, as is shown by the photo taken in Calcutta.

My journal has lately been filled with eulogistic notices of Rolly's regime, which I realise are not strictly becoming for me to chronicle, but from an historical point of view I think it is interesting to have a record of them, and I have only quoted a very limited percentage of the numberous letters and articles that have been written in the same strain. The facts in the following speech made by Mrs Besant are correct, but how she discovered them I am at a loss to conceive.

Mrs BESANT'S EULOGY.

Benares, September 30th.

It will help you to understand the real nature of the Viceroy if I tell you what happened when he rightly hastened to Calcutta without fulfilling his engagement to visit our College for passing urgent legislation for the suppression of sedition. When he got into the carriage at the station surrounded by guards, it went at a gallop through Calcutta streets.Reaching Government House, he asked the reason why such a strange pace was adopted. The answer was:
"Your Excellency there is danger on the streets."
"Is that the way to meet danger, as if you were running away from it?"
"Your Excellency, we removed the Indian guards and replaced them with Scotch."
"Take the Scotchmen away and put on my Indian guards. If we do not trust Indians, how can we hope Indians will trust us?"

Sunday, October 2nd.

Chirol has completed his series of letters on India. They are extremely able and in most cases very fair and will no doubt draw the public's attention to the present situation. He has a cut at Rolly for not consulting his Council sufficiently and for not upholding the authority of the Civil Service. I think he has absolutely no justification for either criticism; the latter is based on the fact that Rolly accepted Sir Bampfylde Fuller's resignation without asking him to reconsider, which would have been encouraging insubordination. As regards his Council, he has invariably consulted them on all necessary measures, but he has had exceptional difficulties to contend with, as it is notorious that some of the Members during the past five years have had no opinions worthy of consideration, and the views that they expressed one day they would contradict the next. In looking through his boxes of papers the other day Rolly came upon Lord Morley's reply to his original despatch about reforms, written on May 17th, 1907. There are 35 clauses under 7 different headings. I quote the opening paragraph; in itself a complete answer to all attempts made by the papers at home to give Lord Morley the credit for proposals that were made on Rolly's initiative.

> "My Lord, I have examined in Council with the care that their high importance demands the five proposals submitted to me in your despatch of 21st March. Those proposals, as Your Excellency assured your Legislative Council on 6th April were not framed in accordance with instructions conveyed to you from home. 'This move in advance has emanated entirely from the Government of India'. This initiative you took as a great step 'towards satisfying the present requirements of the Indian Empire."

Friday, 7th Dhami Camp.

We all feel dreadfully depressed to think that this is really the last camp life that we shall experience in India. It is altogether so different to anything that would be possible in another country. Rolly and I looked round our tents with their luxurious fittings with a real pang, knowing that we shall never see the like again. We said good-bye to the Rana and all the shikaris with regret. The shikari who ran the whole show was a most delightful person. He spoke excellent English and happened also to be the Prime Minister of the State. If he is as good a Prime Minister as he is a shikari, I feel certain that the Rana's affairs must be in a very flourishing condition. These hill-people are such a delightful type, tall and good-looking and marvellously athletic. They took the keenest interest in the sport, and if I chanced to hit a pheasant or to kill a gurul, their faces lit up with a beaming smile. In riding home after the shoot last night we watched the beaters on the opposite side of the valley—a thousand of them walking single-file in their loose khaki clothes, making an elongated serpentine line along the face of the mountain. It is a matter of total indifference to them if they are walking along the level or climbing up the side of a precipice. Even my dandy Jampanis hardly got out of breath in spite of the heavy weight they were carrying. Left camp on our tats at 1.30, and practically galloped the whole way to Jutogh, 8 miles, in 45 minutes. We caught sight of quite a big snake darting across the road, and disappearing into the bushes. I don't know if it was a dangerous one. I have only seen half a dozen snakes all the time I have been in India. I reached Viceregal Lodge only in time to see to all the preparations for the presentation that was to take place at 4.30.

The ladies of India have collected a really lovely pearl necklace to give me as a farewell gift. They have all been so wonderful about it and the Committee have taken untold trouble to get the best value for their money. Every jeweller in India has sent sample pearls, and I think the final selection is really a very beautiful one and matches my own shorter row very well. When all the ladies were assembled in the Ball-room, I came in and stood on the dais, while Lady Dane read the address, which I endeavoured to answer to the best of my ability trying to make them realise how really touched I am by their kindness in giving me such a present.

Monday, 10th. Simla

Spent the morning in seeing to our final packing. The boxes are to leave Simla tomorrow and once all this is done, I feel I shall be able to breathe more freely, but I have to write my thanks to all the absent subscribers to my necklace and the artists who have contributed pictures, which will keep me busy for some days. Rolly's friend from the Kurram, Ghulam Khan, has come the whole way to Simla in order to say good-bye to him. He arrived with an interpreter and said he was the proudest man in Kurram since he had a picture of the Viceroy handing in his house. He brought us fruits from his garden and presented me with a very pretty silver necklace typical of the kind worn by the ladies of his district.

The news of the revolution in Portugal has been very startling. The King and Queen Amélie have escaped on board a man-of-war. Many details are not known. The Governor of Goa, De Costa, who entertained us so hospitably, has had gracefully to retire in favour of the Republican representative, who curiously has the same name. The whole train service throughout France has come to a standstill owing to universal strikes. I hope the country will have resumed a normal condition before December. It would be a great bore to be hung up at Marseille.

Wednesday, 12th.

This week will be a great strain on Rolly. He has three dinners running, which means three speeches. Tonight the Scottish Dinner took place. Mr Robertson acted a Chairman and Francis tells me that Mr Robertson's speech was quite excellent and also Rolly's answer, which he delivered chiefly with a Scotch accent. Between the courses, General Campbell and his son walked up and down the room playing the pipes. Huge bunches of white heather decorated the table. They had written home to England for 20 yards of ribbon made of the Elliot tartan, which they declare is in existence, although I have always been led to believe that the lowland clans do not possess tartans. However the Elliot tartan rug was always to the fore in Canada, and as this ribbon was made of the same shades, I am beginning to believe that the tartan is bona fide. Anyhow the shop wrote back to say that the ribbon which had been ordered would require a special loom, and they consequently could not supply less than 250 yards!! How the remaining 230 yards are to be disposed of I am at a loss to conceive. Rolly's health was drunk with all Highland honours, even old Sir Alfred

Mackenzie, who is nearly 90,[277] managed to stand on his chair. Some of the members danced sword dances after dinner, and at the conclusion of the entertainment they all joined hands, and danced round the room singing Auld Lang Syne. The whole party accompanied Rolly downstairs singing "Will ye noo coom back again." Rolly did not reach home till 1 o'clock, having thoroughly enjoyed his evening. He was especially pleased with himself for having alluded to me as they do on the border as only "just an English body".

Friday, October 14th

While Rolly was being entertained by the United Service Club, I was giving a ladies' dinner party to the members of the Committee who had assisted in collecting subscriptions for my pearl necklace. At the psychological moment I rose, thumped the table to attract attention, and gave the toast of the Queen to the strains of the National Anthem. The ladies then drank my health. Most of the ladies smoked except myself and one or two others, and as I looked round the table at this gathering, I felt I was presiding over a suffragette assembly.

Saturday, 15th.

The heavy luggage has started, transport of the 127 boxes are now on their road to Bombay and will be conveyed to England in a Government transport. Where they are to be unpacked at Minto and where the contents will be stowed away, is a conundrum that will not be easy to solve. Mrs Davies came to luncheon, also Father Hickie, a Catholic priest, a charming man whose acquaintance I much regret I have not made sooner. I found him a very pleasant neighbour at luncheon and extremely human. He was in the Royal Artillery for 16 years before he became a priest, which probably accounts for his being so liberal-minded.

Spent an hour in having some of the horses photographed—a very tedious operation, as they always contrived to stand with their legs huddled beneath them and they refused to make the most of themselves. Waitress starts for England next week. I only hope that she will be able to stand the deep ground at home. In India one canters with impunity on these hard roads, an experiment which would certainly lame most English horses at once.

Tuesday, 18th.

Had a meeting of the Dufferin Fund; it will be the last time I shall preside as Lady President. I feel quite a pang at giving up so many interests that have figured so largely in my life during the past five years. This evening our farewell ball took place. Captain Mackenzie has surpassed himself in the artistic way the tents have been arranged. I made a desperate

277. Sir Alfred Robert Davidson Mackenzie had fought in the Mutiny and wrote *Mutiny Memoirs: Being Personal Reminiscences of the Great Sepoy Revolt of 1857*.

effort throughout the evening to talk to as many people as possible. Although everyone enjoyed themselves very much, one could not help noticing an element of sadness which, I think, everyone felt more or less at this being our real good-bye to Simla society. Dancing was kept up to quite a late hour; it was 2 o'clock before "God save the King" was played.

Wednesday, 26th October.

Captain Cadogan has left, much to our regret. He tells me that Colonel Victor's brother, Alan, who has just been here, is the youngest officer in the Army selected for the Horse Artillery. Apparently it is the ambition of every gunner to get his jacket, and Alan Brooke has been put over the heads of any number of his senior officers. He invented a fuse when he was at Woolwich Academy which was sent up with recommendation to the War Office. At present he is mad about aeroplanes and has also invented an apparatus which enables wild animals to photograph themselves at night. He finds the animal's kill during the day, arranges the necessary paraphernalia, and when the animal comes unsuspectingly to his kill at night, he breaks a string which somehow ignites a flash-light, and at the same time opens the shutter of the camera as he passes.[278]

Friday. 28th.

Had some splendid sets of tennis on the Staff Courts. The Crookes had collected all the best players in Simla. I suppose this will almost be the last time I shall ever play tennis in my life, as I cannot see any prospect of ever having the opportunity of playing in England, besides grandmothers don't play.

Gave our farewell dinner party of 80 people. All the members of the Black Hearts were present in their uniform. They have been so hospitable to us all these five years that we were anxious to show our appreciation of all they had done by asking the members in a body. After "The King" had been drunk, Mr Jenkins got up and proposed our health, which they drank to the strains of: "He is a jolly good fellow", followed by much cheering. Rolly in responding told them how sorry he was that this was the last opportunity he should have of entertaining our friends at Viceregal Lodge. We danced after dinner and just as the clock struck 12 Auld lang syne was played. We made a huge ring round the room, everybody singing with might and main. Mr Butler then again led three cheers for Rolly and me and Eileen, which were responded to with so much enthusiasm that I felt quite a lump in my throat. Mr Butler said that, although he was a most undemonstrative man, he could not help congratulating me on the way things had gone during our regime. He dilated on all the difficulties Rolly had had to contend with, and said that the reforms and the promotion of Indians was undoubtedly distasteful to the Civil Servants and the whole English community,

278. Alan Brooke became Field Marshall Lord Alanbrooke of Brookeborough. He was Chief of the Imperial General Staff 1941-1946 and was a noted ornithologist and photographer.

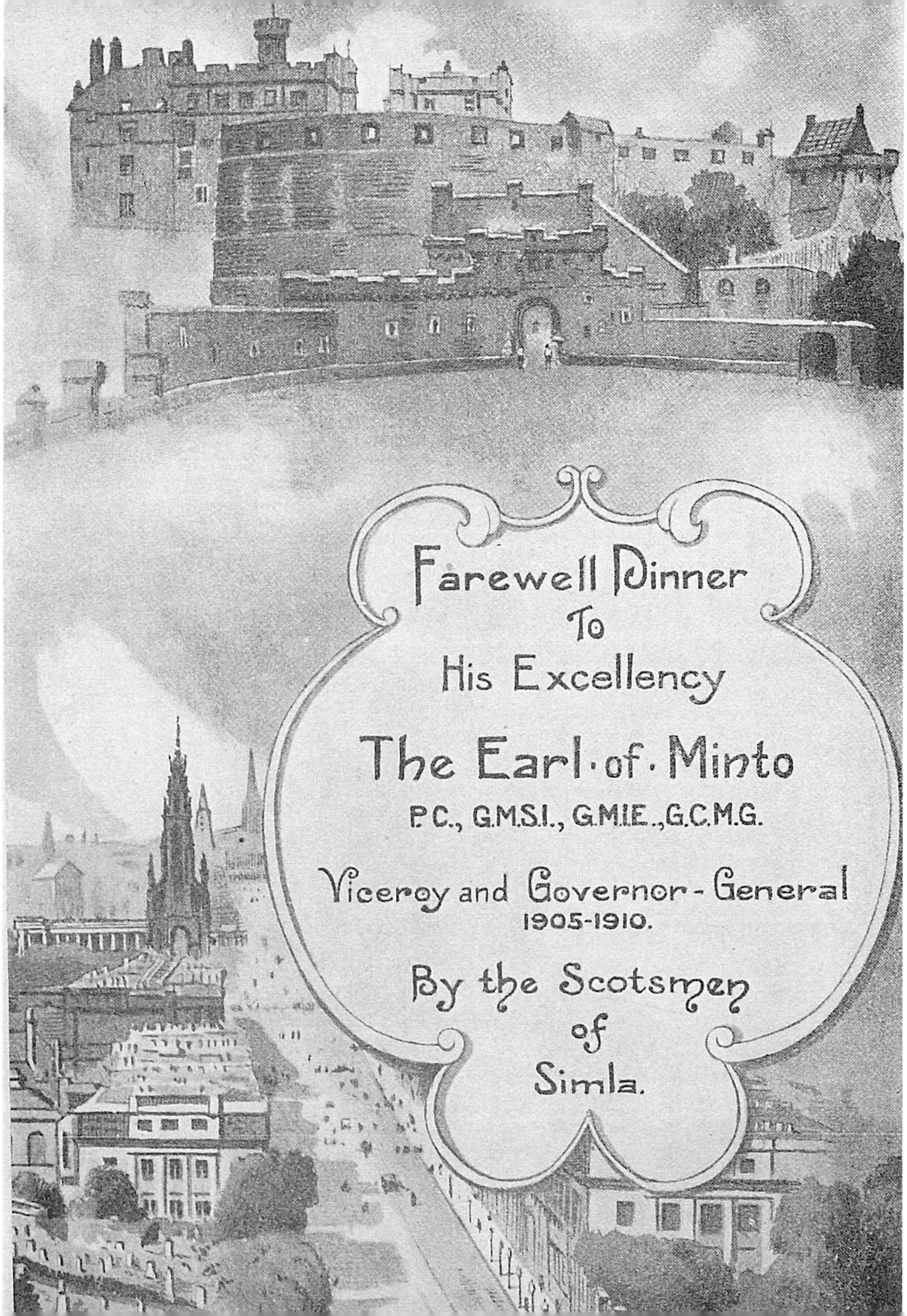
Farewell Dinner
To
His Excellency
The Earl·of·Minto
P.C., G.M.S.I., G.M.I.E., G.C.M.G.
Viceroy and Governor-General
1905-1910.
By the Scotsmen
of
Simla.

and that, although he had expected them to recognise in two or three years that no other course had been possible, he was much surprised that they should have already accepted the situation and taken for granted that Rolly had been right with so little adverse criticism.

The day the deportees were released Mr Butler was dining with one of the cleverest commercial men in Calcutta, Mr Birkrmyre.[279] There was a real scare at the moment in the financial world. Mr Birkmyre said: "I am not a politician, and Lord Minto is not in the trade. He would not ask my opinion on the administration of the country, and I would not want his views on jute. He naturally is totally indifferent to the fact that I consider the release of the deportees a mistake; no doubt if he can prove he was right, he will have scored a big success. "A young subaltern was overheard to say that same evening: "Deuced plucky of Lord Minto letting out those fellows." Mr Butler told me that he considered the way we had entertained people during our five years had been heroic. He told me that an old Mahommedan who had recently been given an interview with Rolly, had returned to him delighted with his conversation and had said to him in Persian: "the Viceroy rained gentlemanliness on me." I had never before seen Mr Butler so moved, for he always appears to be a most phlegmatic person. It was really very upsetting standing in the doorway bidding everyone farewell. One and all endeavoured to say some word of appreciation, and to my intense surprise Mr Butler, who was the last person to leave, suddenly flung himself on his knees and clasped my hand in both his own by way of a farewell.

Captain Mackenzie tells me that every servant in the house has subscribed according to their pay to the King's Memorial because the "Lord Master" had initiated the scheme. I think this is very touching and shows such a nice spirit. A sweeper who gets Rs.8 a month, the equivalent of about £7.00 a year, out of which he has to find his food, cheerfully contributes his mite which no doubt means he has to deny himself and has forfeited his food for a day. How many Englishmen would do this I wonder?

I have with difficulty induced Colonel Victor to be photographed in order to have a record of his term of office amongst the row of past Military Secretaries that adorn the wall of his room. He is passing on most of his servants to Major Maxwell. One man came to him seven years ago as a syce; on being asked if he understood the management of horses, he indignantly replied: "I have played polo." This would be a surprising answer to receive from a helper at home, and would hardly be considered a recommendation. Captain Mackenzie has given me rather an interesting Kodak of a group taken in 1907 of Rolly at Saharanpur surrounded by the riff-raff of the population. This was before anything connected with sedition had eked out, but it shows what risks he ran unconsciously, as it is about the most seditious place in India.

---

279. Became Sir Archibald Birkmyre, Bt and was a jute merchant and member of the Viceroy's Council.

Sunday, 30th.

We all went to church in the morning. I have no real affection for Christ Church. The three service that standout in my mind are Violet's confirmation and the Memorial Services for Lady Curzon and King Edward. A very nice plate has been put up by Lord Curzon to Sir Denzil Ibbetson. The inscription is charming but I cannot help thinking is out of place, as Sir Denzil and the whole of his family were atheists and never set foot inside a church. Mr and Mrs Stanley Reid lunched. He is the editor of the Times of India. We have always considered his paper antagonistic as he is said to be so strong a supporter of Lord Curzon that he thinks no one in the world should question his opinion. I found him extremely pleasant to talk to and Rolly had some conversation with him afterwards and thought his views on the political situation very sound, so no doubt he has been maligned.

Monday, 31st.

Was a very busy day, finishing up everything. My scrap books have been completed as far as possible. We have kept a permanent *daftari*[280] in the house for months pasting in photographs and keeping Rolly's extract book of newspaper cuttings up to date. All the Staff came to a sort of farewell dinner, the only outsiders being Mrs Spence and Lady Haig. We danced the whole evening and enjoyed the beautiful floor and the perfect strains of Herr Büchner's music. Rolly and I had our final dance together, as I quite realise, that on my return to England, I must give up these frivolities. In spite of old age, the empty ball-room and the alluring music still have their attractions for me, but these temptations I shall leave behind me in India.

Tuesday, 1st November.

Two beautiful chandeliers, which I ordered from Jaipur two years ago, have just arrived. These were the finishing touches which the drawing room required and I am glad they arrived in time for me to see how well my instructions have been carried out. The nights are now quite frosty but the herbaceous border is still a blaze of colour. The amphiopsis has grown up to the first storey of the house and is now a gorgeous crimson. I can hardly recall the bleak cheerless aspect of the whole place when we first arrived. Luxuriant creepers and masses of roses have changed the whole appearance. Herr Büchner selected one favourite piece after another and finished up with Tosti's "Good-bye".

---

280. Bookbinder.

Wednesday, 2nd.

Rolly is leaving poor old Dandy behind. When we have gone he is to be quietly got rid of. It is the kindest thing to do, as he is totally blind and is losing the power of his limbs. His little burial place has been selected in a lovely spot amongst the flowering shrubs beyond the tennis court. We took our final walk round the gardens. I said good-bye to every room in the house. Simla has been a real home to us and we all feel a genuine pang at leaving a place that has become almost a part of one's self. At half-past eleven people assembled on the lawn to say good-bye to us. It was a public departure, so all the officials were in uniform. It was most upsetting, as people were so cordial and I really think felt very sad at our departure. There was no time for anything but a hearty hand-shake as we walked round the circle of people, and no doubt we passed by many friends unnoticed. Rolly and I then got into the postillion carriage with a full escort of the body-guard and drove away to the strains of Auld Lang Syne and the enthusiastic cheering of the spectators. All the employees on the place were assembled to see us off, but it was hard to single out any one especially. It was a sad and trying morning which one will remember all one's life. As we passed the Guard at the foot of the hill, we stopped for Rolly to make his last inspection of the Ghurka guard. The landaus were waiting for us two or three miles down the road and we drove in the old-fashioned way the whole way to Kalka, lunching at Khairaghat. Most of the stages had decorations, and as we neared Kalka in the darkness, there were brilliant illuminations. I expect that this will be the last Viceregal trip to Kalka by carriage, as motors in future are sure to supersede the tonga ponies, although I think the road is singularly ill-adapted to such rapid travelling, with its endless curves which makes the motor swing from side to side in a most disagreeable manner.

Thursday, 3rd.

We arrived at Patiala at 9.30 A.M., and were received by the Maharaja, Sir Louis and Lady Dane and a large concourse of officials. There has been a great deal of trouble in the Patiala State. Pretam Singh, the Commander-in-Chief, who is also one of Rolly's Honorary A.D.C.'s, has been encouraging the young Maharaja in his riotous living, presumably in the hopes that he should drink himself to death as his father did before him, so that Pretam should usurp the power in the State. Things have been going from bad to worse and the great question has been whether the Maharaja should after all be given his powers. The decision to postpone the installation would of course disgrace him in the eyes of the whole Indian world and probably drive him further from the path of virtue. It has been difficult enough to obtain reliable information, but it is pretty certain that Pretam has been tampering with the troops, the finest corps of Sikh Imperial Service Troops in India. A week before we left Simla Rolly decided that Pretam was to be banished from Patiala, and another man, Gurdit Singh.

Rolly ordered a full Viceroy's escort to meet him in Patiala, the King's Own Dragoon Guards came from Amballa, and a Battery of Artillery from Meerut, under Colonel Hulton. It was impossible to know what the feeling of the troops might be, or how far Pretam's friends would resent his dethronement, so the guns were loaded as for action and each British soldier carried 100 rounds of ammunition. The Maharaja at first seemed inclined to be sulky. Three hundred guests had been invited to assist at the installation ceremony. Rolly and the whole Staff were in uniform and he and the Maharaja rode together through the crowds for two and half miles to the parade ground. I drove with Sir Louis in a gold and silver carriage drawn by four-horses. Along the route the State elephants, camels, caparisoned horses, were stationed, and armies of bearers in gorgeous uniform, beside gold and silver dandies. It was a lovely sight, and I realised that this was almost my last experience of Eastern magnificence.

We drove back to the Rest-House between the Review and the Durbar and the inevitable photograph was taken. I had never before seen an installation and the whole pageant was most impressive. Presents were exchanged, Mr Butler[281] having to produce gifts valued at many thousands of rupees. The Maharaja presenting the equivalent to the Viceroy, but his gifts alas are taken to the Toshakhana and we can keep nothing unless we pay for it. There was one grim moment when we feared that the sword-belt with which the Maharaja was to be girded was not going to be long enough to encircle his portly figure. Mr Butler and he struggled with it for some moments before it could be fastened—certainly his proportions have become colossal and his waist-band must have needed several yards of gold lace. In announcing the installation, Mr Butler reeled out the Maharaja's titles in the most masterly way without notes:

His Highness Farzand-i-Khas-i-Daulat-i-Inglishia, Mansur-i-Zaman, Amir-ul-Umra, Maharajadhiraj, Rajeshwar, Sri Maharaja-i-Rajagan Bhupindra Singh, Mahindra Bahadur, Sidhu Jat.

The Durbar hall is a very fine room, celebrated for its magnificent chandeliers about which an interesting story is told. The Maharaja's grandfather did not care for any display, dressed simply and went about unattended. One day he strolled into to a big shop in Calcutta called Osier and told the shopman he wished to select some chandeliers. He pointed to some magnificent ones and asked their price. The shopman said "Don't waste my time in asking the price of goods you could not possibly afford to buy." "Oh, couldn't I", replied the Maharaja; "What is the value of the whole of your stock at present in the shop?" "Three million rupees," was the answer; "Very well," said the Maharaja "I will buy it all," and he promptly sat down and wrote out the cheque to the amazement of the discomfited shopman. They hurried to the bank to find out whether the man was a lunatic or if his cheque could be cashed, but as Patiala is one of the richest states in India, the Bank made no difficulty in producing the money.

---

281. Spencer Harcourt Butler, later Governor of the United Provinces.

We had an enormous luncheon, 130 people in a tent, which was proportionately hot and stuffy. It was an evident relief to the Maharaja that everything passed off so well and he became much less sullen and anxious. I hope everything will go well, as I cannot help having affection for the Maharaja. He is so young and has had so many temptations purposely put in his path. I think a strong man could make a really able Ruler of him. He told me as I bade him good-bye that he was anxious to present me with Rs. 10,000 for my nursing scheme, which donation I gratefully accepted.

Friday, November 4th. Rampur.

Reached Rampur at 8.30 in the morning. The Nawab was at the station to meet us—an insignificant-looking man, speaking perfect English, dressed in silk brocades, but with nothing effective in the way of jewellery. After luncheon we drove in motors through the city for several miles along a road with avenues of orange trees to a palace in a lovely garden, where he has recently made a canal circling round the grounds for about a mile. Rampur is quite one of the greenest places I have seen in India, and has excellent irrigation facilities. We stopped to see the palace he has built inside the Fort on our way home. The Nawab is a perfect revelation to one. He has marvellous taste and has nothing but the very best specimens in the various rooms; very fine pictures, statuary, good silver and china. He has travelled enormously and has made the best use of all his experiences. The State Banquet took place in this magnificent palace in the evening and was very well done. The Nawab never drew rein for one moment during dinner. A great part of his conversation was abuse of Sir Anthony Macdonnell who had been Lieutenant-Governor of the United Provinces. He said: "Sir Anthony hated me and I cordially returned the compliment".

The Nawab made a very long speech in proposing Rolly's health and was especially delighted with his answer; it was amusing to watch his expression. He grinned from ear to ear the whole time. After dinner we looked on at the great display of fireworks.

Saturday, 5th.

We went in the morning with the Nawab to the palace, and inspected his jewels which are kept in an enormous strong room. Words fail me to describe the beauty of the gems. He has colossal diamonds of the finest and purest colour, all beautifully set, not a jarring note anywhere. But what impressed me by far the most and made it impossible to obviate breaking the 10th Commandment were the contents of a large leather portmanteau, in which were three deep trays containing countless rows of the most magnificently matched pearls I have ever seen. I hardly realised that so many pearls existed in the world. He carelessly picked up rope after rope of priceless shape and lustre. He showed us four of the largest which his grandfather had bought for under a thousand pounds. These, he told us, he had refused £250,000 for. What appealed me most of all was a huge row of pearls absolutely identical in colour and size. These, he said, he had taken 20 years to collect. After the jewels we inspected the library where the Nawab has a world renowned Arabic collection; books with marvellous illustrations and many interesting autographs dating back to Babar. He showed us a letter from old Lord Minto telling his ancestor that he had been made an Earl. This Nawab has the most up-to-date views; he is having his son taught Persian and Arabic thoroughly first, then English. He told me he did not consider a man was educated unless he was familiar with all the old languages. He seems to get the very best out of the West and the East; he himself dresses in native fashion and adheres to their orthodox customs. His sitting-rooms had the best sofas and easy-chairs from England and his dining-room chairs were Chippendale. He told us when he had taken Lord Curzon round, the first thing he wanted to do was to take possession of his best manuscripts for the Victoria Memorial. He was furious when Lord Curzon said to him: "I suppose you have had everything cleaned up in my honour. I have no doubt I should find it very different if I paid you a surprise visit." He answered: "I am glad to say that whatever time of the day or night Your Excellency condescended to pay me a visit, you would find everything as clean as it is today."

Last night after the banquet we were garlanded with superb golden necklaces, the Nawab had ordered them to be more magnificent than any that had been made before, and I believe they each cost £40. The Nawab interested me personally, as he is evidently an extremely clever man. It was rather touching to hear that during our visit he walked round the camp twice during the night at 1 and 4 A.M. to see if the sentries were at their posts; he himself never alluded to this.

We have known for some days that Lord Morley has decided to resign. The official announcement has appeared today in the papers. I cannot help regretting that Lord Hardinge will not have to work with Lord Morley for six months, although I quite understand him not wishing to begin working with a new Viceroy. The papers are full of panegyrics as to his wisdom and sagacity and all he has done for India. No doubt no one except himself could have kept the House of Commons in order or have managed to carry out the big reform schemes, but no one has any conception how difficult it has been to keep him on the right track and in a good temper. One cannot help feeling that Lord Morley has acted too much on Tallyrand's theory that "speech has been given to man in order to enable him to disguise his thoughts".

Sunday, 6th. Agra.

Here we spent three of the most restful days I have ever had in India. The last evening Rolly and I sat in one of the red minarets of the Taj for an hour overlooking the river, watching

Nawab of Rampur.

the sunset. The foliage of the trees gradually turned black in the twilight while flocks of green parrots flew screeching from twig to twig. We sat on till the young moon began to cast shadows, and then at last we walked sadly back through the gardens, conscious that never again could we gaze on so fair a scene. The Maharaja of Jaipur came to bid us farewell; he was so dignified and fluent in his own language but he cannot speak English. The Maharaja of Dholpur who we have never met before also came. He is quite a young man and speaks excellent English. He is the happy possessor of five marvellous pearls. The Tsar of Russia offered him two million pounds for these but he wouldn't hear of selling them.

Saturday, 12th.

Our visit to Benares has been a disappointing one as far as the weather is concerned as both mornings the rain prevented Rolly making the river expedition. Today in motoring to the Maharaja's Palace we crossed the river by the same bridge that the tram passes over. As the iron gates were being opened to admit the string of motors, some one suggested that the mail train should be due, the official answered: "She has been due some time, but I have held her up till the Viceroy has crossed the bridge!" What would Morley think of this? Yet he recently asked an Indian official how many guns would be accorded him if he visited India. Concealing a smile the official said such an eventuality had never arisen. Morley said: "But the Viceroy gets 31 guns and I am a bigger man than he is." I can only conclude that Morley was proposing to depose the King and assume the role of Cromwell. He also told Mr Butler that people were in the habit of coming into his room without showing the respect he understood was exacted of them by the Viceroy, whom no one could approach without an A.D.C. in uniform introducing. English visitors would no doubt object to do puja at the door even to the Secretary of State, and the deference shown to people in authority in the East is hardly to be expected from a Western race, in whom manners unfortunately are sadly lacking.

Sunday, 13th. Barrackpore.

My birthday brings a nasty jar with it, reminding me of advancing years, but the mail dispelled depression, as I received such delightful letters of good wishes from all the family. After dinner we sat out quite late enjoying the perfect temperature and the moon which lighted up the whole river and made the scene about as ideal as could be imagined. Where the new garden was made last year, a beautiful new fountain, designed by Mr Marshall, has been erected. This is my last finishing touch to the work we have done at Barrackpore and is

State Silver Carriage, Ramnagar.

a great addition to the place. Our pleasure in returning to this heavenly spot is only marred by the knowledge that our time of enjoyment before leaving it for ever is so short.

Tuesday, 15th. Calcutta

Rolly received eight addresses from various parts of India during the morning and replied to many farewell addresses. They are a marvellous tribute to Rolly and all allude to the improved condition that now exists throughout India. The English community that were so bitter in their criticisms of Rolly's policy in connection with the Native Member of Council and the release of the deportees acknowledge that they were wrong, and one cannot be thankful enough that we have been allowed to remain in India long enough to show the public that he was justified in his policy.

We have endeavoured to collect as many of the Staff as possible for our farewell dinner to them which took place this evening. Before going to dinner Colonel Pinhey stepped forward and in the name of the Staff presented us with a beautiful old silver salver, on the back of which is engraved the names of the subscribers, the present and past Staff have all contributed. He made very charming allusions to the harmonious way in which the whole

establishment had worked together and ended by saying that all that they had done in an official capacity had been a labour of love.

I sat between Captain Mackenzie and Captain Jelf, who leave by the midnight train to meet the Hardinges. A great many toasts were proposed and I was at last induced to rise to my feet to return thanks in a few words for the toast which had been proposed by Francis.

Wednesday, November 16th.

Rolly held the last review that I suppose he will ever hold in his life, as he can hardly become Commander-in-Chief. The Artillery and Cavalry galloped past magnificently. Captain Keighley led the first company of the Bodyguard at a terrifying pace. Two mounted men in the second company came down which was a horrid sight to witness but fortunately they were able to get off the ground in time to prevent the next regiment galloping over them. It was a very narrow shave. Tonight the big banquet given to Rolly by the Turf Club took place in the race-course grounds. No ladies were invited to dinner but 130 members were present who came from all parts of India to assist at his farewell. All the grounds had been lit up and practically the whole of Calcutta assembled after dinner. The illuminations were most artistically arranged and I believe nearly the whole electrical power of Calcutta had been turned on to illuminate them.

Mr Larmour lunched. He is Treasurer of the memorial that has been got up for Rolly in Calcutta. He tells me that the subscription list has been unprecedented, the first day nearly a lakh was subscribed, the largest sum that has ever been collected before in so short a time was Rs. 50,000 for Lord Lansdowne. He anticipates that quite a lakh and half will be subscribed. The Maharaja of Bikaner writes to Colonel Pinhey on the subject and says how delighted he is that Rolly has beaten every record for any previous Viceroy. Miss Sorabji tells me that even in the zenana the feeling has undergone a complete change. She says that women are beginning to be anxious to emancipate themselves and have begun to enquire the reason for things instead of accepting all restrictions without a murmur. I was really sorry to say goodbye to her, she has been such a good friend to us and I hope we shall have the opportunity of meeting in England.

Thursday, 17th.

A comparatively quiet day so I went over the entire house to see that all the rooms were arranged to my satisfaction before the new tenants takes possession of them. I have just received a charming letter from the Amir. The brooch that accompanies it is really extremely pretty, formed in the shape of a Gurkha kukri.

Friday, 18th.

Rolly dined at the Calcutta Club. Eileen and i joined the party after dinner. Mr Sinha made an excellent speech and Rolly's answer I heard was most happy. The gardens were lighted up, the trees a mass of coloured electric lights and hundreds of Indian had collected from all parts of India to bid us farewell. The feature of the evening was an illuminated aeroplane which suddenly made its appearance overhead. It hovered in the centre of the garden and from a little box fell an aerial marconigram from the members of the Calcutta Club, "wishing Their Excellencies farewell and bon voyage." Mr Sinha looked after me for most of the evening and brought up everyone of importance. He gives up his post as Legal Member on Monday next and has two cases waiting for him, both of which pay £2,000 down and a fee of £100 a day while the case is on. One can easily realise the pecuniary loss that he has suffered while he has been a Member of Council.

It has been officially announced that the King and Queen intend to come to India in January 1912 to hold a Coronation Durbar. The papers have all received the news with enthusiasm but I expect there will be a great many difficult questions to decide later on, and the expense of the last Delhi Durbar almost ruined some of the smaller States. Mr Blair, the editor of the Empire lunched. He said no greater tribute could be given to Lord Minto after the turbulent condition that the country has been in the the last few year, than that it is considered sufficiently pacified to enable the King to contemplate a visit. Tara Chand, the jeweller, has come from Hyderabad on purpose to say good-bye. His English is not perfect but he told me that: "Viceroy has sprinkled water on the people after the fire which he found. Now everyone happy: Maharajas, Zamindars, and small people, all contented".

The news of the General Election that is to take place at once is rather a bombshell. Parliament is to dissolve on 25th November and we shall return to find England in the throes of a terrible conflict as no doubt party feeling will be running very high.

Saturday, 19th. Barrackpore.

Spent a feverish morning making final arrangements and interviewing people of all sorts. The Maharaja of Darbhanga, who is one of the most wealthy zamindars in Bengal, came to see Rolly. His appearance is most unalluring—he has long black greasy locks and looks as if he had never made the acquaintance of soap and water. As he was leaving the room, he flung himself on his knees, removed his cap and begged Rolly to bless him, which he accordingly did, one hand uplifted to heaven and the other reposing on the oily head invoking a blessing. We motored down to Barrackpore after luncheon. I had my final round of golf and said goodbye to the three little caddies who have always taken the keenest interest in my progress.

Sunday, 20th.

We all went to the 8 o'clock service with very thankful hearts at having so far got through our strenuous five years without any physical breakdown. Spent part of the morning in kodaking the new fountain and the new entrance to the rose garden. After luncheon Rolly and I drove round with Creepy and Crawly and took a sad farewell of the whole place. I think my happiest times in India have been spent at Barrackpore and I am glad to have had one more peaceful day there. We motored back to Calcutta about midnight.

Monday, 21st.

By 10 o'clock the guns were booming out Lord Hardinge's arrival. The officials were all drawn up in their order of precedence, guards-of-honour filled the compound, and at the appointed hour Rolly, Eileen, and I stood at the top of the steps and welcomed Lord and Lady Hardinge, who drove up with the clatter of a full Viceroy's escort. I could hardly realise that it is five years since we first walked up the red carpeted steps between an avenue of the body-guard. They were both most charming and cordial. Rolly presented the Members of Council and the Ruling Princes, and the rest of the introductions were done by the head official of the particular department. It all worked like clock-work and we then took them to their rooms. Rolly had to rush off to his work, but Eileen and I took both Lord and Lady Hardinge on a tour of inspection round the house, and spent most of the morning discussing subjects of interest to us both. I told Lord Hardinge that this was the last holiday he would have for five years, which fact he hardly seems to realise. We were rather amused that the first telegram he sent from Bombay was to order two topees from Ranken. He tells me Dunlop selected his topee for him with a blue puggree which he felt was not so smart or chic as those in which our A.D.C.'s met him, so he was greatly distressed to feel that his first appearance in Calcutta had been inadequate. We were introduced to all their Staff at luncheon. The Maharajas of Bikaner and Scindia are also staying with us, having come the whole way to bid us farewell. Took Lady Hardinge for a drive to the Zoo, and round by the river road. I am quite amazed at her wonderful knowledge of India and its various interests. She seems to have been reading up everything in connection with the Dufferin Fund, Nursing Association, and has already quite a grasp of everything that will be expected of her, and I am sure she will carry on all the various charitable organisations in a most masterful way.[282] We all had tea in the garden together. Diamond[283] is delighted with the dog that Roland begged should be awaiting her on arrival. It is a source of intense delight. She is such a pretty little girl and is thrilled by all her new experiences.

The big dinner took place this evening. The whole official world was assembled, making 119 people all told. The table looked rather bare without any of our silver, but it was covered

282. Winifred (Bena) Hardinge suffered ill health in India and died during a stay in England in 1914. She was closely involved with medical charities and the first medical college for women in India was named after her.

283. The Hardinge's daughter, born in 1900.

INDIA ASHOKYAN MINTO MEMORIAL PILLAR: ALLAHABAD
VICTORIA THE GOOD
EDWARD THE PEACE-MAKER
GEORGE V.
PROCLAMATION 1858
PROCLAMATION 1908
PROCLAMATION 1910
BENTINCK
CANNING
RIPON
MINTO
MINTO INDIA

with a profusion of pink roses and the lovely creeper Antigonum. Rolly introduced Lord Hardinge to everyone and I followed with Lady Hardinge. It is really a very difficult task not to mix up the names of so many people, although Captain Jelf carefully prompted me. Rolly proposed Lord Hardinge's health: he said that he felt sure that everyone was pleased to welcome him here, and went on to say that he must remind Lord Hardinge of where they had originally met many years ago. It was at Walmer Castle, staying with the Governor of the Cinque Ports who happened to be Lord Dufferin. It was curious that the trio should have had such similar careers; Lord Dufferin had been ex-Governor General of Canada and ex-Viceroy of India—he himself came next, had become Governor General of Canada and Viceroy of India, and the youngest Viceroy, he felt sure, would carry on the traditions of his family and be equally successful as Viceroy of India as he had been in his other official capacities. After a graceful allusion to Lady Hardinge we drank their health. Lord Hardinge made a very nice response, and said with what admiration he had watched Lord Minto's career in India and how he hoped to follow the same policy that he had so ably initiated. He felt sure that, as the years went by Lord Minto would receive more credit for all he had achieved, and be handed down to posterity as one of the most successful Viceroys who had ever ruled over India. After dinner we sat in the yellow drawing-room and the Ball-room. I think the evening passed off exceptionally well. The Hardinges have evidently made a most excellent impression and nothing could have been nicer than they both were to everyone—so cordial and so anxious to do the right thing. At the end of the evening Rolly and I stood in the door-way and bid everyone farewell. I think there were a good many tearful eyes, and nothing could be more gratifying to us than the affectionate manner in which eyeryone has expressed their regret at our approaching departure.

So ends our official life in India. It has been one of intense interest and it is natural that one cannot relinquish it without a pang. At the same time the strain on Rolly has been colossal; and however much I regret the loss of the interest of his great position, I am glad to feel that he is returning to a well-earned rest at home with the knowledge that his work has the appreciation of the whole Indian and European community.

Tuesday, 22nd November.

I don't know if the Hardinges take in the difficulties that will arise unless strict supervision of the Government House establishment is maintained. Mr Coryton, who has succeeded dear old Ram Das, has now a complete plan of the house, an illustration of every room with a drawing of the way the furniture is arranged and a list of each article. The godowns are as spick and span as a man-of-war in their neatness, every item has to be accounted for, whereas in the old days there was a glorious confusion; cases of china have lately been discovered, the existence of which no one was aware of, and Ram Das had a lordly way of ordering a thousand ormolu door handles, or a gross of anything I happened to want, with princely recklessness and regardless whether there was a credit or debit balance in the bank of a lakh of rupees. After all it has panned out well. Ram Das with his want of method was

Departure cartoon

very useful to me when we were doing up the house, and it enabled me to get everything I wanted, but with Sir Guy, as Finance Member, it is sounder to have Mr Coryton with an accurate knowledge of the current expenditure.

We had a trying afternoon, giving presents and saying good-bye to everyone who has served us. Everyone was so affected that few words were spoken, and I seized the offering in order to hide my emotion and pressed it into the hands of the recipient. The head servants and khitmatgars were told to assemble in the gallery, and Rolly made them a little speech, which was translated by Colonel Victor. The head khansama made an eloquent reply, and various retainers were given presents in addition to a month's pay, the total of which for the whole establishment mounts up to about £800!!! They all salaamed and wished us God-speed before dispersing. I spent the evening till dinner, giving Bena further information about various charities. It was sad to sit down to dinner for the last time opposite the throne; I fear I rather neglected Scindia who sat on my other side, but when I turned round I invariably found tears trickling from his prominent eyes, which was most upsetting. For the last time we sat in the marble hall and listened to the band, each man seemed to put extra feeling into their instruments as they played our favourite pieces. At the conclusion of the programme Rolly and I went and said good-bye to the men. I find these tearful scenes most trying and shall be heartily glad when we are on board ship.

Wednesday, 23rd.

The whole morning was a nightmare. In the first place, I had had to sit up till 3.30 A.M. writing chits for my favourite servants and correcting my journal, which I was anxious to get printed before leaving India, so my eyes felt hot and too big for their sockets from fatigue. Mrs Spence, Mr Buck and several of our intimate friends begged to come during the morning for a private farewell. I tried to feel as stony as possible, but tearful eyes, the pressure of the hand and a "God bless you" is enough to upset anyone. A great many Indian Princes have come to Calcutta to bid us farewell. The Maharajas of Gwalior, Kashmir, Bikaner, Benares, Jodhpur, Kurupam, Gidhaur, Burdwan, Darbhunga, Vizianagram, the Prince of Arcot, and crowds more Indians whose names I can't cope with. By 12.15 the halls were packed, and Rolly and I took 20 minutes literally fighting our way through the people. At last we reached the top of the marble steps and walked for the last time over the red carpet between the two lines of the splendid Body-guard. The Hardinges stood at the foot of the steps and we both bade them a most cordial farewell. I made them each a curtsy and wished them good luck; he seemed quite overcome, and it really was a moving sight, the enormous escort and the guard-of-honour and the steps thronged by this wonderful concourse of people all eager to give us an enthusiastic send-off. Scindia and Bikaner pressed our hands in both their own but they couldn't speak. We drove through the gates where the band was stationed playing Auld Lang Syne and Büchner's sad face quite haunted me.

As we drove through the streets packed with spectators, cheer after cheer rang out, and occasionally I caught sight of a face I knew at some window or on a balcony, Howrah Bridge was beautifully decorated with palms, as was the railway station; and I found my carriage a bower of flowers. We steamed slowly out of the station amidst cheers and sat down with a sigh of relief but with very mixed feelings of sorrow and gladness. A wonderful chapter in our lives is ended. The guns boomed out our departure and announced the installation of the new Viceroy. The time we have lived through has been a most remarkable one. On our first arrival in 1905 there was an apparent calm before veiled sedition began, and lastly open anarchy. Then came the new repressive measures; the muzzling of the press and the commencement of a new era; the fulfilment of the Queen's Proclamation of 1858 and the recognition that the ambitions of the Indians must be given scope. After less than a year the condition of the country has undergone a complete change, and Lord Hardinge, I hope, will rule over a peaceful India. Rolly and I made Crooke and Francis come and sit at our table at dinner in the train, they are the only two members of the staff who have stayed with us the entire time, and nobody could have been more helpful than they both have been. I am fully aware that I have always had a critical eye on the staff, and the way they have done their work is beyond all praise. Much of the success of the regime is wholly due to them.

Thursday, 24th.On the train.

We are going this time by the Nagpur route, which is new to us, the railway is laid through the loveliest part of India, the luxuriant jungles of the Central Provinces, where Rolly has twice been coming to shoot, but has always been prevented at the last moment. It was so extraordinary to see no files in Rolly's room; but he has not yet begun his holiday, as he had to prepare the answers to the addresses at Bombay. The line as usual was thickly patrolled by police, it was curious to see on going over a bridge made of a double line of iron cross-bars, policemen wedged between them, in a space that looked only wide enough to plant a border of convolvuluses. We have been flooded by farewell telegrams and have received such kind messages from all parts of India. Fryer gave Rolly such a wonderful account of poor old Dandy s funeral at Simla, Mr and Mrs Fryer were the chief mourners. The latter feels Dandy's death so acutely that she fainted across his grave!!! Most wives would hardly show such feeling for their husbands.

HE 1910.

Friday, November 25th. R.I.M.S. Dufferin.

It is hard to believe that we have actually arrived at our last day in India. The huge white train, with every luxury the heart of man can devise, the countless servants ready to fly at one's bidding, has belonged to us for so long and has practically been our home during so many weeks of touring, that it has become very dear to us. The country through which we passed yesterday was lovely. The Central Provinces are the happy hunting ground of the shikar enthusiast. The wooded hills, the grassy glades, the bamboo jungles, with occasional stretches of water, make about as perfect a combination as one could imagine. One of the officials travelling with us, who had also been to Bombay to fetch Lord Hardinge, was greatly amused by one of his Staff, who on hearing that they were in a good tiger country said: "What a pity we are going through in the night!" If he expects to see rows of tigers sitting on their haunches watching the train, I am afraid he will be disappointed.

We reached Bombay at 2.15. Sir George and Lady Clarke were at the station to meet us and dear old Sir Pertab. Rolly received an address from the Chamber of Commerce, and we then motored to Government House. Lady Clarke seems a very nice woman, and Sir George has become quite young and sprightly with his new wife.[284] At 4 o'clock we drove in State with full escort to the Convocation Hall, where the native community had prepared a wonderful farewell reception. They cheered us tremendously as we walked up between the rows of spectators. A very appreciative address was read; we were garlanded, and were then led to a refreshment shamiana where Mr Gokhale proposed the toast of our health most eloquently, and Rolly made a charming impromptu speech in answer. At the Apollo Bunder, Sir George and Lady Clarke, the Admiral and all the officials were drawn up to bid us farewell. The Bombay Corporation gave us our final address and casket, and we commenced saying the good-byes. The dear old Begum had come all the way from Bhopal with the whole of her family to pay her respects, and dear old Sir Pertab was speechless with sadness and emotion, tears were rolling down his cheeks and he looked quite wretched. Mr Cleveland was another official who couldn't speak, but though there were these individual cases of people who really minded, the actual departure was nothing like so trying as the farewells in Calcutta. At last we walked down the red carpeted steps for the last time, got into the launch and steamed away, amidst the ringing cheers of a vast crowd. H.M.S. Hyacinth and the R.I.M. Alert manned their yards as we passed, and all the ships were dressed.

The setting sun lighted up the whole scene and seemed to give us a parting benediction as we came alongside the R.I.M.S. Dufferin. The officers were drawn up to receive us and everything looked very smart. This is a beautiful ship and everything possible has been done for our comfort. We had hard work to answer all the farewell telegrams before sailing and it was heartbreaking saying good-bye to our faithful servants. They all came on board to salaam us for the last time and sadly departed in the launch, all more or less in tears. How terribly I shall miss them. Four of them have been with me for five years and have been

284. Governor of Bombay, his first wife and his daughter had both died in 1909.

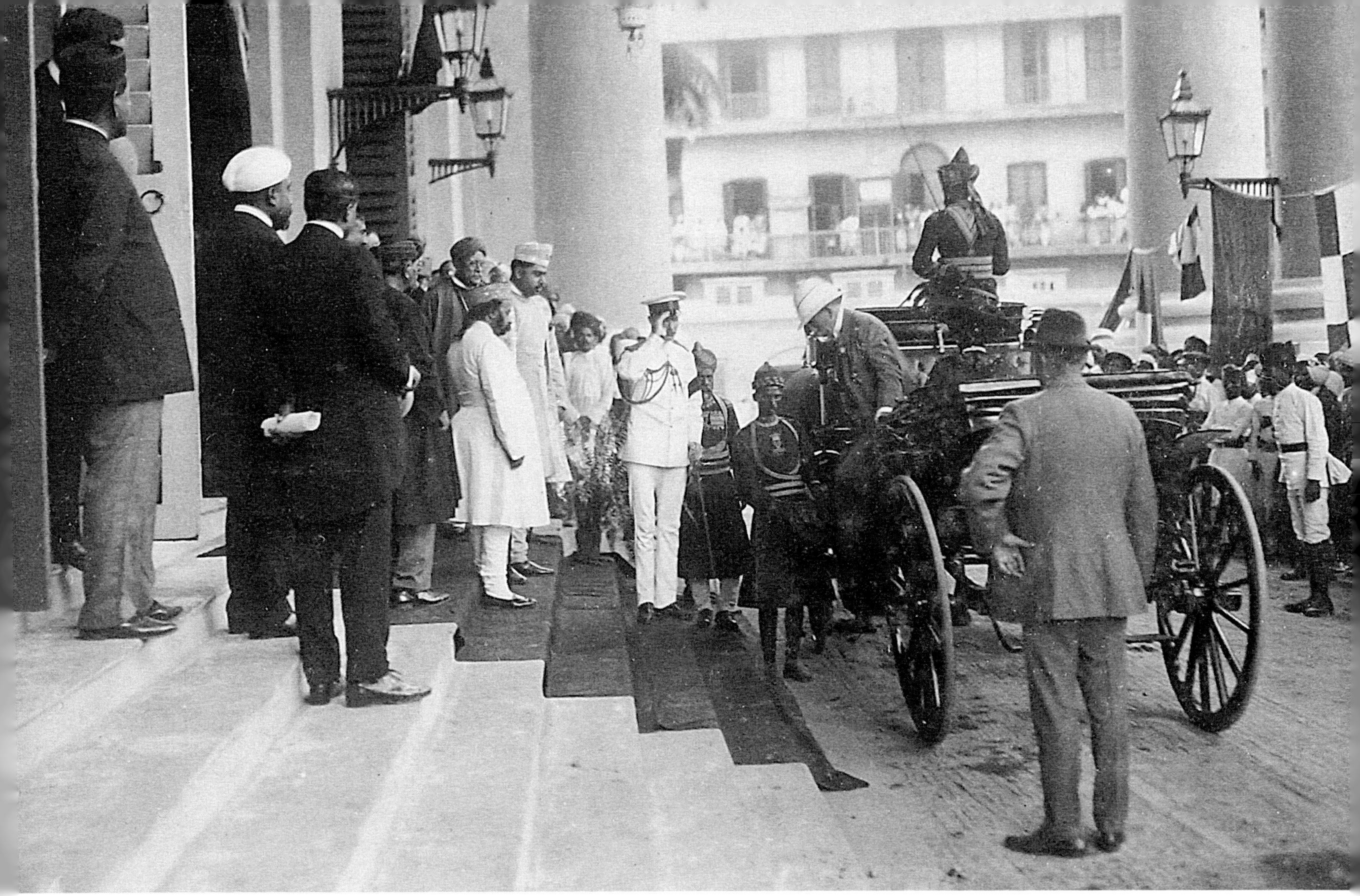

absolutely devoted. The Dufferin began to move out slowly from her moorings, gliding over the tranquil waters. We listened to the strains of "God save the King" played by the band on the Hyacinth for the very last time in Rolly's honour, then three rousing cheers rang out, first from the Alert, then from the Hyacinth. It was a solemn moment, one felt that Rolly was laying down the burden of a great responsibility that he has carried unflinchingly to a successful finish, against overwhelming odds. The evening was a gorgeous one; the sky a deep orange, the glow reflected on the sea and the dark spires and buildings in Bombay stood out in sharp relief. Then came the twilight, and a great calm pervaded the atmosphere. We sat on in the increasing gloom until the great beacons of flame from the revolving light-houses faded away like two stars in the heavens. Nature seemed to understand our mood

Farewell: His Ex. alighting at Town Hall, Calcutta.

and I could not have wished to bid a more perfect farewell to the shores of India. The East has cast her magic spell around us, nothing can fascinate one in quite the same way again.

What a lot there is to think of and talk over! We have never had time for either in the midst of our busy life. Looking back, with all the knowledge of passed events, I don't believe there is a single thing that Rolly would have done differently. Rather a wonderful fact and one for which I thank Providence most devoutly, is that during the entire five years he has never been compelled for one complete day to give up doing some work. Even when he has felt really ill he has always insisted on having his papers brought to him. For myself I have been marvellously lucky, the climate has always agreed with me and only once during five years have I failed to fulfil an engagement which Eileen undertook instead of me. My worst experience was attending our garden party of 1,500 people the day of my bad fall when I broke a bone in my hand and was bruised all over, but I managed to get through it. Bhopendra Nath Basu, the Legislative Member, whose loyalty is always questioned, wrote a long letter to Colonel Pinhey, saying how much he regretted not being present at our farewell, but as a near relation of his had just died, he would have had to appear with bare feet and wearing a dhotee. It is fortunate that he stayed away and spared us this sight.

Tuesday, 29th.

I am sending this journal back to Calcutta to Mr Scott to have it printed, I am anxious not to wind it up until I reach England. What a burden it has been to me all these years I can hardly describe, frequently written at night, or during the few minutes of rest between functions. It has been a heavy task-master and of necessity the long days entailed more writing, but it has almost reached completion now. It has always been hurriedly written, it is badly expressed, and transgresses every rule of composition, but it will be an interesting book of reference, recording, for Rolly and me, by far the most strenuous five years of our lives. At the farewell dinner we gave in Calcutta, some one was tactless enough to say to me: "Well I do hope you will get safely on board ship now, of course the political outlook is much clearer, but there is always the danger of some fanatic wishing by an act of violence to gain notoriety." I am thankful to say I have always been

able to keep such thoughts in the background. If one had allowed them to take possession of one, one's nerves must have become affected. It was perfectly useless to fuss, but this does not prevent me feeling intensely grateful to Providence for watching over us through countless perils, of which we were probably totally unconscious.

Monday, December 5th.

We arrived at Suez about 5 A.M. We have had a wonderfully comfortable voyage, no heat to speak of, and it has been delightful having the whole of this great ship to ourselves with an exceptionally nice lot of officers on board. The last night at dinner Rolly proposed the health of the Captain and officers, and told them how struck he had been by the smartness of the ship and the excellence of the discipline. Captain Dobson is very proud of having managed to keep fresh flowers for the table decoration during the whole voyage, and he presented Eileen and me with a farewell bouquet each, tied up with a Dufferin ribbon, as we left the ship. We walked down the companion ladder over our last bit of red carpet and steamed off in the Dufferin launch, the sailors manning the yards. We have now said goodbye for ever to all our pomp and ceremony, and assume the humble role of ordinary mortals. The Herefordshire Captain received us in the gangway and conducted us to our cabins, which are quite comfortable, but very small and not quite up to Viceregal splendour. They have given us a tiny sitting-room, and made everything as nice as possible. The Steward looking after us, Jenkins by name, a most obliging person, told us he had been our Steward on board the Scotsman in 1898 when we went out to Canada to succeed Lord Aberdeen. It is a curious coincidence that he should have started us on our Viceregal career and attend us again at the close of it. I asked him if he had been put on expressly, and he said, "No," that we happened to be occupying the particular cabins of his beat. The ship is not at all full, only about 50 other passengers, but one cannot help resenting their existence, and their chairs are naturally installed in the most secluded nooks. They of course look upon us as the interlopers, but we must get used to being jostled, and to having no attention paid us. It is very good for us having to find our level, but after 11 years of red carpets and special trains, it is impossible not to feel a vague sense of surprise at being considered of no account. The staff feel it just as much as we do, and quite resent our being treated as ordinary mortals.

The letters from home bring good news on the whole but the doctors think that Larry must not risk coming up to London to meet us and that he will have to be careful for the next six months. This makes us realise that his concussion was much more serious that we at first realised although I am more than thankful that he is as well as he is especially as he has been unfortunate to get concussion twice in one year.

Going home.

Saturday, 10th.

We are within 24 hours of Marseilles, and have had a record passage in perfectly smooth weather. The Mediterranean so far has proved warmer than the Red Sea. We have been able to sit about without coats, and have even played Bridge on deck after dinner enjoying the balmy air. I could not believe it could be so much warmer in December than I have ever experienced it before, even in May and July. We have played skittles, but have not mixed much with our fellow-passengers; they had already made up their various cliques before we got on board, and we are such a big party ourselves that we require no outside addition.

December 11th. R.M.S. Herefordshire.

There was the usual bustle connected with the arrival of the ship. Two motors were provided for us, and Rolly and I, Eileen, Francis, and Colonel Victor drove out to the Reserve Hotel for luncheon, where we thoroughly enjoyed the seductive dishes of their celebrated chef. We motored round Marseilles during the afternoon, got out and explored the various gardens, dined at the Station Hotel and left by an 8 o'clock train for Paris. Rolly and I felt our salon lits rather inadequate and cramped after our spacious Indian carriages, but we managed to get through the night, and reached Paris at 7 A.M. We had to drive across to the Gare de Lyons, where we breakfasted and started for Calais at 9.30. The Mayor greeted us on arrival in a very smart official uniform; we were photographed several times by persistent representatives of various papers, who naturally caught us at the most unbecoming moment. It was a rough crossing with seas breaking over us, but we none of us minded. The three dogs had to be shut up in their houses and Tashi made piteous wails of distress as she was taken off by a stranger who travels with them up to Minto, where they remain in quarantine for three months. Lama, the brown husband, as he is called, having only arrived from Tibet a few days before we left Calcutta, is still very farouche, but made friends with Mrs Fryer on board ship. This isolation is a terrible ordeal for these poor dogs to go through.

Almost before we realised that we had got alongside the pier, Sir Dunlop was on board wecoming us home; it was a real pleasure to see him again. He had ordered a wonderful tea on the train and was so full of information as to all that has been happening that the journey to London appeared quite short. Owing to the numbers of people who proposed to greet us at the station, the accommodation at Charing Cross was not considered sufficient, consequently our carriage was slipped en route, and we came into Victoria Station instead. The sea of faces was quite bewildering, but I soon found Esmond, Violet and, Louisa to my intense delight. Then began a wild endeavour to grasp everyone by the hand, which was no easy task. Everyone was so cordial it did one's heart good to receive such a welcome, and as we drove off in a motor, three lusty cheers rang out. It was a moment never to be forgotten. Mrs Stewart greeted us in Audley Square, looking exactly the same and the house has been kept in apple-pie order. Vi and Charlie dined with us and very thankful we felt to

The Return of Lord and Lady Minto: Lord and Lady Minto and their eldest daughter were photographed at Calais, where they were received on arrival by the British Consul, seen in the photograph wearing Levee dress.

have reached home safely after all our experiences. Rowland had kindly collected a staff of servants for us, and we spent a very cheerful evening. Rolly, on his arrival was greeted with a letter from the Lord Mayor of London offering him the Freedom of the City.

Thursday, 15th.

We were sent for to lunch at Buckingham Palace. Rolly had his audience alone with the King, who presented him with the Order of the Garter, and expressed his great appreciation of the way Rolly had performed his exceptionally difficult task. Meanwhile I sat with the Queen, and after enquiring about many Indian questions, she told me she had a favour to ask me, and then expressed her wish that I should become one of her Ladies-in-Waiting. She begged me to think it well over, but said she hoped very much I should accept. We then had luncheon with them, Princess Victoria and the two eldest boys completing the party. There was nothing stiff or formal, and we both thoroughly enjoyed our visit, as they were so friendly and interested in all we had to tell them about India.

Monday, 19th.

Lord Morley came and lunched with us. Nothing could have been nicer than he was, although I believe he tried to prevent Rolly getting the Garter, and never in the two interviews they have had alluded to it in any way. It is interesting to hear how private influence has been brought to bear on the newspapers. A well-known correspondent went to Dunlop and begged to be given information which would enable him to write a correct

account of the Indian administration of the past five years. Knowing the importance of having reliable knowledge, Dunlop spent hours in giving the required information. Four columns were written for the Times and two for the Daily Mail. Lord Northcliffe meanwhile met an influential official lately connected with the India Office, and the Times' article was reduced to one column, and the Daily Mail editor suddenly said he had changed his mind and would not require one at all. The author was thoroughly disgusted and exacted the uttermost farthing for both articles. The whole cause of the suppression of these articles was the vanity of the said official, who does not wish the public to peep behind the scenes and see for themselves facts as they really are. We had a long talk to Sir Arthur Bigge, who I think realises more each day the difficulties connected with the King's visit to India. I believe half London society wish to go out, and all the questions of precedence will have to be most carefully gone into to avoid heart-burnings.

It is so sad to have had to leave Ruby[285] behind in London, but she is alas not strong enough to come up to Minto. Violet took Larry up by the night train Tuesday night, Rolly, Eileen, Essy and I started Wednesday morning, the 20th. Dunlop and Crooke came to see us off at the station. Arthur and Hubert Elliot[286] joined us at Carlisle. I was quite amazed at the reception Hawick gave us; the town seemed one mass of wild enthusiasm. The streets were packed with people, and a ceaseless roar of cheering was kept up the entire time. It was a happy moment when I saw Rolly standing safe and sound once more under his own roof and I think everyone's heart was very full. His Viceregal career has certainly ended with a gratifying burst of applause, and I feel very proud of him. The old Scotch saying "Safe in" is full of meaning and brings a great sense of relief and thankfulness. The storm has been weathered, the haven reached. India now becomes a sealed book to us. Frontier wars, sedition, conspiracies, plague and famine are no longer nightmares that disturb our peace of mind. The steering gear is in other hands, our ship is safe in port, where there is a great calm, and I hope we may long be spared to enjoy our well earned rest.

Extract from a letter to Lady Antrim from Mr Butler.

> "It is over and it has ended well. There could not have been a better send off. No Viceroy's departure has been more regretted. The Indians to a man from the Nizam downwards feel that they have lost a friend. It was strong personal feeling for the Viceroy which has kept many from joining the enemy and has brought many back to the fold. Lord Minto's personality quieted the atmosphere. And there has been a great outburst of gratitude and affection for Lady Minto. The position of parties is such that, if a Viceroy is popular with Indians, he excites the suspicion of Europeans. It is very extraordinary how many Europeans have already come round. History will judge truly".

285. She had had jaundice.
286. Rolly's brother Arthur and his son.

M.M., His Ex., H.H. the Begum, Bhopal.

A NOTE ON SPELLING

The four volumes of the Indian Journals in their original printed form, plus a slim fifth, the somewhat piecemeal index, have, been cut to ribands, as Mary would have said, to make a manageable book. In the process there has been some attempt to rationalise the spelling throughout the book, to avoid confusion, of words taken from Urdu or Hindustani. In fact even Hobson-Jobson, the bible of Anglo-Indian etymology offers several different spellings of many commonly used expressions and words such as jemadar and Mary probably wrote them accordingly. Where Mary's spelling appears intentionally to be that of her time, it has been left alone. 'Thibet' for instance, was an alternative that crops up in 19th century travel writing and Mary uses it indiscriminately with 'Tibet' although a transcriber or printer may be responsible for the variation. Otherwise obvious errors, either in printing or from the original transcription of Mary's handwriting, have been corrected. The editor has also made occasional changes where a blemish or two on a page may have been transmogrified in print to a rash of random punctuation unintended by its author. The aim throughout has been for Mary's voice and views to stand out as nearly as possible as she first expressed them.

INDEX